SUPREME COURT CASE BRIEFS IN CRIMINAL PROCEDURE

SUPREME COURT CASE BRIEFS IN CRIMINAL PROCEDURE

Michael A. Cretacci

ROWMAN & LITTLEFIELD PUBLISHERS, INC.
Lanham • Boulder • New York • Toronto • Plymouth, UK

ROWMAN & LITTLEFIELD PUBLISHERS, INC.

Published in the United States of America
by Rowman & Littlefield Publishers, Inc.
A wholly owned subsidary of The Rowman & Littlefield Publishing Group, Inc.
4501 Forbes Boulevard, Suite 200, Lanham, Maryland 20706
www.rowmanlittlefield.com

Estover Road
Plymouth PL6 7PY
United Kingdom

British Library Cataloguing in Publication Information Available

Library of Congress Cataloging-in-Publication Data:
Cretacci, Michael A., 1968–
  Supreme Court case briefs in criminal procedures / Michael A. Cretacci.
     p. cm.
  Includes index.
  ISBN-13: 978-0-7425-5860-1 (cloth : alk. paper)
  ISBN-10: 0-7425-5860-6 (cloth : alk. paper)
  ISBN-13: 978-0-7425-5861-8 (pbk. : alk. paper)
  ISBN-10: 0-7425-5861-4 (pbk. : alk. paper)
  1. Criminal procedure—United States—Cases. 2. Searches and seizures—United States—Cases. 3. United
States. Supreme Court. I. Title.
  KF9618.C668 2007
  345.73'05—dc22   2007001217

Printed in the United States of America

♾™ The paper used in this publication meets the minimum requirements of American National Standard
for Information Sciences—Permanence of Paper for Printed Library Materials, ANSI/NISO Z39.48-1992.

Gei Qin Ai De

Contents

Preface and Acknowledgments

THE UNITED STATES SUPREME COURT has sought, over the last fifty to sixty years, to expand its reach over the domain of criminal processing. As a result, the Court has seen its review of cases in this area increase dramatically. Unfortunately, it is often the case that the decisions rendered by the Court are confusing and sometimes contradictory. The end product is frequently difficult to apply in the day-to-day operations of the criminal justice system, especially in the area of law enforcement. Search and seizure and interrogation law have especially become cumbersome and difficult to understand, let alone to apply in fast-developing and sometimes dangerous situations that police officers and other officials routinely face.

While the case materials that the Court reviews continue to increase, an expected result of that issue is that the many textbooks that cover criminal procedure have tended to become more complex. Many excellent texts exist in this area, and they are written by many prominent scholars. However, one of their main drawbacks is that they are often long and complicated, making it very difficult for the average undergraduate student to comprehend. One of the main reasons for this book is to simplify that material and make it easily digestible not only for the average student but also for instructors that are just beginning to develop an interest in criminal procedure. For those who have studied this area for some time, this book also serves as an easy guide to the major issues that are typically covered in such courses. Finally, the organization and presentation of the material also makes this book accessible to police officers and laypersons who might be either required to know criminal processing or have a general interest in it.

Each chapter begins with a brief introduction that summarizes the major issues that will be presented. It describes the issues by both asking and answering questions that the cases will highlight. This method is used primarily to familiarize the reader with the material that will follow in the briefs so as to provide some insight into what the Court has said before getting into the chapter itself. Each brief is composed of four major parts. First, the "Facts," which present the background of the case, the charges, and the actions of the officials that resulted in the decision that was challenged. Second, the "Issue" addresses the major legal point for that particular case. In traditional criminal procedure textbooks, cases are sometimes repeated because they frequently deal with many different issues. However, that approach is avoided here in an attempt to specifically reduce confusion and repetition. Therefore, only one major issue is usually presented and addressed in this section and is done in the form of a question. Third, the "Holding" is essentially the answer to the question presented in the "Issue" part of the brief. It is answered either "yes" or "no." Fourth, the last part of the brief is the "Rationale," and it states the Court's reasoning behind the decision that it made.

The material for this book was taken from Lexis-Nexis and Westlaw, the electronic legal resources. The case facts have been edited from this material and are not direct quotations from those databases. Also, the issues and holdings are frequently reworded so as to provide clarity for the reader. The only material that is quoted from the cases themselves is that presented in the "Rationale" for each of the briefs. However, case citations, parenthetical references, and the like have been omitted. Ellipses (. . .) have been inserted where text has been deleted to improve the clarity of the justification for the decision. The idea throughout is to present the material in as clear and concise a manner as possible in an attempt to foster the greatest amount of understanding and comprehension.

I would like to acknowledge those who have helped me with this project and I dare say that without their assistance, this book would never have been completed. First, I would like to defer to my lovely wife. Without her support, sacrifice, effort, and love, I could accomplish nothing. There is the old saying, "Behind every good man is a good woman." In my case, the good woman "is in front of" the man who is trying to be good but is probably failing miserably!

I am also grateful for the assistance of Rosalie Robertson, former senior editor at AltaMira Press. She was very patient and helpful and gave me clear guidance throughout this process. I am also naturally thankful for Christopher Anzalone, Karen Ackermann, Sarah Walker, and their editorial staff at Rowman & Littlefield, whose effort has been integral to this book's completion. Finally, I would like to thank Mr. Chad Martin and Miss Christy Winchester, who retrieved much of the material that I needed to write the book.

Table of Cases

I

SEIZING PEOPLE

1

Reasonable Suspicion and Stop and Frisk

SEIZING A PERSON FOR THE PURPOSES of conducting an investigation is a serious action. The police routinely stop people; briefly detain them, and sometimes even conduct cursory searches of their clothing and person for several different reasons. First, police can stop an individual as a means to protect themselves (and others), from perceived or impending danger. As one might expect, the police cannot just walk up to someone on the street, or anywhere else for that matter, and stop a person and begin searching them without purpose. They must have some articulable reason for which they have detained an individual. When such a stop is made, the authorities invoke the Fourth Amendment to the United States Constitution, which protects people from unreasonable searches and seizures. A stop, according to the United States Supreme Court, is a seizure within the meaning of the Fourth Amendment and must, therefore, be reasonable for it to be lawful. In addition, after the police lawfully stop someone, they can also conduct a brief search, which also invokes the Fourth Amendment because it too must be reasonable. Several matters associated with reasonable suspicion, brief stops, and these cursory searches are detailed in this chapter.

If the police decide at some point that they wish to stop and search a person, they need to have some facts or information that allows them to think that someone may be engaging in criminal activity. The collection of facts that the police need to briefly stop and detain a person for the purpose of protecting themselves or other citizens is called *reasonable suspicion.*

For example, the Supreme Court has defined reasonable suspicion as a quantum of facts that would lead an average person to believe that criminal activity was happening, has already happened, or is about to happen. One would think that perhaps that definition is pretty clear, but the Court has adopted what it calls a "totality of the circumstances" test to determine whether or not the police had reasonable suspicion when a stop was made. So in reality, determining whether or not police had reasonable suspicion when they detained someone can be a balancing act.

Another matter that is related to the determination of reasonable suspicion is what information can the police use to ascertain if someone may be acting improperly? This matter is just as important as allowing the police to detain a person in the first place. Another way of addressing the issue is saying that the information that the police collect allows them to determine if someone is acting in such a way as to warrant further checking.

The Supreme Court has spoken on the issue quite frequently and in great detail in an effort to help the police determine what kind of behavior can be thought to arouse the need for further investigation. One might ask, can the police use the information given to them by an informant that they verify with other information to stop someone? The Supreme Court has answered that question in the affirmative and has allowed an officer to reach into the waistband of a person who was sitting in his car to seize a gun. Frequently in the media we hear about how the police issue bulletins, which give detailed descriptions of suspected offenders. Can these descriptions amount to enough questionable information about a person to warrant the police stopping someone that resembles the description? The Supreme Court has said that they do. What about an attempt by the police to identify someone not suspected of criminal activity? Can they arrest someone who refuses to identify themselves in such a situation? Not according to the Supreme Court. Additionally, the police can also stop people who are driving in such a way that alerts them to possible criminal activity. Can the police stop people that are suspected of being in the United States illegally? Yes, and they can stop them even at their employer's place of business. Another question might be, how long can the police detain a person after the police obtain reasonable suspicion? The Supreme Court has said that while it would not create a "bright line rule," thirty minutes is not an unreasonable amount of time.

It should now be clear that the police can stop people and briefly detain them in many different kinds of circumstances. It should be equally apparent that the police cannot just stop anyone they want, whenever they want; they must have some information that leads them to believe that something illegal is happening. The next matter that needs to be addressed is, what can the police do, if anything, to a person once they have been lawfully detained?

The Supreme Court has said that once a person is lawfully stopped under the reasonable suspicion standard, the police may conduct a cursory search called a *frisk*. Again, the Court has taken the lead in defining for the police what a frisk entails. A frisk is a light "pat-down" of a person's outer clothing in an attempt to determine if that individual is armed or presents a threat. It takes place rather quickly and cannot be used as a platform by the police to conduct a more invasive search unless evidence of weapons is found. It is designed to confirm or dispel the suspicion of the officer that the person is armed and dangerous, and its length and invasiveness are circumscribed by this suspicion.

A natural question in this area is, what if an officer comes across something on the person of a suspect that has been lawfully stopped but the identity of the object is not immediately apparent to the officer? The Supreme Court has ruled that such situations require that the officer know the identity of the object during the frisk, before he or she may use it against the person. In fact, the Court has stated that if the officer must focus the search on the object in order to identify it by manipulating it in a way that requires additional investigation, the officer may not use it as evidence under the rules governing frisks.

A. What Is Reasonable Suspicion?

1. Objective Amount of Information

United States v. Sokolow, 490 U.S. 1 (1989)
Vote: 7-2
FACTS: Upon his arrival at Honolulu International Airport, Andrew Sokolow was stopped by Drug Enforcement Administration (DEA) agents. The agents knew that (1) Sokolow paid $2,100 for two airplane tickets from a roll of $20 bills; (2) he traveled under a name that did not match the name under which his telephone number was listed; (3) his original destination was Miami, a source city for illicit drugs; (4) he stayed in Miami for only forty-eight hours, even though a round-trip flight from Honolulu to Miami takes twenty hours; (5) he appeared nervous during his trip; and (6) he checked none of his luggage. The agents found 1,063 grams of cocaine in his carry-on luggage. Sokolow was subsequently charged with possessing cocaine with intent to distribute and entered a conditional guilty plea.
ISSUE: Is the reasonable suspicion level of objective information greater than a hunch?
HOLDING: Yes.
RATIONALE: "Reasonable suspicion entails some minimal level of objective justification for making a stop—that is, something more than an inchoate and unparticularized suspicion or 'hunch,' but less than the level of suspicion required for probable cause."

"[T]he police can stop and briefly detain a person for investigative purposes if they have a reasonable suspicion supported by articulable facts that criminal activity 'may be afoot,' even if they lack probable cause under the Fourth Amendment."

"The concept of reasonable suspicion, like probable cause, is not 'readily, or even usefully, reduced to a neat set of legal rules. . . .' The process does not deal with hard certainties, but with probabilities. Long before the law of probabilities was articulated as such, practical people formulated certain common-sense conclusions about human behavior; jurors as fact-finders are permitted to do the same—and so are law enforcement officers."

"Paying $2,100 in cash for two airplane tickets is out of the ordinary, and it is even more out of the ordinary to pay that sum from a roll of $20 bills containing nearly twice that amount of cash. Most business travelers, we feel confident, purchase airline tickets by credit card or check so as to have a record for tax or business purposes, and few vacationers carry with them thousands of dollars in $20 bills. We also think the agents had a reasonable ground to believe that respondent was traveling under an alias; the evidence was by no means conclusive, but it was sufficient to warrant consideration. While a trip from Honolulu to Miami, standing alone, is not a cause for any sort of suspicion, here there was more: surely few residents of Honolulu travel from that city for 20 hours to spend 48 hours in Miami during the month of July."

"Any one of these factors is not by itself proof of any illegal conduct and is quite consistent with innocent travel. But we think taken together they amount to reasonable suspicion."

2. Is There a Test for Obtaining Reasonable Suspicion?

United States v. Arvizu, 534 U.S. 266 (2002)
Vote: 9-0

FACTS: Border Patrol Agent Clinton Stoddard saw a minivan, a type of automobile favored by smugglers, slow dramatically as it approached his patrol car. The driver, Ralph Arvizu, appeared stiff and his posture very rigid. He did not look at Stoddard and seemed to be trying to pretend that he was not there. Stoddard followed the car and observed that the passengers in the vehicle—children—waved to him in an unusual, mechanical way. He stopped the van after it made an abrupt turn, and after finding out that the van was registered to a location just above the Mexican border that is known for drug trafficking, Arvizu consented to a search of the vehicle, where Stoddard found nearly 130 pounds of marijuana. Arvizu entered a conditional guilty plea to the charge of possession with intent to distribute.

ISSUE: Is the test for obtaining reasonable suspicion "totality of the circumstances"?
HOLDING: Yes.

RATIONALE: "When discussing how reviewing courts should make the reasonable-suspicion determinations, we have repeatedly said that they must look at the 'totality of the circumstances' of each case to see whether the detaining officer has a 'particularized and objective basis' for suspecting legal wrongdoing. . . . This process allows officers to draw on their own experience and specialized training to make inferences from and deductions about the cumulative information available. . . ."

"We think that the approach taken by the Court of Appeals here departs sharply from the teachings of these cases. The court's evaluation and rejection of seven of the listed factors in isolation from each other does not take into account the 'totality of the circumstances.'"

"The Court of Appeals' view that it was necessary to 'clearly delimit' an officer's consideration of certain factors to reduce 'troubling . . . uncertainty . . .' also runs counter to our cases and underestimates the usefulness of the reasonable-suspicion standard in guiding officers in the field."

"Having considered the totality of the circumstances and given due weight to the factual inferences drawn by the law enforcement officer and District Court Judge, we hold that Stoddard had reasonable suspicion to believe that respondent was engaged in illegal activity."

B. Stop and Frisk Defined

Terry v. Ohio, 392 U.S. 1 (1968)
Vote: 8-1

FACTS: Martin McFadden, a Cleveland detective, observed John Terry and Richard Chilton on a street corner. He saw them proceed alternately back and forth along an identical route, pausing to stare in the same store window, which they did many times.

Each completion of the route was followed by a conference between the two, and then at one point they were joined by a third man, who quickly left. Suspecting the two men of impending criminal activity, McFadden followed them and saw them rejoin the third man in front of a store. The officer approached them, identified himself, and asked their names. McFadden spun Terry around, patted down his outside clothing, and found a pistol. He also found one on Chilton. Both men were convicted of carrying a concealed weapon.

ISSUE: Is a search of the outer clothing for weapons violative of the Fourth Amendment?

HOLDING: No.

RATIONALE: "Where a reasonably prudent officer is warranted in the circumstances of a given case in believing that his safety or that of others is endangered, he may make a reasonable search for weapons of the person believed by him to be armed and dangerous regardless of whether he has probable cause to arrest. . . . Though the police must whenever practicable secure a warrant to make a search and seizure, that procedure cannot be followed where swift action based upon on-the-spot observations of the officer on the beat is required. . . . The officer here was performing a legitimate function of investigating suspicious conduct when he decided to approach petitioner and his companions. . . . An officer justified in believing that an individual whose suspicious behavior he is investigating at close range is armed may, to neutralize the threat of physical harm, take necessary measures to determine whether that person is carrying a weapon."

"The officer's search was confined to what was minimally necessary to determine whether the men were armed, and the intrusion, which was made for the sole purpose of protecting himself and others nearby, was confined to ascertaining the presence of weapons."

C. Scope of a Stop and Frisk

1. Searching Outside the Bounds of Terry

Minnesota v. Dickerson, 508 U.S. 366 (1993)

Vote: 9-0

FACTS: Two Minneapolis police officers observed Timothy Dickerson leave a building. One of the officers identified the building as a crack house. Initially, Dickerson made eye contact but quickly shifted his direction and moved down an alley away from the officers, who then decided to investigate further. The officers used their car to block Dickerson's exit from the alley and ordered him to submit to a pat-down. The officer found no weapons but felt a lump in his pocket. After manipulating the object, the officer opened the pocket and discovered a package, which contained crack cocaine. Dickerson was charged and convicted with possession of a controlled substance.

ISSUE: If it is determined that the drugs seized by police exceed the bounds of *Terry*, can the evidence be used for a conviction?

HOLDING: No.

RATIONALE: "Rather, a protective search—permitted without a warrant and on the basis of reasonable suspicion less than probable cause—must be strictly 'limited to that which is necessary for the discovery of weapons which might be used to harm the officer or others nearby. . . .' If the protective search goes beyond what is necessary to determine if the suspect is armed, it is no longer valid. . . ."

"[I]t is clear that the court was correct in holding that the police officer in this case overstepped the bounds of the 'strictly circumscribed' search for weapons. . . . Where, as here, 'an officer who is executing a valid search for one item seizes a different item,' this Court rightly 'has been sensitive to the danger' . . . that officers will enlarge a specific authorization. . . . Here, the officer's continued exploration of respondent's pocket after having concluded that it contained no weapon was unrelated to '[t]he sole justification of the search [under *Terry*.] the protection of the police officer and others nearby. . . .' It therefore amounted to the sort of evidentiary search that *Terry* [*v. Ohio*, 392 U.S. 1 (1968)] expressly refused to authorize, and that we have condemned. . . ."

2. Presence in a High-Crime Area

Illinois v. Wardlow, 528 U.S. 119 (2000)

Vote: 5-4

FACTS: Chicago police officers, Nolan and Harvey, were driving the last car of a four-car caravan converging on an area known for heavy narcotics trafficking. Officer Nolan observed respondent Sam Wardlow standing next to a building holding an opaque bag. Wardlow looked in the direction of the officers and fled. Nolan and Harvey turned their car southbound, watched him as he ran through the alley, and cornered him on the street. Nolan exited his car and stopped Wardlow. He immediately conducted a protective pat-down search for weapons. During the frisk, Nolan squeezed the bag respondent was carrying and felt a heavy, hard object similar to the shape of a gun. The officer then opened the bag and discovered a .38 caliber handgun with five live rounds of ammunition. Wardlow was convicted of unlawful use of a weapon by a felon.

ISSUE: Is mere presence in an area known for crime enough to support reasonable suspicion to justify a stop and frisk?

HOLDING: No.

RATIONALE: "An individual's presence in area of expected criminal activity, standing alone, is not enough to support reasonable, particularized suspicion that person is committing a crime . . . But officers are not required to ignore relevant characteristics of location in determining whether circumstances are sufficiently suspicious to warrant further investigation."

"In this case, moreover, it was not merely respondent's presence in an area of heavy narcotics trafficking that aroused the officers' suspicion, but his unprovoked flight upon noticing the police. Our cases have also recognized that nervous, evasive behavior is a pertinent factor in determining reasonable suspicion. . . . Headlong flight—wherever it occurs—is the consummate act of evasion. . . . Thus, the determination of reasonable suspicion must be based on commonsense judgments and inferences about human behavior. . . . Flight, by its very nature, is not 'going about one's business;' in fact, it is just the opposite."

3. Does a Tip Equate to Reasonable Suspicion?

Florida v. J.L., 529 U.S. 266 (2000)
Vote: 9-0
FACTS: An anonymous caller reported to the Miami-Dade Police that a young, black male, wearing a plaid shirt, was carrying a gun. There was no audio recording of the tip, and nothing was known about the informant. Sometime after the police received the tip—the record does not say how long—two officers responded. They arrived at the bus stop and saw three black males "just hanging out [there]." One of the men, J.L., was indeed wearing a plaid shirt, but apart from that fact the officers had no reason to suspect any of the three of engaging in criminality. The officers did not see a firearm, and J.L. made no unusual movements. One of the officers approached J.L., told him to put his hands up, frisked him, and seized a gun from his pocket. The second officer frisked the others and found nothing. Fifteen-year-old, J.L. was charged with carrying a concealed firearm without a license and possession of a firearm.
ISSUE: Is an anonymous tip that a person is carrying a gun sufficient to justify a stop-and-frisk based on reasonable suspicion?
HOLDING: No.
RATIONALE: "[T]ip provided no predictive information that would provide police with means to test informant's knowledge or credibility, so that all police had to rely on was bare report of an unknown, unaccountable informant who neither explained how he knew about gun nor supplied any basis for believing he had inside information."

"Here, the officers' suspicion that J.L. was carrying a weapon arose not from their own observations but solely from a call made from an unknown location by an unknown caller. The tip lacked sufficient indicia of reliability to provide reasonable suspicion to make a *Terry* [*v. Ohio*, 392 U.S. 1 (1968)] stop: It provided no predictive information and therefore left the police without means to test the informant's knowledge or credibility."

"The reasonableness of official suspicion must be measured by what the officers knew before they conducted their search."

"An accurate description of a subject's readily observable location and appearance is of course reliable in this limited sense: It will help the police correctly identify the person whom the tipster means to accuse. Such a tip, however, does not show that the tipster has knowledge of concealed criminal activity."

D. Under What Circumstances Can Reasonable Suspicion Be Obtained and a Stop Executed?

1. Reasonable Suspicion and the Informant

Adams v. Williams, 407 U.S. 143 (1972)

Vote: 6-3

FACTS: Police officer John Connolly was on patrol in Bridgeport, Connecticut. A person known to Connolly approached and informed him that an individual in a nearby vehicle was carrying narcotics and had a gun at his waist. After calling for assistance, Connolly approached, tapped on the car window, and asked Robert Williams to open the door. When Williams rolled down the window instead, the sergeant reached into the car and removed a fully loaded revolver in precisely the place indicated by the informant. A search incident to that arrest revealed substantial quantities of heroin on Williams and in the car, and they found a machete and a second revolver hidden in the automobile. Williams was arrested and convicted of unlawful possession of a handgun and possession of heroin.

ISSUE: Can police justifiably act on a tip provided by a previously reliable informant?

HOLDING: Yes.

RATIONALE: "So long as the officer is entitled to make a forcible stop, and has reason to believe that the suspect is armed and dangerous, he may conduct a weapons search limited in scope to this protective purpose."

"In reaching this conclusion, we reject respondent's argument that reasonable cause for a stop and frisk can only be based on the officer's personal observation, rather than on information supplied by another person. Informants' tips, like all other clues and evidence coming to a policeman on the scene, may vary greatly in their value and reliability. One simple rule will not cover every situation. . . . But in some situations—for example, when the victim of a street crime seeks immediate police aid and gives a description of his assailant, or when a credible informant warns of a specific impending crime—the subtleties of the hearsay rule should not thwart an appropriate police response."

"[T]he policeman found Williams in possession of a gun in precisely the place predicted by the informant. This tended to corroborate the reliability . . . and, together with the surrounding circumstances, certainly suggested no lawful explanation for possession of the gun."

2. Reasonable Suspicion and the Wanted Flyer

United States v. Hensley, 469 U.S. 221 (1985)

Vote: 9-0

FACTS: Two armed men robbed a tavern in St. Bernard, Ohio. Six days later, police officer Kenneth Davis, interviewed an informant who passed along information that Thomas Hensley had driven the getaway car during the robbery. Davis obtained a written statement from the informant and immediately issued a "wanted flyer" to other police departments in the area. The flyer twice stated that Hensley was wanted for aggravated robbery. It described both Hensley and the date and location of the robbery, and asked other departments to pick up and hold Hensley for the St. Bernard police. The flyer also warned departments to consider Hensley armed and dangerous.

The "wanted flyer" was received in the Covington Police Department and read aloud at each change of shift. Officer Terence Eger saw Hensley in the driver's seat of a white Cadillac and asked him to move on. As he drove away, Eger inquired whether there was a warrant and two other officers said that there might be a robbery warrant outstanding. Officers Daniel Cope and David Rassache, testified that they had heard or read the flyer, that they recalled that the flyer sought a stop and that the issuance of such a flyer was usually followed by the issuance of a warrant. Cope reported that he had sighted a white Cadillac and turned on his flashing lights and Hensley pulled over. Cope approached Hensley's car with his service revolver drawn and had Hensley and passenger Albert Green step out. Moments later, Rassache stepped up to the open passenger door and observed the butt of a revolver. Green was then arrested. A search of the car uncovered a second handgun and a third handgun in the back seat. After the discovery of these weapons, Hensley was also arrested and convicted of possession of a firearm by a convicted felon.

ISSUE: Can police make a *Terry* stop based on reasonable suspicion from a "wanted flyer"?

HOLDING: Yes.

RATIONALE: "If a 'wanted flyer' has been issued on the basis of articulable facts supporting a reasonable suspicion that the person wanted has committed an offense, then reliance on that flyer justifies a stop to check identification, to pose questions, or to detain the person briefly."

"In an era when criminal suspects are increasingly mobile and increasingly likely to flee across jurisdictional boundaries, this rule is a matter of common sense: it minimizes the volume of information concerning suspects that must be transmitted to other jurisdictions and enables police in one jurisdiction to act promptly."

"The law enforcement interests promoted by allowing one department to make investigatory stops based upon another department's bulletins or flyers are considerable, while the intrusion on personal security is minimal."

"We hold that the evidence uncovered in the course of the stop is admissible if the police who *issued* the flyer or bulletin possessed a reasonable suspicion justifying a stop. . . ."

3. Reasonable Suspicion and Identification

a. Identification Statutes Unsupported by Reasonable Suspicion

Brown v. Texas, 443 U.S. 47 (1979)

Vote: 9-0

FACTS: Two police officers, Venegas and Sotelo, observed two men walking away from one another in an alley in an area with high levels of trafficking. They stopped and asked Brown to identify himself. One officer testified that he stopped him because he "looked suspicious and we had never seen that subject in that area before." The police did not suspect Brown of engaging in criminality, nor did they believe that he was armed. When Brown refused to identify himself, he was arrested and convicted for violation of a Texas statute that made it a crime for a person to refuse to give his name and address to an officer who has lawfully stopped him.

ISSUE: Can police conduct a *Terry* stop under the auspices of a statute that requires a person to identify themselves when police do not suspect that the person is engaging in criminality?

HOLDING: No.

RATIONALE: "An individual's reasonable expectation of privacy is not subject to arbitrary invasions solely at the unfettered discretion of officers . . . a seizure must be based on specific, objective facts. . . . The State . . . maintains that the officers were justified in stopping appellant because they had a 'reasonable, articulable suspicion that a crime had just been, was being, or was about to be committed. ' . . . [W]e have required the officers to have a reasonable suspicion, based on objective facts, that the individual is involved in criminal activity."

"The flaw in the State's case is that none of the circumstances preceding the officers' detention of appellant justified a reasonable suspicion that he was involved in criminal conduct. Officer Venegas . . . was unable to point to any facts supporting that conclusion. There is no indication in the record that it was unusual for people to be in the alley. The fact that appellant was in a neighborhood frequented by drug users, standing alone, is not a basis for concluding that appellant himself was engaged in criminal conduct. . . . Officer Venegas acknowledged that the only reason he stopped appellant was to ascertain his identity."

b. Identification Statutes Supported by Reasonable Suspicion

Hiibel v. Sixth Judicial District Court, 542 U.S. 177 (2004)
Vote: 5-4

FACTS: The sheriff's department got a call reporting an assault. The caller reported seeing a man strike a woman in a truck on a certain road. Deputy Sheriff Lee Dove arrived and found a truck matching the description at the side of the road and marks on the road indicated that the truck had stopped suddenly. Larry Dudley Hiibel appeared drunk and when asked on several occasions to identify himself, refused to do so. He became agitated and insisted that he had done nothing wrong. Dove explained that he was conducting an investigation concerning a fight and that continuing to refuse in light of his condition would result in arrest. Hiibel was charged and convicted of willfully resisting, delaying, or obstructing a police officer in discharging or attempting to discharge any legal duty of his office in conjunction with Nevada's "stop and identify" statute.

ISSUE: Can the police make an arrest based upon a "failure to identify" statute during the course of a legitimate *Terry* stop?

HOLDING: Yes.

RATIONALE: "The principles of *Terry* [*v. Ohio*, 392 U.S. 1 (1968)] permit a State to require a suspect to disclose his name in the course of a *Terry* stop. The reasonableness of a seizure under the Fourth Amendment is determined 'by balancing its intrusion on the individual's Fourth Amendment interests against its promotion of legitimate government interests. . . .' The Nevada statute satisfies that standard. The request for identity has an immediate relation to the purpose, rationale, and practical demands of a *Terry* stop. The threat of criminal sanction helps ensure that the request for identity does not become a legal nullity. . . . A state law requiring a suspect to disclose his name in the course of a valid *Terry* stop is consistent with Fourth Amendment."

"Here, the initial stop was based on reasonable suspicion, satisfying the Fourth Amendment requirements. . . ."

4. Reasonable Suspicion and the Corroboration of Anonymous Tips

Alabama v. White, 496 U.S 325 (1990)
Vote: 6-3

FACTS: Corporal B. H. Davis of the Montgomery Police Department received a call from an anonymous person, stating that Vanessa White would be leaving 235-C Lynwood Terrace Apartments in a brown station wagon with the right taillight lens broken, that she would be going to Dobey's Motel, and that she would be in possession of cocaine inside a brown attaché case. Davis and his partner, P. A. Reynolds, proceeded to the complex and saw a brown Plymouth station wagon with a broken right taillight in front of the 235 building. Davis and Reynolds observed White leave the 235 building and enter the car. They followed the vehicle as it took the most direct route to Dobey's Motel. Reynolds requested a unit to stop the vehicle. He asked if they could look for cocaine, and received consent to do so. The officers found a brown attaché case in the car, and White provided the combination. At the station, the officers found three milligrams of cocaine in her purse. She filed a conditional guilty plea to the charges of possession of marijuana and cocaine.

ISSUE: Can an anonymous tip, corroborated by the police and independent investigation, amount to reasonable suspicion?

HOLDING: Yes.

RATIONALE: "[I]nformant's veracity, reliability and basis of knowledge, are highly relevant. These factors are also relevant in the reasonable suspicion context. . . . [I]n this case there is more than the tip itself."

"Reasonable suspicion . . . is dependent upon both the content of information possessed by police and its degree of reliability. Both factors—quantity and quality—are considered in the 'totality of the circumstances—the whole picture.' . . . Contrary to the court below, we conclude that when the officers stopped respondent, the anonymous tip had been sufficiently corroborated to furnish reasonable suspicion that respondent was engaged in criminal activity and that the investigative stop therefore did not violate the Fourth Amendment."

"[B]ecause an informant is shown to be right about some things, he is probably right about other facts that he has alleged, including the claim that the object of the tip is engaged in criminal activity . . . the independent corroboration by the police of significant aspects of the informer's predictions imparted some degree of reliability to the other allegations."

"What was important was the caller's ability to predict respondent's *future behavior,* because it demonstrated inside information."

5. Reasonable Suspicion and Automobile Stops

Delaware v. Prouse, 440 U.S. 648 (1979)
Vote: 8-1
FACTS: A Delaware policeman stopped Prouse's car and smelled marihuana smoke as he was walking toward it. Upon arriving at the driver's side of the vehicle he seized marihuana in plain view on the floor. Prouse was indicted for illegal possession of a controlled substance. At a hearing on Prouse's motion to suppress the marihuana, the officer testified that prior to stopping the car he had not observed any suspected activity that was in violation of the law but that he made the stop only to check the driver's license and registration. The officer was not acting in conjunction with any police procedures.
ISSUE: May the police stop a vehicle and detain the driver for a license check absent reasonable suspicion that the driver has violated the law?
HOLDING: No.
RATIONALE: "Stopping an automobile and detaining its occupants constitute a 'seizure. . . .' The essential purpose of the proscriptions in the Fourth Amendment is to impose a standard of 'reasonableness' upon the exercise of discretion by government officials, including law enforcement agents, in order to 'safeguard the privacy and security of individuals against arbitrary invasions.'"

"To insist neither upon an appropriate factual basis for suspicion directed at a particular automobile nor upon some other substantial and objective standard or rule to govern the exercise of discretion 'would invite intrusions upon constitutionally guaranteed rights based on nothing more substantial than inarticulate hunches. . . .' By hypothesis, stopping apparently safe drivers is necessary only because the danger presented by some drivers is not observable at the time of the stop. When there is not probable cause to believe that a driver is violating any one of the multitude of applicable traffic and equipment regulations—or other articulable basis amounting to reasonable suspicion that the driver is unlicensed or his vehicle unregistered—we cannot conceive of any legitimate basis upon which a patrolman could decide that stopping a particular driver for a spot check would be more productive than stopping any other driver."

"Accordingly, we hold that except in those situations in which there is at least articulable and reasonable suspicion that a motorist is unlicensed or that an automobile is not registered, or that either the vehicle or an occupant is otherwise subject to seizure for violation of law, stopping an automobile and detaining the driver in order to check his driver's license and the registration of the automobile are unreasonable under the Fourth Amendment."

6. Reasonable Suspicion and the Questioning of Suspected Illegal Aliens

United States v. Brignoni-Ponce, 422 U.S. 873 (1975)
Vote: 9-0
FACTS: Two Border Patrol agents were observing northbound traffic in Southern California from a car at the side of the highway and they were using the car's lights to illuminate passing cars. They stopped respondent's car because its three occupants appeared to be Mexican. The officers questioned Brignoni-Ponce and his two passengers about their citizenship and learned that the passengers were illegals. Brignoni-Ponce was charged with and convicted of two counts of knowingly transporting illegal immigrants.
ISSUE: May a roving border patrol stop a vehicle and question the occupants solely on their appearance?
HOLDING: No.
RATIONALE: "[W]e hold that when an officer's observations lead him reasonably to suspect that a particular vehicle may contain aliens who are illegally in the country, he may stop the car briefly and investigate the circumstances that provoke suspicion. As in *Terry*, the stop and inquiry must be 'reasonably related in scope to the justification for their initiation. . . .'"

"We are unwilling to let the Border Patrol dispense entirely with the requirement that officers must have a reasonable suspicion to justify roving-patrol stops. In the context of border area stops, the reasonableness requirement of the Fourth Amendment demands something more than the broad and unlimited discretion sought by the Government. Roads near the border carry not only aliens seeking to enter the country illegally, but a large volume of legitimate traffic as well. . . . To approve roving-patrol stops of all vehicles in the border area, without any suspicion that a particular vehicle is carrying illegal immigrants, would subject the residents of these and other areas to potentially unlimited interference. . . ."

"[T]he nature of illegal alien traffic and the characteristics of smuggling operations tend to generate articulable grounds for identifying violators. Consequently, a requirement of reasonable suspicion for stops allows the Government adequate means of guarding the public interest and also protects residents of the border areas. . . ."

"In this case the officers relied on a single factor to justify stopping respondent's car: the apparent Mexican ancestry of the occupants. We cannot conclude that this furnished reasonable grounds to believe that the three occupants were aliens. . . . [T]his factor alone would justify neither a reasonable belief that they were aliens, nor a reasonable belief that the car concealed other aliens."

7. Reasonable Suspicion and the Questioning of Illegal Aliens at Their Employer

Immigration and Naturalization Service v. Delgado, 466 U.S. 210 (1984)

FACTS: Acting on search warrants, the Immigration and Naturalization Service (INS) conducted two "factory surveys" of the employees in two factories. A third was conducted with the employer's consent at another location. Each survey lasted from one to two hours. Agents positioned themselves near the exits while others moved through the factory asking the employees questions pertaining to their citizenship. If an employee was a citizen or permanent resident, the agent moved on. While the survey was being conducted, the employees continued their work and were free to walk around. Some employees and their union filed actions alleging that the factory surveys conducted by the INS violated the Fourth Amendment.

ISSUE: Are "factory surveys" conducted by INS agents, seizures under the Fourth Amendment requiring reasonable suspicion before questioning of employees can take place?

HOLDING: No.

RATIONALE: "We conclude that these factory surveys did not result in the seizure of the entire work forces, and that the individual questioning of the respondents in this case by INS agents concerning their citizenship did not amount to a detention or seizure under the Fourth Amendment."

"The Fourth Amendment does not proscribe all contact between the police and citizens, but is designed 'to prevent arbitrary and oppressive interference by enforcement officials. . . .' 'Obviously, not all personal intercourse between policemen and citizens involves "seizures" of persons. Only when the officer, by means of physical force or show of authority, has restrained the liberty of a citizen may we conclude that a "seizure" has occurred. . . .'"

"[O]ur recent decision in [*Florida v. Royer*, 460 U.S. 491 (1983)], plainly implies that interrogation relating to one's identity or a request for identification by the police does not, by itself, constitute a Fourth Amendment seizure."

"We reject the claim that the entire work forces of the two factories were seized. . . . Ordinarily, when people are at work their freedom to move about has been meaningfully restricted, not by the actions of law enforcement officials, but by the workers' voluntary obligations to their employers. The record indicates that when these surveys were initiated, the employees were about their ordinary business, operating machinery and performing other job assignments. While the surveys did cause some disruption, including the efforts of some workers to hide, the record also indicates that workers were not prevented by the agents from moving about the factories."

"The record indicates that the INS agents' conduct in this case consisted simply of questioning employees and arresting those they had probable cause to believe were unlawfully present in the factory. . . ."

"[T]he mere possibility that they would be questioned if they sought to leave the buildings should not have resulted in any reasonable apprehension by any of them that they would be seized or detained in any meaningful way."

8. Reasonable Suspicion and the Length of Detention

a. Several Minutes and the Legitimacy of Detention

United States v. Sharpe, 470 U.S. 675 (1985)
Vote: 7-2

FACTS: DEA agent Cooke noticed an overloaded truck with an attached camper traveling with a blue Pontiac Bonneville. Savage was driving the truck; Sharpe was driving the car. After following the two vehicles for some time, Cooke decided to make a stop and radioed the South Carolina State Highway Patrol for assistance. When Officer Thrasher attempted to stop them, the car pulled over, but the truck continued. Thrasher continued after the truck while Cooke stayed with the car. After obtaining identification from Sharpe, Cooke unsuccessfully tried to radio Thrasher. Meanwhile, Thrasher had stopped the truck and told Savage that he would be held until the agent arrived, which was about fifteen minutes later. After smelling marihuana, Cooke opened the camper and observed some forty-three bales of marijuana. Approximately thirty to forty minutes had elapsed between the time Cooke stopped the Pontiac and the time he returned to arrest Sharpe. Savage and Sharpe were convicted of possession of a controlled substance with intent to distribute.

ISSUE: Is a twenty-minute *Terry* stop reasonable under the Fourth Amendment?

HOLDING: Yes.

RATIONALE: "In assessing whether a detention is too long in duration to be justified as an investigative stop, we consider it appropriate to examine whether the police diligently pursued a means of investigation that was likely to confirm or dispel their suspicions quickly. . . . A court making this assessment should take care to consider whether the police are acting in a swiftly developing situation. . . ."

"Agent Cooke pursued his investigation in a diligent and reasonable manner. During most of Savage's 20-minute detention, Cooke was attempting to contact Thrasher and enlisting the help of the local police who remained with Sharpe while Cooke left to pursue Officer Thrasher and the pickup. Once Cooke reached Officer Thrasher and Savage, he proceeded expeditiously: within the space of a few minutes, he examined Savage's driver's license and the truck's bill of sale, requested (and was denied) permission to search the truck, stepped on the rear bumper and noted that the truck did not move, confirming his suspicion that it was probably overloaded."

"It was appropriate for Officer Thrasher to hold Savage for the brief period pending Cooke's arrival. Thrasher could not be certain that he was aware of all of the facts that had aroused Cooke's suspicions. . . ."

"The delay in this case was attributable almost entirely to the evasive actions of Savage. . . ."

"We reject the notion that a 20-minute stop is unreasonable when the police have acted diligently and a suspect's actions contribute to the added delay about which he complains."

b. Length of Detention and Luggage

United States v. Place, 462 U.S. 696 (1983)

Vote: 9-0

FACTS: On one particular Friday, Raymond J. Place waited at the Miami International Airport to buy a ticket to La Guardia Airport in New York City. Law enforcement officers, suspicious of Place's behavior, approached him and requested his ticket and identification. Place consented to a search of two bags but the officers decided not to conduct the search. The officers did notify the Drug Enforcement Agency (DEA) in NYC to make them aware of the situation and Place's arrival. When Place refused to consent to a search of his luggage, the agents seized the luggage in order to take it to a federal judge to obtain a search warrant. Before that, however, the agents subjected the luggage to a "sniff test" by a trained narcotics detection dog, which reacted positively to one of the suitcases. Approximately ninety minutes transpired between the seizure and the "sniff test." Waiting until the following Monday, the agents obtained a search warrant for that suitcase and upon opening it discovered more than a thousand grams of cocaine. Place was arrested and convicted of possession of narcotics.

ISSUE: Can police detain luggage for ninety minutes so that a dog can sniff it for drugs?

HOLDING: No.

RATIONALE: "In sum, we conclude that when an officer's observations lead him reasonably to believe that a traveler is carrying luggage that contains narcotics, the principles of *Terry* and its progeny would permit the officer to detain the luggage briefly to investigate the circumstances that aroused his suspicion, provided that the investigative detention is properly limited in scope."

"The length of the detention of respondent's luggage alone precludes the conclusion that the seizure was reasonable in the absence of probable cause. Although we have recognized the reasonableness of seizures longer than the momentary ones involved in *Terry* [*v. Ohio*, 392 U.S. 1 (1968)], *Adams* [*v. Williams*, 407 U.S. 143 (1972)], and [*United States v. Brignoni-Ponce*, 422 U.S. 873 (1975)], the brevity of the invasion of the individual's Fourth Amendment interests is an important factor in determining whether the seizure is so minimally intrusive as to be justifiable on reasonable suspicion. Moreover, in assessing the effect of the length of the detention, we take into account whether the police diligently pursue their investigation. We note that here the New York agents knew the time of Place's scheduled arrival at La Guardia, had ample time to arrange for their additional investigation at that location, and thereby could have minimized the intrusion on respondent's Fourth Amendment interests. Thus, although we decline to adopt any outside time limitation for a permissible *Terry* stop, we have never approved a seizure of the person for the prolonged 90-minute period involved here and cannot do so on the facts presented by this case."

9. Reasonable Suspicion and Searching Patrons in a Tavern Named in a Search Warrant

Ybarra v. Illinois, 444 U.S. 85 (1979)
Vote: 6-3

FACTS: On the strength of information obtained from a confidential informant a judge issued a search warrant for the Aurora Tap Tavern and its bartender. The warrant authorized the police to search for evidence of possession of narcotics. Several officers went to the tavern and notified everyone that they were going to conduct a search for weapons. One of the officers patted down the customers while the others searched the building. An officer felt some objects in a cigarette pack on Ventura Ybarra on his first search and proceeded to the other patrons. A short while later, he returned to Ybarra and conducted a second search, which yielded the package and pieces of tinfoil, which contained heroin. Ybarra was convicted for the unlawful possession of a controlled substance.

ISSUE: May the police conduct a pat-down of a patron in a bar named in a search warrant and seize evidence from a second search of the same patron if no reasonable suspicion existed that the patron was engaged in criminality?

HOLDING: No.

RATIONALE: "The *Terry* [*v. Ohio*, 392 U.S. 1 (1968)] case created an exception to the requirement of probable cause, an exception whose 'narrow scope' this Court 'has been careful to maintain.' Under that doctrine a law enforcement officer, for his own protection and safety, may conduct a pat-down to find weapons that he reasonably believes or suspects are then in the possession of the person he has accosted. . . . The 'narrow scope' of the *Terry* exception does not permit a frisk for weapons on less than reasonable belief or suspicion directed at the person to be frisked, even though that person happens to be on premises where an authorized narcotics search is taking place."

"[W]e are asked to construe the Fourth and Fourteenth Amendments to permit evidence searches of persons who, at the commencement of the search, are on 'compact' premises subject to a search warrant, at least where the police have a 'reasonable belief' that such persons 'are connected with' drug trafficking. . . ."

"[H]ere the police possessed a warrant authorizing the search of the Aurora Tap Tavern. Moreover, in [*United States v. Di Re*, 332 U.S. 581 (1948)] the Government conceded that its officers could not search all the persons in a house being searched pursuant to a search warrant."

"For these reasons, we conclude that the searches of Ybarra and the seizure of what was in his pocket contravened the Fourth and Fourteenth Amendments."

2

Probable Cause

As was the case in the previous chapter, police must have an objective basis for detaining a suspect. In this chapter, *probable cause* will be addressed, as it is the requirement that the authorities must meet prior to making an arrest. Once again, when an arrest is made, the protection against unreasonable searches and seizures is invoked. However, the standard that police must attain for making an arrest is higher for probable cause than it is for reasonable suspicion. Recall from the last chapter that reasonable suspicion was defined as information that led a reasonable person to believe that criminal activity was afoot. Several issues that define the contours of probable cause also need attention.

Most importantly, the Supreme Court has defined probable cause in relatively clear terms. The police need to have a workable standard that can be applied quickly, in rapidly changing circumstances on the street. If they desire to make an arrest, they need to know when they have probable cause and that it revolves around delineable offenses and identifiable offenders. The Court has said that probable cause, like reasonable suspicion, is a quantum of facts. However, probable cause is more specific. In order to have probable cause, the authorities must be able to articulate that a *particular person* has committed a *particular offense.* And like the definition for reasonable suspicion, the Court has taken the "totality of the circumstances" approach, meaning that all the information that the officer(s) have at their disposal at the time the arrest is made will be used to determine whether or not the officer(s) had probable cause at the time of the arrest.

Another issue for consideration is what information the police can use to ascertain whether or not probable cause exists. The Supreme Court has spoken on the issue several times in an effort to give the police a clear standard by which to operate. Once again, police may use information that they can verify from an informant. Before the police can obtain an arrest or search warrant, they must file an affidavit swearing that the information that they are in possession of is truthful and that it has been honestly collected. The Supreme Court has also issued guidelines on how probable cause can be obtained for these important documents. Like information collectible for reasonable suspicion, police can also use furtive movement in their calculation for probable cause. One might also ask whether the police can use prior knowledge of criminal conduct in their determination. The Supreme Court has said that the police may do so.

While it may seem that the Court is willing to let the police do almost whatever they want in obtaining probable cause, that would not be true. In fact, the Court has ruled that the police may not formally arrest anyone without probable cause and they also may not engage in activity that amounts to arrest without probable cause. An example of this type of conduct is spiriting someone to the police station against their will in order to obtain their fingerprints.

A. Probable Cause Defined

Brinegar v. United States, 338 U.S. 160 (1949)
Vote: 5-4

FACTS: Officers Malsed and Creehan were parked in a car beside a highway when Brinegar drove past. Malsed had arrested him about five months earlier for illegally transporting liquor; had seen him loading liquor into a vehicle on at least two occasions during the preceding six months; and knew him to have a reputation for hauling liquor. Malsed recognized Brinegar as the driver of the passing car. Both agents later testified that the car, appeared to be "heavily loaded" and "weighted down with something." Brinegar increased his speed as he passed the officers and they gave chase and pulled him over. Malsed said, "Hello, Brinegar, how much liquor have you got in the car?" or "How much liquor have you got in the car this time?" Brinegar replied, "Not too much," or "Not so much," and eventually admitted that he had twelve cases in the car. Malsed testified that one case was visible from outside the car. Twelve more cases were found under and behind the front seat. Brinegar was convicted of importing liquor in violation of the Liquor Enforcement Act of 1936.

ISSUE: Is probable cause a reasonable belief that an offense has been committed?

HOLDING: Yes.

RATIONALE: "[U]nder the Fourth Amendment, a valid search of a vehicle moving on a public highway may be had without a warrant, but only if probable cause for the search exists."

"In dealing with probable cause . . . we deal with probabilities. These are not technical; they are the factual and practical considerations of everyday life on which reasonable and prudent men, not legal technicians, act."

"'The substance of all the definitions' of probable cause 'is a reasonable ground for belief of guilt. . . .' And this 'means less than evidence which would justify condemnation' or conviction. . . . [I]t has come to mean more than bare suspicion: Probable cause exists where 'the facts and circumstances within their (the officers') knowledge and of which they had reasonably trustworthy information (are) sufficient in themselves to warrant a man of reasonable caution in the belief that' an offense has been or is being committed."

"The rule of probable cause is a practical, nontechnical conception affording the best compromise that has been found for accommodating these often opposing interests. Requiring more would unduly hamper law enforcement. To allow less would be to leave law-abiding citizens at the mercy of the officers' whim or caprice."

B. How is Probable Cause Obtained?

1. Informant Information and Corroboration

Draper v. United States, 358 U.S. 307 (1959)
Vote: 6-1

FACTS: Marsh had employed Hereford as an occasional informant and over time real-ized that he had provided accurate information concerning violation of narcotics laws. Hereford told Marsh that James Draper was selling drugs in Denver. On September 7, 1956, Hereford told Marsh that Draper had gone to Chicago the day before, that he was going to bring back heroin, and that he would return to Denver on the 8th or by train. Hereford also gave Marsh a detailed description of Draper and of the clothing he would be wearing and said that he would be carrying "a tan zipper bag" and that he "walked real fast." The police found no one matching Hereford's description on the 8th but did find someone on the 9th. After verifying Hereford's information, Draper was stopped and the subsequent search revealed heroin and a syringe. Hereford died shortly there-after and did not testify at the hearing. Draper was convicted of knowingly concealing and transporting narcotics.

ISSUE: Can police use information provided by an informant to obtain probable cause?

HOLDING: Yes.

RATIONALE: "Petitioner . . . contends . . . that the information given by Hereford to Marsh was 'hearsay' and, because hearsay is not legally competent evidence in a criminal trial . . . , should have been put out of mind by Marsh in assessing whether he had 'probable cause. . . .'"

"We find petitioner entirely in error. . . . 'The so-called distinction places a wholly unwarranted emphasis upon the criterion of admissibility in evidence, to prove the ac-cused's guilt, of the facts relied upon to show probable cause.'"

"Nor can we agree with petitioner's second contention that Marsh's information was insufficient to show probable cause. . . . The information given to narcotic agent Marsh by 'special employee' Hereford may have been hearsay to Marsh, but coming from one employed for that purpose and whose information had always been found accurate and reliable, it is clear that Marsh would have been derelict in his duties had he not pursued it. And when, in pursuing that information, he saw a man, having the exact physical attributes and wearing the precise clothing and carrying the tan zipper bag that Hereford had described, alight from one of the very trains from the very place stated by Hereford and start to walk at a 'fast' pace toward the station exit, Marsh had personally verified every facet of the information given him by Hereford except whether petitioner had accomplished his mission and had the three ounces of heroin on his person or in his bag. And surely, with every other bit of Hereford's information being thus personally verified, Marsh had 'reasonable grounds' to believe that the re-maining unverified bit of Hereford's information—that Draper would have the heroin with him—was likewise true."

2. Probable Cause and Affidavits

Illinois v. Gates, 462 U.S. 213 (1983)

Vote: 6-3

FACTS: On May 3, 1978, the Bloomingdale, Illinois, Police Department received an anonymous letter that included statements purporting that Lance and Susan Gates were engaged in selling drugs; that Susan Gates would drive their car to Florida on May 3 to load it with drugs, and her husband would fly down in a few days to drive the car back; that the car's trunk would be loaded with drugs; and that the Gateses presently had over $100,000 worth of drugs in their basement. Acting on the tip, a police officer determined the Gates's address and learned that the husband made a reservation on a May 5 flight to Florida. Arrangements for surveillance of the flight were made with an agent of the Drug Enforcement Administration (DEA), and the surveillance disclosed that the husband took the flight, stayed overnight in a motel room registered in the wife's name, and left the following morning with a woman in a car bearing an Illinois license plate issued to the husband, heading north on an interstate highway used by travelers to the Bloomingdale area. A search warrant for the Gates's residence and automobile was then obtained from an Illinois state-court judge, based on the Bloomingdale police officer's affidavit setting forth the foregoing facts and a copy of the anonymous letter. When the Gateses arrived at their home, the police were waiting and discovered marihuana and other contraband in the trunk of Gates's car and home. State drug charges were brought against the couple.

ISSUE: Is the test for probable cause for informant information the "totality of the circumstances" approach?

HOLDING: Yes.

RATIONALE: "Although an informant's 'veracity,' 'reliability,' and 'basis of knowledge' are all highly relevant in determining the value of his report in showing probable cause for the issuance of a search warrant, these elements are not entirely separate and independent requirements to be rigidly exacted in every case but should be understood simply as close intertwined issues that may usefully illuminate the common sense, practical question as to whether under the totality of the circumstances there is 'probable cause' to believe that contraband or evidence is located in a particular place."

"An informant's 'veracity' or 'reliability' and his 'basis of knowledge' are relevant considerations in the totality of circumstances analysis which is to be used to determine whether probable cause exists for the issuance of a search warrant; a deficiency in one of these elements may be compensated for, in determining the overall reliability of a tip, by a strong showing as to the other, or by some other indicia of reliability."

"The task of a magistrate issuing a search warrant is to make a practical, common-sense decision whether, given all the circumstances set before him, including the 'veracity' and 'basis of knowledge' of persons supplying hearsay information, there is a fair probability that contraband or evidence of a crime will be found in a particular place and the duty of a reviewing court is simply to ensure that the magistrate had a substantial basis for concluding probable cause existed."

"Under a 'totality of circumstances' test for the determination of probable cause, magistrates are free to exact assurances that the information in the affidavits supporting the request for a search warrant has been obtained in a reliable way by an honest or credible person."

3. Furtive Movement and Flight

Wong Sun v. United States, 371 U.S. 471 (1963)
Vote: 5-4
FACTS: On the morning of June 4, 1959, federal agents in San Francisco arrested Hom Way and found heroin in his possession. He stated that he had bought heroin from "Blackie Toy," owner of a laundry. At about 6 a.m., agents went to "Oye's Laundry," operated by James Wah Toy. Agent Wong told him that he was calling for laundry and dry cleaning and Toy started to close the door. Agent Wong then identified himself and Toy immediately "slammed the door and started running" to his living quarters. Agent Wong and the others followed and when Toy reached into a nightstand, Agent Wong arrested him. There was nothing in the drawer, and a search uncovered no narcotics. One of the agents said to Toy, "[Hom Way] says he got narcotics from you." Toy responded, "No, I haven't been selling any narcotics at all. However, I do know somebody who has." When asked who that was, Toy said, "I only know him as Johnny. I don't know his last name." However, Toy described a house where he said Johnny lived. The agents left and located the house. They entered and found Johnny Yee in the bedroom. After a discussion, Yee gave the agents heroin and stated that it had been brought by Toy and "Sea Dog." Toy said that "Sea Dog" was Wong Sun. Toy pointed out the house where Wong Sun lived. Agent Wong identified himself to a woman on the landing and asked "for Mr. Wong." She said that Wong Sun was "in the back room sleeping." An agent removed Wong Sun from the bedroom in handcuffs. A thorough search of the apartment followed, but no narcotics were discovered. Petitioners were convicted of fraudulent and knowing transportation and concealment of heroin.
ISSUE: Can a suspect's flight when approached by narcotics agents by itself justify an inference of guilt sufficient for probable cause to arrest?
HOLDING: No.
RATIONALE: "A suspect's flight when several narcotics officers appeared at the door of his laundry and living quarters does not justify an inference of guilt sufficient to generate probable cause for his arrest, where one of the officers, before identifying himself as such, misrepresented his mission by stating that he had come for laundry and dry cleaning and never adequately dispelled the misimpression engendered by his own ruse, and moreover, made no effort to ascertain whether the suspect was identical with the person whom an informer had described as a violator of the narcotics laws; hence a finding by the Court of Appeals that the officers' uninvited entry into the suspect's living quarters was unlawful is justified by the evidence."

"A vague suspicion cannot be transformed into probable cause for arrest by reason of the suspect's ambiguous conduct which the arresting officers themselves have provoked. . . . It is urged that Toy's flight down the hall when the supposed customer at the door revealed that he was a narcotics agent adequately corroborates the suspicion generated by Hom Way's accusation. . . . We noted in that case that the lawfulness of an officer's entry to arrest without a warrant 'must be tested by criteria identical with those embodied in 18 U.S.C. §3109, which deals with entry to execute a search warrant.' That statute requires that an officer must state his authority and his purpose at the threshold, and be refused admittance, before he may break open the door. We held that when an officer insufficiently or unclearly identifies his office or his mission, the occupant's flight from the door must be regarded as ambiguous conduct. . . . In the instant case, Toy's flight from the door afforded no surer an inference of guilty knowledge. . . ."

"Toy's refusal to admit the officers and his flight down the hallway thus signified a guilty knowledge no more clearly than it did a natural desire to repel an apparently unauthorized intrusion. . . . [T]he Government claims no extraordinary circumstances—such as the imminent destruction of vital evidence, or the need to rescue a victim in peril—which excused the officer's failure truthfully to state his mission before he broke in."

4. Admissions of Criminal Activity

Rawlings v. Kentucky, 448 U.S. 98 (1980)
Vote: 7-2
FACTS: Police executed a warrant to arrest Lawrence Marquess and found another resident and four visitors, including David Rawlings at the home. While unsuccessfully searching for Marquess, officers smelled marihuana and saw seeds. Two officers left to obtain a search warrant while other officers detained the occupants, allowing them to leave only if they consented to a body search. About forty-five minutes later, the officers returned with the search warrant; which was read to the remaining occupants, including Rawlings, and they were also given *Miranda* warnings. Cox, an occupant, was ordered to empty her purse, which contained drugs. Cox told Rawlings, who was standing nearby, "to take what was his," and Rawlings claimed ownership of the drugs. At that time, an officer searched Rawlings, finding $4,500 in cash and a knife. He was then arrested and later convicted of possession with intent to sell controlled substances.
ISSUE: Can admission of ownership of evidence amount to probable cause for arrest?
HOLDING: Yes.
RATIONALE: "Petitioner also contends that the search of his person that uncovered the money and the knife was illegal. Like the Supreme Court of Kentucky, we have no difficulty upholding this search as incident to petitioner's formal arrest. Once petitioner admitted ownership of the sizable quantity of drugs found in Cox's purse, the police clearly had probable cause to place petitioner under arrest. Where the formal arrest followed quickly on the heels of the challenged search of petitioner's person, we do not believe it particularly important that the search preceded the arrest rather than vice versa. . . ."

5. Known Criminality in Combination with Other Activities

Ker v. California, 374 U.S. 23 (1963)
Vote: 5-4

FACTS: Sergeant Cook of the Los Angeles County Sheriff's Office, in purchasing marijuana from Terrhagen, accompanied him to a bowling alley on July 26, 1960, where
they were to meet Terrhagen's "connection." Terrhagen stated that the "connection"
kept his supply of narcotics "somewhere up in the hills." The deputy recognized the
driver of the vehicle as Roland Murphy, whom he knew from other narcotics officers to
be a large-scale dealer. At the officer's house, Terrhagen cut one pound of marijuana
and gave it to Cook, who had previously paid him. The next day, Officer Warthen, who
had observed the Terrhagen-Murphy episode, and Officer Markman were assigned to
keep Murphy under surveillance. They observed him engage in activities similar to the
night before, and at the same location, the officers observed a parked automobile
whose lone occupant was George Douglas Ker. Murphy "appeared to have conversation
with him." Soon thereafter Ker drove away. The officers followed him but lost him;
however, they recovered his address through the DMV. Officer Berman was given this
information after he had observed the meeting between Ker and Murphy and knew
from previous occasions that Ker was an active dealer. Based on Berman's knowledge
and Murphy's meetings, he and other officers proceeded to the address they had obtained through Ker's license number. They found the automobile that they had been
following parked in the lot of the apartment complex and also ascertained that there
was someone in the Kers' apartment. They then obtained a passkey to the apartment.
Finding Ker sitting in the living room, Berman stated that they were narcotics officers.
Berman testified that he repeated his identification to Diane Ker and observed marijuana. After refusing to answer questions, he arrested the Kers. They were convicted of
possessing marijuana.

ISSUE: Can knowledge of prior criminality be used to ascertain probable cause?

HOLDING: Yes.

RATIONALE: "The lawfulness of the arrest without warrant, in turn, must be based
upon probable cause, which exists 'where "the facts and circumstances within their [the
officers'] knowledge and of which they had reasonably trustworthy information [are]
sufficient in themselves to warrant a man of reasonable caution in the belief that" an
offense has been or is being committed. . . .' The information within the knowledge
of the officers at the time they arrived at the Kers' apartment, as California's courts
specifically found, clearly furnished grounds for a reasonable belief that petitioner
George Ker had committed and was committing the offense of possession of marijuana. Officers Markman and Warthen observed a rendezvous between Murphy and
Ker on the evening of the arrest which was a virtual reenactment of the previous night's
encounter between Murphy, Terrhagen, and Sergeant Cook, which concluded in the
sale by Murphy to Terrhagen and the Sergeant of a package of marijuana of which the
latter had paid Terrhagen for one pound which he received from Terrhagen after the
encounter with Murphy. To be sure, the distance and lack of light prevented the officers from seeing and they did not see any substance pass between the two men, but the

virtual identity of the surrounding circumstances warranted a strong suspicion that the one remaining element—a sale of narcotics —was a part of this encounter as it was the previous night. But Ker's arrest does not depend upon this single episode with Murphy. When Ker's U-turn thwarted the officer's pursuit, they learned his name and address from the Department of Motor Vehicles and reported the occurrence to Officer Berman. Berman, in turn, revealed information from an informer whose reliability had been tested previously, as well as from other sources, not only that Ker had been selling marijuana from his apartment but also that his likely source of supply was Murphy himself. That this information was hearsay does not destroy its role in establishing probable cause. . . ."

"[T]he California court specifically found and the record supports both that the officers entered the apartment for the purpose of arresting George Ker and that they had probable cause to make that arrest prior to the entry."

C. Transportation to the Police Station without Probable Cause

Hayes v. Florida, 470 U.S. 811 (1985)
Vote: 8-0
FACTS: A series of burglary-rapes occurred in Punta Gorda, Florida. Police found fingerprints on the doorknob of the bedroom of one of the victims, which they believed belonged to the assailant. The police also found a shoe print near the victim's porch. Although they had little information to tie Hayes to the scene, after police interviewed him, the investigators came to consider him a suspect. They visited his home to obtain his fingerprints or to arrest him. They did not seek a warrant. Arriving at his house, Hayes expressed reluctance to accompany them for printing, and an investigator explained that he would be arrested. Hayes then stated that he would rather go to the station than be arrested. Officers seized tennis shoes in plain view. Hayes was taken to the station, printed, and arrested after a determination that his prints matched those left at the scene. Hayes was later convicted of burglary and rape.
ISSUE: May a suspect be taken to the police station for fingerprinting without probable cause?
HOLDING: No.
RATIONALE: "[T]here was no probable cause to arrest, no consent to the journey to the police station, and no judicial authorization for such a detention for fingerprinting purposes. . . ."

"None of our later cases have undercut the holding in *Davis* [*v. Mississippi*, 394 U.S. 721 (1969)] that transportation to and investigative detention at the station house without probable cause or judicial authorization together violate the Fourth Amendment."

"There is no doubt that at some point in the investigative process, police procedures can qualitatively and quantitatively be so intrusive with respect to a suspect's freedom of movement and privacy interests as to trigger the full protection of the Fourth and

Fourteenth Amendments. . . . And our view continues to be that the line is crossed when the police, without probable cause or a warrant, forcibly remove a person from his home or other place in which he is entitled to be and transport him to the police station, where he is detained, although briefly, for investigative purposes. We adhere to the view that such seizures, at least where not under judicial supervision, are sufficiently like arrests to invoke the traditional rule that arrests may constitutionally be made only on probable cause."

3

Arrest

THE TERM PROBABLE CAUSE, discussed in the previous chapter, serves as a foundation for two very important activities that the police engage in: arresting of suspected law breakers and searching for evidence related to their crimes. In this chapter, *arrest* will be examined in detail. Before the police can arrest anyone in the formal sense that we think of the concept (transportation of the suspect to the police station, handcuffing the suspect, reading of the *Miranda* warnings etc.), they must first have obtained probable cause. As stated previously, probable cause is a bit more difficult to attain than reasonable suspicion because it requires a greater degree of specificity. Once an officer is able to make such a connection, he or she may then make a formal arrest and take a person into custody. As one might expect, several issues have cropped up over the years that the United States Supreme Court has dealt with, some successfully, some not so successfully.

Aside from the fact that the Court has been quite clear as to what probable cause is, it also has given the authorities some guidance as to what an arrest is. In fact, the Supreme Court has said that an arrest (not a stop-and-frisk) is the most intrusive seizure that the police can make. So, first of all, an arrest is a seizure and, therefore, it is protected by the Fourth Amendment to the U.S. Constitution. In other words, certain standards must be met before the police can make an arrest or else it will be deemed unconstitutional or illegal.

The Supreme Court has also addressed several other matters related to arrest. For example, one might ask if a person has to be notified of the officer's intentions prior to arresting a person. The Supreme Court has said "no," the individual being arrested does not have to be notified of the intentions of the officer prior to the making of an arrest. The Court has also ruled on the issue of who is allowed to make probable-cause determinations with regard to issuing warrants. It is not only judges that have the right to issue warrants and make determinations as to whether the police have probable cause. The Court has held that various types of judicial officers can make probable-cause determinations for the purpose of issuing warrants.

Further, this chapter will address the question of what police do in the area of arrest if they do not have a warrant. The Supreme Court has also addressed this area and has stated that as long as the police have probable cause, they can make an arrest, even without a warrant. Usually these warrantless arrests occur as the result of some emergency that makes it impossible for the police to obtain one. However, the Court has ruled that police can make an arrest without a warrant, even in a public place, even if there was enough time for them to obtain one. However, it has also ruled that if the police take that route, the arrestee must be brought before a judge to determine if in fact the police did have probable cause to make the arrest in the first place. Usually that determination must be made within forty-eight hours unless some unforeseen emergency circumstance intervenes and prevents the police from doing so. So some safeguards do exist for assuring that the police follow the rules when making an arrest.

One of the biggest issues that the Court has been asked to decide is what the police can do when making an arrest when they enter either the arrestee's or a third party's home. These issues are quite sensitive, and the Court has indicated that unless a very pressing emergency exists, police *must have a warrant* to enter someone's home. In addition, the Court has also stated that the seriousness of the offense for which the police wish to make an arrest is a consideration as to whether or not the police can enter a home without a warrant.

The Court has also ruled on whether or not the police can make arrests for relatively minor offenses. Regardless of the seriousness of the offense, when police arrest a suspect, they must use some degree of force. While there certainly are issues as to what kind of force can be used and the degree to which that force can be used, the Supreme Court has made specific landmark decisions concerning when deadly force can be used. Finally, the Court has also sought to be proactive in the area of nonlethal force by holding that the test for determining whether an amount of force is appropriate is an objective one, not one determined by the subjective feelings of a court or particular person.

A. Arrest Defined

California v. Hodari D., 499 U.S. 621 (1991)
Vote: 7-2
FACTS: Officers Brian McColgin and Jerry Pertoso were on patrol in Oakland. They were dressed in street clothes but wearing police jackets. As they rounded the corner in their unmarked car, they saw a group huddled around a parked car. When the group saw the officers' car, they apparently panicked and fled. Hodari D. ran through an alley. The officers gave chase and Pertoso left the car and ran in the opposite direction down a different alley to cut off Hodari. Hodari did not turn and see Pertoso until he was almost upon him, whereupon he tossed away what appeared to be a small rock. A moment later, Pertoso tackled Hodari, handcuffed him, and radioed for assistance. Hodari was found to be carrying $130 and a pager, and the rock he had discarded was found to be crack cocaine. The State of California initiated juvenile proceedings against Hodari D. as a result.
ISSUE: Does an arrest take place when the police chase a suspect and the suspect does not yield or when the police do not apply physical force to restrain a suspect?
HOLDING: No.
RATIONALE: "To constitute an arrest, however—the quintessential 'seizure of the person' under our Fourth Amendment jurisprudence—the mere grasping or application of physical force with lawful authority, whether or not it succeeded in subduing the arrestee, was sufficient. . . ."

"The present case . . . does not involve the application of any physical force; Hodari was untouched by Officer Pertoso at the time he discarded the cocaine. His defense relies instead upon the proposition that a seizure occurs 'when the officer, by means of physical force *or show of authority*, has in some way restrained the liberty of a citizen. . . .' The narrow question before us is whether, with respect to a show of authority as with respect to application of physical force, a seizure occurs even though the subject does not yield. We hold that it does not."

"The language of the Fourth Amendment, of course, cannot sustain respondent's contention. The word 'seizure' readily bears the meaning of a laying on of hands or application of physical force to restrain movement. . . . It does not remotely apply, however, to the prospect of a policeman yelling 'Stop, in the name of the law!' at a fleeing form that continues to flee. That is no seizure. Nor can the result respondent wishes to achieve be produced—indirectly, as it were—by suggesting that Pertoso's uncomplied-with show of authority was a common-law arrest, and then appealing to the principle that all common-law arrests are seizures. An arrest requires *either* physical force (as described above) *or*, where that is absent, *submission* to the assertion of authority."

"'[A]n assertion of authority and purpose to arrest followed by submission of the arrestee constitutes an arrest. . . .'"

"We do not think it desirable, even as a policy matter, to stretch the Fourth Amendment beyond its words and beyond the meaning of arrest. . . ."

"Respondent contends that his position is sustained by the so-called [*United States v. Mendenhall*, 446 U.S. 544 (1980)] test. . . . '[A] person has been "seized" within the meaning of the Fourth Amendment only if, in view of all the circumstances surrounding the incident, a reasonable person would have believed that he was not free to leave. . . .' In seeking to rely upon that test here, respondent fails to read it carefully. It says that a person has been seized 'only if,' not that he has been seized 'whenever'; it states a *necessary*, but not a *sufficient*, condition for seizure—or, more precisely, for seizure effected through a 'show of authority.' *Mendenhall* establishes that the test for existence of a 'show of authority' is an objective one: not whether the citizen perceived that he was being ordered to restrict his movement, but whether the officer's words and actions would have conveyed that to a reasonable person."

"In sum, assuming that Pertoso's pursuit in the present case constituted a 'show of authority' enjoining Hodari to halt, since Hodari did not comply with that injunction he was not seized until he was tackled."

B. Components of an Arrest

1. Seizure

Michigan v. Chesternut, 486 U.S. 567 (1988)
Vote: 9-0
FACTS: Four police officers riding in a marked cruiser observed a car pull over to the curb. A man got out of the car and approached Michael Mose Chesternut, who was standing on the corner. When Chesternut saw the patrol car, he began to run. As Officer Peltier later testified, the patrol car followed Chesternut "to see where he was going." The cruiser drove alongside him for a short distance. As they drove, the officers observed Chesternut discard a number of packets he pulled from his pocket. Officer Peltier got out to examine the packets and discovered that they contained pills. While Peltier was engaged in this inspection, Chesterut then stopped and Peltier arrested him for the possession of narcotics. During an ensuing search, the police discovered in Chesternut's hatband another packet of pills, heroin, and a needle. Chesternut was charged with possession of controlled substances.
ISSUE: Is the test for determining whether or not someone has been seized within the meaning of the Fourth Amendment a situation "where given all the circumstances a reasonable person would not feel free to leave," and does that determination vary according to police conduct and the setting in which it occurs?
HOLDING: Yes.
RATIONALE: "'Obviously, not all personal intercourse between policemen and citizens involves "seizures" of persons.'"

"The test provides that the police can be said to have seized an individual 'only if, in view of all of the circumstances surrounding the incident, a reasonable person would have believed that he was not free to leave.'"

"Moreover, what constitutes a restraint on liberty prompting a person to conclude that he is not free to 'leave' will vary, not only with the particular police conduct at issue, but also with the setting in which the conduct occurs."

"Applying the Court's test to the facts of this case, we conclude that respondent was not seized by the police before he discarded the packets containing the controlled substance. . . . [T]he police conduct involved here would not have communicated to the reasonable person an attempt to capture or otherwise intrude upon respondent's freedom of movement. The record does not reflect that the police activated a siren or flashers; or that they commanded respondent to halt, or displayed any weapons; or that they operated the car in an aggressive manner to block respondent's course or otherwise control the direction or speed of his movement. . . . [T]his kind of police presence does not, standing alone, constitute a seizure. . . . Without more, the police conduct here—a brief acceleration to catch up with respondent, followed by a short drive alongside him—was not 'so intimidating' that respondent could reasonably have believed that he was not free to disregard the police presence and go about his business. The police therefore were not required to have 'a particularized and objective basis for suspecting [respondent] of criminal activity,' in order to pursue him."

2. Intention of the Officer to Seize

Brower v. County of Inyo, 489 U.S. 593 (1989)
Vote: 9-0
FACTS: William James Caldwell Brower was killed when the stolen car that he had been driving at high speeds in an effort to elude police crashed into a roadblock. His heirs brought a civil action under 42 U.S.C. § 1983, claiming that the police used "brutal, excessive, unreasonable and unnecessary physical force" in establishing the roadblock, and thus effected an unreasonable seizure of Brower, in violation of the Fourth Amendment. The heirs alleged that the police (1) caused an eighteen-wheel tractor-trailer to be placed across both lanes of a two-lane highway in the path of Brower's flight, (2) effectively concealed this roadblock by placing it behind a curve and leaving it unilluminated, and (3) positioned a police car, with its headlights on, between Brower's oncoming vehicle and the truck, so that Brower would be "blind" on his approach. It was further alleged that Brower's fatal collision with the truck was "a proximate result" of this official conduct.
ISSUE: Is the intent of the police to seize a suspect relevant to the determination as to whether or not a Fourth Amendment seizure took place?
HOLDING: Yes.
RATIONALE: "Violation of the Fourth Amendment requires an intentional acquisition of physical control. A seizure occurs even when an unintended person or thing is the object of the detention or taking . . . but the detention or taking itself must be willful. This is implicit in the word 'seizure,' which can hardly be applied to an unknowing act. . . ."

"It is clear, in other words, that a Fourth Amendment seizure does not occur whenever there is a governmentally caused termination of an individual's freedom of movement (the innocent passerby), nor even whenever there is a governmentally caused and governmentally *desired* termination of an individual's freedom of movement (the fleeing felon), but only when there is a governmental termination of freedom of movement *through means intentionally applied.*"

"We think it enough for a seizure that a person be stopped by the very instrumentality set in motion or put in place in order to achieve that result. It was enough here, therefore, that, according to the allegations of the complaint, Brower was meant to be stopped by the physical obstacle of the roadblock—and that he was so stopped. . . ."

"The complaint here sufficiently alleges that respondents, under color of law, sought to stop Brower by means of a roadblock and succeeded in doing so. That is enough to constitute a 'seizure' within the meaning of the Fourth Amendment."

3. Authority to Arrest with a Warrant

Shadwick v. City of Tampa, 407 U.S. 345 (1972)
Vote: 9-0
FACTS: Shadwick was arrested for impaired driving on a warrant issued by a clerk of the municipal court. He filed a motion for the court to quash the warrant on the ground that it was issued by a nonjudicial officer in violation of the Fourth and Fourteenth Amendments.
ISSUE: Does the issuance of an arrest warrant by a municipal court clerk for the violation of a municipal ordinance contravene the requirement of the Fourth Amendment that warrants shall only be issued by a neutral and detached magistrate?
HOLDING: No.
RATIONALE: "There is some suggestion in appellant's brief that a judicial officer must be a lawyer or the municipal court judge himself."

"Past decisions of the Court have mentioned review by a judicial officer prior to issuance of a warrant. . . ."

"In some cases the term judicial officer appears to have been used interchangeably with that of magistrate. . . . In others, it was intended simply to underscore the now accepted fact that someone independent of the police and prosecution must determine probable cause. . . . The very term 'judicial officer' implies, of course, some connection with the judicial branch. But it has never been held that only a lawyer or judge could grant a warrant, regardless of the court system or the type of warrant involved."

"An examination of the Court's decisions reveals that the terms 'magistrate' and 'judicial officer' have been used interchangeably. Little attempt was made to define either term, to distinguish the one from the other, or to advance one as the definitive Fourth Amendment requirement. We find no commandment in either term, however, that all warrant authority must reside exclusively in a lawyer or judge."

"The substance of the Constitution's warrant requirements does not turn on the labeling of the issuing party. The warrant traditionally has represented an independent assurance that a search and arrest will not proceed without probable cause to believe that a crime has been committed and that the person or place named in the warrant is involved in the crime. Thus, an issuing magistrate must meet two tests. He must be neutral and detached, and he must be capable of determining whether probable cause exists. . . ."

"The requisite detachment is present in the case at hand. Whatever else neutrality and detachment might entail, it is clear that they require severance and disengagement from activities of law enforcement. There has been no showing whatever here of partiality, or affiliation of these clerks with prosecutors or police. The record shows no connection with any law enforcement activity or authority which would distort the independent judgment the Fourth Amendment requires. Appellant himself expressly refused to allege anything to that effect. The municipal court clerk is assigned not to the police or prosecutor but to the municipal court judge for whom he does much of his work. In this sense, he may well be termed a 'judicial officer.' While a statutorily specified term of office and appointment by someone other than 'an executive authority' might be desirable, the absence of such features is hardly disqualifying."

"Appellant likewise has failed to demonstrate that these clerks lack capacity to determine probable cause. The clerk's authority extends only to the issuance of arrest warrants for breach of municipal ordinances. We presume from the nature of the clerk's position that he would be able to deduce from the facts on an affidavit before him whether there was probable cause to believe a citizen guilty of impaired driving, breach of peace, drunkenness, trespass, or the multiple other common offenses covered by a municipal code. There has been no showing that this is too difficult a task for a clerk to accomplish."

4. Authority to Arrest without a Warrant

a. Probable Cause Determination in Warrantless Arrests

County of Riverside v. McLaughlin, 500 U.S. 44 (1991)
Vote: 5-4
FACTS: Donald Lee McLaughlin filed a class action suit under 42 U.S.C. § 1983 in the United States District Court for the Central District of California, where he sought injunctive and declaratory relief on behalf of himself and all others similarly situated. A second complaint named three additional plaintiffs and alleged that each plaintiff had been arrested without a warrant, had not received prompt probable cause or bail hearings, and was still in custody. The district court granted class certification and issued a preliminary injunction requiring the county to provide a judicial determination of probable cause within thirty-six hours of arrest to all persons arrested without a warrant, except in exigent circumstances. The United States Court of Appeals for the Ninth Circuit affirmed the injunction and held that the policy of providing probable cause determinations at arraignment within forty-eight hours was not in accordance with the constitutional requirement that such determinations be made promptly. The U.S. Supreme Court vacated and remanded the judgment.
ISSUE: Are jurisdictions providing judicial determinations of probable cause for warrantless arrests within forty-eight hours, meeting the Constitutional requirement of promptness?
HOLDING: Yes.
RATIONALE: "[T]his Court held that the Fourth Amendment requires a prompt judicial determination of probable cause as a prerequisite to an extended pretrial detention following a warrantless arrest. . . ."

"Significantly, the Court stopped short of holding that jurisdictions were constitutionally compelled to provide a probable cause hearing immediately upon taking a suspect into custody and completing booking procedures."

"Plainly, if a probable cause hearing is constitutionally compelled the moment a suspect is finished being 'booked,' there is no room whatsoever for 'flexibility and experimentation by the States.'"

"The Court of Appeals for the Ninth Circuit held that no flexibility was permitted. It construed *Gerstein* [*v. Pugh*, 420 U.S. 103 (1975)] as 'requiring a probable cause determination to be made *as soon as the administrative steps incident to arrest were completed*, and that such steps should require only a brief period. . . .' The foregoing discussion readily demonstrates the error of this approach. *Gerstein* held that probable cause determinations must be prompt—not immediate. . . ."

"Although we hesitate to announce that the Constitution compels a specific time limit, it is important to provide some degree of certainty so that States and counties may establish procedures with confidence that they fall within constitutional bounds. Taking into account the competing interests articulated in *Gerstein*, we believe that a jurisdiction that provides judicial determinations of probable cause within 48 hours of arrest will, as a general matter, comply with the promptness requirement of *Gerstein*."

b. Suspects in Public

1. Entering a Home after a Suspect Was Outside

United States v. Santana, 427 U.S. 38 (1976)
Vote: 7-2
FACTS: Officer Michael Gilletti arranged a heroin "buy" with Patricia McCafferty, and she told him it would cost $115 "and we will go down to Mom Santana's for the dope." Gilletti met McCafferty at a prearranged location. She got in his car and directed him to drive to Santana's residence. McCafferty took the money and went inside the house, came out, and gave Gilletti the heroin. Gilletti then placed McCafferty under arrest, and she told him, "Mom has the money." Officer Pruitt and the others then drove to Santana's house, and after the police identified themselves, Santana fled into the hallway of the house. The officers followed, and as she tried to continue her flight heroin packets fell to the floor. When Santana was told to empty her pockets she produced seventy dollars of Gilletti's marked money. She was indicted for possession of heroin with intent to distribute.
ISSUE: Can the police enter a home to make a warrantless arrest, justified by probable cause, if the suspect was in public first but retreated to the house to avoid the police?
HOLDING: Yes.
RATIONALE: "While it may be true that under the common law of property the threshold of one's dwelling is 'private,' as is the yard surrounding the house, it is nonetheless clear that under the cases interpreting the Fourth Amendment Santana was in a 'public' place. She was not in an area where she had any expectation of privacy. 'What a person knowingly exposes to the public, even in his own house or office, is not a subject of Fourth Amendment protection. . . .' She was not merely visible to the

public but was as exposed to public view, speech, hearing, and touch as if she had been standing completely outside her house. . . . Thus, when the police, who concededly had probable cause to do so, sought to arrest her, they merely intended to perform a function which we have approved. . . ."

"The only remaining question is whether her act of retreating into her house could thwart an otherwise proper arrest. We hold that it could not. . . . [W]e recognized the right of police, who had probable cause to believe that an armed robber had entered a house a few minutes before, to make a warrantless entry to arrest the robber and to search for weapons. . . . [T]he need to act quickly here is even greater than in that case while the intrusion is much less."

"We thus conclude that a suspect may not defeat an arrest which has been set in motion in a public place. . . ."

c. Failing to Obtain a Warrant

United States v. Watson, 423 U.S. 411 (1976)
Vote: 6-2
FACTS: Khoury, an informant, telephoned a postal inspector and told him that Watson was in possession of a stolen credit card and had asked him to cooperate in using the card. Khoury had provided the inspector with reliable information on inspection matters, some involving Watson. Khoury delivered the card to the inspector later that day and upon learning that Watson had agreed to provide other cards, the inspector asked Khoury to arrange a meeting at a restaurant with Watson. Prior to the meeting, Khoury was told that if Watson had additional cards, he was to give a signal. He gave it and Watson was arrested. He was removed from the restaurant to the street where he was Mirandized and where a search revealed that Watson had no credit cards on his person. The inspector asked if he could look inside Watson's car. Watson said, "Go ahead," even after the inspector cautioned, "If I find anything, it is going to go against you." Watson provided the keys, and the inspector found an envelope containing two credit cards under the floor mat. Watson was charged with and convicted of possession of stolen mail.
ISSUE: Can the police make an arrest based on probable cause in public without a warrant, even if they had time to get one but failed to?
HOLDING: Yes.
RATIONALE: "Watson's arrest was not invalid because executed without a warrant. Title 18 U.S.C. §3061(a)(3) expressly empowers the Board of Governors of the Postal Service to authorize Postal Service officers and employees 'performing duties related to the inspection of postal matters' to 'make arrests without warrant for felonies cognizable under the laws of the United States if they have reasonable grounds to believe that the person to be arrested has committed or is committing such a felony. . . .' Because there was probable cause in this case . . . the inspector and his subordinates, in arresting Watson, were acting strictly in accordance with the governing statute and regulations."

"'The usual rule is that a police officer may arrest without warrant one believed by the officer upon reasonable cause to have been guilty of a felony. . . .' The necessary inquiry, therefore, was not whether there was a warrant or whether there was time to get one, but whether there was probable cause for the arrest."

"The cases construing the Fourth Amendment thus reflect the ancient common-law rule that a peace officer was permitted to arrest without a warrant for a misdemeanor or felony committed in his presence as well as for a felony not committed in his presence if there was reasonable ground for making the arrest. . . . This has also been the prevailing rule under state constitutions and statutes."

"They do not conflict with the authority of constables or other peace officers, or private persons under proper limitations, to arrest without warrant those who have committed felonies. The public safety, and the due apprehension of criminals, charged with heinous offences, imperiously require that such arrests should be made without warrant. . . .'"

"The balance struck by the common law in generally authorizing felony arrests on probable cause, but without a warrant, has survived substantially intact. It appears in almost all of the States in the form of express statutory authorization. In 1963, the American Law Institute undertook the task of formulating a model statute governing police powers and practice in criminal law enforcement and related aspects of pretrial procedure. In 1975, after years of discussion, A Model Code of Pre-arraignment Procedure was proposed. Among its provisions was § 120.1, which authorizes an officer to take a person into custody if the officer has reasonable cause to believe that the person to be arrested has committed a felony, or has committed a misdemeanor or petty misdemeanor in his presence. The commentary to this section said: 'The Code thus adopts the traditional and almost universal standard for arrest without a warrant.'"

"This is the rule Congress has long directed its principal law enforcement officers to follow. Congress has plainly decided against conditioning warrantless arrest power on proof of exigent circumstances."

2. Arrest for an Unrelated Crime

Devenpeck v. Alford, 543 U.S. 146 (2004)
Vote: 8-0
FACTS: A disabled automobile was stranded on the shoulder of a highway in Pierce County, Washington. Jerome Alford pulled his car off the road and activated his headlights. Officer Joi Haner of the Washington State Patrol, passed the disabled car from the opposite direction. He turned around to check on the motorists, and when he arrived, Alford, who had begun helping change a flat tire, hurried back to his car and drove away. The motorists asked Haner if Alford was a "cop"; they said that his statements and his lights had given them that impression. They also informed Haner that as Alford fled he left his flashlight behind.

On the basis of this information, Haner radioed Sergeant Gerald Devenpeck that he was concerned that Alford was a "wannabe cop." He then pursued Alford's vehicle, pulled it over, and observed that he was listening to a police radio and that handcuffs and a police scanner were in the car, which bolstered Haner's belief that Alford was impersonating a police officer. Haner thought, moreover, that he also seemed untruthful and evasive because he told Haner that he had worked previously for the "State Patrol" but later claimed instead to have worked in policing in Texas and at a shipyard. He stated that his headlights were part of a car-alarm system, and acted as though he was unable to trigger them.

Devenpeck arrived and inquired about the headlights, and as before, Alford stated that they were part of his alarm system. Devenpeck noticed a tape recorder on the passenger seat with the recording button depressed and ordered Haner to remove Alford from the car. They played the tape, and found that he had been recording his conversations with the police. Devenpeck told Alford, that he was under arrest for a violation of the Washington Privacy Act. Alford protested that a court decision, a copy of which he claimed was in his glove box, allowed him to record roadside conversations with police. Devenpeck returned to his car, reviewed the Privacy Act, and attempted unsuccessfully to confirm that the arrest was lawful. Believing that the text of the Privacy Act confirmed that the recording was illegal, he directed Haner to take Alford to jail.

Devenpeck reached Mark Lindquist, a deputy county prosecutor, by phone, and they discussed possible offenses, including violation of the Privacy Act. Lindquist stated that probable cause existed. Haner charged Alford with violating the State Privacy Act and issued a ticket to him for his flashing headlights. The state trial court dismissed both charges. Alford filed a 1983 suit alleging that he was falsely imprisoned and arrested in violation of the Fourth Amendment.

ISSUE: Does an arrest in public for an offense that is not closely related to the originally stated crime violate the Fourth Amendment?

HOLDING: No.

RATIONALE: "A warrantless arrest by a law officer is reasonable under the Fourth Amendment where there is probable cause to believe that a criminal offense has been or is being committed. . . . In this case, the Court of Appeals held that the probable-cause inquiry is further confined to the known facts bearing upon the offense actually invoked at the time of arrest, and that (in addition) the offense supported by these known facts must be 'closely related' to the offense that the officer invoked. . . . We find no basis in precedent or reason for this limitation."

"Our cases make clear that an arresting officer's . . . subjective reason for making the arrest need not be the criminal offense as to which the known facts provide probable cause. As we have repeatedly explained, 'the fact that the officer does not have the state of mind which is hypothecated by the reasons which provide the legal justification for the officer's action does not invalidate the action taken as long as the circumstances, viewed objectively, justify that action.'"

"The rule that the offense establishing probable cause must be 'closely related' to, and based on the same conduct as, the offense identified by the arresting officer at the time of arrest is inconsistent with this precedent. Such a rule makes the lawfulness of an arrest turn upon the motivation of the arresting officer. . . . This means that the constitutionality of an arrest under a given set of known facts will 'vary from place to place and from time to time . . .' depending on whether the arresting officer states the reason for the detention and, if so, whether he correctly identifies a general class of offense for which probable cause exists."

"Those who support the 'closely related offense' rule say that, although it is aimed at rooting out the subjective vice of arrests made for the wrong reason, it does so by objective means—that is, by reference to the arresting officer's statement of his reason. . . . Subjective intent of the arresting officer . . . is simply no basis for invalidating an arrest. Those are lawfully arrested whom the facts known to the arresting officers give probable cause to arrest."

"Finally, the 'closely related offense' rule is condemned by its perverse consequences. While it is assuredly good police practice to inform a person of the reason for his arrest at the time he is taken into custody, we have never held that to be constitutionally required. Hence, the . . . consequence of a rule limiting the . . . inquiry to offenses closely related to . . . those identified by the arresting officer is . . . that officers will cease providing reasons for arrest."

c. Entering the Suspect's Home

1. For Felonies

Payton v. New York, 445 U.S. 573 (1980)
Vote: 6-3
FACTS: New York City detectives established probable cause to believe that Theodore Payton had murdered the manager of a gas station. Six officers went to Payton's apartment, with the intention to arrest him, but they had not obtained a warrant. Although light and music emanated from the apartment, there was no response to their knock. They summoned emergency assistance and used crowbars to open the door. No one was home, but in plain view was a .30 caliber shell casing that was seized. Payton was later convicted for murder.
ISSUE: May the police make a warrantless, nonconsensual entry into suspect's home for the purpose of making a routine, felony arrest?
HOLDING: No.
RATIONALE: "It is a 'basic principle of Fourth Amendment law' that searches and seizures inside a home without a warrant are presumptively unreasonable."

"'It is one thing to seize without a warrant property resting in an open area or seizable by levy without an intrusion into privacy, and it is quite another thing to effect a warrantless seizure of property, even that owned by a corporation, situated on private premises to which access is not otherwise available for the seizing officer.'"

"The Fourth Amendment protects the individual's privacy in a variety of settings. In none is the zone of privacy more clearly defined than when bounded by the unambiguous physical dimensions of an individual's home—a zone that finds its roots in clear and specific constitutional terms: 'The right of the people to be secure in their . . . houses . . . shall not be violated.' That language unequivocally establishes the proposition that '[at] the very core [of the Fourth Amendment] stands the right of a man to retreat into his own home and there be free from unreasonable governmental intrusion. . . .' In terms that apply equally to seizures of property and to seizures of persons, the Fourth Amendment has drawn a firm line at the entrance to the house. Absent exigent circumstances, that threshold may not reasonably be crossed without a warrant."

2. Minor Offenses

Welsh v. Wisconsin, 466 U.S. 740 (1984)

Vote: 6-3

FACTS: Randy Jablonic observed a car being driven erratically, and the car eventually swerved off the road. Jablonic drove his truck up behind the car so as to block it from returning to the road. Another passerby also stopped and Jablonic asked her to call the police. The driver of the car asked Jablonic for a ride but then walked away. Jablonic told one officer what he had seen and the officer then checked registration of the car and learned that it was registered to Edward G. Welsh. Without obtaining a warrant, the police proceeded to the Welsh home and gained entry from Welsh's stepdaughter. Proceeding upstairs to Welsh's bedroom, they found him in bed. At this point, he was arrested for driving under the influence. Welsh had his license suspended by the trial court in a hearing pursuant to his refusal to take a breathalyzer.

ISSUE: Can the police enter a home without exigent circumstances to make a warrantless, nighttime arrest for a nonjailable offense?

HOLDING: No.

RATIONALE: "[T]he Court has recognized, as 'a "basic principle of Fourth Amendment law[,]" that searches and seizures inside a home without a warrant are presumptively unreasonable.'"

"Consistently with these long-recognized principles . . . warrantless felony arrests in the home are prohibited by the Fourth Amendment, absent probable cause and exigent circumstances . . . and that the police bear a heavy burden when attempting to demonstrate an urgent need that might justify warrantless searches or arrests."

"Our hesitation in finding exigent circumstances, especially when warrantless arrests in the home are at issue, is particularly appropriate when the underlying offense for which there is probable cause to arrest is relatively minor. Before agents of the government may invade the sanctity of the home, the burden is on the government to demonstrate exigent circumstances that overcome the presumption of unreasonableness that attaches to all warrantless home entries. . . . When the government's interest is only to arrest for a minor offense, that presumption of unreasonableness is difficult to rebut, and the government usually should be allowed to make such arrests only with a warrant issued upon probable cause by a neutral and detached magistrate."

"It is to me a shocking proposition that private homes, even quarters in a tenement, may be indiscriminately invaded at the discretion of any suspicious police officer engaged in following up offenses that involve no violence or threats of it. While I should be human enough to apply the letter of the law with some indulgence to officers acting to deal with threats or crimes of violence which endanger life or security, it is notable that few of the searches found by this Court to be unlawful dealt with that category of crime. . . . When an officer undertakes to act as his own magistrate, he ought to be in a position to justify it by pointing to some real immediate and serious consequences if he postponed action to get a warrant."

"Consistently with this approach, the lower courts have looked to the nature of the underlying offense as an important factor to be considered in the exigent-circumstances calculus. . . . Without approving all of the factors included in the standard adopted by that court, it is sufficient to note that many other lower courts have also considered the gravity of the offense an important part of their constitutional analysis."

"But of those courts addressing the issue, most have refused to permit warrantless home arrests for nonfelonious crimes. . . . [W]e note that it is difficult to conceive of a warrantless home arrest that would not be unreasonable under the Fourth Amendment when the underlying offense is extremely minor."

"Application of this principle to the facts of the present case is relatively straightforward. The petitioner was arrested in the privacy of his own bedroom for a non criminal, traffic offense. . . . On the facts of this case, however, the claim of hot pursuit is unconvincing because there was no immediate or continuous pursuit of the petitioner from the scene of a crime. Moreover, because the petitioner had already arrived home, and had abandoned his car at the scene of the accident, there was little remaining threat to the public safety."

3. Entering a Third Person's Home

Steagald v. United States, 451 U.S. 204 (1981)
Vote: 7-2
FACTS: An informant told a DEA agent that he might be able to locate Ricky Lyons, who was wanted on drug charges. The informant contacted the agent a second time and gave him a phone number in Atlanta where Lyons could be reached. The agent called Agent Kelly Goodowens and relayed the information he had obtained. Goodowens then contacted the phone company and secured the address corresponding to the number. Goodowens also discovered that Lyons was the subject of an arrest warrant.

Goodowens and other officers went to the address two days later to search for Lyons. Hoyt Gaultney and Gary Steagald were standing outside the house. The officers approached, frisked both men, and determined that neither man was Lyons. Several officers proceeded to the house, where Gaultney's wife answered the door. She was told to place her hands against the wall while one agent searched the house. Lyons was not found, but during the search of the house the agent observed cocaine. Agent Goodowens sent an officer to obtain a warrant and in the meantime conducted a second search, which uncovered additional evidence. During a third search conducted pursuant to the warrant, the agents uncovered forty-three pounds of cocaine. Steagald was indicted and convicted of federal drug charges.

ISSUE: Can the police search for the subject of an arrest warrant in the home of a third party without a search warrant?

HOLDING: No.

RATIONALE: "The question before us is a narrow one. The search at issue here took place in the absence of consent or exigent circumstances. Except in such special situations, we have consistently held that the entry into a home to conduct a search or make an arrest is unreasonable under the Fourth Amendment unless done pursuant to a warrant."

"The purpose of a warrant is to allow a neutral judicial officer to assess whether the police have probable cause to make an arrest or conduct a search. As we have often explained, the placement of this checkpoint between the Government and the citizen implicitly acknowledges that an 'officer engaged in the often competitive enterprise of ferreting out crime . . . ,' may lack sufficient objectivity to weigh correctly the strength of the evidence supporting the contemplated action against the individual's interests in protecting his own liberty and the privacy of his home."

"To be sure, the warrant embodied a judicial finding that there was probable cause to believe that Ricky Lyons had committed a felony, and the warrant therefore authorized the officers to seize Lyons. However, the agents sought to do more than use the warrant to arrest Lyons in a public place or in his home; instead, they relied on the warrant as legal authority to enter the home of a third person based on their belief that Ricky Lyons might be a guest there. Regardless of how reasonable this belief might have been, it was never subjected to the detached scrutiny of a judicial officer. Thus, while the warrant in this case may have protected Lyons from an unreasonable seizure, it did absolutely nothing to protect petitioner's privacy interest in being free from an unreasonable invasion and search of his home. Instead, petitioner's only protection from an illegal entry and search was the agent's personal determination of probable cause. In the absence of exigent circumstances, we have consistently held that such judicially untested determinations are not reliable enough to justify an entry into a person's home to arrest him without a warrant, or a search of a home for objects in the absence of a search warrant."

"In this case, for example, Agent Goodowens knew the address of the house to be searched two days in advance, and planned the raid from the federal courthouse in Atlanta where, we are informed, three fulltime magistrates were on duty. In routine search cases such as this, the short time required to obtain a search warrant from a magistrate will seldom hinder efforts to apprehend a felon."

"Whatever practical problems remain, however, cannot outweigh the constitutional interests at stake. Any warrant requirement impedes to some extent the vigor with which the Government can seek to enforce its laws, yet the Fourth Amendment recognizes that this restraint is necessary in some cases to protect against unreasonable searches and seizures. We conclude that this is such a case."

4. Minor Criminal Offenses in General

Atwater v. City of Lago Vista, 532 U.S. 318 (2001)
Vote: 5-4
FACTS: Gail Atwater was driving with none of her children wearing seatbelts. Police officer Bart Turek pulled her over and "yelled," "we've met before" and "you're going to jail." He asked for her license and insurance. Atwater said that she did not have the cards because her purse had been stolen and Turek said that he had "heard that story two-hundred times." Atwater then asked to take her children to a friend's but Turek said, "you're not going anywhere." The friend arrived and took the children. Turek handcuffed Atwater, drove her to the station, and put her in a cell, after which she was released on $310 bond. She pleaded no contest to the seatbelt violations and paid a $50 fine.
ISSUE: Can police make warrantless arrests for minor crimes if probable cause exists?
HOLDING: Yes.
RATIONALE: "[I]n the years leading up to American independence, Parliament repeatedly extended express warrantless arrest authority to cover misdemeanor-level offenses not amounting to or involving any violent breach of the peace."

"In *Carroll* [v. *United States*, 267 U.S. 132 (1925)] itself we spoke of the common-law rule as only 'sometimes expressed' that way . . . , and, indeed, in the very same paragraph, we conspicuously omitted any reference to a breach-of-the-peace limitation in stating that the 'usual rule' at common law was that 'a police officer [could] arrest without warrant . . . one guilty of a misdemeanor if committed in his presence.'"

"As will be seen later, the view of warrantless arrest authority as extending to at least 'some misdemeanors' beyond breaches of the peace was undoubtedly informed by statutory provisions authorizing such arrests, but it reflected common law in the strict, judge-made sense as well. . . ."

"Accordingly, we confirm today what our prior cases have intimated: the standard of probable cause 'applies to all arrests, without the need to "balance" the interests and circumstances involved in particular situations. . . .' If an officer has probable cause to believe that an individual has committed even a very minor criminal offense in his presence, he may, without violating the Fourth Amendment, arrest the offender."

"Atwater's arrest satisfied constitutional requirements. There is no dispute that Officer Turek had probable cause to believe that Atwater had committed a crime in his presence. She admits that neither she nor her children were wearing seat belts, as required by Tex. Tran. Code Ann. § 545.413 (1999)."

"Nor was the arrest made in an 'extraordinary manner, unusually harmful to [her] privacy or . . . physical interests.' As our citations in *Whren* [v. *United States*, 517 U.S. 806 (1996)] make clear, the question whether a search or seizure is 'extraordinary' turns, above all else, on the manner in which the search or seizure is executed. . . . Atwater's arrest was surely 'humiliating,' as she says in her brief, but it was no more 'harmful to . . . privacy or . . . physical interests' than the normal custodial arrest."

C. Use of Force When Conducting an Arrest

1. Unarmed Felons

Tennessee v. Garner, 471 U.S. 1 (1985)
Vote: 6-3
FACTS: Memphis Officers Elton Hymon and Leslie Wright answered a "prowler inside call." Upon arriving they saw a woman gesturing toward the adjacent house. She told them she had heard glass breaking and that "they" or "someone" was breaking in. While Wright radioed the dispatcher, Hymon went behind the house. He saw someone run across the backyard. The fleeing suspect, Edward Garner, stopped at a fence at the edge of the yard. Hymon was able to see Garner's face and hands but saw no sign of a weapon, and, was "reasonably sure" that Garner was unarmed. Hymon called "Police, halt!" and took a few steps toward him. Garner then began to climb over the fence. Convinced that Garner would elude capture, Hymon shot him. Garner died on the operating table. Garner's father then brought an action seeking damages under 42 U.S.C. §1983 for asserted violations of the Fourth, Fifth, Sixth, Eighth, and Fourteenth Amendments.
ISSUE: Can the police use deadly force to prevent the escape of an unarmed felon?
HOLDING: No.
RATIONALE: "The use of deadly force to prevent the escape of all felony suspects, whatever the circumstances, is constitutionally unreasonable. It is not better that all felony suspects die than that they escape. Where the suspect poses no immediate threat to the officer and no threat to others, the harm resulting from failing to apprehend him does not justify the use of deadly force to do so. . . . The Tennessee statute is unconstitutional insofar as it authorizes the use of deadly force against such fleeing suspects."

"It is not, however, unconstitutional on its face. Where the officer has probable cause to believe that the suspect poses a threat of serious physical harm, either to the officer or to others, it is not constitutionally unreasonable to prevent escape by using deadly force. Thus, if the suspect threatens the officer with a weapon or there is probable cause to believe that he has committed a crime involving the infliction or threatened infliction of serious physical harm, deadly force may be used if necessary to prevent escape, and if, where feasible, some warning has been given."

"It has been pointed out many times that the common-law rule is best understood in light of the fact that it arose at a time when virtually all felonies were punishable by death. 'Though effected without the protections and formalities of an orderly trial and conviction, the killing of a resisting or fleeing felon resulted in no greater consequences than those authorized for punishment of the felony of which the individual was charged or suspected. . . .' Courts have also justified the common-law rule by emphasizing the relative dangerousness of felons."

"Neither of these justifications makes sense today. Almost all crimes formerly punishable by death no longer are or can be. . . . And while in earlier times 'the gulf between the felonies and the minor offences was broad and deep . . . ,' today the distinction is minor and often arbitrary."

"There is an additional reason why the common-law rule cannot be directly translated to the present day. The common-law rule developed at a time when weapons were rudimentary. Deadly force could be inflicted almost solely in a hand-to-hand struggle during which, necessarily, the safety of the arresting officer was at risk. Handguns were not carried by police officers until the latter half of the last century. . . ."

"Actual departmental policies are important for an additional reason. We would hesitate to declare a police practice of long standing 'unreasonable' if doing so would severely hamper effective law enforcement. But the indications are to the contrary. There has been no suggestion that crime has worsened in any way in jurisdictions that have adopted, by legislation or departmental policy, rules similar to that announced today. *Amici* note that '[after] extensive research and consideration, [they] have concluded that laws permitting police officers to use deadly force to apprehend unarmed, nonviolent fleeing felony suspects actually do not protect citizens or law enforcement officers, do not deter crime or alleviate problems caused by crime, and do not improve the crime-fighting ability of law enforcement agencies.'"

"Officer Hymon could not reasonably have believed that Garner—young, slight, and unarmed—posed any threat."

"Hymon did not have probable cause to believe that Garner, whom he correctly believed to be unarmed, posed any physical danger to himself or others."

2. Standard for Excessive Force Claims

Graham v. Connor, 490 U.S. 386 (1989)
Vote: 9-0
FACTS: Dethorne Graham felt the onset of an insulin reaction and asked a friend, William Berry, to drive him to a store so he could buy orange juice. When Graham entered the store and saw a number of people ahead of him, he hurried out of the store.

Police officer Connor saw Graham hastily enter and leave the store, became suspicious and followed Berry's car. Although Berry told Connor that Graham was suffering from a reaction, the officer ordered Berry and Graham to wait. When Connor returned to his car Graham got out, ran around it twice, and sat down on the curb, where he passed out.

Other officers arrived and one rolled Graham over on the sidewalk and cuffed his hands ignoring Berry's pleas to get him some sugar. Another officer said: "I've seen a lot of people with sugar diabetes that never acted like this. Ain't nothing wrong with the M. F. but drunk. Lock the S. B. up." Several officers then lifted Graham up carried him over to Berry's car, and placed him face down on the hood. Graham asked the officers to check his wallet for a diabetic decal and one of the officers told him to "shut up" and shoved his face down against the hood. Four officers threw him headfirst into the police car. A friend of Graham's brought some orange juice but the officers refused to let him have it. Finally, Connor received a report that Graham had done nothing wrong at the store, and the officers drove him home and released him. At some point during his encounter, Graham sustained a broken foot, cuts on his wrists, a bruised forehead, and an injured shoulder; he also claims to have developed a loud ringing in his right ear. Graham filed suit alleging excessive force in violation of his Fourteenth Amendment rights.

ISSUE: Is the standard of analysis for claims alleging excessive force against the police "objective reasonableness"?

HOLDING: Yes.

RATIONALE: "Where, as here, the excessive force claim arises in the context of an arrest or investigatory stop of a free citizen, it is most properly characterized as one invoking the protections of the Fourth Amendment, which guarantees citizens the right 'to be secure in their persons . . . against unreasonable . . . seizures' of the person. . . . Today we make explicit what was implicit in [*Tennessee v. Garner*, 471 U.S. 1 (1985)]'s analysis, and hold that *all* claims that law enforcement officers have used excessive force—deadly or not—in the course of an arrest, investigatory stop, or other 'seizure' of a free citizen should be analyzed under the Fourth Amendment and its 'reasonableness' standard, rather than under a 'substantive due process' approach. Because the Fourth Amendment provides an explicit textual source of constitutional protection against this sort of physically intrusive governmental conduct, that Amendment, not the more generalized notion of 'substantive due process,' must be the guide for analyzing these claims."

"The 'reasonableness' of a particular use of force must be judged from the perspective of a reasonable officer on the scene, rather than with the 20/20 vision of hindsight. . . . With respect to a claim of excessive force, the same standard of reasonableness at the moment applies: 'Not every push or shove, even if it may later seem unnecessary in the peace of a judge's chambers . . . ,' violates the Fourth Amendment. The calculus of reasonableness must embody allowance for the fact that police officers are often forced to make split-second judgments—in circumstances that are tense, uncertain, and rapidly evolving—about the amount of force that is necessary in a particular situation."

"As in other Fourth Amendment contexts, however, the 'reasonableness' inquiry in an excessive force case is an objective one: the question is whether the officers' actions are 'objectively reasonable' in light of the facts and circumstances confronting them, without regard to their underlying intent or motivation. . . . An officer's evil intentions will not make a Fourth Amendment violation out of an objectively reasonable use of force; nor will an officer's good intentions make an objectively unreasonable use of force constitutional."

"Because petitioner's excessive force claim is one arising under the Fourth Amendment, the Court of Appeals erred in analyzing it under the four-part *Johnson v. Glick* [481 F.2d 1028] test. That test, which requires consideration of whether the individual officers acted in 'good faith' or 'maliciously and sadistically for the very purpose of causing harm,' is incompatible with a proper Fourth Amendment analysis. We do not agree . . . that the 'malicious and sadistic' inquiry is merely another way of describing conduct that is objectively unreasonable under the circumstances. Whatever the empirical correlations between 'malicious and sadistic' behavior and objective unreasonableness may be, the fact remains that the 'malicious and sadistic' factor puts in issue the subjective motivations of the individual officers, which our prior cases make clear has no bearing on whether a particular seizure is 'unreasonable' under the Fourth Amendment."

II

THE FOURTH AMENDMENT—
SEARCH AND SEIZURE

4

Searches and Seizures with Warrants

I N THE PREVIOUS CHAPTERS, the focus of study hinged upon seizures of persons and the quantum of evidence that was required of the police before they could seize an individual. In chapters 4–8, the discussion will be founded upon what the police can do once they have determined that they have reached the threshold amount of evidence when investigating suspected criminality. In this chapter, the most important area to be addressed is the area of searching and seizing with and without warrants.

This chapter begins with a brief introduction to what the Supreme Court refers to when it is asked to examine the fairness of a search or seizure and what tests the Court has used in the past for defining those terms. Historically, the Supreme Court's jurisprudence in these areas has been guided by two general tests that determine whether or not the police have engaged in some activity that requires the protection of the Fourth Amendment. The first of those tests is called the *trespass doctrine*. This rule basically states that the Fourth Amendment only protects the list of things specifically mentioned in the Fourth Amendment. That is, the Fourth Amendment acts as a shield against the "searching for and seizing of" "persons, houses, papers, and effects." If the police tried to obtain material that was deemed not a part of that narrow list, then it was found not to be a protectable search or a seizure. That way of looking at the problem lasted until *Katz v. United States*, 389 U.S. 347 (1967). That case overturned the trespass doctrine and instituted a new way of determining whether or not the police had committed a search or seizure. This new rule is called the *privacy doctrine*, which is founded on the idea that people have an expectation of privacy in many things, not just those few articles listed in the Fourth Amendment. The test for determining whether or not a valid expectation exists is whether the individual has a subjective expectation of privacy in the thing searched for or seized and whether society as a whole is prepared to recognize that subjective expectation.

While the privacy doctrine is the current test, before the police can search for and seize evidence, in many cases they need to have a *warrant*. A warrant is basically a written order by a judge, or someone with the authority to do so, that directs the police to either seize a person or materials that are suspected of being involved in the further-ance of criminal activity. To obtain such an order, the police again need to have prob-able cause, but the Supreme Court has held that they may not lie to obtain it because they can be held liable if the lie injures someone (*Franks v. Delaware*, 438 U.S. 154 [1978] and *Malley v. Briggs*, 475 U.S. 336 [1986]). However, there are other things that the police must specify in the warrants to make them valid. For example, the police must specify the person that they would like to seize and the places that they wish to search for that person or the evidence they wish to find.

While it may seem that the warrant process is complicated, it really isn't. In fact, in many cases, it doesn't take long at all. The only hindrances to obtaining the warrant are the different rules that the police must follow, but if they are doing a good job of in-vestigating, they likely have all of the information that they need prior to applying for the warrant in the first place. While that may make some more at ease with their un-derstanding of this process, it is also the case that the police do need to follow a few rules before the warrant will be signed. More specifically, the police cannot obtain a warrant from a judge who is paid to issue warrants but not paid to not issue them, nor may they obtain one from a person who will also participate in the search. The police must also announce that they are at a home (unless a specific emergency exception ex-ists). Additionally, they may also detain a person while they are conducting a search so that they are not interfered with while the search is taking place.

Regarding the specific task of searching a home, the authorities also have particular rules that must be followed. For example, the Court has ruled to what extent a house can be "secured" while the police attempt to obtain a warrant. It has also decided that police can conduct "protective sweeps" inside a home when looking for dangerous sus-pects.

The last topic for discussion is electronic surveillance and what the police must do before getting permission to conduct it and what instruments they may use. More to the point, the Court has ruled under what conditions the police may listen to conver-sations between people via the use of a wire. It has also stated that the use of a pen reg-ister to collect phone numbers is also acceptable and with some reluctance has allowed for the planting of "beepers" on vehicles or in materials considered evidence. While it may seem that the Court is quite liberal in its allowing the police to engage in these ac-tivities, remember that it also requires judicial oversight of these special circumstances and that the police must, as in all of the other instances where they seek to perform searches and obtain evidence, have probable cause that criminality is taking place be-fore they can proceed.

A. Bedrock Concepts

1. What Is a Search?

Kyllo v. United States, 533 U.S. 27 (2001)
Vote: 5-4
FACTS: Agent William Elliott of the United States Department of the Interior came to suspect that marijuana was being grown in Danny Kyllo's home. Agents Elliott and Dan Haas used a thermal imager to scan the triplex. The scan of Kyllo's home took a few minutes and was performed from Elliott's vehicle across the street. The scan showed that the roof over the garage and a sidewall were relatively hot compared to the rest of the home. Elliott concluded that Kyllo was using lights to grow marijuana in his house. Based on tips from informants, utility bills, and the imaging, a judge issued a search warrant and the agents found more than 100 plants. Kyllo entered a conditional guilty plea to a charge of manufacturing marijuana.
ISSUE: Is a search a violation of a subjective expectation of privacy that society recognizes as reasonable? Does the use of a thermal imaging device constitute a search?
HOLDING: Yes.
RATIONALE: "[T]he antecedent question whether a Fourth Amendment 'search' has occurred is not so simple. . . ."

"But in fact we have held that visual observation is no 'search' at all. . . . We held that the Fourth Amendment nonetheless protected *Katz* [*v. United States*, 389 U.S. 347 (1967)] from the warrantless eavesdropping because he 'justifiably relied' upon the privacy of the telephone booth. As Justice Harlan's oft-quoted concurrence described it, a Fourth Amendment search occurs when the government violates a subjective expectation of privacy that society recognizes as reasonable. We have subsequently applied this principle to hold that a Fourth Amendment search does *not* occur—even when the explicitly protected location of a *house* is concerned—unless 'the individual manifested a subjective expectation of privacy in the object of the challenged search,' and 'society [is] willing to recognize that expectation as reasonable.'"

"The present case involves officers on a public street engaged in more than naked-eye surveillance of a home. We have previously reserved judgment as to how much technological enhancement of ordinary perception from such a vantage point, if any, is too much."

"The question we confront today is what limits there are upon this power of technology to shrink the realm of guaranteed privacy."

"[T]here is a ready criterion, with roots deep in the common law, of the minimal expectation of privacy that *exists*, and that is acknowledged to be *reasonable*. To withdraw protection of this minimum expectation would be to permit police technology to erode the privacy guaranteed by the Fourth Amendment. We think that obtaining by sense-enhancing technology any information regarding the interior of the home that could not otherwise have been obtained without physical 'intrusion into a constitutionally protected area,' constitutes a search—at least where (as here) the technology in question is not in general public use. This assures preservation of that degree of privacy against government that existed when the Fourth Amendment was adopted. On the basis of this criterion, the information obtained by the thermal imager in this case was the product of a search."

"'The Fourth Amendment is to be construed in the light of what was deemed an unreasonable search and seizure when it was adopted, and in a manner which will conserve public interests as well as the interests and rights of individual citizens.'"

"Where, as here, the Government uses a device that is not in general public use, to explore details of the home that would previously have been unknowable without physical intrusion, the surveillance is a 'search' and is presumptively unreasonable without a warrant."

2. Does Questioning Bus Passengers Constitute a Seizure?

Florida v. Bostick, 501 U.S. 429 (1991)
Vote: 6-3
FACTS: Two Broward County, Florida, police officers, with badges, insignia, and one of them holding a zipper pouch containing a pistol, boarded a bus bound from Miami to Atlanta in Fort Lauderdale. Eyeing the passengers, the officers, without suspicion, picked out Bostick and asked to inspect his ticket and identification. The ticket matched his identification and both were returned. However, the officers explained their presence as narcotics agents and then requested consent to search his luggage. Consent was granted and contraband was found. Bostick entered a conditional guilty plea to charges of cocaine trafficking.
ISSUE: Does an encounter on a bus initiated by police who are clearly identifiable but lacking in reasonable suspicion, constitute a seizure within the meaning of the Fourth Amendment if the passenger is told that he does not have to give consent to search?
HOLDING: No.
RATIONALE: "So long as a reasonable person would feel free 'to disregard the police and go about his business,' the encounter is consensual and no reasonable suspicion is required. The encounter will not trigger Fourth Amendment scrutiny unless it loses its consensual nature."

"Since *Terry* [*v. Ohio*, 392 U.S. 1 (1968)], we have held repeatedly that mere police questioning does not constitute a seizure."

"[T]here is no doubt that if this same encounter had taken place before Bostick boarded the bus or in the lobby of the bus terminal, it would not rise to the level of a seizure. . . . We have stated that even when officers have no basis for suspecting a particular individual, they may generally ask questions of that individual."

"When police attempt to question a person who is walking down the street or through an airport lobby, it makes sense to inquire whether a reasonable person would feel free to continue walking. But when the person is seated on a bus and has no desire to leave, the degree to which a reasonable person would feel that he or she could leave is not an accurate measure of the coercive effect of the encounter."

"Here, for example, the mere fact that Bostick did not feel free to leave the bus does not mean that the police seized him. Bostick was a passenger on a bus that was scheduled to depart. He would not have felt free to leave the bus even if the police had not been present. Bostick's movements were 'confined' in a sense, but this was the natural result of his decision to take the bus; it says nothing about whether or not the police conduct at issue was coercive."

". . . Bostick's freedom of movement was restricted by a factor independent of police conduct—*i.e.*, by his being a passenger on a bus. Accordingly, the 'free to leave' analysis on which Bostick relies is inapplicable. In such a situation, the appropriate inquiry is whether a reasonable person would feel free to decline the officers' requests or otherwise terminate the encounter. This formulation follows logically from prior cases and breaks no new ground. We have said before that the crucial test is whether, taking into account all of the circumstances surrounding the encounter, the police conduct would 'have communicated to a reasonable person that he was not at liberty to ignore the police presence and go about his business.' Where the encounter takes place is one factor, but it is not the only one."

"We adhere to the rule that, in order to determine whether a particular encounter constitutes a seizure, a court must consider all the circumstances surrounding the encounter to determine whether the police conduct would have communicated to a reasonable person that the person was not free to decline the officers' requests or otherwise terminate the encounter. That rule applies to encounters that take place on a city street or in an airport lobby, and it applies equally to encounters on a bus."

3. The Trespass Doctrine and Protected Places

Olmstead v. United States, 277 U.S. 438 (1928)
Vote: 5-4
FACTS: The case involves a conspiracy to import, possess, and sell liquor unlawfully by using vessels and property around Seattle. The liquor was transported as far north as British Columbia. Olmstead was the leading conspirator and the general manager of the business. There were telephones in an office of the manager in his own home, at the homes of his associates, and at other places in the city. Communication was had frequently with Vancouver, British Columbia. At times the sales amounted to 200 cases of liquor per day.

The information that led to the discovery of the conspiracy was obtained by intercepting messages on the telephones of the conspirators by four federal prohibition officers. Small wires were inserted along the ordinary telephone wires from the residences of four of the petitioners and those leading from the chief office. The insertions were made without trespass upon any property of the defendants. They were made in the basement of a large office building. The taps from house lines were made in the streets near the houses.

Conversations were testified to by the government witnesses. They revealed the large business transactions of the partners and their subordinates. Men at the wires heard the orders given for liquor by customers and the acceptances; they became auditors of the conversations between the partners. Olmstead and his associates were convicted of conspiracy to violate the National Prohibition Act.

ISSUE: Is the tapping of telephone wires off the premises of the accused a violation of the Fourth Amendment's protection against illegal searches and seizures?

HOLDING: No.

RATIONALE: "The well known historical purpose of the Fourth Amendment, directed against general warrants and writs of assistance, was to prevent the use of governmental force to search a man's house, his person, his papers and his effects; and to prevent their seizure against his will."

"*Gouled v. United States* [255 U.S. 298 (1921)] carried the inhibition against unreasonable searches and seizures to the extreme limit. Its authority is not to be enlarged by implication and must be confined to the precise state of facts disclosed by the record. . . . There was actual entrance into the private quarters of defendant and the taking away of something tangible. Here we have testimony only of voluntary conversations secretly overheard."

"The Amendment itself shows that the search is to be of material things—the person, the house, his papers or his effects. The description of the warrant necessary to make the proceeding lawful, is that it must specify the place to be searched and the person or *things* to be seized."

"It is plainly within the words of the Amendment to say that the unlawful rifling by a government agent of a sealed letter is a search and seizure of the sender's papers or effects. The letter is a paper, an effect, and in the custody of a Government that forbids carriage except under its protection."

"The United States takes no such care of telegraph or telephone messages as of mailed sealed letters. The Amendment does not forbid what was done here. There was no searching. There was no seizure. The evidence was secured by the use of the sense of hearing and that only. There was no entry of the houses of offices of the defendants."

"By the invention of the telephone, fifty years ago, and its application for the purpose of extending communications, one can talk with another at a far distant place. The language of the Amendment cannot be extended and expanded to include telephone wires reaching to the whole world from the defendant's house of office. The intervening wires are not part of his house of office any more than are the highways along which they are stretched."

"The reasonable view is that one who installs in his house a telephone instrument with connecting wires intends to project his voice to those quite outside, and that the wires beyond his house and messages while passing over them are not within the protection of the Fourth Amendment. Here those who intercepted the projected voices were not in the house of either party to the conversation."

"Neither the cases we have cited nor any of the many federal decisions brought to our attention hold the Fourth Amendment to have been violated as against a defendant unless there has been an official search and seizure of his person, or such a seizure of his papers or his tangible material effects, or an actual physical invasion of his house 'or curtilage' for the purpose of making a seizure."

4. The Privacy Doctrine and the Expectation of Privacy

a. Is There a Right to Privacy in Telephone Conversations from Public Phone Booths?

Katz v. United States, 389 U.S. 347 (1967)

Vote: 7-1

FACTS: Katz was convicted in the District Court for the Southern District of California under an eight-count indictment charging him with transmitting wagering information by telephone from Los Angeles to Miami and Boston. The Government introduced evidence of his telephone conversations, overheard by FBI agents who had attached a listening and recording device to the outside of the public telephone booth from which he had placed his calls. In affirming his conviction, the court of appeals rejected the contention that the recordings had been obtained in violation of the Fourth Amendment, because "there was no physical entrance into the area occupied by [the petitioner]."

ISSUE: Does the Fourth Amendment protection against unreasonable searches and seizures only extend to tangible items?

HOLDING: No.

RATIONALE: "[T]he correct solution of Fourth Amendment problems is not necessarily promoted by incantation of the phrase 'constitutionally protected area. . . .'"

"For the Fourth Amendment protects people, not places. What a person knowingly exposes to the public, even in his own home or office, is not a subject of Fourth Amendment protection. . . . But what he seeks to preserve as private, even in an area accessible to the public, may be constitutionally protected."

"But what he sought to exclude when he entered the booth was not the intruding eye—it was the uninvited ear. He did not shed his right to do so simply because he made his calls from a place where he might be seen. No less than an individual in a business office, in a friend's apartment, or in a taxicab, a person in a telephone booth may rely upon the protection of the Fourth Amendment. One who occupies it, shuts the door behind him, and pays the toll that permits him to place a call is surely entitled to assume that the words he utters into the mouthpiece will not be broadcast to the world."

"The Government contends, however, that the activities of its agents in this case should not be tested by Fourth Amendment requirements, for the surveillance technique they employed involved no physical penetration of the telephone booth from which the petitioner placed his calls. But 'the premise that property interests control the right of the Government to search and seize has been discredited . . .' on which that decision rested. Once this much is acknowledged, and once it is recognized that the Fourth Amendment protects people—and not simply 'areas'—against unreasonable searches and seizures, it becomes clear that the reach of that Amendment cannot turn upon the presence or absence of a physical intrusion into any given enclosure."

"We conclude that the underpinnings of *Olmstead* and *Goldman* [*v. United States*, 316 U.S. 129 (1942)] have been so eroded by our subsequent decisions that the 'trespass' doctrine there enunciated can no longer be regarded as controlling. The Government's activities in electronically listening to and recording the petitioner's words violated the privacy upon which he justifiably relied while using the telephone booth and thus constituted a 'search and seizure' within the meaning of the Fourth Amendment."

b. Is There a Right to Privacy in Individual Bank Records?

United States v. Miller, 425 U.S. 435 (1976)
Vote: 7-2
FACTS: In response to an informant's tip, a deputy sheriff from Houston County, Georgia, stopped a van occupied by two of Mitch Miller's co-conspirators. The truck contained a distillery apparatus and material. On January 9, 1973, a fire broke out in a Kathleen, Georgia, warehouse rented to Miller. During the fire, officials discovered a 7,500-gallon-capacity distillery, 175 gallons of non-tax-paid whiskey, and related paraphernalia.

Two weeks later, agents of the Treasury Department's Alcohol, Tobacco and Firearms Bureau presented grand jury subpoenas to two banks where Miller maintained accounts. The subpoenas required "all records of accounts, i.e., savings, checking, loan or otherwise, in the name of Mr. Mitch Miller." The banks did not advise respondent but ordered their employees to make the records available and to provide copies of any documents the agents desired. Agents were shown microfilm records of the relevant account and provided with copies of deposit check slips. These included all checks, deposit slips, two financial statements, and three monthly statements. Miller was convicted of possessing an unregistered still, carrying on the business of a distiller without giving bond and with intent to defraud the Government of whiskey tax, possessing 175 gallons of whiskey upon which no taxes had been paid, and conspiring to defraud the United States of tax revenues.
ISSUE: Do individuals have a right to privacy in bank records?
HOLDING: No.
RATIONALE: "On their face, the documents subpoenaed here are not respondent's 'private papers.' Unlike the claimant in *Boyd* [*v. United States*, 116 U.S. 616 (1886)], respondent can assert neither ownership nor possession. Instead, these are the business records of the banks."

"Even if we direct our attention to the original checks and deposit slips, rather than to the microfilm copies actually viewed and obtained by means of the subpoena, we perceive no legitimate 'expectation of privacy' in their contents. The checks are not confidential communications but negotiable instruments to be used in commercial transactions. All of the documents obtained, including financial statements and deposit slips, contain only information voluntarily conveyed to the banks. . . ."

"The depositor takes the risk, in revealing his affairs to another, that the information will be conveyed by that person to the Government."

"Since no Fourth Amendment interests of the depositor are implicated here, this case is governed by the general rule that the issuance of a subpoena to a third party to obtain the records of that party does not violate the rights of a defendant. . . ."

c. Is There an Individual Right to Privacy in Phone Numbers Sent to the Phone Company?

Smith v. Maryland, 442 U.S. 735 (1979)

Vote: 5-3

FACTS: On March 5, 1976, Patricia McDonough was robbed. She gave the police a description of the robber and of a 1975 Monte Carlo. After the robbery, McDonough began receiving obscene phone calls from a man identifying himself as the robber. On one occasion, the caller asked that she step out on her front porch; she did so, and saw the 1975 Monte Carlo she had described. On March 16, police spotted a man who met McDonough's description driving a 1975 Monte Carlo in her area. By tracing the plate, police learned that the car was registered to Michael Lee Smith.

The phone company, at police request but without a warrant, installed a pen register to record the numbers dialed from Smith's home. It revealed that on March 17 a call was placed from Smith's home to McDonough's phone. The police obtained a search warrant for Smith's residence, which revealed that a page in his phone book was turned down to the name and number of McDonough. Petitioner was arrested and identified by McDonough in a lineup. He was convicted of robbery.

ISSUE: Is there a constitutional expectation of privacy in numbers dialed from a phone?

HOLDING: No.

RATIONALE: "[T]his Court uniformly has held that the application of the Fourth Amendment depends on whether the person invoking its protection can claim a 'justifiable,' a 'reasonable,' or a 'legitimate expectation of privacy' that has been invaded by government. . . . This inquiry . . . embraces two discrete questions. The first is . . . whether . . . the individual has shown that "he seeks to preserve [something] as private." The second question is whether the individual's subjective expectation of privacy is 'one that society is prepared to recognize as 'reasonable. . . .'"

"Since the pen register was installed on telephone company property at the telephone company's central offices, petitioner obviously cannot claim that his 'property' was invaded or that police intruded into a 'constitutionally protected area. . . .' [P]en registers do not acquire the *contents* of communications."

"First, we doubt that people in general entertain any actual expectation of privacy in the numbers they dial. All telephone users realize that they must 'convey' phone numbers to the telephone company, since it is through telephone company switching equipment that their calls are completed. All subscribers realize, moreover, that the phone company has facilities for making permanent records of the numbers they dial. . . . [I]t is too much to believe that telephone subscribers, under these circumstances, harbor any general expectation that the numbers they dial will remain secret."

"Second, even if petitioner did harbor some subjective expectation that the phone numbers he dialed would remain private, this expectation is not 'one that society is prepared to recognize as 'reasonable. . . .' This Court consistently has held that a person has no legitimate expectation of privacy in information he voluntarily turns over to third parties. . . ."

"We therefore conclude that petitioner in all probability entertained no actual expectation of privacy in the phone numbers he dialed, and that, even if he did, his expectation was not 'legitimate.' The installation and use of a pen register, consequently, was not a 'search. . . .'"

d. Is There a Right to Privacy in Garbage Placed at the Curb?

California v. Greenwood, 486 U.S. 35 (1988)
Vote: 6-2

FACTS: In early 1984, Laguna Beach police officer, Jenny Stracner, received information indicating that Greenwood might be engaged in narcotics trafficking. Stracner learned that a suspect had informed an agent in February that a truck filled with drugs was en route to Greenwood's address. Neighbors also complained of heavy traffic late at night in front of Greenwood's home. Stracner sought to investigate this information by conducting a surveillance of Greenwood's home and observed several vehicles make brief stops at the house during the late-night and early morning hours. She also followed a truck to a residence that had previously been under investigation as a narcotics-trafficking location.

Stracner asked the trash collector to pick up the plastic garbage bags that Greenwood had left on the curb and to turn the bags over to her without mixing their contents with other garbage. The trash collector complied with her request. She found items indicative of narcotics use and used it in an affidavit in support of a search warrant for Greenwood's home. Police officers encountered both respondents at the house later that day when they arrived to execute the warrant. The police discovered quantities of cocaine and hashish during their search of the house. The residents were arrested on felony narcotics charges. They subsequently posted bail. Another warrant was secured for Greenwood's home based on the information from a second trash search. The police found more narcotics and evidence of trafficking and Greenwood was again arrested.

ISSUE: Is there a constitutional right to privacy in garbage bags placed at the curb?

HOLDING: No.

RATIONALE: "The warrantless search and seizure of the garbage bags left at the curb outside the Greenwood house would violate the Fourth Amendment only if respondents manifested a subjective expectation of privacy in their garbage that society accepts as objectively reasonable."

"Here, we conclude that respondents exposed their garbage to the public sufficiently to defeat their claim to Fourth Amendment protection. It is common knowledge that plastic garbage bags left on or at the side of a public street are readily accessible to animals, children, scavengers, snoops, and other members of the public. . . . Moreover, respondents placed their refuse at the curb for the express purpose of conveying it to a third party, the trash collector, who might himself have sorted through respondents' trash or permitted others, such as the police, to do so. Accordingly, having deposited their garbage 'in an area particularly suited for public inspection and, in a manner of speaking, public consumption, for the express purpose of having strangers take it . . . ,' respondents could have had no reasonable expectation of privacy in the inculpatory items that they discarded."

"Our conclusion that society would not accept as reasonable respondents' claim to an expectation of privacy in trash left for collection in an area accessible to the public is reinforced by the unanimous rejection of similar claims by the Federal Courts of Appeals. . . . '[T]he overwhelming weight of authority rejects the proposition that a reasonable expectation of privacy exists with respect to trash discarded outside the home and the curtilage thereof.' In addition, of those state appellate courts that have considered the issue, the vast majority have held that the police may conduct warrantless searches and seizures of garbage discarded in public areas. . . .'"

e. Does a Suspect in a Crime Have an Expectation of Privacy as an Overnight Guest?

Minnesota v. Olson, 495 U.S. 91 (1990)
Vote: 7-2
FACTS: A gunman robbed a gas station in Minneapolis and fatally shot the manager. An officer suspected Joseph Ecker. The officer and his partner drove to Ecker's home, arriving at about the same time as another car. The driver took evasive action, and spun out of control and came to a stop. Two men fled the car on foot, and Ecker was captured inside his home. The second man escaped. Inside the car, police found money and the murder weapon. They also found a title with the name Rob Olson crossed out, a letter addressed to a Roger R. Olson of 3151 Johnson Street, and a videotape rental receipt made out to Rob Olson and dated two days earlier. The police verified that Robert Olson lived at the address.

Dianna Murphy called the police and said that Olson drove the car and that he was planning to leave town by bus. She called again, gave her address and phone number, and said that a man named Rob had told a Maria and two other women, Louanne and Julie, that he was the driver. The caller stated that Louanne was Julie's mother and that the two women lived at 2406 Fillmore Northeast. The detective sent police to the address. Police spoke to Louanne's mother, Helen Niederhoffer, who lived in the lower unit. She confirmed that an Olson had been staying upstairs but was not present. She promised to call the police when Olson returned. A "probable cause arrest bulletin," was issued for Olson. The police were instructed to stay away from the duplex.

Niederhoffer called police and said Olson had returned. The detective instructed police to surround the house. He then telephoned Julie from headquarters and told her Rob should come out. The detective heard a male voice say, "tell them I left." Julie stated that Rob had left, whereupon at 3 p.m. the detective ordered the police to enter. Without seeking permission and with weapons drawn, the police entered the upper unit and found respondent hiding in a closet. Less than an hour after his arrest, respondent made an inculpatory statement at police headquarters. He was convicted of murder, armed robbery, and assault.

ISSUE: Does a suspect have a right to privacy when he is an overnight guest?

HOLDING: Yes.

RATIONALE: "We need go no further than to conclude, as we do, that Olson's status as an overnight guest is alone enough to show that he had an expectation of privacy in the home that society is prepared to recognize as reasonable."

"To hold that an overnight guest has a legitimate expectation of privacy in his host's home merely recognizes the everyday expectations of privacy that we all share. Staying overnight in another's home is a longstanding social custom that serves functions recognized as valuable by society. We stay in others' homes when we travel to a strange city for business or pleasure, when we visit our parents, children, or more distant relatives out of town, when we are in between jobs or homes, or when we house-sit for a friend. We will all be hosts and we will all be guests many times in our lives. From either perspective, we think that society recognizes that a houseguest has a legitimate expectation of privacy in his host's home."

"From the overnight guest's perspective, he seeks shelter in another's home precisely because it provides him with privacy, a place where he and his possessions will not be disturbed by anyone but his host and those his host allows inside."

"That the guest has a host who has ultimate control of the house is not inconsistent with the guest having a legitimate expectation of privacy. The houseguest is there with the permission of his host, who is willing to share his house and his privacy with his guest. It is unlikely that the guest will be confined to a restricted area of the house; and when the host is away or asleep, the guest will have a measure of control over the premises. . . . The point is that hosts will more likely than not respect the privacy interests of their guests, who are entitled to a legitimate expectation of privacy despite the fact that they have no legal interest in the premises and do not have the legal authority to determine who may or may not enter the household."

"Because respondent's expectation of privacy in the Bergstrom home was rooted in 'understandings that are recognized and permitted by society . . . ,' it was legitimate, and respondent can claim the protection of the Fourth Amendment."

f. Does a Suspect Have an Expectation of Privacy When He Is in a Home by Consent Only?

Minnesota v. Carter, 525 U.S. 83 (1998)
Vote: 6-3

FACTS: James Thielen, a police officer in Eagan, Minnesota, went to an apartment building to investigate a tip. The informant said that he had walked by the window of an apartment and had seen people putting a white powder into bags. Thielen looked in the same window through a gap in the closed blind and observed the bagging operation. He then notified headquarters, which began preparing affidavits for a search warrant while he returned to the apartment building. When two men left the building in a previously identified Cadillac, the police stopped the car. Inside were Wayne Thomas Carter and Melvin Johns. As the police opened the door of the car to let Johns out, they observed a black pouch and a loaded handgun. Carter and Johns were arrested, and a later search of the vehicle discovered pagers, a scale, and forty-seven grams of cocaine in plastic sandwich bags. After seizing the car, the police returned to the apartment and arrested Kimberly Thompson. A search of the apartment pursuant to a warrant revealed cocaine residue on the kitchen table and plastic baggies. Thielen identified Carter, Johns, and Thompson as the three people he had observed placing the powder into baggies. The police later learned that while Thompson was the lessee of the apartment, Carter and Johns lived in Chicago and had come to the apartment for the purpose of packaging the cocaine. Carter and Johns had never been to the apartment before and were only in the apartment for two and a half hours. Carter and Johns were convicted of both conspiracy to commit a controlled substance crime in the first degree and aiding and abetting in a controlled substance crime in the first degree.

ISSUE: Does a suspect "merely present" in a home by consent of the owner have a recognized right to privacy in the home?

HOLDING: No.

RATIONALE: "We have held that 'capacity to claim the protection of the Fourth Amendment depends . . . upon whether the person who claims the protection of the Amendment has a legitimate expectation of privacy in the invaded place.'"

"But while the holding of *Jones* [*v. United States*, 362 U.S. 257 (1960)]—that a search of the apartment violated the defendant's Fourth Amendment rights—is still valid, its statement that 'anyone legitimately on the premises where a search occurs may challenge its legality . . .' was expressly repudiated. . . . Thus an overnight guest in a home may claim the protection of the Fourth Amendment, but one who is merely present with the consent of the householder may not."

"Property used for commercial purposes is treated differently for Fourth Amendment purposes than residential property. 'An expectation of privacy in commercial premises, however, is different from, and indeed less than, a similar expectation in an individual's home.' And while it was a 'home' in which respondents were present, it was not their home."

"But the purely commercial nature of the transaction engaged in here, the relatively short period of time on the premises, and the lack of any previous connection between respondents and the householder, all lead us to conclude that respondents' situation is closer to that of one simply permitted on the premises. We therefore hold that any search which may have occurred did not violate their Fourth Amendment rights."

"[W]e conclude that respondents had no legitimate expectation of privacy in the apartment. . . ."

5. Particularity (Property Owners and the Description of their Criminality)

Zurcher v. Stanford Daily, 436 U.S. 547 (1978)

Vote: 5-4

FACTS: Officers of the Palo Alto Police Department and of the Santa Clara County Sheriff's Department responded to a call from the director of the Stanford University Hospital requesting the removal of a large group of demonstrators. The police chose to force their way in, and as they did so, a group of demonstrators emerged, armed with sticks and clubs, and attacked the group of officers. One officer was knocked to the floor and struck repeatedly on the head; another suffered a broken shoulder. All nine were injured.

A special edition of the *Stanford Daily* carried articles and photographs devoted to the protest and the district attorney's office secured a warrant for an immediate search of the *Daily*'s offices for negatives, film, and pictures. The warrant affidavit contained no allegation or indication that members of the staff were involved in unlawful acts. The officers had not been advised by the staff that the areas they were searching contained confidential materials. The search revealed only the photographs that had already been published. The staff brought a civil action under 42 U.S.C. § 1983 against the police officers, the chief of police, the district attorney and one of his deputies, and the judge who had issued the warrant.

ISSUE: Does a search warrant have to claim that the owner of the property named in the warrant is responsible for criminal activity for the warrant to be valid?

HOLDING: No.

RATIONALE: "As heretofore understood, the Amendment has not been a barrier to warrants to search property on which there is probable cause to believe that fruits, instrumentalities, or evidence of crime is located, whether or not the owner or possessor of the premises to be searched is himself reasonably suspected of complicity in the crime being investigated."

"In situations where the State does not seek to seize 'persons' but only those 'things' which there is probable cause to believe are located on the place to be searched, there is no apparent basis in the language of the Amendment for also imposing the requirements for a valid arrest—probable cause to believe that the third party is implicated in the crime."

"Search warrants are not directed at persons; they authorize the search of '[places]' and the seizure of 'things,' and as a constitutional matter they need not even name the person from whom the things will be seized."

"[T]he premise of the District Court's holding appears to be that state entitlement to a search warrant depends on the culpability of the owner or possessor of the place to be searched and on the State's right to arrest him. The cases are to the contrary."

"The critical element in a reasonable search is not that the owner of the property is suspected of crime but that there is reasonable cause to believe that the specific 'things' to be searched for and seized are located on the property to which entry is sought."

"Against this background, it is untenable to conclude that property may not be searched unless its occupant is reasonably suspected of crime and is subject to arrest."

"We do hold, however, that the courts may not, in the name of Fourth Amendment reasonableness, prohibit the States from issuing warrants to search for evidence simply because the owner or possessor of the place to be searched is not then reasonably suspected of criminal involvement."

"[A]s we have said, it is apparent that whether the third-party occupant is suspect or not, the State's interest in enforcing the criminal law and recovering the evidence remains the same. . . ."

6. Particularity (Things to be Seized)

a. Description of Materials and Relationship to Crime

Stanford v. Texas, 379 U.S. 476 (1965)
Vote: 9-0

FACTS: Texas police officers presented themselves at John William Stanford Jr.'s home for the purpose of searching it under authority of a warrant. They seized some 2,000 of Stanford's books, pamphlets, and papers. The warrant was issued under the Suppression Act, which was a law that, among other things, outlawed the Communist Party and created various individual criminal offenses, each punishable by imprisonment for up to twenty years. Section 9 authorized the issuance of a warrant "for the purpose of searching for and seizing any books, records, pamphlets, cards, receipts, lists, memoranda, pictures, recordings, or any written instruments showing that a person or organization is violating or has violated any provision of this Act."

Stanford was not at home when the officers arrived, but his wife let the officers in after one of them had read the warrant to her. After some delay, occasioned by an unsuccessful effort to locate Stanford, the search began. Authorities took a number of books from his personal library. The books and pamphlets taken comprised approximately 300 separate titles. Among the books taken were works by such diverse writers as Karl Marx, Jean Paul Sartre, Theodore Draper, Fidel Castro, Earl Browder, Pope John XXIII, and Mr. Justice Hugo L. Black. The officers also took possession of many of the petitioner's private documents and papers, including his marriage certificate, his insurance policies, his household bills and receipts, and files of his personal correspondence. The officers did not find any "records of the Communist Party" or any "party lists and dues payments." Stanford attacked the validity of the search.

ISSUE: Is a search warrant that describes books, records, pamphlets, cards, receipts, lists, memoranda, pictures, recordings, and other written instruments not particularly describing their relationship to the offense, valid?

HOLDING: No.

RATIONALE: "For we think it is clear that this warrant was of a kind which it was the purpose of the Fourth Amendment to forbid—a general warrant."

"[W]hat this history indispensably teaches is that the constitutional requirement that warrants must particularly describe the 'things to be seized' is to be accorded the most scrupulous exactitude when the 'things' are books, and the basis for their seizure is the ideas which they contain. . . . No less a standard could be faithful to First Amendment freedoms. The constitutional impossibility of leaving the protection of those freedoms to the whim of the officers charged with executing the warrant is dramatically underscored by what the officers saw fit to seize under the warrant in this case."

"The point is that it was not any contraband of that kind which was ordered to be seized, but literary material—'books, records, pamphlets, cards, receipts, lists, memoranda, pictures, recordings and other written instruments concerning the Communist Party of Texas, and the operations of the Communist Party in Texas.' The indiscriminate sweep of that language is constitutionally intolerable."

b. Description of Things to Be Seized in the Warrant

Groh v. Ramirez, 540 U.S. 551 (2004)

Vote: 5-4

FACTS: Joseph Ramirez and his family live in Butte-Silver Bow County, Montana. Jeff Groh is an agent for the Bureau of Alcohol, Tobacco and Firearms (ATF). A citizen informed Groh that on a number of visits to Ramirez's ranch the visitor had seen an automatic rifle, grenades, a grenade launcher, and a rocket launcher. Groh's warrant application stated that the search was for "any automatic firearms or parts to automatic weapons, destructive devices to include but not limited to grenades, grenade launchers, rocket launchers, and any and all receipts pertaining to the purchase or manufacture of automatic weapons or explosive devices or launchers." Groh also supported the application with a detailed affidavit. Groh then obtained a warrant from a judge.

Although the application described the place to be searched and items to be seized, the warrant failed to identify any of the items. The part of the form that called for a description of the items referred to Ramirez's house. Groh led police on the search, which turned up nothing illegal. Ramirez's wife was given a copy of the search warrant, but not a copy of the application. The following day, Groh faxed Ramirez's attorney a copy of the application, but no charges were ever filed. The Ramirezes sued Groh for a violation of the Fourth Amendment.

ISSUE: Does a warrant that fails to describe the things to be seized, even though the application does, violate the particularity clause of the Fourth Amendment?

HOLDING: Yes.

RATIONALE: "The warrant was plainly invalid. The Fourth Amendment states unambiguously that 'no Warrants shall issue, but upon probable cause, supported by Oath or affirmation, and *particularly describing* the place to be searched, and *the persons or things to be seized*.' The warrant in this case complied with the first three of these requirements: It was based on probable cause and supported by a sworn affidavit, and it described particularly the place of the search. On the fourth requirement, however, the warrant failed altogether. Indeed, petitioner concedes that 'the warrant . . . was deficient in particularity because it provided no description of the type of evidence sought.'"

"The fact that the *application* adequately described the 'things to be seized' does not save the *warrant* from its facial invalidity. The Fourth Amendment by its terms requires particularity in the warrant, not in the supporting documents. . . . And for good reason: 'The presence of a search warrant serves a high function . . . and that high function is not necessarily vindicated when some other document, somewhere, says something about the objects of the search, but the contents of that document are neither known to the person whose home is being searched nor available for her inspection. . . .'"

"Petitioner argues that even though the warrant was invalid, the search nevertheless was 'reasonable' within the meaning of the Fourth Amendment. . . ."

"We disagree . . . the warrant did not describe the items to be seized *at all*. In this respect the warrant was so obviously deficient that we must regard the search as 'warrantless' within the meaning of our case law. . . . [O]ur cases have firmly established the '"basic principle of Fourth Amendment law" that searches and seizures inside a home without a warrant are presumptively unreasonable. . . .' Thus, 'absent exigent circumstances, a warrantless entry to search for weapons or contraband is unconstitutional even when a felony has been committed and there is probable cause to believe that incriminating evidence will be found within.'"

"We have clearly stated that the presumptive rule against warrantless searches applies with equal force to searches whose only defect is a lack of particularity in the warrant."

"[U]nless the particular items described in the affidavit are also set forth in the warrant itself (or at least incorporated by reference, and the affidavit present at the search), there can be no written assurance that the Magistrate actually found probable cause to search for, and to seize, every item mentioned in the affidavit."

"A particular warrant also 'assures the individual whose property is searched or seized of the lawful authority of the executing officer, his need to search, and the limits of his power to search.'"

"But as we observed in the companion case to [*Massachusetts v. Sheppard*, 468 U.S. 981 (1984)] 'a warrant may be so facially deficient—*i.e.*, in failing to particularize the place to be searched or the things to be seized—that the executing officers cannot reasonably presume it to be valid. . . .' This is such a case."

c. Anticipatory Warrants and Particularity

United States v. Grubbs, 126 S.Ct. 1494 (2006)
Vote: 8-0
FACTS: Grubbs purchased a tape containing child pornography from a website operated by an undercover postal inspector. The Postal Inspection Service arranged a controlled delivery of the videotape to his home. A postal inspector submitted a search warrant application describing the operation in detail. The affidavit stated that the warrant would not be executed until the package had been received and taken into the home. The affidavit referred to two attachments that described the home and the items that would be seized. The attachments but not the affidavit were incorporated into the warrant. Grubbs's wife received the package, and Grubbs was detained as he was leaving the house. Grubbs confessed and was given a copy of the warrant, which had the attachments. At his suppression hearing on the charge of receiving a visual depiction of a minor engaged in sexually explicit conduct, Grubbs argued that the warrant was invalid because it failed to list the triggering condition. Grubbs pleaded guilty but reserved his right to appeal the denial of his suppression motion.
ISSUE: Does an anticipatory warrant for a house that does not list the trigger condition, violate the Fourth Amendment?
HOLDING: No.
RATIONALE: "The Fourth Amendment, however, does not set forth some general 'particularity requirement.' It specifies only two matters that must be 'particularly describ[ed]' in the warrant: 'the place to be searched' and 'the persons or things to be

seized.' We have previously rejected efforts to expand the scope of this provision to embrace unenumerated matters. . . . The language of the Fourth Amendment is likewise decisive here; its particularity requirement does not include the conditions precedent to execution of the warrant."

"The Fourth Amendment does not require that the warrant set forth the magistrate's basis for finding probable cause, even though probable cause is the quintessential 'precondition to the valid exercise of executive power.' Much less does it require description of a triggering condition."

"This argument assumes that the executing officer must present the property owner with a copy of the warrant before conducting his search. . . . In fact, however, neither the Fourth Amendment nor Rule 41 of the Federal Rules of Criminal Procedure imposes such a requirement. . . . 'The absence of a constitutional requirement that the warrant be exhibited at the outset of the search, or indeed until the search has ended, is . . . evidence that the requirement of particular description does not protect an interest in monitoring searches. . . .' The Constitution protects property owners not by giving them license to engage the police in a debate over the basis for the warrant, but by interposing, the 'deliberate, impartial judgment of a judicial officer . . . between the citizen and the police.'"

B. Execution of a Search Warrant

1. Obtaining Probable Cause

a. False Statements by Police to Obtain Probable Cause

Franks v. Delaware, 438 U.S. 154 (1978)
Vote: 7-2
FACTS: Cynthia Bailey told police that she had been confronted in her home earlier that morning by a man with a knife, and that he had sexually assaulted her. She described her assailant's age, race, height, build, and facial hair, and gave a detailed description of his clothing as consisting of a white thermal undershirt, black pants with a silver or gold buckle, a brown leather three-quarter-length coat, and a dark knit cap that he wore pulled down around his eyes. Jerome Franks coincidentally was taken into custody for an assault involving a fifteen-year-old girl six days earlier and stated to police that he was surprised that his hearing was about her because he said "that he knew her." He also said, "I thought you said Bailey. I don't know her." It was this statement that gave police a clue as to his involvement with Bailey.

The affidavit for the search of Frank's home alleged that he typically wore the same clothes as those described by the victim. This was supported by statements by the police in the affidavit, which stated: "On Tuesday, 3/9/76, your affiant contacted Mr. James Williams and Mr. Wesley Lucas of the Delaware Youth Center where Jerome Franks is employed and did have personal conversation with both these people." and "Mr. James

Williams revealed to your affiant that the normal dress of Jerome Franks does consist of a white knit thermal undershirt and a brown leather jacket," and "Mr. Wesley Lucas revealed to your affiant that in addition to the thermal undershirt and jacket, Jerome Franks often wears a dark green knit hat." The defense attacked these statements as being false and that the individuals were never contacted by the particular officers and that information that they did proffer to other officers was different from that in the affidavit. Clothes matching the description of those of the assailant were found at Frank's home and introduced at trial where he was convicted of rape, kidnapping, and burglary.

ISSUE: Can police make false statements to obtain probable cause for search warrants?

HOLDING: No.

RATIONALE: "In the event that at that hearing the allegation of perjury or reckless disregard is established by the defendant by a preponderance of the evidence, and, with the affidavit's false material set to one side, the affidavit's remaining content is insufficient to establish probable cause, the search warrant must be voided and the fruits of the search excluded to the same extent as if probable cause was lacking on the face of the affidavit."

"'When the Fourth Amendment demands a factual showing sufficient to comprise "probable cause," the obvious assumption is that there will be a *truthful* showing.' This does not mean 'truthful' in the sense that every fact recited in the warrant affidavit is necessarily correct, for probable cause may be founded upon hearsay and upon information received from informants, as well as upon information within the affiant's own knowledge that sometimes must be garnered hastily. But surely it is to be 'truthful' in the sense that the information put forth is believed or appropriately accepted by the affiant as true. . . . Because it is the magistrate who must determine independently whether there is probable cause. . . . [I]t would be an unthinkable imposition upon his authority if a warrant affidavit, revealed after the fact to contain a deliberately or recklessly false statement, were to stand beyond impeachment."

"The requirement that a warrant not issue 'but upon probable cause, supported by Oath or affirmation,' would be reduced to a nullity if a police officer was able to use deliberately falsified allegations to demonstrate probable cause, and, having misled the magistrate, then was able to remain confident that the ploy was worthwhile."

b. Can Officers Be Held Liable for Failing to Obtain Probable Cause When Applying for a Warrant?

Malley v. Briggs, 475 U.S. 336 (1986)

Vote: 7-2

FACTS: Rhode Island State Police were conducting a court-authorized wiretap on Paul Driscoll's telephone. Police intercepted a call to Driscoll from an unknown individual who identified himself as "Dr. Shogun." The police logsheet summarized the call: "General conversation re. a party they went to last night . . . caller says I can't believe I was token [*sic*] in front of Jimmy Briggs—caller states he passed it to Louisa . . . Paul says

Nancy was sitting in his lap rolling her thing." Edward Malley was the trooper in charge of the investigation of Driscoll and decided after reviewing the logsheet that the call from "Dr. Shogun" was incriminating, because "toking" means smoking marihuana and "rolling her thing" refers to rolling a marihuana cigarette. Petitioner also concluded that another call showed that the party discussed by Driscoll and "Dr. Shogun" took place at respondents' house. He drew up complaints and presented them to a judge. The judge signed warrants for the arrest of respondents and twenty others. Respondents were arrested but charges were dropped when the grand jury did not return an indictment. Respondents brought an action under 42 U.S.C. § 1983 charging that Malley, in applying for warrants for their arrest, violated their rights under the Fourth and Fourteenth Amendments.

ISSUE: Are police entitled to absolute immunity if they make an arrest that is lacking in probable cause?

HOLDING: No.

RATIONALE: "Our cases also make plain that '[for] executive officers in general, . . . qualified immunity represents the norm . . .' Like federal officers, state officers who 'seek absolute exemption from personal liability for unconstitutional conduct must bear the burden of showing that public policy requires an exemption of that scope.'"

"Although we have previously held that police officers sued under § 1983 for false arrest are qualifiedly immune. . . . [P]etitioner urges that he should be absolutely immune because his function in seeking an arrest warrant was similar to that of a complaining witness. The difficulty with this submission is that complaining witnesses were not absolutely immune at common law. In 1871, the generally accepted rule was that one who procured the issuance of an arrest warrant by submitting a complaint could be held liable if the complaint was made maliciously and without probable cause. Given malice and the lack of probable cause, the complainant enjoyed no immunity. The common law thus affords no support for petitioner."

"Defendants will not be immune if, on an objective basis, it is obvious that no reasonably competent officer would have concluded that a warrant should issue. . . ."

"We find it reasonable to require the officer applying for the warrant to minimize this danger by exercising reasonable professional judgment."

2. Can Evidence of a Separate Crime Be Seized?

Andresen v. Maryland, 427 U.S. 463 (1976)
Vote: 7-2

FACTS: A fraud unit began an investigation of real estate settlement activities in Maryland. Andresen was an attorney who specialized in real estate settlements. During the investigation, Andresen's activities came under scrutiny; particularly in connection with a transaction involving Lot 13T in the Potomac Woods subdivision. The investigation disclosed that he had defrauded the purchaser of the lot. Investigators, concluding that there was probable cause to believe that Andresen had committed crimes of false pretenses, applied for warrants. The application sought permission to search for specified documents pertaining to the sale and conveyance of the lot. A judge issued the warrants. The searches of the two offices were conducted simultaneously and Andresen was present during the search of his law office. His counsel was present during the latter half of the search. The State introduced evidence not related to Lot 13T at the trial that resulted in his convictions on several counts of false pretenses and other charges. Although, four of the five convictions were reversed. One count remained of false pretenses and three counts of misappropriation.

ISSUE: Can material unrelated to the crime alleged in a search warrant be seized and used against a defendant at trial to prove the indicated crime?

HOLDING: Yes.

RATIONALE: "Under investigation was a complex real estate scheme whose existence could be proved only by piecing together many bits of evidence. Like a jigsaw puzzle, the whole 'picture' of petitioner's false pretense scheme with respect to Lot 13T could be shown only by placing in the proper place the many pieces of evidence that, taken singly, would show comparatively little."

"Petitioner charges that the seizure of documents pertaining to a lot other than Lot 13T violated the principles of *Warden v. Hayden* [387 U.S. 294 (1967)] and therefore should have been suppressed. His objection appears to be that these papers were not relevant to the Lot 13T charge and were admissible only to prove another crime with which he was charged after the search. The fact that these documents were used to help form the evidentiary basis for another charge, it is argued, shows that the documents were seized solely for that purpose."

"In this case, we conclude that the trained special investigators reasonably could have believed that the evidence specifically dealing with another lot in the Potomac Woods subdivision could be used to show petitioner's intent with respect to the Lot 13T transaction."

"In the present case, when the special investigators secured the search warrants, they had been informed of a number of similar charges against petitioner arising out of Potomac Woods transactions. And, by reading numerous documents and records supplied by the Lot 13T and other complainants, and by interviewing witnesses, they had become familiar with petitioner's method of operation. Accordingly, the relevance of documents pertaining specifically to a lot other than Lot 13T, and their admissibility to show the Lot 13T offense, would have been apparent."

3. Knock-and-Announce Rule

a. Is the Knock-and-Announce Rule Part of the Reasonableness Requirement of the Fourth Amendment?

Wilson v. Arkansas, 514 U.S. 927 (1995)
Vote: 9-0
FACTS: Sharlene Wilson made narcotics sales of marijuana and methamphetamine to an informant under the direction of the Arkansas State Police at the home that Wilson shared with Bryson Jacobs. The informant telephoned Wilson at her home and

arranged to meet her at a local store to buy some marijuana. Wilson pulled a semiau-tomatic pistol at this meeting and waved it in the informant's face, threatening to kill her if she turned out to be working for the police. She then sold the informant a bag of marijuana. Police obtained search and arrest warrants. Affidavits stated that Jacobs had previously been convicted of arson and firebombing. Police officers found the main door to Wilson's home open. While opening an unlocked screen door and entering the residence, they identified themselves as police officers and stated that they had a war-rant. Once inside the home, the officers seized drugs, firearms, and ammunition. Wil-son was in the bathroom, flushing marijuana down the toilet. Wilson and Jacobs were arrested and charged with delivery of marijuana, delivery of methamphetamine, pos-session of drug paraphernalia, and possession of marijuana and convicted.

ISSUE: Is the knock-and-announce rule part of the Fourth Amendment reasonable-ness requirement?

HOLDING: Yes.

RATIONALE: "An examination of the common law of search and seizure leaves no doubt that the reasonableness of a search of a dwelling may depend in part on whether law enforcement officers announced their presence and authority prior to entering."

"'But before he breaks it, he ought to signify the cause of his coming, and to make request to open doors . . . , for the law without a default in the owner abhors the de-struction or breaking of any house. . . .'"

"Several prominent founding-era commentators agreed on this basic principle. Ac-cording to Sir Matthew Hale, the 'constant practice' at common law was that 'the offi-cer may break open the door, if he be sure the offender is there, if after acquainting them of the business, and demanding the prisoner, he refuses to open the door. . . .' '[T]he law doth never allow' an officer to break open the door of a dwelling 'but in cases of necessity,' that is, unless he 'first signify to those in the house the cause of his com-ing, and request them to give him admittance.'"

"Our own cases have acknowledged that the common-law principle of announce-ment is 'embedded in Anglo-American law. . . .' [B]ut we have never squarely held that this principle is an element of the reasonableness inquiry under the Fourth Amendment. We now so hold. Given the longstanding common-law endorsement of the practice of announcement, we have little doubt that the Framers of the Fourth Amendment thought that the method of an officer's entry into a dwelling was among the factors to be considered in assessing the reasonableness of a search or seizure."

b. Is There a Blanket Exception to the Knock-and-Announce Rule for Drug Cases?

Richards v. Wisconsin, 520 U.S. 385 (1997)
Vote: 9-0
FACTS: Police in Madison, Wisconsin, obtained a search warrant for Steiney Richards's hotel room for drugs. The warrant was the culmination of an investigation that had

uncovered evidence that Richards was one of several individuals dealing drugs out of hotel rooms in Madison. The police requested a warrant that would have given advance authorization for a "no-knock" entry into the hotel room, but the magistrate explicitly deleted those portions of the warrant.

The officers arrived at the hotel and Officer Pharo knocked on Richards's door and, responding to the query from inside the room, stated that he was a maintenance man. With the chain still on the door, Richards cracked it open. Richards acknowledges that when he opened the door he saw the man in uniform standing behind Pharo. He quickly slammed the door closed and, after waiting two or three seconds, the officers began kicking and ramming the door to gain entry to the locked room. The officers testified that they identified themselves as police while they were kicking the door in. When they finally did break into the room, the officers caught Richards trying to escape through the window. They also found cash and cocaine hidden in plastic bags above the bathroom ceiling tiles. Richards pled guilty to possession with intent to deliver. The Wisconsin Supreme Court held that a blanket exception to the knock-and-announce rule existed for drug cases.

ISSUE: Is there a blanket exception to the knock-and-announce rule for drug cases?

HOLDING: No.

RATIONALE: "First, the exception contains considerable overgeneralization. For example, while drug investigation frequently does pose special risks to officer safety and the preservation of evidence, not every drug investigation will pose these risks to a substantial degree."

"A second difficulty with permitting a criminal-category exception to the knock-and-announce requirement is that the reasons for creating an exception in one category can, relatively easily, be applied to others. . . . If a *per se* exception were allowed for each category of criminal investigation that included a considerable—albeit hypothetical—risk of danger to officers or destruction of evidence, the knock-and-announce element of the Fourth Amendment's reasonableness requirement would be meaningless."

"Thus, the fact that felony drug investigations may frequently present circumstances warranting a no-knock entry cannot remove from the neutral scrutiny of a reviewing court the reasonableness of the police decision not to knock and announce in a particular case. Instead, in each case, it is the duty of a court confronted with the question to determine whether the facts and circumstances of the particular entry justified dispensing with the knock-and-announce requirement."

"In order to justify a 'no-knock' entry, the police must have a reasonable suspicion that knocking and announcing their presence, under the particular circumstances, would be dangerous or futile, or that it would inhibit the effective investigation of the crime by, for example, allowing the destruction of evidence. This standard—as opposed to a probable cause requirement—strikes the appropriate balance between the legitimate law enforcement concerns at issue in the execution of search warrants and the individual. . . ."

c. Is a Fifteen-Second Wait after Knock-and-Announce Sufficient?

United States v. Banks, 540 U.S. 31 (2003)

Vote: 9-0

FACTS: North Las Vegas Police and FBI agents got a warrant to search Lashawn Lowell Banks's apartment based on information that he was selling cocaine from inside. As soon as they arrived, officers called out "police search warrant" and rapped hard enough on the door to be heard by officers at the back door. There was no indication whether anyone was home, and after waiting for fifteen to twenty seconds, the officers broke open the front door. Banks was in the shower and testified that he heard nothing until the door was broken, which brought him out to confront the police. The search produced weapons, cocaine, and evidence of drug dealing. Banks moved to suppress the evidence, arguing that the officers waited an unreasonably short time before forcing entry and as a result, violated the Fourth Amendment. The judge denied the motion, and Banks pleaded guilty, reserving the right to challenge the search on appeal.

ISSUE: Does a fifteen-to-twenty-second wait in conjunction with the knock-and-announce rule satisfy the Fourth Amendment?

HOLDING: Yes.

RATIONALE: "The question is whether their 15-to-20-second wait before a forcible entry satisfied the Fourth Amendment. . . . We hold that it did."

"[T]he issue comes down to whether it was reasonable to suspect imminent loss of evidence after the 15 to 20 seconds the officers waited prior to forcing their way. Though we agree with Judge Fisher's dissenting opinion that this call is a close one . . . we think that after 15 or 20 seconds without a response, police could fairly suspect that cocaine would be gone if they were reticent any longer. Courts of appeals have, indeed, routinely held similar wait times to be reasonable in drug cases with similar facts including easily disposable evidence."

"And the argument that 15 to 20 seconds was too short for Banks to have come to the door ignores the very risk that justified prompt entry. . . . In this case, however, the police claim exigent need to enter, and the crucial fact in examining their actions is not time to reach the door but the particular exigency claimed. On the record here, what matters is the opportunity to get rid of cocaine, which a prudent dealer will keep near a commode or kitchen sink. The significant circumstances include the arrival of the police during the day, when anyone inside would probably have been up and around, and the sufficiency of 15 to 20 seconds for getting to the bathroom or the kitchen to start flushing cocaine down the drain. That is, when circumstances are exigent because a pusher may be near the point of putting his drugs beyond reach, it is imminent disposal, not travel time to the entrance, that governs when the police may reasonably enter; since the bathroom and kitchen are usually in the interior of a dwelling, not the front hall, there is no reason generally to peg the travel time to the location of the door, and no reliable basis for giving the proprietor of a mansion a longer wait than the resident of a bungalow, or an apartment like Banks'. And 15 to 20 seconds does not seem an unrealistic guess about the time someone would need to get in a position to rid his quarters of cocaine."

"Once the exigency had matured, of course, the officers were not bound to learn anything more or wait any longer before going in, even though their entry entailed some harm to the building."

d. Is There a Higher Standard for No-Knock Entries When the Police Damage Property?

United States v. Ramirez, 523 U.S. 65 (1998)
Vote: 9-0
FACTS: Alan Shelby was a prisoner serving concurrent state and federal sentences. The Tillamook County Sheriff's Office took custody of Shelby, expecting to transport him to the Tillamook County Courthouse, where he was scheduled to testify. On the way to the courthouse, he escaped. He was reported to have made threats to kill witnesses and police officers, to have tortured people with a hammer, and to have said that he would "not do federal time."

An informant told ATF agent George Kim that on the previous day he had seen a person he believed to be Shelby at Hernan Ramirez's home. Kim and the informant then drove to an area near Ramirez's home, from where Kim observed a man who resembled Shelby.

A deputy U.S. Marshal received a "no-knock" warrant granting permission to enter and search Ramirez's home. The confidential informant also told authorities that respondent might have a stash of guns and drugs hidden in his garage. Forty-five officers gathered to execute the warrant. The officers announced that they had a warrant. Simultaneously, they broke a single window in the garage and pointed a gun through the opening, hoping thereby to dissuade any of the occupants from rushing to the weapons the officers believed might be in the garage.

Ramirez and his family were asleep inside the house. He believed that they were being burglarized and ran to his utility closet, grabbed a pistol, and fired it into the ceiling of his garage. The officers fired back and shouted "police." At that point, Ramirez ran to the living room, threw his pistol away, and threw himself onto the floor. Shortly thereafter, he, his wife, and their child were taken into police custody. Shelby was not found. Ramirez was subsequently indicted for being a felon in possession of firearms.
ISSUE: Are police held to a higher standard of objective reasonableness for no-knock entries when they destroy property?
HOLDING: No.
RATIONALE: "In this case, we must decide whether the Fourth Amendment holds officers to a higher standard than this when a 'no-knock' entry results in the destruction of property. We hold that it does not."

"'[I]n order to justify a 'no-knock' entry, the police must have a reasonable suspicion that knocking and announcing their presence, under the particular circumstances, would be dangerous or futile, or that it would inhibit the effective investigation of the crime by, for example, allowing the destruction of evidence.'"

"Neither of these cases explicitly addressed the question whether the lawfulness of a no-knock entry depends on whether property is damaged in the course of the entry. It is obvious from their holdings, however, that it does not. Under *Richards* [*v. Wisconsin*, 520 U.S. 385 (1997)], a no-knock entry is justified if police have a 'reasonable suspicion' that knocking and announcing would be dangerous, futile, or destructive to the purposes of the investigation. Whether such a 'reasonable suspicion' exists depends in no way on whether police must destroy property in order to enter."

"Applying these principles to the facts at hand, we conclude that no Fourth Amendment violation occurred. A reliable confidential informant had notified the police that Alan Shelby might be inside respondent's home, and an officer had confirmed this possibility. Shelby was a prison escapee with a violent past who reportedly had access to a large supply of weapons. He had vowed that he would 'not do federal time.' The police certainly had a 'reasonable suspicion' that knocking and announcing their presence might be dangerous to themselves or to others."

e. Knock-and-Announce and the Exclusionary Rule

Hudson v. Michigan 126 S.Ct. 2159 (2006)
Vote: 5-4
FACTS: Police obtained a warrant to search Hudson's home, and he was charged with drugs and firearms possession after he was found with a loaded handgun in the chair he was sitting in. Police announced their presence, but waited only a few seconds before opening the door without knocking. Hudson filed a motion to suppress and the Michigan trial court granted it. The Michigan Court of Appeals reversed, relying on Michigan Supreme Court cases that stated that suppression is inappropriate when entry is made pursuant to a valid warrant but in violation of the knock-and-announce rule. Hudson was convicted of drug possession and the court of appeals rejected his claim that his Fourth Amendment rights were violated.
ISSUE: Does the Fourth Amendment require the suppression of all evidence if the knock-and-announce rule is violated?
HOLDING: No.
RATIONALE: "'Subsequent case law has rejected this reflexive application of the exclusionary rule.' We had said as much in *Leon*, a decade earlier, when we explained that '[w]hether the exclusionary sanction is appropriately imposed in a particular case, . . . is "an issue separate from the question whether the Fourth Amendment rights of the party seeking to invoke the rule were violated by police conduct."'"

"In other words, exclusion may not be premised on the mere fact that a constitutional violation was a 'but-for' cause of obtaining evidence. Our cases show that but-for causality is only a necessary, not a sufficient, condition for suppression. . . . We have 'never held that evidence is "fruit of the poisonous tree" simply because "it would not have come to light but for the illegal actions of the police. . . ."' Rather, but-for cause, or 'causation in the logical sense alone . . .' can be too attenuated to justify exclusion."

"Attenuation also occurs when, even given a direct causal connection, the interest protected by the constitutional guarantee that has been violated would not be served by suppression of the evidence obtained."

"For this reason, cases excluding the fruits of unlawful warrantless searches . . . say nothing about the appropriateness of exclusion to vindicate the interests protected by the knock-and-announce requirement. . . . The interests protected by the knock-and-announce requirement are quite different—and do not include the shielding of potential evidence from the government's eyes."

"One of those interests is the protection of human life and limb, because an unannounced entry may provoke violence in supposed self-defense by the surprised resident."

"What the knock-and-announce rule has never protected, however, is one's interest in preventing the government from seeing or taking evidence described in a warrant. Since the interests that *were* violated in this case have nothing to do with the seizure of the evidence, the exclusionary rule is inapplicable."

C. Searching Premises

1. Detaining People and Search Warrants

a. Can People Be Detained at the Place to Be Searched?

Michigan v. Summers, 452 U.S. 692 (1981)
Vote: 6-3
FACTS: Detroit police officers encountered Summers descending the front steps of his house as they were about to execute a warrant. They requested his assistance in gaining entry and detained him while they searched. After the occupants of the house were detained, a search revealed two bags of suspected narcotics under the bar in the basement. A custodial search conducted by Officer Conant revealed a plastic bag containing suspected heroin in the defendant's jacket pocket. It is this heroin, discovered on Summers' person that forms the basis of the possession charge.
ISSUE: Can police detain people in the vicinity of a house while conducting a search?
HOLDING: Yes.
RATIONALE: "The detention of one of the residents while the premises were searched, although admittedly a significant restraint on his liberty, was surely less intrusive than the search itself. Indeed, we may safely assume that most citizens—unless they intend flight to avoid arrest—would elect to remain in order to observe the search of their possessions. Furthermore, the type of detention imposed here is not likely to be exploited by the officer or unduly prolonged in order to gain more information, because the information the officers seek normally will be obtained through the search and not through the detention. Moreover, because the detention in this case was in respondent's own residence, it could add only minimally to the public stigma associated with the search itself and would involve neither the inconvenience nor the indignity associated with a compelled visit to the police station."

"[B]oth the law enforcement interest and the nature of the 'articulable facts' supporting the detention are relevant. Most obvious is the legitimate law enforcement interest in preventing flight in the event that incriminating evidence is found. Less obvious, but sometimes of greater importance, is the interest in minimizing the risk of harm to the officers. Although no special danger to the police is suggested by the evidence in this record, the execution of a warrant to search for narcotics is the kind of transaction that may give rise to sudden violence or frantic efforts to conceal or destroy evidence. The risk of harm to both the police and the occupants is minimized if the officers routinely exercise unquestioned command of the situation. . . . Finally, the orderly completion of the search may be facilitated if the occupants of the premises are present. Their self-interest may induce them to open locked doors or locked containers to avoid the use of force that is not only damaging to property but may also delay the completion of the task at hand."

"The existence of a search warrant, however, also provides an objective justification for the detention."

b. Length of Detention at Place to Be Searched

Muehler v. Mena, 544 U.S. 93 (2005)
Vote: 9-0
FACTS: Based on an investigation of a gang-related, drive-by shooting, Officers Muehler and Brill believed that at least one member of the West Side Locos gang lived at 1363 Patricia Avenue. Muehler then obtained a search warrant for the address, which authorized a search of the house for deadly weapons and evidence of gang membership. In light of the high degree of risk involved in searching a house suspected of housing gang members, a Special Weapons and Tactics (SWAT) team was used to secure the residence before the search. The SWAT team with other officers executed the warrant while Iris Mena was asleep in her bed. Officers entered her bedroom and placed her in handcuffs at gunpoint. The team also handcuffed three other people and took them and Mena into a converted garage. While the search continued, officers guarded the four detainees, who were allowed to move around the garage but remained in handcuffs.

Aware that the gang was composed mostly of illegal immigrants, the officers notified the Immigration and Naturalization Service (INS) and an INS agent accompanied the officers during the search. During their detention, an agent asked several identifying questions and later asked for their documentation. The search yielded a .22 caliber handgun with ammunition, a box of .25 caliber ammunition, several baseball bats with gang symbols, gang paraphernalia, and a bag of marijuana. Before the officers left the area, Mena was released. In her § 1983 suit against the officers she argued that she was detained for an unreasonable amount of time and in an unreasonable manner in violation of the Fourth Amendment, and appellate courts agreed.
ISSUE: Does detaining a suspect in a home for two to three hours in handcuffs while a search is being conducted violate the Fourth Amendment?
HOLDING: No.
RATIONALE: "We hold that Mena's detention in handcuffs for the length of the search was consistent with our opinion in *Michigan v. Summers* [452 U.S. 692 (1981)] . . .

and that the officers' questioning during that detention did not violate her Fourth Amendment rights."

"In *Summers* . . . we held that officers executing a search warrant for contraband have the authority 'to detain the occupants of the premises while a proper search is conducted. . . .' We made clear that the detention of an occupant is 'surely less intrusive than the search itself,' and the presence of a warrant assures that a neutral magistrate has determined that probable cause exists to search the home."

"An officer's authority to detain incident to a search is categorical; it does not depend on the 'quantum of proof justifying detention or the extent of the intrusion to be imposed by the seizure. . . .' Thus, Mena's detention for the duration of the search was reasonable under *Summers* because a warrant existed to search 1363 Patricia Avenue and she was an occupant of that address at the time of the search."

"Inherent in *Summers'* authorization to detain an occupant of the place to be searched is the authority to use reasonable force to effectuate the detention."

"The officers' use of force in the form of handcuffs . . . as well as the detention of the three other occupants, was reasonable because the governmental interests outweigh the marginal intrusion. . . . The imposition of correctly applied handcuffs . . . was undoubtedly a separate intrusion in addition to detention in the converted garage."

"The governmental interests in not only detaining, but using handcuffs, are at their maximum when, as here, a warrant authorizes a search for weapons and a wanted gang member resides on the premises. In such inherently dangerous situations, the use of handcuffs minimizes the risk of harm to both officers and occupants. . . . Though this safety risk inherent in executing a search warrant for weapons was sufficient to justify the use of handcuffs, the need to detain multiple occupants made the use of handcuffs all the more reasonable."

"However, the 2- to 3-hour detention in handcuffs in this case does not outweigh the government's continuing safety interests. . . . We conclude that the detention of Mena in handcuffs during the search was reasonable."

c. Securing a Home While a Warrant Is Being Sought

Segura v. United States, 468 U.S. 796 (1984)
Vote: 5-4
FACTS: New York Drug Enforcement agents began surveillance of Andres Segura and Luz Marina Colon. They observed Colon deliver a bulky package to Esther Parra at a fast-food restaurant parking lot while Segura and Enrique Rivudalla-Vidal visited inside. The agents followed Parra and Rivudalla-Vidal to their apartment and stopped them. Parra was found to possess cocaine, and she and Rivudalla-Vidal were arrested. After being advised of his rights, Rivudalla-Vidal admitted that he had purchased the cocaine from Segura and confirmed that Colon had made the delivery at the restaurant parking lot. Agents were advised that a search warrant for Segura's and Colon's apartment probably could not be obtained until the following day but that the agent should secure the premises. Later that day, the agents arrested Segura in the lobby of his apartment, knocked on the door, and, when it was opened by Colon, entered the apartment.

The agents then conducted a limited security check and observed drug paraphernalia. Colon was then arrested, and both petitioners were taken into custody. Two agents remained in the apartment awaiting the warrant, but because of 'administrative delay' the warrant was not issued until nineteen hours later. In the search pursuant to the warrant, the agents discovered cocaine. These items were seized, together with those observed during the security check. Segura and Colon were convicted of conspiring to distribute cocaine and of possessing with intent to distribute cocaine.

ISSUE: If police have probable cause, can they secure a place while they seek a warrant?

HOLDING: Yes.

RATIONALE: "[T]he Court has frequently approved warrantless seizures of property, on the basis of probable cause, for the time necessary to secure a warrant, where a warrantless search was either held to be or likely would have been held impermissible."

"Underlying these decisions is a belief that society's interest in the discovery and protection of incriminating evidence from removal or destruction can supersede, at least for a limited period, a person's possessory interest in property, provided that there is probable cause to believe that that property is associated with criminal activity."

"However, in two cases we have suggested that securing of premises under these circumstances does not violate the Fourth Amendment, at least when undertaken to preserve the status quo while a search warrant is being sought."

"We see no reason, as *Mincey* [*v. Arizona*, 437 U.S. 385 (1978)] and *Rawlings* [*v. Kentucky*, 448 U.S. 98 (1980)] would suggest, why the same principle applied in *Chambers* [*v. Maroney*, 399 U.S. 42 (1970)], [*United States v. Chadwick*, 433 U.S. 1 (1977)], and [*Arkansas v. Sanders*, 442 U.S. 753 (1979)], should not apply where a dwelling is involved."

"We hold, therefore, that securing a dwelling, on the basis of probable cause, to prevent the destruction or removal of evidence while a search warrant is being sought is not itself an unreasonable seizure of either the dwelling or its contents."

d. Restraining Suspects from Entering Their Homes

Illinois v. McArthur, 531 U.S. 326 (2001)
Vote: 8-1

FACTS: Tera McArthur asked police to accompany her to the trailer where she lived with her husband, Charles, so that they could keep the peace while she removed her belongings. Tera went inside, where Charles was present. The officers remained outside. When Tera emerged, she spoke to Assistant Chief John Love, who was on the porch. She suggested he check the trailer because "Chuck had dope in there." She added (in Love's words) that she had seen Chuck "slide some dope underneath the couch." Love knocked on the trailer door, told Charles what Tera had said, and asked for permission to search, which Charles denied. Love then sent an officer with Tera to get a warrant. Love told Charles, who was on the porch, that he could not reenter the trailer unless a police officer accompanied him. Love subsequently reentered the trailer two or three times with Charles to observe what Charles did. Police returned with the warrant and searched the trailer. The officers found a pipe, a box for marijuana, and a small amount of marijuana. They then arrested him and he was charged with unlawfully possessing drug paraphernalia and marijuana.

ISSUE: May police restrain a suspect from going into his house, for two to three hours while they obtain a search warrant?

HOLDING: Yes.

RATIONALE: "In the circumstances of the case before us, we cannot say that the warrantless seizure was *per se* unreasonable. It involves a plausible claim of specially pressing or urgent law enforcement need. . . . Moreover, the restraint at issue was tailored to that need, being limited in time and scope. . . ."

"We conclude that the restriction at issue was reasonable, and hence lawful. . . ."

"[T]he police imposed the restraint for a limited period of time, namely, two hours. . . . As far as the record reveals, this time period was no longer than reasonably necessary for the police, acting with diligence, to obtain the warrant. . . ."

"Our conclusion that the restriction was lawful finds significant support in this Court's case law. . . . [B]oth majority and minority assumed, at least for argument's sake, that the police, armed with reliable information that the apartment contained drugs, might lawfully have sealed the apartment from the outside, restricting entry into the apartment while waiting for the warrant. . . ."

"In various other circumstances, this Court has upheld temporary restraints where needed to preserve evidence until police could obtain a warrant. . . ."

"We have found no case in which this Court has held unlawful a temporary seizure that was supported by probable cause and was designed to prevent the loss of evidence while the police diligently obtained a warrant in a reasonable period of time."

"We have explained above why we believe that the need to preserve evidence of a 'jailable' offense was sufficiently urgent or pressing to justify the restriction upon entry that the police imposed."

"In sum, the police officers in this case had probable cause to believe that a home contained contraband, which was evidence of a crime. They reasonably believed that the home's resident, if left free of any restraint, would destroy that evidence. And they imposed a restraint that was both limited and tailored reasonably to secure law enforcement needs while protecting privacy interests. In our view, the restraint met the Fourth Amendment's demands."

2. Can Media "Ride-Along" during Execution of a Search Warrant for a Home?

Wilson v. Layne, 526 U.S. 603 (1999)
Vote: 8-1

FACTS: United States Marshals and Montgomery County, Maryland, police executed arrest warrants for Dominic Wilson. They were accompanied by a reporter and photographer from the *Washington Post*. The officers and the media entered the dwelling. Charles Wilson ran into the living room to investigate. Discovering at least five men with guns in his living room, he demanded that they state their business. Believing him to be Dominic Wilson, the officers subdued him on the floor. Geraldine Wilson entered the living room and observed her husband being restrained. When their sweep was completed, the officers learned that Dominic was not there. The photographer took pictures, and the reporter was in the living room. At no time, were the reporter or photographer involved in the execution of the warrant. The Wilsons sued the officials for money damages under *Bivens v. Six Unknown Federal Narcotics Agents* [403 U.S. 388 (1971)] and contended that bringing members of the media to observe and record the execution of the warrant violated their Fourth Amendment rights.

ISSUE: Can police bring media representatives along to record the execution of warrants?

HOLDING: No.

RATIONALE: "[T]he Fourth Amendment does require that police actions in execution of a warrant be related to the objectives of the authorized intrusion. . . ."

"Certainly the presence of reporters inside the home was not related to the objectives of the authorized intrusion. Respondents concede that the reporters did not engage in the execution of the warrant, and did not assist the police in their task. The reporters therefore were not present for any reason related to the justification for police entry into the home—the apprehension of Dominic Wilson."

"It may well be that media ride-alongs further the law enforcement objectives of the police in a general sense, but that is not the same as furthering the purposes of the search. Were such generalized 'law enforcement objectives' themselves sufficient to trump the Fourth Amendment, the protections guaranteed by that Amendment's text would be significantly watered down."

"Surely the possibility of good public relations for the police is simply not enough, standing alone, to justify the ride-along intrusion into a private home. And even the need for accurate reporting on police issues in general bears no direct relation to the constitutional justification for the police intrusion into a home in order to execute a felony arrest warrant."

"The *Washington Post* reporters in the Wilsons' home were working on a story for their own purposes. They were not present for the purpose of protecting the officers, much less the Wilsons. A private photographer was acting for private purposes, as evidenced in part by the fact that the newspaper and not the police retained the photographs. Thus, although the presence of third parties during the execution of a warrant may in some circumstances be constitutionally permissible . . . the presence of *these* third parties was not."

"The reasons advanced by respondents, taken in their entirety, fall short of justifying the presence of media inside a home. We hold that it is a violation of the Fourth Amendment for police to bring members of the media or other third parties into a home during the execution of a warrant when the presence of the third parties in the home was not in aid of the execution of the warrant."

3. May Police Search the Home of a Member of an Indian Reservation in Conjunction with an Offense That Took Place off the Reservation?

Nevada v. Hicks, 533 U.S. 353 (2001)
Vote: 9-0
FACTS: Floyd Hicks resided on a tribal reservation and came under suspicion of having killed, off the reservation, a particular sheep, a gross misdemeanor under Nevada law. A game warden obtained from state court a search warrant that required "validation" from the tribal court according to the issuing judge. A search warrant was obtained from the tribal court, and the warden, accompanied by a tribal officer, searched respondent's yard, uncovering only the head of a different species. Approximately one year later, a tribal officer reported to the warden that he had observed two mounted bighorn sheep heads in Hicks's home. The warden again obtained a search warrant from state court; though this warrant did not explicitly require permission from the tribal court, and Hicks's home was again (unsuccessfully) searched. Hicks brought suit against several officials remedial under 42 U.S.C. § 1983, one of which argued that the search was unreasonable under the Fourth Amendment. He later dropped the suits against the officials in their official capacities, leaving only his suit against those officials in their individual capacities. The tribal court held that it had jurisdiction over the claims, a holding affirmed by the tribal appeals court.
ISSUE: Can police search the home of a reservation member for an offense that took place off the reservation?
HOLDING: Yes.
RATIONALE: "We conclude today, in accordance with these prior statements, that tribal authority to regulate state officers in executing process related to the violation, off reservation, of state laws is not essential to tribal self-government or internal relations—to "the right to make laws and be ruled by them." The State's interest in execution of process is considerable, and even when it relates to Indian-fee lands it no more impairs the tribe's self-government than federal enforcement of federal law impairs state government. . . . [A] State 'can act only through its officers and agents,' and if a tribe can 'affix penalties to acts done under the immediate direction of the [state] government, and in obedience to its laws,' 'the operations of the [state] government may at any time be arrested at the will of the [tribe].'"

"Nothing in the federal statutory scheme prescribes, or even remotely suggests, that state officers cannot enter a reservation (including Indian-fee land) to investigate or prosecute violations of state law occurring off the reservation."

4. Do Police Have to Give Notice of Remedies for Return of Seized Property?

City of West Covina v. Perkins, 525 U.S. 234 (1999)
Vote: 9-0
FACTS: Police officers of the City of West Covina, California, acting pursuant to a valid search warrant, seized property. The property belonged to Lawrence Perkins and his

family. The suspect in the crime was Marcus Marsh, who had been a boarder. After leaving their home, and unknown to them, he became the subject of a homicide investigation. During the search of Perkins's home, the police seized photos of Marsh, an address book, a 12-gauge shotgun, a starter pistol, ammunition, and $2,629 in cash. At the conclusion of the search, the officers left Perkins a form and an itemized list of property seized. Perkins called Ferrari, one of the detectives listed on the notice, and inquired about return of the seized property. One of the detectives told Perkins he needed to obtain a court order authorizing the property's return. About a month after the search, Perkins went to the court to see Judge Dan Oki, who had issued the warrant. He learned that Oki was on vacation. He tried to have another judge release his property but was told the court had nothing under Perkins's name. Perkins filed suit against the city and the officers who conducted the search. After ruling for the city, briefs were filed that addressed the issue of the appropriateness of remedies for the return of seized property.

ISSUE: Do the police have to provide notice to the owners of property seized for its return?

HOLDING: No.

RATIONALE: "When the police seize property for a criminal investigation, however, due process does not require them to provide the owner with notice of state law remedies."

"No similar rationale justifies requiring individualized notice of state-law remedies which, like those at issue here, are established by published, generally available state statutes and case law. Once the property owner is informed that his property has been seized, he can turn to these public sources to learn about the remedial procedures available to him. The City need not take other steps to inform him of his options. . . . In prior cases in which we have held that postdeprivation state-law remedies were sufficient to satisfy the demands of due process and the laws were public and available, we have not concluded that the State must provide further information about those procedures."

"The Court of Appeals' far-reaching notice requirement not only lacks support in our precedent but also conflicts with the well-established practice of the States and the Federal Government. The notice required by the Court of Appeals far exceeds that which the States and the Federal Government have traditionally required their law enforcement agencies to provide. Indeed, neither the Federal Government nor any State requires officers to provide individualized notice of the procedures for seeking return of seized property."

D. Warrants for Electronic Surveillance

1. Is Use of a Tape Recorder Constitutional?

Osborn v. United States, 385 U.S. 323 (1966)

Vote: 7-1

FACTS: Osborn, a lawyer, was indicted for trying to influence a jury. He directed Robert D. Vick to contact Ralph A. Elliott, a member of the petit jury panel, and to offer Elliott $10,000 to vote for an acquittal if he should be selected. The primary evidence against Osborn consisted of a tape recording of a conversation between himself and Vick. The judges jointly issued a warrant for the recording to be made once Vick made it known to them that the integrity of their court was at risk. Osborn was convicted of one count of endeavoring to bribe a member of the jury panel in a prospective federal criminal trial. He challenged the admission of the tape.

ISSUE: Can police use a tape recorder to record conversations if they obtain a warrant?

HOLDING: Yes.

RATIONALE: "The situation which faced the two judges of the District Court when they were presented with Vick's affidavit . . . [was that] 'The affidavit contained information which reflected seriously upon a member of the bar of this court, who had practiced in my court ever since I have been on the bench. I decided that some action had to be taken to determine whether this information was correct or whether it was false. It was the most serious problem that I have had to deal with since I have been on the bench. I could not sweep it under the rug.'"

"[I]n response to a detailed factual affidavit alleging the commission of a specific criminal offense . . . the judges of that court jointly authorized the use of a recording device for the narrow and particularized purpose of ascertaining the truth of the affidavit's allegations. As the district judges recognized, it was imperative to determine whether the integrity of their court was being undermined, and highly undesirable that this determination should hinge on the inconclusive outcome of a testimonial contest between the only two people in the world who knew the truth—one an informer, the other a lawyer of previous good repute. There could hardly be a clearer example of 'the procedure of antecedent justification before a magistrate that is central to the Fourth Amendment' as 'a precondition of lawful electronic surveillance.'"

"We hold on these facts that the use of the recording device was permissible. . . ."

2. Is the Use of a Receiver to Overhear a Conversation by One Consenting to Wear a Wire Constitutional?

United States v. White, 401 U.S. 745 (1971)

Vote: 6-3

FACTS: On four occasions, conversations between James A. White and Harvey Jackson took place in Jackson's home. Each time, the conversations were overheard by an agent concealed in a kitchen closet with Jackson's consent and by a second agent outside the house using a radio receiver. Four other conversations—one in White's home, one in a restaurant, and two in Jackson's car—were overheard by the use of radio equipment. White was convicted for various illegal transactions in narcotics.

ISSUE: Do police need a warrant to record a conversation between individuals if one has granted consent to wear a wire?

HOLDING: No.

RATIONALE: "[H]owever strongly a defendant may trust an apparent colleague, his expectations in this respect are not protected by the Fourth Amendment when it turns out that the colleague is a government agent regularly communicating with the authorities. In these circumstances, 'no interest legitimately protected by the Fourth Amendment is involved,' for that amendment affords no protection to 'a wrongdoer's misplaced belief that a person to whom he voluntarily confides his wrongdoing will not reveal it. . . .' No warrant to 'search and seize' is required in such circumstances, nor is it when the Government sends to defendant's home a secret agent who conceals his identity and makes a purchase of narcotics from the accused . . . or when the same agent, unbeknown to the defendant, carries electronic equipment to record the defendant's words and the evidence so gathered is later offered in evidence."

"Concededly a police agent who conceals his police connections may write down for official use his conversations with a defendant and testify concerning them, without a warrant authorizing his encounters with the defendant and without otherwise violating the latter's Fourth Amendment rights. . . ."

"If the law gives no protection to the wrongdoer whose trusted accomplice is or becomes a police agent, neither should it protect him when that same agent has recorded or transmitted the conversations which are later offered in evidence to prove the State's case. . . ."

"At least there is no persuasive evidence that the difference in this respect between the electronically equipped and the unequipped agent is substantial enough to require discrete constitutional recognition, particularly under the Fourth Amendment which is ruled by fluid concepts of 'reasonableness.'"

"It is thus untenable to consider the activities and reports of the police agent himself, though acting without a warrant, to be a 'reasonable' investigative effort and lawful under the Fourth Amendment but to view the same agent with a recorder or transmitter as conducting an 'unreasonable' and unconstitutional search and seizure."

3. Is Use of a Beeper to Track a Person a Search?

United States v. Knotts, 460 U.S. 276 (1983)
Vote: 9-0
FACTS: Having reason to believe that Tristan Armstrong was purchasing chloroform to be used in the illegal manufacture of drugs, Minnesota police arranged with the seller to place a beeper inside a chloroform container that was sold to Armstrong. Officers then followed the car in which the chloroform was placed, maintaining contact by tracing the chloroform, by beeper monitoring, to Knotts's cabin in Wisconsin. Following three days of visual surveillance of the cabin, officers obtained a search warrant

and discovered the chloroform container and a drug laboratory in the cabin, including chemicals and formulas for producing amphetamine. Knotts was convicted for conspiring to manufacture controlled substances.

ISSUE: Is the use of a beeper by police to track a person a search?

HOLDING: No.

RATIONALE: "The governmental surveillance conducted by means of the beeper in this case amounted principally to the following of an automobile on public streets and highways. We have commented more than once on the diminished expectation of privacy in an automobile. . . . 'It travels public thoroughfares where both its occupants and its contents are in plain view.'"

"The fact that the officers in this case relied not only on visual surveillance, but also on the use of the beeper to signal the presence of [Darryl] Petschen's automobile to the police receiver, does not alter the situation. Nothing in the Fourth Amendment prohibited the police from augmenting the sensory faculties bestowed upon them at birth with such enhancement as science and technology afforded them in this case."

"We think that respondent's contentions . . . lose sight of the limited use which the government made of the signals from this particular beeper. As we have noted, nothing in this record indicates that the beeper signal was received or relied upon after it had indicated that the drum containing the chloroform had ended its automotive journey at rest on respondent's premises in rural Wisconsin. . . . But scientific enhancement of this sort raises no constitutional issues which visual surveillance would not also raise."

"[D]id monitoring the beeper signals complained of by respondent invade any legitimate expectation of privacy on his part . . . ? [W]e hold it did not. Since it did not, there was neither a 'search' nor a 'seizure' within the contemplation of the Fourth Amendment."

a. Can Beepers Be Used to Monitor Evidence Suspects in Private Residences without a Warrant?

United States v. Karo, 468 U.S. 705 (1984)

Vote: 6-3

FACTS: After DEA agent Rottinger learned that James Karo, Richard Horton, and William Harley had ordered fifty gallons of ether, Carl Muehlenweg, an informant, told Rottinger that it was to be used to extract cocaine from clothing. The Government obtained an order authorizing the installation and monitoring of a beeper in one of the cans. With Muehlenweg's consent, DEA agents substituted their own can containing a beeper for one of the others. Agents saw Karo pick up the ether, followed him home, and determined by using the beeper that the ether was inside the house, where it was monitored. The ether then moved to two other houses, including Horton's, before it was moved to a locker in a storage facility and then to a locker in another such facility. Both lockers were rented by Horton and Harley. The ether was removed from the second storage facility by Gene Rhodes and a woman and transported in Horton's truck to Rhodes's house and then to a house rented by Horton, Harley, and Michael Steele. Using the beeper, agents determined that the can was inside the house and obtained a search warrant based in part on information derived through use of the beeper. The warrant was executed and Horton, Harley, Steele, Karo, and Evan Roth were arrested, and cocaine was seized. All were indicted for conspiracy to possess cocaine with intent to distribute.

ISSUE: Can police use beepers to monitor activity inside a private residence without a warrant?

HOLDING: No.

RATIONALE: "We cannot accept the Government's contention that it should be completely free from the constraints of the Fourth Amendment to determine by means of an electronic device, without a warrant and without probable cause or reasonable suspicion, whether a particular article—or a person, for that matter—is in an individual's home at a particular time. Indiscriminate monitoring of property that has been withdrawn from public view would present far too serious a threat to privacy interests in the home to escape entirely some sort of Fourth Amendment oversight."

"Surely if the Government surreptitiously plants a listening device on an unsuspecting household guest or family member and then monitors conversations with the homeowner, the homeowner could challenge the monitoring of the conversations regardless of the fact that he did not have power 'to give effective consent to the search' of the visitor. . . ." [T]here is a substantial distinction between '[revelations] to the Government by a party to conversations with the defendant' and eavesdropping on conversations without the knowledge or consent of either party to it. A homeowner takes the risk that his guest will cooperate with the Government but not the risk that a trustworthy friend has been bugged by the Government without his knowledge or consent."

"In sum, we discern no reason for deviating from the general rule that a search of a house should be conducted pursuant to a warrant."

"As we have said, by maintaining the beeper the agents verified that the ether was actually located in the Taos house and that it remained there while the warrant was sought. This information was obtained without a warrant and would therefore be inadmissible at trial against those with privacy interests in the house—Horton, Harley, Steele, and Roth."

5

Searches and Seizures without Warrants

IN THE PRIOR CHAPTER, the area of inquiry centered upon the concepts of search and seizure using warrants. This is the preferred method of conducting these activities, as one could argue that the protection provided is a bit stronger than under other circumstances. That is, if the police have obtained a warrant to either make an arrest or to conduct a search, they are pretty much assured that the warrant will be valid and that upon challenge in court, its validity will be affirmed. Naturally, the fruit of the search is subject to exclusion based upon the manner in which the search was conducted, regardless of the validity of the underlying warrant. However, the law also recognizes that exceptions to the immediate requirement of a judicial determination of probable cause do exist. Sometimes situations and circumstances develop so quickly and with so great an amount of danger that police just do not have time to obtain warrants. That is the subject of this chapter.

The easiest way for the police to be able to search and seize is to obtain consent, and not surprisingly, the Supreme Court has sanctioned such activities. In fact, several circumstances exist where the Court has allowed police to seize evidence or individuals within this context. For example, motorists that are lawfully stopped do not have to be told that they do not have to give consent before they can leave. The Court has also addressed the areas that can be searched within this context and if the consent can be withdrawn. The Court has also delved into the matter of who may give consent in situations where the direct property owner is not present but someone who is using the property gives consent to search. Here, under some circumstances, the police are allowed to accept such consent.

An additional situation where the police do not have to obtain warrants are when they conduct searches incident to lawful arrests. Under such circumstances, police may search the individual arrested and their immediate surroundings for evidence or possible instrumentalities of criminal activity, including weapons. The Supreme Court has taken special care to limit these kinds of searches, even when they are incidental to lawful arrests, when they are conducted in the home. Adding to these sometimes complicated actions, the Court has ruled that the searches must be contemporaneous to the arrest. That is, the searches must be close in time to the original arrest, without too much delay, in order for the evidence to be admitted at trial without the warrant.

Finally, there are also many other situations where the police may conduct searches and make seizures without warrants. These include what the Court has called "special needs searches" and certain types of vehicle searches. However, due to the complex nature of these topics, each has it's own separate chapter (chapters 6 and 7, respectively).

A. What Is Consent?

Schneckloth v. Bustamonte, 412 U.S. 218 (1973)
Vote: 6-3

FACTS: Officer James Rand stopped a car when he observed that a headlight and its license plate light were burned out. Six men were in the vehicle. Joe Alcala and Robert Bustamonte were in the front seat with Joe Gonzales, the driver. Three older men were in the backseat. When Gonzales could not produce a license, Rand asked if any of the other five had any identification. Only Alcala produced a license, and he explained that the car was his brother's. After the occupants stepped out of the car at the officer's request and after two additional officers arrived, Rand asked Alcala if he could search the car. Alcala replied, "Sure, go ahead." Prior to the search no one was threatened with arrest and, according to Officer Rand, it "was all very congenial at this time." Gonzales testified that Alcala actually helped in the search of the car, by opening the trunk and glove compartment. In Gonzales's words: "The police officer asked Joe [Alcala], he goes, 'Does the trunk open?' And Joe said, 'Yes.' He went to the car and got the keys and opened up the trunk." The officers found three checks that had previously been stolen from a car wash.

ISSUE: Does consent give authority to police to search as an exception to the requirements of probable cause and search warrants? Must consent be voluntary before it can be valid, and is it ascertained by the "totality of the circumstances"?

HOLDING: Yes.

RATIONALE: "It is equally well settled that one of the specifically established exceptions to the requirements of both a warrant and probable cause is a search that is conducted pursuant to consent. . . . The constitutional question in the present case concerns the definition of 'consent. . . .'"

"'The appellate court found that 'in the instant case the prosecution met the necessary burden of showing consent . . . since there were clearly circumstances from which the trial court could ascertain that consent had been freely given without coercion or submission to authority. Not only officer Rand, but Gonzales, the driver of the automobile, testified that Alcala's assent to the search of his brother's automobile was freely, even casually given. At the time of the request to search the automobile the atmosphere, according to Rand, was "congenial" and there had been no discussion of any crime.'"

"Similar considerations lead us to agree with the courts of California that the question whether a consent to a search was in fact 'voluntary' or was the product of duress or coercion, express or implied, is a question of fact to be determined from the totality of all the circumstances. . . ."

"In situations where the police have some evidence of illicit activity, but lack probable cause to arrest or search, a search authorized by a valid consent may be the only means of obtaining important and reliable evidence. And in those cases where there is probable cause to arrest or search, but where the police lack a warrant, a consent search may still be valuable. If the search is conducted and proves fruitless, that in itself may convince the police that an arrest with its possible stigma and embarrassment is unnecessary. . . . In short, a search pursuant to consent may result in considerably less inconvenience for the subject of the search, and, properly conducted, is a constitutionally permissible and wholly legitimate aspect of effective police activity."

"But the Fourth and Fourteenth Amendments require that a consent not be coerced, by explicit or implicit means, by implied threat or covert force."

"[I]t is only by analyzing all the circumstances of an individual consent that it can be ascertained whether in fact it was voluntary or coerced. It is this careful sifting of the unique facts and circumstances of each case that is evidenced in our prior decisions involving consent searches."

"Conversely, if under all the circumstances it has appeared that the consent was not given voluntarily—that it was coerced by threats or force, or granted only in submission to a claim of lawful authority—then we have found the consent invalid and the search unreasonable. . . ."

"In this case, there is no evidence of any inherently coercive tactics—either from the nature of the police questioning or the environment in which it took place. There is no reason to believe, under circumstances such as are present here, that the response to a policeman's question is presumptively coerced; and there is, therefore, no reason to reject the traditional test for determining the voluntariness of a person's response."

"Our decision today is a narrow one. We hold only that when the subject of a search is not in custody and the State attempts to justify a search on the basis of his consent, the Fourth and Fourteenth Amendments require that it demonstrate that the consent was in fact voluntarily given, and not the result of duress or coercion, express or implied. Voluntariness is a question of fact to be determined from all the circumstances, and while the subject's knowledge of a right to refuse is a factor to be taken into account, the prosecution is not required to demonstrate such knowledge as a prerequisite to establishing a voluntary consent."

B. Consent Obtained via False Authority

Bumper v. North Carolina, 391 U.S. 543 (1968)
Vote: 8-1
FACTS: Bumper lived with his grandmother, Hattie Leath, in a house located in a rural area at the end of an isolated road. Two days after an alleged rape but prior to the arrest, four officers—the county sheriff, two of his deputies, and a state investigator—went to this house and found Leath with some young children. She met the officers at the front door. One of them announced, "I have a search warrant to search your house." Mrs. Leath responded, "Go ahead," and opened the door. In the kitchen the officers found the rifle that was later introduced in evidence at Bumper's trial after a motion to suppress had been denied. He was charged with rape. The jury found Bumper guilty.

ISSUE: Can the police obtain valid consent from a person to search a home when they lie about their possession of a search warrant prior to obtaining the consent?

HOLDING: No.

RATIONALE: "The issue thus presented is whether a search can be justified as lawful on the basis of consent when that 'consent' has been given only after the official conducting the search has asserted that he possesses a warrant. We hold that there can be no consent under such circumstances."

"A search conducted in reliance upon a warrant cannot later be justified on the basis of consent if it turns out that the warrant was invalid. The result can be no different when it turns out that the State does not even attempt to rely upon the validity of the warrant, or fails to show that there was, in fact, any warrant at all."

"When a law enforcement officer claims authority to search a home under a warrant, he announces in effect that the occupant has no right to resist the search. The situation is instinct with coercion—albeit colorably lawful coercion. Where there is coercion there cannot be consent."

"We hold that Mrs. Leath did not consent to the search, and that it was constitutional error to admit the rifle in evidence against the petitioner. . . ."

C. Informing Suspects in Vehicles of Their Freedom to Leave Prior to Obtaining Consent

1. Automobiles

Ohio v. Robinette, 519 U.S. 33 (1996)

Vote: 8-1

FACTS: This case arose on a stretch of Interstate 70 north of Dayton, Ohio, where the posted speed limit was forty-five miles per hour because of construction. Robert D. Robinette was clocked at sixty-nine miles per hour as he drove his car along this stretch of road, and was stopped by Deputy Roger Newsome of the Montgomery County Sheriff's office. Newsome received Robinette's license, and he ran a computer check, which indicated that Robinette had no previous violations. Newsome then asked Robinette to step out of his car, turned on his camera, issued a verbal warning to Robinette, and returned his license.

At this point, Newsome asked, "One question before you get gone: Are you carrying any illegal contraband in your car? Any weapons of any kind, drugs, anything like that?" Robinette answered "No" to these questions, after which Newsome asked if he could search the car. Robinette consented. Newsome discovered a small amount of marijuana and, in a film container, a pill that was later determined to be methamphetamine. Robinette was then arrested and charged with knowing possession of a controlled substance. He then pleaded "no contest," and was found guilty.

ISSUE: Do police have to notify suspects of their right to refuse consent to search for it to be valid?

HOLDING: No.

RATIONALE: "We are here presented with the question whether the Fourth Amendment requires that a lawfully seized defendant must be advised that he is 'free to go' before his consent to search will be recognized as voluntary. We hold that it does not."

"We have previously rejected a *per se* rule very similar to that adopted by the Supreme Court of Ohio in determining the validity of a consent to search. In *Schneckloth v. Bustamonte* [412 U.S. 218 (1973)] . . . it was argued that such a consent could not be valid unless the defendant knew that he had a right to refuse the request. We rejected this argument: 'While knowledge of the right to refuse consent is one factor to be taken into account, the government need not establish such knowledge as the *sine qua non* of an effective consent. . . .' And just as it 'would be thoroughly impractical to impose on the normal consent search the detailed requirements of an effective warning . . .' so too would it be unrealistic to require police officers to always inform detainees that they are free to go before a consent to search may be deemed voluntary."

2. Buses

United States v. Drayton, 536 U.S. 194 (2002)
Vote: 6-3

FACTS: Christopher Drayton and Clifton Brown Jr. were traveling on a bus from Fort Lauderdale to Detroit which made a stop in Tallahassee. As he left, the driver allowed three members of the Tallahassee Police Department, who were dressed in plain clothes and carried concealed weapons and visible badges, to board the bus. Officer Hoover knelt on the driver's seat and faced the rear of the bus. He could observe the passengers and ensure the safety of the other officers without blocking the aisle or exit. Officers Lang and Blackburn went to the rear of the bus and Blackburn remained stationed there, facing forward. Lang asked the passengers about their travel and sought to match passengers with luggage. To avoid blocking the aisle, Lang stood next to or just behind each passenger. According to Lang's testimony, passengers who declined to cooperate or who chose to exit the bus would have been allowed to do so. On the day in question, Lang did not inform passengers of their right to refuse to cooperate.

Drayton was in the aisle seat, Brown in the seat next to the window. Lang approached them from the rear and leaned over Drayton's shoulder. He held up his badge long enough for them to identify him as a police officer. Lang spoke in a soft voice: "I'm Investigator Lang with the Tallahassee Police Department. We're conducting bus interdiction [*sic*], attempting to deter drugs and illegal weapons being transported on the bus. Do you have any bags on the bus?" Both men pointed to a single bag and Lang asked, "Do you mind if I check it?" and Brown responded, "Go ahead." Lang handed the bag to Blackburn to check. The bag contained no contraband.

Lang then asked "Do you mind if I check your person?" Brown answered, "Sure," and cooperated. In both thigh areas, Lang detected hard objects similar to drug packages detected on other occasions. Lang arrested and handcuffed Brown. Officer Hoover escorted Brown from the bus. Lang then asked Drayton, "Mind if I check you?" Drayton responded by lifting his hands about eight inches from his legs. Lang conducted a pat-down of Drayton's thighs and detected hard objects similar to those found on Brown. He arrested Drayton and escorted him from the bus. A further search revealed that respondents had duct-taped plastic bundles of powder cocaine between several pairs of their boxer shorts. Both men were charged with conspiring to distribute cocaine and with possessing cocaine with intent to distribute it.

ISSUE: Can the police conduct warrantless searches on a bus without notifying passengers of their right to refuse to cooperate?

HOLDING: Yes.

RATIONALE: "The Fourth Amendment permits police officers to approach bus passengers at random to ask questions and to request their consent to searches, provided a reasonable person would understand that he or she is free to refuse. . . ."

"Law enforcement officers do not violate the Fourth Amendment's prohibition of unreasonable seizures merely by approaching individuals on the street or in other public places and putting questions to them if they are willing to listen. . . . Even when law enforcement officers have no basis for suspecting a particular individual, they may pose questions, ask for identification, and request consent to search luggage—provided they do not induce cooperation by coercive means. . . ."

"We turn now . . . to . . . [whether] their consent to the suspicionless search was involuntary. In circumstances such as these, where the question of voluntariness pervades both the search and seizure inquiries, the respective analyses turn on very similar facts. And, as the facts above suggest, respondents' consent to the search of their luggage and their persons was voluntary."

"The Court has rejected in specific terms the suggestion that police officers must always inform citizens of their right to refuse when seeking permission to conduct a warrantless consent search. . . . Nor do this Court's decisions suggest that even though there are no *per se* rules, a presumption of invalidity attaches if a citizen consented without explicit notification that he or she was free to refuse to cooperate. Instead, the Court has repeated that the totality of the circumstances must control, without giving extra weight to the absence of this type of warning. . . ."

D. Scope of Consent Searches

1. Area Allowed to Search

a. Can Police Use the Fruit of a Consensual Search If a Suspect Was Illegally Detained?

Florida v. Royer, 460 U.S. 491 (1983)
Vote: 5-4
FACTS: Royer was observed at Miami International Airport by two detectives, and they believed that Royer fit the "drug courier profile." He purchased a one-way ticket to New York City and checked his suitcases, placing on each a tag bearing the name "Holt" and

the destination "La Guardia." As Royer walked to the concourse the detectives identified themselves and asked if Royer had a "moment" to speak with them; he said "Yes."

Upon request, but without oral consent, Royer produced his ticket and license. The ticket, bore the name "Holt," while the license had "Royer." When the detectives asked about the discrepancy, Royer explained that a friend had made the reservation. Royer became more nervous, whereupon the detectives informed him that they were narcotics investigators and that they had reason to suspect him of transporting narcotics.

The detectives did not return Royer's ticket and identification but asked him to accompany them to a room. Royer said nothing but went. The room was described as a "large storage closet," located in the stewardesses' lounge. Without his consent, Detective Johnson retrieved Royer's luggage. Royer was asked if he would consent to a search of the suitcases. Without orally responding, Royer produced a key and unlocked one of the suitcases, which one detective opened without seeking further assent. Marihuana was found in that suitcase. According to Johnson, Royer stated that he did not know the combination to the lock on the second suitcase. When asked if he objected to opening the suitcase, Royer said "[No], go ahead," and did not object when told that the suitcase might have to be broken. The suitcase was pried open and more marihuana was found. Royer was arrested and convicted of possession of marijuana.

ISSUE: Can police obtain valid consent from a suspect who has been illegally detained?

HOLDING: No.

RATIONALE: "Several factors led the court to conclude that respondent's confinement was tantamount to arrest. Royer had 'found himself in a small enclosed area being confronted by two police officers—a situation which presents an almost classic definition of imprisonment. . . .' The detectives' statement to Royer that he was suspected of transporting narcotics also bolstered the finding that Royer was 'in custody' at the time the consent to search was given. In addition, the detectives' possession of Royer's airline ticket and their retrieval and possession of his luggage made it clear, in the District Court of Appeal's view, that Royer was not free to leave."

"[T]he State had conceded at oral argument before that court that 'the officers would not have permitted Royer to leave the room even if he had erroneously thought he could.'"

"The State proffers three reasons for holding that when Royer consented to the search of his luggage, he was not being illegally detained. First, it is submitted that the entire encounter was consensual and hence Royer was not being held against his will at all. We find this submission untenable. Asking for and examining Royer's ticket and his driver's license were no doubt permissible in themselves, but when the officers identified themselves as narcotics agents, told Royer that he was suspected of transporting narcotics, and asked him to accompany them to the police room, while retaining his ticket and driver's license and without indicating in any way that he was free to depart, Royer was effectively seized for the purposes of the Fourth Amendment. These circumstances surely amount to a show of official authority such that 'a reasonable person would have believed that he was not free to leave.'"

"What had begun as a consensual inquiry in a public place had escalated into an investigatory procedure in a police interrogation room, where the police, unsatisfied with previous explanations, sought to confirm their suspicions. The officers had Royer's ticket, they had his identification, and they had seized his luggage. Royer was never informed that he was free to board his plane if he so chose, and he reasonably believed that he was being detained. At least as of that moment, any consensual aspects of the encounter had evaporated. . . .'"

"It appears, rather, that the primary interest of the officers was not in having an extended conversation with Royer but in the contents of his luggage, a matter which the officers did not pursue orally with Royer until after the encounter was relocated to the police room."

"Because we affirm the Florida District Court of Appeal's conclusion that Royer was being illegally detained when he consented to the search of his luggage, we agree that the consent was tainted by the illegality and was ineffective to justify the search."

b. Can the Police Search a Closed Container within a Car Pursuant to a Consent Search?

Florida v. Jimeno, 500 U.S. 248 (1991)
Vote: 7-2

FACTS: Dade County officer Frank Trujillo overheard Enio Jimeno arranging a drug transaction over a public phone. Believing that he might be involved in drug trafficking, Trujillo followed his car. The officer observed him make a right turn at a red light without stopping and then pulled Jimeno over. Trujillo told Jimeno that he had been stopped for committing a traffic infraction but also said that he had reason to believe that he had drugs in the car and asked permission to search it. He explained that Jimeno did not have to consent to the search and Jimeno stated that he had nothing to hide and gave Trujillo permission. After his wife Luz stepped out of the car, Trujillo went to the passenger side, opened the door, and saw a folded, brown paper bag on the floorboard. The officer picked up the bag, opened it, and found a kilogram of cocaine inside. The Jimenos were charged with possession with intent to distribute cocaine.

ISSUE: May the police use the fruit of a consensual car search if they open a closed container that may hide the object of the search?

HOLDING: Yes.

RATIONALE: "[W]e decide whether a criminal suspect's Fourth Amendment right to be free from unreasonable searches is violated when, after he gives a police officer permission to search his automobile, the officer opens a closed container found within the car that might reasonably hold the object of the search. We find that it is not. The Fourth Amendment is satisfied when, under the circumstances, it is objectively reasonable for the officer to believe that the scope of the suspect's consent permitted him to open a particular container within the automobile."

"The standard for measuring the scope of a suspect's consent . . . is . . . what would the typical reasonable person have understood by the exchange between the officer and the suspect . . . ? The question before us, then, is whether it is reasonable for an officer to consider a suspect's general consent to a search of his car to include consent to examine a paper bag lying on the floor of the car. We think that it is."

"A suspect may of course delimit as he chooses the scope of the search to which he consents. But if his consent would reasonably be understood to extend to a particular container, the Fourth Amendment provides no grounds for requiring a more explicit authorization."

2. May Police Obtain Consent from a Third Party?

a. Girlfriend?

United States v. Matlock, 415 U.S. 164 (1974)
Vote: 6-3

FACTS: William Matlock was arrested in the yard in front of the home he leased from Mr. and Mrs. Marshall. Living in the home were Mrs. Marshall, several of her children, including her daughter Gayle Graff, Gayle's three-year-old son, and Matlock. Although the officers were aware at the time of the arrest that he lived in the house, they did not ask him which room he occupied or whether he would consent to a search. Three officers went to the door of the house and were admitted by Mrs. Graff. The officers told her they were looking for money and a gun and asked if they could search the house. Although denied by Mrs. Graff at the suppression hearings, it was found that she consented voluntarily to the search of the house, including the east bedroom on the second floor, which she said was jointly occupied by Matlock and herself. The east bedroom was searched and the evidence at issue here, $4,995 in cash, was found in a diaper bag in the only closet in the room. The issue came to be whether Mrs. Graff's relationship to the east bedroom was sufficient to make her consent to the search valid against Matlock. He was indicted for bank robbery in Wisconsin. He filed a motion to suppress evidence seized by police.

ISSUE: May police obtain consent to search from a third party that has common authority over the property sought?

HOLDING: Yes.

RATIONALE: "[B]ut more recent authority here clearly indicates that the consent of one who possesses common authority over premises or effects is valid as against the absent, nonconsenting person with whom that authority is shared. . . . These cases at least make clear that when the prosecution seeks to justify a warrantless search by proof of voluntary consent, it is not limited to proof that consent was given by the defendant, but may show that permission to search was obtained from a third party who possessed common authority over or other sufficient relationship to the premises or effects sought to be inspected."

"As an initial matter we fail to understand why, on any approach to the case, the out-of-court representations of respondent himself that he and Gayle Graff were husband and wife were considered to be inadmissible against him. Whether or not Mrs. Graff's statements were hearsay, the respondent's own out-of-court admissions would surmount all objections based on the hearsay rule both at the suppression hearings and at the trial itself, and would be admissible for whatever inferences the trial judge could reasonably draw concerning joint occupancy of the east bedroom."

b. Landlord?

Chapman v. United States, 365 U.S. 610 (1961)
Vote: 8-1

FACTS: Bridgaman and a friend owned a house near Macon, Georgia, which they rented through a rental agency. Understanding that the house had been rented to a new tenant, Bridgaman, went to the house for the purpose of inviting the tenants to attend church. Upon arrival he noted a strong "odor of mash" about the house. There was no response to his knock, and, although he tried to do so, he was unable to see into the house. He then returned to his home and advised the local police of his observations. Soon afterward two officers arrived and the three then went to the rented house and noticed a strong odor of "whiskey mash" coming from the house. After their knock at the door failed to produce a response, they walked around the house and tried to look into it but were unable to do so. They found that the windows were locked, except for one in the bathroom. Upon entering the house, an officer saw a distillery and 1,300 gallons of mash located in the living room. After federal officers were called and en route, Chapman drove up, unlocked the front door, entered the house and was immediately arrested. The federal officers soon arrived and took custody of Chapman. None of the officers had a warrant. He was convicted of violation of federal liquor laws.

ISSUE: May police obtain consent from a landlord to enter without a warrant, the room of a tenant who is suspected of engaging in crime?

HOLDING: No.

RATIONALE: "'It has also been said that [the landlord] may enter to "view waste," that is, to determine whether waste has been committed, *provided at least that this does not involve the breaking of windows or doors. . . .*' There are several answers to this contention. First, here the landlord and the officers forced open a window to gain entry to the premises. Second, 'their purpose in entering was [not to view waste but] to search for distilling equipment. . . .' Third, to uphold such an entry, search and seizure 'without a warrant would reduce the [Fourth] Amendment to a nullity and leave [tenants'] homes secure only in the discretion of [landlords]'"

"After pointing to the fact that a Georgia statute provides that the unlawful manufacture of distilled liquor on rented premises shall work a forfeiture of the rights of the tenant, at the option of the landlord, and that another provides that use of a structure for that purpose constitutes a nuisance, the Government argues that, inasmuch as he used the demised premises for the illicit manufacture of distilled liquor, petitioner had forfeited all rights in the premises, and the landlord thus acquired the right forcibly to enter to abate the nuisance, and that he could and did delegate that right to the officers. But it is clear that, before the officers made the forcible entry, the landlord did not know that the premises were being used for the manufacture of liquor, nor had he exercised his statutory option to forfeit the tenancy for such a cause."

c. Hotel Clerk?

Stoner v. California, 376 U.S. 483 (1964)

Vote: 8-1

FACTS: The Budget Town Food Market in Monrovia, California, was robbed by two men, one of whom was described by eyewitnesses as carrying a gun and wearing horn-rimmed glasses and a gray jacket. Soon after the robbery a checkbook belonging to Joey L. Stoner was found in an adjacent parking lot and turned over to the police. Two of the stubs indicated that checks had been drawn to the order of the Mayfair Hotel in Pomona. Pursuing this lead, officers learned from the Pomona police that Stoner had a record, and they obtained from the Pomona police a picture of him. They showed it to the two witnesses, who both stated that the picture looked like the man who had carried the gun. On the basis of this information the officers went to the Mayfair Hotel in Pomona with neither search nor arrest warrants.

Police asked the clerk if Stoner was staying, to which he replied, "Yes," but that he was out. The police asked for permission to search the room and told the clerk that they wanted to arrest someone involved in a robbery. Let in by the clerk, the officers entered the room and made a thorough search. They found a pair of horn-rimmed glasses, a gray jacket, and a .45 caliber pistol with a clip and several cartridges in the bottom of a bureau drawer. Stoner was arrested two days later and was convicted of armed robbery.

ISSUE: Can a hotel clerk give police consent to search the room of a suspect?

HOLDING: No.

RATIONALE: "[T]he argument is made that the search of the hotel room, although conducted without the petitioner's consent, was lawful because it was conducted with the consent of the hotel clerk. We find this argument unpersuasive."

"Even if it be assumed that a state law which gave a hotel proprietor blanket authority to authorize the police to search the rooms of the hotel's guests could survive constitutional challenge, there is no intimation in the California cases cited by the respondent that California has any such law. Nor is there any substance to the claim that the search was reasonable because the police, relying upon the night clerk's expressions of consent, had a reasonable basis for the belief that the clerk had authority to consent to the search."

"It is important to bear in mind that it was the petitioner's constitutional right which was at stake here, and not the night clerk's nor the hotel's. It was a right, therefore, which only the petitioner could waive by word or deed, either directly or through an agent. It is true that the night clerk clearly and unambiguously consented to the search. But there is nothing in the record to indicate that the police had any basis whatsoever to believe that the night clerk had been authorized by the petitioner to permit the police to search the petitioner's room."

"At least twice this Court has explicitly refused to permit an otherwise unlawful police search of a hotel room to rest upon consent of the hotel proprietor."

"It is true, as was said in [*United States v. Jeffers*, 342 U.S. 49 (1951)], that when a person engages a hotel room he undoubtedly gives 'implied or express permission' to 'such persons as maids, janitors or repairmen' to enter his room 'in the performance of their duties. . . .' But the conduct of the night clerk and the police in the present case was of an entirely different order."

"No less than a tenant of a house, or the occupant of a room in a boarding house . . . a guest in a hotel room is entitled to constitutional protection against unreasonable searches and seizures. . . . That protection would disappear if it were left to depend upon the unfettered discretion of an employee of the hotel. It follows that this search without a warrant was unlawful."

d. Consent to Search Given by Spouses

Georgia v. Randolph 126 S.Ct. 1515 (2006)
Vote: 5-3
FACTS: Scott Randolph separated from his wife in late May 2001 and returned in July. She complained to police that her husband took her son and that he used cocaine. Scott told police that he took the boy away to prevent his wife from taking him out of the country, denied cocaine use, and stated that it was his wife that used. Mrs. Randolph offered that "items of drug evidence" were in the house. Scott refused permission to search the house. However, Mrs. Randolph did consent and led the police to the drugs. An officer went to retrieve an evidence bag from his car and was thereafter refused permission by Mrs. Randolph to search any further. The police took the couple and a straw with powder on it to the police station and obtained a warrant for the home. After the subsequent search, more drugs were found, and Scott was charged with possession. The trial court denied his motion to suppress, ruling that Mrs. Randolph had common authority to consent to the search. The Court of Appeals of Georgia reversed, and the Supreme Court of Georgia sustained.
ISSUE: Does a physically present spousal occupant's refusal to grant permission to search a home invalidate consent given by another spousal occupant?
HOLDING: Yes.
RATIONALE: "In resolving the defendant's objection to use of the evidence taken in the warrantless search, we said that 'the consent of one who possesses common authority over premises or effects is valid as against the absent, nonconsenting person with whom that authority is shared. . . .' Consistent with our prior understanding that Fourth Amendment rights are not limited by the law of property . . . we explained that the third party's 'common authority' is not synonymous with a technical property interest."

"[W]hen people living together disagree over the use of their common quarters, a resolution must come through voluntary accommodation, not by appeals to authority. Unless the people living together fall within some recognized hierarchy, like a household of parent and child or barracks housing military personnel of different grades, there is no societal understanding of superior and inferior. . . . In sum, there is no common understanding that one co-tenant generally has a right or authority to prevail over the express wishes of another. . . ."

"Since the co-tenant wishing to open the door to a third party has no recognized authority in law or social practice to prevail over a present and objecting co-tenant, his disputed invitation, without more, gives a police officer no better claim to reasonableness in entering than the officer would have in the absence of any consent at all. Accordingly, in the balancing of competing individual and governmental interests entailed by the bar to unreasonable searches . . . the cooperative occupant's invitation adds nothing to the government's side to counter the force of an objecting individual's claim to security against the government's intrusion into his dwelling place."

"But nothing in social custom or its reflection in private law argues for placing a higher value on delving into private premises to search for evidence in the face of disputed consent, than on requiring clear justification before the government searches private living quarters over a resident's objection. We therefore hold that a warrantless search of a shared dwelling for evidence over the express refusal of consent by a physically present resident cannot be justified as reasonable as to him on the basis of consent given to the police by another resident."

E. Searches Incident to Arrest

1. Scope

Chimel v. California, 395 U.S. 752 (1969)
Vote: 7-2
FACTS: Three officers arrived at Chimel's home with an arrest warrant for the burglary of a coin shop. The officers knocked on the door, identified themselves to his wife, and asked if they might come inside. She ushered them into the house, where they waited ten or fifteen minutes until Chimel came home from work. When he entered the house, one of the officers handed him the arrest warrant and asked for permission to "look around." The petitioner objected, but was told that "on the basis of the lawful arrest," the officers would conduct a search. No search warrant had been issued.

Accompanied by Chimel's wife, the officers looked through the entire house, including the attic, the garage, and a small workshop. In the master bedroom and sewing room, the officers directed Chimel's wife to open drawers and "to physically move contents of the drawers from side to side so that [they] might view any items that would have come from [the] burglary." After completing the search, they seized numerous items—primarily coins, but also several medals, tokens, and a few other objects. Chimel was tried and convicted of burglary.

ISSUE: May the police search the entire house of a suspect on the authority of a lawful arrest if they do not have a warrant?

HOLDING: No.

RATIONALE: "'[T]he scope of [a] search must be "strictly tied to and justified by" the circumstances which rendered its initiation permissible.'"

"When an arrest is made, it is reasonable for the arresting officer to search the person arrested in order to remove any weapons that the latter might seek to use in order to resist arrest or effect his escape. Otherwise, the officer's safety might well be endangered, and the arrest itself frustrated. In addition, it is entirely reasonable for the arresting officer to search for and seize any evidence on the arrestee's person in order to prevent its concealment or destruction. And the area into which an arrestee might reach in order to grab a weapon or evidentiary items must, of course, be governed by a like rule. A gun on a table or in a drawer in front of one who is arrested can be as dangerous to the arresting officer as one concealed in the clothing of the person arrested. There is ample justification, therefore, for a search of the arrestee's person and the area 'within his immediate control'—construing that phrase to mean the area from within which he might gain possession of a weapon or destructible evidence.'"

"There is no comparable justification, however, for routinely searching any room other than that in which an arrest occurs—or, for that matter, for searching through all the desk drawers or other closed or concealed areas in that room itself. Such searches, in the absence of well-recognized exceptions, may be made only under the authority of a search warrant."

"No consideration relevant to the Fourth Amendment suggests any point of rational limitation, once the search is allowed to go beyond the area from which the person arrested might obtain weapons or evidentiary items. The only reasoned distinction is one between a search of the person arrested and the area within his reach on the one hand, and more extensive searches on the other."

"'After arresting a man in his house, to rummage at will among his papers in search of whatever will convict him, appears to us to be indistinguishable from what might be done under a general warrant. . . .'"

2. Can Police Conduct Protective Sweeps of Homes?

Maryland v. Buie, 494 U.S. 325 (1990)
Vote: 7-2
FACTS: Two men committed an armed robbery of a pizza restaurant in Prince George's County. And one of the robbers was wearing a red jogging suit. Police obtained arrest warrants for Edward Buie and his suspected accomplice, Lloyd Allen. Buie's house was placed under surveillance. The police executed the warrant for Buie but first had a police secretary call his house to verify his presence. She initially spoke to a female, then to Buie, whereupon several officers proceeded to the house and fanned out through both floors. Officer James Rozar stated that he would "freeze" the basement so that no one could come up. With his revolver drawn, Rozar twice shouted into the basement. When a voice asked who was speaking, Rozar announced three times, "This is the police. Show me your hands." A pair of hands appeared around the stairwell, and Buie emerged. Rozar arrested him. After Buie was in custody, Officer Joseph Frolich entered the basement to see if anyone else remained and noticed a red running suit in plain view on a stack of clothing and seized it.
ISSUE: Can the police conduct, incident to arrest, a protective sweep of a home?
HOLDING: Yes.
RATIONALE: "A 'protective sweep' is a quick and limited search of premises, incident to an arrest and conducted to protect the safety of police officers or others. It is

narrowly confined to a cursory visual inspection of those places in which a person might be hiding."

"We conclude that the Fourth Amendment would permit the protective sweep undertaken here if the searching officer 'possessed a reasonable belief based on "specific and articulable facts which, taken together with the rational inferences from those facts, reasonably warranted" the officer in believing . . .' that the area swept harbored an individual posing a danger to the officer or others."

"We agree with the State, as did the court below, that a warrant was not required. We also hold that as an incident to the arrest the officers could, as a precautionary matter and without probable cause or reasonable suspicion, look in closets and other spaces immediately adjoining the place of arrest from which an attack could be immediately launched. Beyond that, however, we hold that there must be articulable facts which, taken together with the rational inferences from those facts, would warrant a reasonably prudent officer in believing that the area to be swept harbors an individual posing a danger to those on the arrest scene."

"We should emphasize that such a protective sweep, aimed at protecting the arresting officers, if justified by the circumstances, is nevertheless not a full search of the premises, but may extend only to a cursory inspection of those spaces where a person may be found. The sweep lasts no longer than is necessary to dispel the reasonable suspicion of danger and in any event no longer than it takes to complete the arrest and depart the premises."

3. Arrestee

United States v. Robinson, 414 U.S. 218 (1973)
Vote: 6-3
FACTS: Richard Jenks of the District of Columbia Metropolitan Police Department observed Willie Robinson driving and, as a result of an investigation of Robinson's license four days earlier, determined there was reason to believe that he should not be driving. Jenks pulled Robinson over and all three of the occupants emerged from the car. At that point Jenks informed respondent that he was under arrest for "operating after revocation and obtaining a permit by misrepresentation." Jenks then began to search Robinson. During this pat-down, Jenks felt an object in the left breast pocket of the coat Robinson was wearing, but testified that he "couldn't tell what it was" and also that he "couldn't actually tell the size of it." Jenks then reached into the pocket and pulled out the object, which turned out to be a "crumpled-up cigarette package." He then opened the cigarette pack and found fourteen capsules of powder, which proved to be heroin. Robinson was convicted of the possession and facilitation of concealment of heroin.
ISSUE: Can police conduct a search of a person lawfully arrested without a warrant?
HOLDING: Yes.
RATIONALE: "We conclude that the search conducted by Jenks in this case did not offend the limits imposed by the Fourth Amendment. . . ."

"It is well settled that a search incident to a lawful arrest is a traditional exception to the warrant requirement of the Fourth Amendment. This general exception has historically been formulated into two distinct propositions. The first is that a search may be made of the *person* of the arrestee by virtue of the lawful arrest. The second is that a search may be made of the area within the control of the arrestee."

"'The right without a search warrant contemporaneously to search persons lawfully arrested while committing crime and to search the place where the arrest is made in order to find and seize things connected with the crime as its fruits or as the means by which it was committed, as well as weapons and other things to effect an escape from custody, is not to be doubted.'"

"'When an arrest is made, it is reasonable for the arresting officer to search the person arrested in order to remove any weapons that the latter might seek to use in order to resist arrest or effect his escape. Otherwise, the officer's safety might well be endangered, and the arrest itself frustrated. In addition, it is entirely reasonable for the arresting officer to search for and seize any evidence on the arrestee's person in order to prevent its concealment or destruction.'"

"[T]here is a 'distinction in purpose, character, and extent between a search incident to an arrest and a limited search for weapons.'"

"'The former, although justified in part by the acknowledged necessity to protect the arresting officer from assault with a concealed weapon . . . is also justified on other grounds . . . and can therefore involve a relatively extensive exploration of the person.'"

"The justification or reason for the authority to search incident to a lawful arrest rests quite as much on the need to disarm the suspect in order to take him into custody as it does on the need to preserve evidence on his person for later use at trial."

"It is scarcely open to doubt that the danger to an officer is far greater in the case of the extended exposure which follows the taking of a suspect into custody and transporting him to the police station than in the case of the relatively fleeting contact resulting from the typical *Terry* [*v. Ohio*, 392 U.S. 1 (1968)]-type stop. This is an adequate basis for treating all custodial arrests alike for purposes of search justification."

"A custodial arrest of a suspect based on probable cause is a reasonable intrusion under the Fourth Amendment; that intrusion being lawful, a search incident to the arrest requires no additional justification. It is the fact of the lawful arrest which establishes the authority to search, and we hold that in the case of a lawful custodial arrest a full search of the person is not only an exception to the warrant requirement of the Fourth Amendment, but is also a 'reasonable' search under that Amendment."

4. Contemporaneousness

United States v. Edwards, 415 U.S. 800 (1974)
Vote: 5-4
FACTS: Shortly after 11 p.m. Edwards was lawfully arrested and charged with attempting to break into a Post Office. He was taken to the local jail and placed in a cell. Shortly

thereafter, investigation revealed that the attempted entry had been made through a wooden window, which apparently had been pried up with a pry bar, leaving paint chips on the windowsill. The next morning, trousers and a T-shirt were purchased for Edwards to substitute for the clothing he had been wearing at the time of, and since his arrest. His clothing was then taken from him and held as evidence. Examination of the clothes revealed paint chips matching the samples taken from the window. This evidence and his clothing were received at trial over Edwards's objection and he was convicted.

ISSUE: Can a search of a suspect's clothes that takes place several hours after arrest be considered contemporaneous to the arrest?

HOLDING: Yes.

RATIONALE: "It is also plain that searches and seizures that could be made on the spot at the time of arrest may legally be conducted later when the accused arrives at the place of detention."

"The courts of appeals have followed this same rule, holding that both the person and the property in his immediate possession may be searched at the station house after the arrest has occurred at another place and if evidence of crime is discovered, it may be seized and admitted in evidence. Nor is there any doubt that clothing or other belongings may be seized upon arrival of the accused at the place of detention and later subjected to laboratory analysis or that the test results are admissible at trial."

"[O]nce the accused is lawfully arrested and is in custody, the effects in his possession at the place of detention that were subject to search at the time and place of his arrest may lawfully be searched and seized without a warrant even though a substantial period of time has elapsed between the arrest and subsequent administrative processing, on the one hand, and the taking of the property for use as evidence, on the other. This is true where the clothing or effects are immediately seized upon arrival at the jail, held under the defendant's name in the 'property room' of the jail, and at a later time searched and taken for use at the subsequent criminal trial. The result is the same where the property is not physically taken from the defendant until sometime after his incarceration."

6

Searches and Seizures without Warrants II—Special Needs

S EARCHING FOR AND SEIZING EVIDENCE without warrants continues in this chapter. While in chapter 5, the discussion focused on different individual circumstances where police were not required to obtain warrants prior to initiating a search, this chapter will highlight a special *category* of searches that also do not require warrants. These searches are called *special needs* searches, and because the governmental interest markedly outweighs the privacy interests of individuals in this area, the Supreme Court has granted the police a great deal of leeway in conducting these searches. In fact, these types of searches are so important to the general functioning of a governmental entity that sometimes these kinds of procedures are referred to as "suspicionless searches." It is this aspect of these types of searches that stand in marked contrast to the other types of governmental invasions that we have discussed so far.

Recall that in earlier chapters we discussed the general requirement that police must have a quantum of evidence before they can search or seize people or things. That amount of evidence was either probable cause or reasonable suspicion. In this chapter, we discuss instances where the police do not need to meet either one of these thresholds before they can take action against a person.

For example, vehicle searches can be quite complicated, but for present purposes police can do what is called an inventory search of a lawfully impounded car, pursuant to proper procedures, without a warrant or probable cause. Law enforcement agencies can also conduct searches at the U.S. border without warrants because the need to control who (and what) comes into (and goes out of) the country is an important governmental function. Another important area of discussion is what the government can do in this area to persons who are in its custody. Individuals have a very limited right to privacy in many of these situations; therefore, law enforcement can "search and seize" almost at will. Similarly, governmental employees, while certainly in possession of Fourth Amendment protections, have diminished protections while working in a law enforcement capacity. As a result, the government can impose urine and blood tests on its employees in certain circumstances. Additionally, students also have a lesser degree of privacy and protection while they are at school, and as a result school administrators have the authority to search their belongings. Finally, since the government has an interest in strictly regulating certain businesses, such as gun dealers, these places are also subjected to special kinds of administrative searches.

A. Automobile Inventory Searches

1. Are Bags Found in Cars during a Lawfully Conducted Inventory Subject to Search?

Colorado v. Bertine, 479 U.S. 367 (1987)
Vote: 7-2
FACTS: A Boulder, Colorado, police officer arrested Steven Lee Bertine for driving while under the influence of alcohol. After Bertine was taken into custody and before the arrival of a tow truck to take his van, a backup officer inventoried the van in accordance with departmental procedures. He found a backpack directly behind the front seat of the van. The officer observed inside the pack a nylon bag containing metal canisters and discovered that they contained cocaine, methaqualone tablets, cocaine paraphernalia, and $700 in cash. In an outside zippered pouch of the backpack he also found $210 in cash in a sealed envelope. After completing the inventory of the van, the officer had the van towed and brought the backpack, money, and contraband to the police station. Bertine was subsequently charged with driving while under the influence of alcohol; unlawful possession of cocaine with intent to dispense, sell, and distribute; and unlawful possession of methaqualone.
ISSUE: Can police search closed containers pursuant to a lawful inventory search?
HOLDING: Yes.
RATIONALE: "In [*South Dakota v. Opperman*, 428 U.S. 364 (1976)], this Court assessed the reasonableness of an inventory search of the glove compartment in an abandoned automobile impounded by the police. We found that inventory procedures serve to protect an owner's property while it is in the custody of the police, to insure against claims of lost, stolen, or vandalized property, and to guard the police from danger. In light of these strong governmental interests and the diminished expectation of privacy in an automobile, we upheld the search. In reaching this decision, we observed that our cases accorded deference to police caretaking procedures designed to secure and protect vehicles and their contents within police custody."

"In the present case, as in *Opperman* and [*Illinois v. Lafayette*, 462 U.S. 640 (1983)], there was no showing that the police, who were following standardized procedures, acted in bad faith or for the sole purpose of investigation. In addition, the governmental interests justifying the inventory searches in *Opperman* and *Lafayette* are nearly the same as those which obtain here. In each case, the police were potentially responsible for the property taken into their custody. By securing the property, the police protected the property from unauthorized interference. Knowledge of the precise nature of the property helped guard against claims of theft, vandalism, or negligence. Such knowledge also helped to avert any danger to police or others that may have been posed by the property."

2. Can Police Open Containers during Inventories When No Policy Concerning Them Exists?

Florida v. Wells, 495 U.S. 1 (1990)

Vote: 9-0

FACTS: A Florida Highway Patrol trooper stopped Wells for speeding and, after smelling alcohol on his breath, arrested him for driving under the influence. Wells then agreed to accompany the trooper to take a breathalyzer. The trooper informed Wells that his car would be impounded and obtained his permission to open the trunk. At the impound facility, an inventory search of the car turned up two marijuana butts in an ashtray and a locked suitcase in the trunk. Under the trooper's direction, employees forced open the suitcase and discovered a garbage bag containing a large amount of marijuana. Wells was charged with possession of a controlled substance and pleaded nolo contendere but reserved his right to appeal the denial of the motion to suppress.

ISSUE: Can police open closed containers during an inventory search without a warrant if the department does not have a policy about such containers?

HOLDING: No.

RATIONALE: "[A]n inventory search must not be a ruse for a general rummaging in order to discover incriminating evidence. The policy or practice governing inventory searches should be designed to produce an inventory. The individual police officer must not be allowed so much latitude that inventory searches are turned into 'a purposeful and general means of discovering evidence of crime.'"

"[W]hile policies of opening all containers or of opening no containers are unquestionably permissible, it would be equally permissible, for example, to allow the opening of closed containers whose contents officers determine they are unable to ascertain from examining the containers' exteriors."

"[T]he Supreme Court of Florida found that the Florida Highway Patrol had no policy whatever with respect to the opening of closed containers encountered during an inventory search. We hold that absent such a policy, the instant search was not sufficiently regulated to satisfy the Fourth Amendment and that the marijuana which was found in the suitcase, therefore, was properly suppressed."

—

B. International Borders

1. Searching Alimentary Canal Smugglers

United States v. Montoya de Hernandez, 473 U.S. 531 (1985)

Vote: 7-2

FACTS: Rosa Montoya de Hernandez arrived at Los Angeles International Airport on a flight from Bogota and passed through Immigration to U.S. Customs. At customs, she encountered Inspector Talamantes, who noticed that she had made at least eight recent trips to Miami or Los Angeles. Talamantes referred her for further questioning and he and another agent asked her about the purpose of her trip. She revealed that she spoke no English and had no family or friends in the United States. She explained that she had come to purchase goods for her husband's store. She had $5,000 in mostly $50 bills and indicated that she had no appointments with vendors but planned to ride around Los Angeles in cabs visiting stores. She also admitted that she had no hotel, planned to stay at a Holiday Inn, could not recall how her ticket was purchased, and had no other shoes than the ones she was wearing.

A female inspector took her to a private area and conducted a pat-down and strip search. The inspector felt her abdomen and noticed a firm fullness. The inspector in charge told her that he suspected she was smuggling drugs in her alimentary canal. She agreed to the inspector's request that she be x-rayed but stated that she was pregnant and then withdrew consent. The inspector then gave her the option of returning to Colombia, agreeing to be x-rayed, or remaining in detention until she produced a bowel movement.

The airline refused to transport her because she lacked a Mexican visa and she was then told that she would be detained until she agreed to an x-ray or her bowels moved. She refused food and drink and refused to use the toilet. Almost sixteen hours after her flight had landed, customs officials sought a court order authorizing a pregnancy test, an x-ray, and a rectal examination. She was taken to a hospital and given a pregnancy test, which was negative. A physician conducted a rectal examination and removed a balloon containing a foreign substance. She was then arrested and over the course of the next four days, passed eighty-eight balloons containing pure cocaine. She was convicted of possession of cocaine with intent to distribute and unlawful importation of cocaine.

ISSUE: May customs officials detain an individual at the border if they reasonably suspect that they are smuggling narcotics in their alimentary canal?

HOLDING: Yes.

RATIONALE: "Here the seizure of respondent took place at the international border. Since the founding of our Republic, Congress has granted the Executive plenary authority to conduct routine searches and seizures at the border, without probable cause or a warrant, in order to regulate the collection of duties and to prevent the introduction of contraband into this country. . . . This Court has long recognized Congress' power to police entrants at the border. . . . Historically such broad powers have been necessary to prevent smuggling and to prevent prohibited articles from entry."

"[T]he Fourth Amendment's balance of reasonableness is qualitatively different at the international border than in the interior. Routine searches of the persons and effects of entrants are not subject to any requirement of reasonable suspicion, probable cause, or warrant. . . ."

"This concern is, if anything, heightened by the veritable national crisis in law enforcement caused by smuggling of illicit narcotics . . . and in particular by the increasing utilization of alimentary canal smuggling. This desperate practice appears to be a relatively recent addition to the smugglers' repertoire of deceptive practices, and it also appears to be exceedingly difficult to detect."

"[T]he Fourth Amendment balance between the interests of the Government and the privacy right of the individual is also struck much more favorably to the Government at the border."

"We hold that the detention of a traveler at the border, beyond the scope of a routine customs search and inspection, is justified at its inception if customs agents, considering all the facts surrounding the traveler and her trip, reasonably suspect that the traveler is smuggling contraband in her alimentary canal."

"The 'reasonable suspicion' standard has been applied in a number of contexts and effects a needed balance between private and public interests when law enforcement officials must make a limited intrusion on less than probable cause. It thus fits well into the situations involving alimentary canal smuggling at the border: this type of smuggling gives no external signs and inspectors will rarely possess probable cause to arrest or search, yet governmental interests in stopping smuggling at the border are high indeed. Under this standard officials at the border must have a 'particularized and objective basis for suspecting the particular person' of alimentary canal smuggling."

"The facts, and their rational inferences, known to customs inspectors in this case clearly supported a reasonable suspicion that respondent was an alimentary canal smuggler."

2. Does Authority to Inspect Vehicles at International Borders Include Authority to Disassemble Automobiles?

United States v. Flores-Montano, 541 U.S. 149 (2004)

Vote: 9-0

FACTS: Manuel Flores-Montano was driving a Ford Taurus station wagon and attempted to enter the United States at the Otay Mesa Port of Entry in Southern California. A customs inspector requested Flores-Montano to leave the vehicle, and the vehicle was then taken to an inspection station. At the station, a second inspector examined the gas tank and noted that it sounded solid. The inspector requested a mechanic from customs to come to the station to remove the tank. After the gas tank was removed, the inspector removed an access plate and found a little more than eighty-one pounds of marijuana. The process took fifteen to thirty minutes altogether. Flores-Montano was indicted on one count of unlawfully importing marijuana and one count of possession of marijuana with intent to distribute. Flores-Montano filed a motion to suppress the marijuana and a divided court of appeals held that the removal of a gas tank requires reasonable suspicion in order to be consistent with the Fourth Amendment.

ISSUE: Does the search of a vehicle's gas tank at an international border require reasonable suspicion?

HOLDING: No.

RATIONALE: "We hold that the search in question did not require reasonable suspicion."

"The Court of Appeals seized on language from our opinion in *United States v. Montoya de Hernandez* [473 U.S. 531 (1985)] . . . in which we used the word 'routine'. . . and . . . fashioned a new balancing test, and extended it to searches of vehicles. But the reasons that might support a requirement of some level of suspicion in the case of highly intrusive searches of the person—dignity and privacy interests of the person being searched—simply do not carry over to vehicles. Complex balancing tests to determine what is a 'routine' search of a vehicle, as opposed to a more 'intrusive' search of a person, have no place in border searches of vehicles."

"The Government's interest in preventing the entry of unwanted persons and effects is at its zenith at the international border. Time and again, we have stated that 'searches made at the border, pursuant to the longstanding right of the sovereign to protect itself by stopping and examining persons and property crossing into this country, are reasonable simply by virtue of the fact that they occur at the border. . . .'"

"That interest in protecting the borders is illustrated in this case by the evidence that smugglers frequently attempt to penetrate our borders with contraband secreted in their automobiles' fuel tank. . . . In addition, instances of persons smuggled in and around gas tank compartments are discovered at the ports of entry of San Ysidro and Otay Mesa at a rate averaging 1 approximately every 10 days."

"Respondent asserts . . . that the suspicionless disassembly of his tank is an invasion of his privacy. But on many occasions, we have noted that the expectation of privacy is less at the border than it is in the interior. . . . We have long recognized that automobiles seeking entry into this country may be searched. . . . It is difficult to imagine how the search of a gas tank, which should be solely a repository for fuel, could be more of an invasion of privacy than the search of the automobile's passenger compartment."

"Second, respondent argues . . . that the disassembly and reassembly of his gas tank is a significant deprivation of his property interest because it may damage the vehicle. He does not, and on the record cannot, truly contend that the procedure of removal, disassembly, and reassembly of the fuel tank in this case or any other has resulted in serious damage to, or destruction of, the property."

"A gas tank search involves a brief procedure that can be reversed without damaging the safety or operation of the vehicle. If damage to a vehicle were to occur, the motorist might be entitled to recovery. . . . While the interference with a motorist's possessory interest is not insignificant when the Government removes, disassembles, and reassembles his gas tank, it nevertheless is justified by the Government's paramount interest in protecting the border."

"For the reasons stated, we conclude that the Government's authority to conduct suspicionless inspections at the border includes the authority to remove, disassemble, and reassemble a vehicle's fuel tank. While it may be true that some searches of property are so destructive as to require a different result, this was not one of them."

3. Is There an Objective Standard of Proof Required for Routine Border Searches?

United States v. Ramsey, 431 U.S. 606 (1977)
Vote: 6-3

FACTS: Charles W. Ramsey and James W. Kelly operated a heroin-by-mail enterprise in the Washington, D.C., area. The process involved their obtaining heroin from Bangkok and having it sent to various locations in D.C. for collection. West Germany intercepted several trans-Atlantic conversations between Sylvia Bailey and Ramsey during which their narcotics operation was discussed. By late January 1974, Bailey and William Ward had gone to Thailand. Thai officials observed Ward mailing letter-sized envelopes, and Bailey and Ward were arrested by Thai officials.

Two days after this arrest, U.S. Customs Inspector George Kallnischkies, inspected a sack of mail from Thailand and spotted eight envelopes that were bulky and that he believed might contain merchandise. Based on the fact that the letters were from Thailand and were "rather bulky," he suspected that the envelopes might contain contraband. He weighed one of the envelopes, and found it weighed three to six times the normal weight. He then opened that envelope and found heroin in it and found it in several others as well.

The envelopes were then sent to Washington where DEA agents, after obtaining a warrant, opened the envelopes and removed most of the heroin. The envelopes were then resealed, and six of them were delivered under surveillance. After Kelly collected the envelopes from the three different addressees, rendezvoused with Ramsey, and gave Ramsey a brown paper bag, federal agents arrested both of them. The bag contained the six envelopes with heroin, $1,100 in cash, and "cutting" material for the heroin.

ISSUE: Do customs officials need probable cause to conduct border searches?

HOLDING: No.

RATIONALE: "Border searches, then, from before the adoption of the Fourth Amendment, have been considered to be 'reasonable' by the single fact that the person or item in question had entered into our country from outside. There has never been any additional requirement that the reasonableness of a border search depended on the existence of probable cause. This longstanding recognition that searches at our borders without probable cause and without a warrant are nonetheless 'reasonable' has a history as old as the Fourth Amendment itself."

"The border-search exception is grounded in the recognized right of the sovereign to control, subject to substantive limitations imposed by the Constitution, who and what may enter the country. It is clear that there is nothing in the rationale behind the border-search exception, which suggests that the mode of entry will be critical. It was conceded at oral argument that customs officials could search, without probable cause and without a warrant, envelopes carried by an entering traveler, whether in his luggage or on his person. . . . Surely no different constitutional standard should apply simply because the envelopes were mailed, not carried. The critical fact is that the envelopes cross the border and enter this country, not that they are brought in by one mode of transportation rather than another. It is their entry into this country from without it that makes a resulting search 'reasonable.'"

"Nor do we agree that, under the circumstances presented by this case, First Amendment considerations dictate a full panoply of Fourth Amendment rights prior to the border search of mailed letters. There is, again, no reason to distinguish between letters mailed into the country, and letters carried on the traveler's person. More fundamentally, however, the existing system of border searches has not been shown to invade protected First Amendment rights, and hence there is no reason to think that the potential presence of correspondence makes the otherwise constitutionally reasonable search 'unreasonable.'"

C. Persons in State Custody

1. Do Prisoners Have an Expectation of Privacy in their Cells?

Hudson v. Palmer, 468 U.S. 517 (1984)
Vote: 5-4
FACTS: Palmer, an inmate at the Bland Correctional Center in Bland, Virginia, was serving sentences for forgery, uttering, grand larceny, and bank robbery. Hudson, an officer at the Correctional Center, with a fellow officer, conducted a "shakedown" search of respondent's prison locker and cell for contraband. During the process, the officers discovered a ripped pillowcase in a trashcan near Palmer's bed. Prison disciplinary procedures were filed against Palmer for destroying property. Palmer was found guilty on the charge and was ordered to reimburse the State for the cost of the material destroyed and a reprimand was entered on his prison record.
ISSUE: Do inmates have a subjective right of privacy in their cells entitling them to the protection of the Fourth Amendment against unreasonable searches?
HOLDING: No.
RATIONALE: "*Bell v. Wolfish* [441 U.S. 520 (1979)] . . . authorized irregular unannounced shakedown searches of prison cells."

"[W]e hold that society is not prepared to recognize as legitimate any subjective expectation of privacy that a prisoner might have in his prison cell and that, accordingly, the Fourth Amendment proscription against unreasonable searches does not apply within the confines of the prison cell. The recognition of privacy rights for prisoners in their individual cells simply cannot be reconciled with the concept of incarceration and the needs and objectives of penal institutions."

"The administration of a prison, we have said, is 'at best an extraordinarily difficult undertaking. . . .' But it would be literally impossible to accomplish the prison objectives identified above if inmates retained a right of privacy in their cells. Virtually the only place inmates can conceal weapons, drugs, and other contraband is in their cells. Unfettered access to these cells by prison officials, thus, is imperative if drugs and contraband are to be ferreted out and sanitary surroundings are to be maintained."

"Determining whether an expectation of privacy is 'legitimate' or 'reasonable' necessarily entails a balancing of interests. The two interests here are the interest of society in the security of its penal institutions and the interest of the prisoner in privacy within his cell. The latter interest, of course, is already limited by the exigencies of the circumstances: A prison 'shares none of the attributes of privacy of a home, an automobile, an office, or a hotel room. . . .' We strike the balance in favor of institutional security, which we have noted is 'central to all other corrections goals.' A right of privacy in traditional Fourth Amendment terms is fundamentally incompatible with the close and continual surveillance of inmates and their cells required to ensure institutional security and internal order. We are satisfied that society would insist that the prisoner's expectation of privacy always yield to what must be considered the paramount interest in institutional security."

"The uncertainty that attends random searches of cells renders these searches perhaps the most effective weapon of the prison administrator in the constant fight against the proliferation of knives and guns, illicit drugs, and other contraband."

"A requirement that even random searches be conducted pursuant to an established plan would seriously undermine the effectiveness of this weapon. It is simply naive to believe that prisoners would not eventually decipher any plan officials might devise for 'planned random searches,' and thus be able routinely to anticipate searches."

"[W]e conclude that prisoners have no legitimate expectation of privacy and that the Fourth Amendment's prohibition on unreasonable searches does not apply in prison cells."

2. Are Body Cavity Searches of Inmates Reasonable without Warrants?

Bell v. Wolfish, 441 U.S. 520 (1979)
Vote: 5-4
FACTS: A class action lawsuit was brought in federal court based on numerous complaints that implicated the Metropolitan Correctional Center (MCC). Respondents charged that they had been deprived of their rights due to overcrowding conditions, length of confinement, illegal searches, inadequate recreational opportunities, insufficient staff, and restrictions on the purchase and receipt of personal items and books. The court of appeals mostly affirmed the district court and in the process held that under the Due Process Clause of the Fifth Amendment, pretrial detainees may "be subjected to only those 'restrictions and privations' which 'inhere in their confinement itself or which are justified by compelling necessities of jail administration.'"
ISSUE: Are body cavity searches of inmates unreasonable under the Fourth Amendment?
HOLDING: No.
RATIONALE: "[M]aintaining institutional security and preserving internal order and discipline are essential goals that may require limitation or retraction of the retained constitutional rights of both convicted prisoners and pretrial detainees. . . . Prison officials must be free to take appropriate action to ensure the safety of inmates and corrections personnel and to prevent escape or unauthorized entry."

"Corrections officials testified that visual cavity searches were necessary not only to discover but also to deter the smuggling of weapons, drugs, and other contraband into the institution."

"[W]e nonetheless conclude that these searches do not violate that Amendment. The Fourth Amendment prohibits only unreasonable searches . . . and under the circumstances, we do not believe that these searches are unreasonable."

"We do not underestimate the degree to which these searches may invade the personal privacy of inmates. Nor do we doubt, as the district court noted, that on occasion a security guard may conduct the search in an abusive fashion. . . . Such abuse cannot be condoned. The searches must be conducted in a reasonable manner. . . . But we deal here with the question whether visual body-cavity inspections as contemplated by the MCC rules can *ever* be conducted on less than probable cause. Balancing the significant and legitimate security interests of the institution against the privacy interests of the inmates, we conclude that they can."

3. Are Warrantless Searches of Probationers Homes Allowed?

a. Searches of Probationers and "Special Needs"

Griffin v. Wisconsin, 483 U.S. 868 (1987)
Vote: 5-4
FACTS: While Joseph Griffin was still on probation, Michael Lew, the supervisor of Griffin's probation officer, received information from a detective that guns might be in Griffin's apartment. Unable to find Griffin's officer, Lew, accompanied by another probation officer and three plainclothes policemen, went to the apartment. When he answered, Lew told him who they were and informed him that they were going to search his home. During the subsequent search—carried out entirely by the probation officers under the authority of Wisconsin's probation regulation—they found a handgun. Griffin was charged with and convicted of possession of a firearm by a convicted felon.
ISSUE: Does the administration of a probation system qualify as a "special need" that justifies the elimination of the warrant requirement when searching probationers' homes?
HOLDING: Yes.
RATIONALE: "We think the Wisconsin Supreme Court correctly concluded that this warrantless search did not violate the Fourth Amendment."

"A probationer's home, like anyone else's, is protected by the Fourth Amendment's requirement that searches be 'reasonable.' Although we usually require that a search be undertaken only pursuant to a warrant (and thus supported by probable cause, as the Constitution says warrants must be). . . . We have also held, for similar reasons, that in certain circumstances government investigators conducting searches pursuant to a regulatory scheme need not adhere to the usual warrant or probable-cause requirements as long as their searches meet 'reasonable legislative or administrative standards. . . .'"

"A State's operation of a probation system, like its operation of a school, government office or prison, or its supervision of a regulated industry, likewise presents 'special needs' beyond normal law enforcement that may justify departures from the usual warrant and probable-cause requirements. . . . To a greater or lesser degree, it is always true of probationers (as we have said it to be true of parolees) that they do not enjoy 'the absolute liberty to which every citizen is entitled, but only . . . conditional liberty properly dependent on observance of special [probation] restrictions.'"

"We think it clear that the special needs of Wisconsin's probation system make the warrant requirement impracticable and justify replacement of the standard of probable cause by 'reasonable grounds,' as defined by the Wisconsin Supreme Court."

"A warrant requirement would interfere to an appreciable degree with the probation system, setting up a magistrate rather than the probation officer as the judge of how close a supervision the probationer requires. Moreover, the delay inherent in obtaining a warrant would make it more difficult for probation officials to respond quickly to evidence of misconduct . . . and would reduce the deterrent effect that the possibility of expeditious searches would otherwise create."

"We think that the probation regime would also be unduly disrupted by a requirement of probable cause. . . . The probationer would be assured that so long as his illegal (and perhaps socially dangerous) activities were sufficiently concealed as to give rise to no more than reasonable suspicion, they would go undetected and uncorrected."

"In such circumstances it is both unrealistic and destructive of the whole object of the continuing probation relationship to insist upon the same degree of demonstrable reliability of particular items of supporting data, and upon the same degree of certainty of violation, as is required in other contexts. In some cases—especially those involving drugs or illegal weapons—the probation agency must be able to act based upon a lesser degree of certainty than the Fourth Amendment would otherwise require in order to intervene before a probationer does damage to himself or society."

"The search of Griffin's residence was 'reasonable' within the meaning of the Fourth Amendment because it was conducted pursuant to a valid regulation governing probationers."

b. Probation Conditions, Searches, and Reasonable Suspicion

United States v. Knights, 534 U.S. 112 (2001)
Vote: 9-0
FACTS: Mark James Knights was sentenced to probation for a drug offense and the probation order included the condition that he would submit himself and property to a search with or without a warrant at anytime by any probation or law enforcement officer.

Three days after Knights was placed on probation, a Pacific Gas & Electric (PG&E) transformer and telecommunications vault were pried open and set on fire. Padlocks had been removed and gasoline had been used to start the fire. Suspicion focused on Knights and his friend. The incidents began after PG&E had filed a theft-of-services complaint against Knights and discontinued his electrical service. Detective Todd Hancock had noticed that the vandalism coincided with Knights's court appearance. And just a week before the arson, a sheriff's deputy had stopped Knights and Steven Simoneau near a PG&E gas line and observed pipes and gasoline in Simoneau's pickup truck.

A sheriff's deputy drove by Knights's residence and saw Simoneau's truck. He felt the hood of the truck and it was warm. Hancock decided to set up surveillance, and early the next morning, Simoneau left the apartment with three cylindrical items. Hancock believed the items were pipe bombs. Simoneau walked across the street to the Napa River, and Hancock heard three splashes. Simoneau returned without the cylinders and drove away. Hancock followed Simoneau, who stopped in a driveway, parked, and left. Hancock entered the driveway and saw a number of objects in the truck: a Molotov cocktail, explosive materials, a gas can, and two padlocks that fit the description of those removed from the transformer. Hancock decided to conduct a search of Knights's apartment and believed that a warrant was not necessary. The search revealed several items used for making bombs. A grand jury indicted him for conspiracy to commit arson, possession of an unregistered destructive device, and being a felon in possession of ammunition.

ISSUE: May probation officers search a probationer's home pursuant to a probation condition, supported by reasonable suspicion, without a warrant?

HOLDING: Yes.

RATIONALE: "In Knights's view, apparently shared by the Court of Appeals, a warrantless search of a probationer satisfies the Fourth Amendment only if it is just like the search at issue in *Griffin* [v. *Wisconsin*, 483 U.S. 868 (1987)]—i.e., a 'special needs' search conducted by a probation officer monitoring whether the probationer is complying with probation restrictions. This dubious logic—that an opinion upholding the constitutionality of a particular search implicitly holds unconstitutional any search that is not like it—runs contrary to *Griffin*'s express statement that its 'special needs' holding made it 'unnecessary to consider whether' warrantless searches of probationers were otherwise reasonable within the meaning of the Fourth Amendment."

"[W]e conclude that the search of Knights was reasonable under our general Fourth Amendment approach of 'examining the totality of the circumstances . . .' with the probation search condition being a salient circumstance."

"We hold that the balance of these considerations requires no more than reasonable suspicion to conduct a search of this probationer's house. . . . When an officer has reasonable suspicion that a probationer subject to a search condition is engaged in criminal activity, there is enough likelihood that criminal conduct is occurring that an intrusion on the probationer's significantly diminished privacy interests is reasonable."

c. Parolee Searches

Samson v. California 126 S.Ct. 2193 (2006)
Vote: 6-3

FACTS: In September 2002, Samson was on parole for a conviction of being a felon in possession of a firearm. Officer Rohleder saw Samson walking with a woman and a child. Based on prior information, Rohleder knew that Samson was on parole and thought that he had an outstanding warrant. Rohleder then stopped him, and Samson stated that no outstanding warrant existed. Officer Rohleder confirmed that no warrant existed but, based solely on Samson's parolee status, conducted a search and found a baggie that contained methamphetamine in Samson's left breast pocket. Samson was charged with possession, the court denied his motion to suppress, and he was subsequently convicted. The California Court of Appeal affirmed, holding that the search was valid because it was not arbitrary, capricious, or harassing.

ISSUE: Do suspicionless police searches of parolees violate the Fourth Amendment?

HOLDING: No.

RATIONALE: "[P]arolees are on the 'continuum' of state-imposed punishments. . . . Parolees have fewer expectations of privacy than probationers, because parole is more akin to imprisonment than probation is to imprisonment. . . . 'Parole is an established variation on imprisonment of convicted criminals. . . . The essence of parole is release from prison, before the completion of sentence, on the condition that the prisoner abides by certain rules during the balance of the sentence.'"

"[A]n inmate-turned-parolee remains in the legal custody of the California Department of Corrections through the remainder of his term and must comply with all of the terms and conditions of parole, including mandatory drug tests, restrictions on association with felons or gang members, and mandatory meetings with parole officers. . . . Parolees may also be subject to . . . '[a]ny other condition deemed necessary. . . .' These conditions clearly demonstrate that parolees . . . have severely diminished expectations of privacy by virtue of their status."

"[T]he parole search condition under California law—requiring inmates who opt for parole to submit to suspicionless searches by a parole officer or other peace officer 'at any time . . .' was 'clearly expressed.'"

D. Government Searches of Employees, Hospital Patients, and Students

1. Employees Seeking Transfers to Sensitive Jobs

National Treasury Employees Union v. Von Raab, 489 U.S. 656 (1989)
Vote: 5-4
FACTS: The United States Customs Commissioner announced implementation of a drug-testing program for employment in positions that involve direct involvement in drug interdiction, require the employee to carry firearms, or require the employee to handle "classified" material. The lab tests for the presence of marijuana, cocaine, opiates, amphetamines, and phencyclidine. Customs employees who test positive and who can offer no acceptable explanation are subject to dismissal. Test results may not be turned over to any other agency or prosecutors without written consent. A federal employee and an official filed suit on behalf of customs employees who sought covered positions by alleging that the drug-testing program violated the Fourth Amendment.

ISSUE: Does a U.S. Customs Service policy requiring a urinalysis from employees who seek transfer or promotion to sensitive positions violate the Fourth Amendment?

HOLDING: No.

RATIONALE: "It is clear that the Customs Service's drug-testing program is not designed to serve the ordinary needs of law enforcement. Test results may not be used in a criminal prosecution of the employee without the employee's consent. The purposes of the program are to deter drug use among those eligible for promotion to sensitive positions within the Service and to prevent the promotion of drug users to those positions. These substantial interests, no less than the Government's concern for safe rail transportation at issue in [*Skinner v. Railway Labor Executives*, 489 U.S. 602 (1989),] present a special need that may justify departure from the ordinary warrant and probable-cause requirements."

"We have recognized before that requiring the Government to procure a warrant for every work-related intrusion 'would conflict with 'the common-sense realization that government offices could not function if every employment decision became a constitutional matter.'"

"Furthermore, a warrant would provide little or nothing in the way of additional protection of personal privacy. . . . Because the Service does not make a discretionary determination to search based on a judgment that certain conditions are present, there are simply 'no special facts for a neutral magistrate to evaluate.'"

"We think the Government's need to conduct the suspicionless searches required by the Customs program outweighs the privacy interests of employees engaged directly in drug interdiction, and of those who otherwise are required to carry firearms."

"The Government has a compelling interest in ensuring that front-line interdiction personnel are physically fit, and have unimpeachable integrity and judgment. Indeed, the Government's interest here is at least as important as its interest in searching travelers entering the country. This national interest in self-protection could be irreparably damaged if those charged with safeguarding it were, because of their own drug use, unsympathetic to their mission of interdicting narcotics. A drug user's indifference to the Service's basic mission or, even worse, his active complicity with the malefactors, can facilitate importation of sizable drug shipments or block apprehension of dangerous criminals. The public interest demands effective measures to bar drug users from positions directly involving the interdiction of illegal drugs."

"We hold that the suspicionless testing of employees who apply for promotion to positions directly involving the interdiction of illegal drugs, or to positions that require the incumbent to carry a firearm, is reasonable. The Government's compelling interests in preventing the promotion of drug users to positions where they might endanger the integrity of our Nation's borders or the life of the citizenry outweigh the privacy interests of those who seek promotion to these positions, who enjoy a diminished expectation of privacy by virtue of the special, and obvious, physical and ethical demands of those positions."

2. Can a State Hospital Use Drug Test Results against Women for Evidentiary Purposes?

Ferguson v. Charleston, 532 U.S. 67 (2001)
Vote: 6-3

FACTS: Staff at the Medical University of South Carolina (MUSC) became concerned about cocaine use by pregnant patients. When the incidence of cocaine use remained unchanged, staff offered to cooperate with police in prosecuting mothers whose children tested positive. MUSC representatives, police, and officials developed a policy that set forth procedures for identifying and testing pregnant patients suspected of drug use, procedures for arresting patients who tested positive, and prescribed prosecutions for drug offenses and/or child neglect. Ten patients filed suit to challenge the legality of the policy, four of whom were arrested during initial implementation and were not offered treatment. The others six failed to comply with treatment or tested positive a second time.

ISSUE: Is a state hospital's performance of a urine test to obtain evidence of a patient's criminal conduct for police purposes a "special needs" search?

HOLDING: No.

RATIONALE: "The critical difference between those four drug-testing cases and this one, however, lies in the nature of the 'special need' asserted as justification for the warrantless searches. In each of those earlier cases, the 'special need' that was advanced as a justification for the absence of a warrant or individualized suspicion was one divorced from the State's general interest in law enforcement. . . . [T]he central and indispensable feature of the policy from its inception was the use of law enforcement to coerce the patients into substance abuse treatment."

"Tellingly, the document codifying the policy incorporates the police's operational guidelines. It devotes its attention to the chain of custody, the range of possible criminal charges, and the logistics of police notification and arrests. Nowhere, however, does the document discuss different courses of medical treatment for either mother or infant, aside from treatment for the mother's addiction."

"[T]he immediate objective of the searches was to generate evidence *for law enforcement purposes*. Given the primary purpose of the Charleston program, which was to use the threat of arrest and prosecution in order to force women into treatment, and given the extensive involvement of law enforcement officials at every stage of the policy, this case simply does not fit within the closely guarded category of 'special needs.'"

"While state hospital employees, like other citizens, may have a duty to provide the police with evidence of criminal conduct that they inadvertently acquire in the course of routine treatment, when they undertake to obtain such evidence from their patients *for the specific purpose of incriminating those patients*, they have a special obligation to make sure that the patients are fully informed about their constitutional rights, as standards of knowing waiver require.

3. Students

a. Can School Officials Conduct Searches That Are Related to Disciplinary Policies?

New Jersey v. T.L.O., 469 U.S. 325 (1985)

Vote: 6-3

FACTS: A teacher at a Piscataway High School in Middlesex County, New Jersey, discovered two girls smoking in a lavatory. One of the two girls was T.L.O. (her initials were used because of her age). The teacher took the two girls to the office, where they met with Assistant Vice Principal Theodore Choplick. After questioning, T.L.O.'s friend admitted that she was smoking, while T.L.O. denied it. Choplick demanded to see her purse and, upon searching it, found a pack of cigarettes, rolling papers, marihuana, a pipe, plastic bags, money, a list of students who owed her money, and letters that implicated her in marihuana dealing. Choplick notified T.L.O.'s mother and turned the evidence over to police. T.L.O.'s mother took her to police headquarters, where T.L.O. confessed that she had been selling marihuana. On the basis of the confession and the evidence seized by Choplick, the State brought delinquency charges against T.L.O., whereupon she was adjudicated delinquent and sentenced to a year's probation.

ISSUE: Do school officials need a warrant to search a student under their authority if they reasonably believe that the student has committed a rule violation?

HOLDING: No.

RATIONALE: "It is evident that the school setting requires some easing of the restrictions to which searches by public authorities are ordinarily subject. The warrant requirement, in particular, is unsuited to the school environment: requiring a teacher to obtain a warrant before searching a child suspected of an infraction of school rules (or of the criminal law) would unduly interfere with the maintenance of the swift and informal disciplinary procedures needed in the schools. Just as we have in other cases dispensed with the warrant requirement when 'the burden of obtaining a warrant is likely to frustrate the governmental purpose behind the search . . . ,' we hold today that school officials need not obtain a warrant before searching a student who is under their authority."

"We join the majority of courts that have examined this issue in concluding that the accommodation of the privacy interests of schoolchildren with the substantial need of teachers and administrators for freedom to maintain order in the schools does not require strict adherence to the requirement that searches be based on probable cause to believe that the subject of the search has violated or is violating the law. Rather, the legality of a search of a student should depend simply on the reasonableness, under all the circumstances, of the search."

"[T]he reasonableness standard should ensure that the interests of students will be invaded no more than is necessary to achieve the legitimate end of preserving order in the schools."

"Our review of the facts surrounding the search leads us to conclude that the search was in no sense unreasonable for Fourth Amendment purposes."

b. Can Schools Require Athletes to Take Drug Tests?

Vernonia School District v. Acton, 515 U.S. 646 (1995)

Vote: 6-3

FACTS: Teachers and administrators observed a sharp increase in drug use at Vernonia High School in Vernonia, Oregon, which resulted in more disciplinary problems, and despite attempts to quell the problem, incidents persisted. Officials then began considering a drug-testing program. After consultations, parents gave their unanimous approval. The policy's purpose is to prevent athletes from using drugs, to protect their health and safety, and to provide users with assistance. The policy applies to all students participating in athletics, and students wishing to play must sign a form and obtain written consent from their parents. Athletes are tested at the beginning of the season. In addition, once each week 10 percent of the athletes are randomly tested. Those selected are notified and tested. The samples are sent to an independent lab, which tests for amphetamines, cocaine, and marijuana.

If a sample tests positive, a second test is administered to confirm the result. If the second test is negative, no further action is taken. If the second test is positive, the parents are notified and the school principal convenes a meeting with the student and his parents, at which the student either agrees to (1) participating in an assistance program or (2) suspension from athletics for the remainder of the current season and the next. Additional positive tests result in different penalties. James Acton, then a seventh grader, signed up to play football at a covered school but was denied because he and his parents refused to sign the forms.

ISSUE: May schools require student athletes to submit to a drug tests without a warrant?

HOLDING: Yes.

RATIONALE: "A search unsupported by probable cause can be constitutional, we have said, 'when special needs, beyond the normal need for law enforcement, make the warrant and probable-cause requirement impracticable.'"

"[T]herefore, 'students within the school environment have a lesser expectation of privacy than members of the population generally.'"

"Legitimate privacy expectations are even less with regard to student athletes. School sports are not for the bashful. They require 'suiting up' before each practice or event, and showering and changing afterwards. Public school locker rooms, the usual sites for these activities, are not notable for the privacy they afford. The locker rooms in Vernonia are typical: No individual dressing rooms are provided; shower heads are lined up along a wall, unseparated by any sort of partition or curtain; not even all the toilet stalls have doors."

"Somewhat like adults who choose to participate in a 'closely regulated industry,' students who voluntarily participate in school athletics have reason to expect intrusions upon normal rights and privileges, including privacy."

"[W]hen the government acts as guardian and tutor the relevant question is whether the search is one that a reasonable guardian and tutor might undertake. Given the findings of need made by the District Court, we conclude that in the present case it is."

E. Administrative Searches and Inspections

1. Gun Dealers

United States v. Biswell, 406 U.S. 311 (1972)

Vote: 8-1

FACTS: The Gun Control Act of 1968 authorizes official entry during business hours into "the premises (including places of storage) of any firearms or ammunition . . . dealer . . . for the purpose of inspecting or examining (1) any records or documents required to be kept . . . and (2) any firearms or ammunition kept or stored by such . . . dealer . . . at such premises." Biswell was licensed to deal in weapons and was visited by a city policeman and a Federal Treasury agent who identified himself, inspected Biswell's books, and requested entry into a locked gun storeroom. Biswell asked if the agent had a search warrant, and the investigator told him that he did not but that a law authorized such inspections. Biswell was given a copy of the section and replied, "Well, that's what it says so I guess it's okay." He unlocked the storeroom, and the agent found and seized two sawed-off rifles, which Biswell was not licensed to possess. He was indicted and convicted for dealing in firearms without having paid tax.

ISSUE: Can police conduct warrantless inspections of gun dealers based on a statute?

HOLDING: Yes.

RATIONALE: "When the officers asked to inspect respondent's locked storeroom, they were merely asserting their statutory right, and respondent was on notice as to their identity and the legal basis for their action. Respondent's submission to *lawful* authority and his decision to step aside and permit the inspection rather than face a criminal prosecution is analogous to a householder's acquiescence in a search pursuant to a warrant when the alternative is a possible criminal prosecution for refusing entry or a forcible entry. In neither case does the lawfulness of the search depend on consent; in both, there is lawful authority independent of the will of the householder who might, other things being equal, prefer no search at all."

"It is also apparent that if the law is to be properly enforced and inspection made effective, inspections without warrant must be deemed reasonable official conduct under the Fourth Amendment. . . . Here, if inspection is to be effective and serve as a credible deterrent, unannounced, even frequent, inspections are essential. In this context, the prerequisite of a warrant could easily frustrate inspection; and if the necessary flexibility as to time, scope, and frequency is to be preserved, the protections afforded by a warrant would be negligible."

"It is also plain that inspections for compliance with the Gun Control Act pose only limited threats to the dealer's justifiable expectations of privacy. When a dealer chooses to engage in this pervasively regulated business and to accept a federal license, he does so with the knowledge that his business records, firearms, and ammunition will be subject to effective inspection. Each licensee is annually furnished with a revised compilation of ordinances that describe his obligations and define the inspector's authority."

"We have little difficulty in concluding that where, as here, regulatory inspections further urgent federal interest, and the possibilities of abuse and the threat to privacy are not of impressive dimensions, the inspection may proceed without a warrant where specifically authorized by statute."

7

Automobile Searches and Seizures

S EIZURES OF AUTOMOBILES AND SUBSEQUENT SEARCHES can be complex. As a result, the Supreme Court has been asked on many different occasions exactly what police can and cannot do in conjunction with stopping a vehicle. At first glance, the different rules that the Court has crafted may seem cumbersome and confusing, but eventually, some clarity of purpose can be ascertained. Once again, the Court has special concerns about vehicles; for example, they possess an inherent ability to transport contraband and they can readily leave a jurisdiction due to their mobility. As a result, the Court has created circumstances where the police may not need a warrant to search a car. This, of course, is a general exception to the rule that police must have a warrant, but they must have probable cause. However, as we have shown previously, there are always exceptions to every rule.

For example, police may stop a vehicle on less than probable cause for investigative purposes when suspicion has been aroused of smuggling of illegal aliens. The Supreme Court has said that in such circumstances the police only need to have reasonable suspicion that such activity is taking place. The test for making that determination is the totality of the circumstances, examining all of the information available at the time the stop occurred. The Court has also determined that individuals have a lesser expectation of privacy when using their cars because they are open to the public in the sense that people can see inside them as they are traveling.

Relatedly, police can do several things after they have lawfully stopped a vehicle. Specifically, they can order both the driver and passengers out of the car so that any interaction with the police enhances the safety and well-being of the officer. They may also ask questions of the occupants as part of the investigation for making the stop. Additionally, they may also search the bags of a passenger for any items that the officer has probable cause to search for. Police can also locate and examine the Vehicle Identification number (VIN) of the car. The Supreme Court has also been asked to specifically deal with how the police must conduct themselves when they wish to search the interior of the car (passenger compartment). The Court has ruled on when the police can search the *entire vehicle*, including the trunk and when they can search the passenger compartment and any containers found in the passenger compartment. Searches "incident to citation" are also covered here. In fact, so are searches of motorboats, buses, and checkpoints.

A. General Rules Surrounding Vehicle Stops

1. Levels of Proof

United States v. Cortez, 449 U.S. 411 (1981)
Vote: 9-0

FACTS: Border Patrol officers believed a person whom they designated as "Chevron," helped smuggle people across a part of the border known for alien traffic. The agents ascertained that the illegals met at a predetermined point and were picked up. Their information also pointed to the likelihood that their suspect traveled around on weekends, early in the morning. The officers stationed themselves close to the area they suspected and observed a truck with a camper pass and then return within the approximate time it would take to make a round trip from the pick-up spot. The officers stopped the vehicle, driven by Jesus Cortez, in which a passenger was wearing shoes suspected of making prints observed at the pick-up spot. Cortez voluntarily opened the door of the camper, and the officers discovered the aliens. Respondents were charged with six counts of transporting illegal aliens and convicted.

ISSUE: Can the Border Patrol stop a car if the stop is based on reasonable suspicion?

HOLDING: Yes.

RATIONALE: "The Fourth Amendment applies to seizures of the person, including brief investigatory stops such as the stop of the vehicle. . . ."

"The totality of the circumstances—the whole picture—must be taken into account. Based upon that whole picture the detaining officers must have a particularized and objective basis for suspecting the particular person stopped of criminal activity. . . ."

"The limited purpose of the stop in this case was to question the occupants of the vehicle about their citizenship and immigration status and the reasons for the round trip in a short time span in a virtually deserted area. No search of the camper or any of its occupants occurred until after respondent Cortez voluntarily opened the back door of the camper; thus, only the stop, not the search is at issue here. The intrusion upon privacy associated with this stop was limited and was 'reasonably related in scope to the justification for [its] initiation. . . .'"

"We have recently held that stops by the Border Patrol may be justified under circumstances less than those constituting probable cause for arrest or search. . . . [T]he question is whether, based upon the whole picture, they, as experienced Border Patrol officers, could reasonably surmise that the particular vehicle they stopped was engaged in criminal activity. On this record, they could so conclude."

2. Do Searches of Vehicles Have to Be Contemporaneous to the Seizure?

United States v. Johns, 469 U.S. 478 (1985)
Vote: 7-2

FACTS: Pursuant to a smuggling operation, a customs officer went to Duarte's residence in Tucson, where he saw two pickup trucks. The officer contacted others, who conducted ground and air surveillance of the trucks as they traveled to a remote airstrip. Soon after the trucks arrived, a small aircraft landed and officers in the air informed those on the ground that one of the trucks had approached the airplane. After a time, a second plane landed and departed. Two officers on the ground saw an individual at the rear of one truck covering the contents with a blanket. The officers ordered them to come out and to lie on the ground. The officers smelled marihuana and saw packages wrapped in plastic and tape. Several individuals were arrested at the scene. The customs aircraft followed the two airplanes back to Tucson where Johns and Hearron, the pilots, were arrested. The officers did not search the trucks at the airstrip. Instead, they took the trucks back to DEA headquarters in Tucson. The packages were removed from the trucks and placed in a DEA warehouse. Without obtaining a search warrant, DEA agents opened some of the packages and took samples that proved to be marihuana. The parties do not dispute that the search occurred three days after the packages were seized from the trucks. Respondents were indicted for conspiracy to possess and possession of marihuana with intent to distribute.

ISSUE: Do police have to search a vehicle contemporaneously with its lawful seizure if they had probable cause to search the vehicle when it was seized?

HOLDING: No.

RATIONALE: "[*United States v. Ross*, 456 U.S. 798 (1982)] . . . establishes that the Customs officers could have lawfully searched the packages when they were first discovered inside the trucks at the desert airstrip. Moreover, our previous decisions indicate that the officers acted permissibly by waiting until they returned to DEA headquarters before they searched the vehicles and removed their contents. There is no requirement that the warrantless search of a vehicle occur contemporaneously with its lawful seizure. . . . '[The] justification to conduct such a warrantless search does not vanish once the car has been immobilized. . . .' A vehicle lawfully in police custody may be searched on the basis of probable cause to believe that it contains contraband, and there is no requirement of exigent circumstances to justify such a warrantless search."

"The Court of Appeals concluded that *Ross* allows warrantless searches of containers only if the search occurs 'immediately' as part of the vehicle inspection or 'soon thereafter. . . .' Neither *Ross* nor our other vehicle search cases suggest any such limitation. The Court concluded that the police were entitled to open the containers discovered inside without first obtaining a warrant. *Ross* did not suggest that this conclusion was affected by the fact that the leather pouch was not searched until after the police had impounded the vehicle or by the existence of exigent circumstances that might have made it impractical to secure a warrant for the search of the container. Instead, *Ross* indicated that the legality of the search was determined by reference to the exception to the warrant requirement."

"Because the Customs officers had probable cause to believe that the pickup trucks contained contraband, any expectation of privacy in the vehicles or their contents was subject to the authority of the officers to conduct a warrantless search."

"[W]here police officers are entitled to seize the container and continue to have probable cause to believe that it contains contraband, we do not think that delay in the execution of the warrantless search is necessarily unreasonable."

"Inasmuch as the Government was entitled to seize the packages and could have searched them immediately without a warrant, we conclude that the warrantless search three days after the packages were placed in the DEA warehouse was reasonable. . . ."

3. Warrants and Vehicle Searches

a. Is a Warrant Required to Search a Vehicle If Police Have Probable Cause?

Carroll v. United States, 267 U.S. 132 (1925)
Vote: 7-2
FACTS: Officers Cronenwett and Scully were in an apartment in Grand Rapids when three men arrived who wished to sell whiskey. The three men (two of whom were John Carroll and George Kiro) said they had to go to the east end of Grand Rapids to get the liquor and that they would be back in half or three-quarters of an hour. One of the men returned and stated that they could not get it that day but that they could the next. The proposed vendors did not return the next day and the evidence disclosed no explanation of their failure to do so. However, the officers noted their car and plate number. On a different occasion, Cronenwett and his subordinates were engaged in patrolling the road leading from Detroit to Grand Rapids, looking for violations of the Prohibition Act, and Carroll and Kiro passed Cronenwett and Scully some distance out from Grand Rapids. The officers followed but lost trace of them. Two months later, Kiro and Carroll passed them in the same automobile traveling toward Grand Rapids from the direction of Detroit. The agents followed the defendants to a point some sixteen miles east of Grand Rapids, where they stopped them and searched the car. They found behind the upholstering of the seats, the filling of which had been removed, sixty-eight bottles. When the defendants were arrested, Carroll said to Cronenwett, "Take the liquor and give us one more chance and I will make it right with you," and he pulled out a roll of bills.
ISSUE: Do police need a warrant to stop a car and search for contraband if they have probable cause?
HOLDING: No.
RATIONALE: "On reason and authority the true rule is that if the search and seizure without a warrant are made upon probable cause, that is, upon a belief, reasonably arising out of circumstances known to the seizing officer, that an automobile or other vehicle contains that which by law is subject to seizure and destruction, the search and seizure are valid."

"[W]e find in the first Congress, and in the following Second and Fourth Congresses, a difference made as to the necessity for a search warrant between goods subject to forfeiture, when concealed in a dwelling house or similar place, and like goods in course of transportation and concealed in a movable vessel where they readily could be put out of reach of a search warrant."

"[S]ince the beginning of the Government, [the Court's rulings can be seen] as recognizing a necessary difference between a search of a store, dwelling house or other structure in respect of which a proper official warrant readily may be obtained, and a search of a ship, motor boat, wagon or automobile, for contraband goods, where it is not practicable to secure a warrant because the vehicle can be quickly moved out of the locality or jurisdiction. . . ."

"The measure of legality of such a seizure is, therefore, that the seizing officer shall have reasonable or probable cause for believing that the automobile which he stops and seizes has contraband liquor therein which is being illegally transported. . . ."

"In cases where seizure is impossible except without warrant, the seizing officer acts unlawfully and at his peril unless he can show the court probable cause."

"In the light of these authorities, and what is shown by this record, it is clear the officers here had justification for the search and seizure."

b. Does a Warrantless Search of a Car That Takes Place at the Police Station after an Arrest Violate the Fourth Amendment?

Chambers v. Maroney, 399 U.S. 42 (1970)
Vote: 7-1

FACTS: A gas station was robbed by two men, each of whom displayed a gun and took money from the cash register. Two teenagers saw the car speed away from a parking lot, and about the same time, they learned that the station had been robbed. They reported to police that four men were in the car and one was wearing a green sweater. Stephen Kovacich told the police that one of the men was wearing a green sweater and the other was wearing a trench coat. A description of the car and the two robbers was broadcast over the police radio. A light blue compact station wagon mirroring the description and carrying four men was stopped by the police. Chambers was one of the men in the car and was wearing a green sweater. A trench coat was also in the car. The occupants were arrested and the car was driven to the police station where it was searched and where police found two revolvers, a glove containing small change, and cards bearing the name of an attendant at a different station. During the warrant-authorized search of Chambers's home, police seized other evidence and he was convicted of both robberies.

ISSUE: Can police conduct a warrantless search of a car at the station after an arrest?
HOLDING: Yes.
RATIONALE: "[F]or the police had probable cause to believe that the robbers, carrying guns and the fruits of the crime, had fled the scene in a light blue compact station wagon which would be carrying four men, one wearing a green sweater and another wearing a trench coat. As the state courts correctly held, there was probable cause to arrest the occupants of the station wagon that the officers stopped; just as obviously was there probable cause to search the car for guns and stolen money."

"On the facts before us, the blue station wagon could have been searched on the spot when it was stopped since there was probable cause to search and it was a fleeting target for a search. The probable-cause factor still obtained at the station house."

c. Do Police Need a Warrant to Search a Car If They Have Probable Cause That Drugs Are Present?

Pennsylvania v. LaBron, 518 U.S. 938 (1996)
Vote: 7-2
FACTS: Police observed Edwin Labron and others engaging in drug transactions. They arrested them and searched the trunk of a car from which the drugs had been produced. In it they found bags of cocaine. The Pennsylvania Supreme Court agreed with the trial court that the drugs should be suppressed, interpreting the law as requiring probable cause and exigent circumstances before the police could conduct a warrantless search of a car.

In an associated case, *Pennsylvania v. Kilgore,* an informant agreed to buy drugs from Kelly Jo Kilgore. Kilgore drove from the parking lot where the deal was made to a farmhouse where she met with Randy Kilgore and obtained the drugs. After the drugs were delivered and the Kilgores were arrested, police searched the farmhouse with the consent of its owner and searched Randy's truck; they had seen the Kilgores walking to and from the truck, which was parked in the driveway of the farmhouse. The search turned up cocaine on the truck's floor.

ISSUE: Do police need to obtain a warrant to search a car if they have probable cause but no exigency to justify the lack of a warrant?

HOLDING: No.

RATIONALE: "In these two cases, the Supreme Court of Pennsylvania held that the Fourth Amendment, as applied to the States through the Fourteenth, requires police to obtain a warrant before searching an automobile unless exigent circumstances are present. Because the holdings rest on an incorrect reading of the automobile exception to the Fourth Amendment's warrant requirement, we . . . reverse."

"The Supreme Court of Pennsylvania held the rule permitting warrantless searches of automobiles is limited to cases where 'unforeseen circumstances involving the search of an automobile [are] coupled with the presence of probable cause. . . .' This was incorrect. Our first cases establishing the automobile exception to the Fourth Amendment's warrant requirement were based on the automobile's 'ready mobility,' an exigency sufficient to excuse failure to obtain a search warrant once probable cause to conduct the search is clear. . . . If a car is readily mobile and probable cause exists to believe it contains contraband, the Fourth Amendment thus permits police to search the vehicle without more. . . . As the state courts found, there was probable cause in both of these cases. . . ."

4. Expectation of privacy

Cardwell v. Lewis, 417 U.S. 583 (1974)
Vote: 5-4
FACTS: Paul Radcliffe's body was found near his car on the banks of the Olentangy River in Delaware County, Ohio. The car had gone over the embankment and had come to rest in brush. Radcliffe had died from shotgun wounds. Casts were made of

tire tracks at the scene and foreign paint scrapings were removed from the right rear fender of his car. The investigation focused on Arthur Ben Lewis Jr. because he had known Radcliffe. Apparently, Lewis had been negotiating the sale of a business and the purchaser employed Radcliffe to examine Lewis's books. Police went to Lewis's place of business to question him and observed the model and color of his car with the thought that it might have been used to push Radcliffe's car over the embankment. Several months later Lewis was asked to appear at the police station. An arrest warrant was obtained and the determination was also made that police also had probable cause to believe that Lewis's car was used in the crime.

Police were in possession of the arrest warrant for the entire period that Lewis was present, he was not arrested until late afternoon. A tow truck took the car to the impoundment lot. The impounded car was examined the next day and the tread of its right rear tire was found to match the cast of a tire impression made at the scene of the crime. Additionally, the technician testified that the foreign paint on the fender of Radcliffe's car was not different from the paint samples taken from Lewis's vehicle.

ISSUE: Does an individual have the same right to privacy in their car as in their home?

HOLDING: No.

RATIONALE: "There is still another distinguishing factor. 'The search of an automobile is far less intrusive on the rights protected by the Fourth Amendment than the search of one's person or of a building. . . .' One has a lesser expectation of privacy in a motor vehicle because its function is transportation and it seldom serves as one's residence or as the repository of personal effects. A car has little capacity for escaping public scrutiny. It travels public thoroughfares where both its occupants and its contents are in plain view. . . . 'What a person knowingly exposes to the public, even in his own home or office, is not a subject of Fourth Amendment protection. . . .'"

"In the present case, nothing from the interior of the car and no personal effects, which the Fourth Amendment traditionally has been deemed to protect, were searched or seized and introduced in evidence. With the 'search' limited to the examination of the tire on the wheel and the taking of paint scrapings from the exterior of the vehicle left in the public parking lot, we fail to comprehend what expectation of privacy was infringed. . . . Under circumstances such as these, where probable cause exists, a warrantless examination of the exterior of a car is not unreasonable under the Fourth and Fourteenth Amendments."

B. Actions Officer May Take after Stopping a Vehicle

1. Ordering a Driver Out of the Car

Pennsylvania v. Mimms, 434 U.S. 106 (1977)
Vote: 6-3
FACTS: Two Philadelphia officers observed Harry Mimms driving a car with an expired license plate. They stopped the vehicle to issue a traffic ticket. One of the officers

approached Mimms and asked him to step out of the car and produce his license and registration. The officer noticed a bulge under Mimms's jacket. Suspecting that the bulge might be a weapon, the officer frisked Mimms and discovered a loaded .38 caliber revolver. The other occupant was also carrying a gun. Mimms was indicted and convicted for carrying a concealed weapon and for unlawfully carrying a firearm without a license.

ISSUE: Can police order a driver out of a car during a lawful traffic stop?

HOLDING: Yes.

RATIONALE: "Rather than conversing while standing exposed to moving traffic, the officer prudently may prefer to ask the driver of the vehicle to step out of the car and off onto the shoulder of the road where the inquiry may be pursued with greater safety to both."

"Against this important interest we are asked to weigh the intrusion into the driver's personal liberty . . . by the order to get out of the car. We think this additional intrusion can only be described as *de minimis*. The driver is being asked to expose to view very little more of his person than is already exposed. The police have already lawfully decided that the driver shall be briefly detained; the only question is whether he shall spend that period sitting in the driver's seat of his car or standing alongside it. Not only is the insistence of the police on the latter choice not a 'serious intrusion upon the sanctity of the person,' but it hardly rises to the level of a 'petty indignity. . . .' What is at most a mere inconvenience cannot prevail when balanced against legitimate concerns for the officer's safety."

2. Ordering Passengers Out of the Car

Maryland v. Wilson 519 U.S. 408 (1997)

Vote: 7-2

FACTS: Maryland State Trooper David Hughes observed a car driving sixty-four miles per hour in an area posted with a speed limit of fifty-five. The car had no license tag and there was a piece of paper reading "Enterprise Rent-A-Car" hanging from its rear. He signaled the car to pull over, but it continued driving for another mile and a half. Hughes noticed that two of three passengers looked at him several times, ducking below sight level and then reappearing. As Hughes approached the car, the driver, Jerry Lee Wilson, exited the car and met Hughes. Wilson appeared nervous but produced a license, and Hughes told him to return to the car and retrieve the rental documents. While the driver was looking for the papers, Hughes ordered the passengers out of the car. When one of them exited, cocaine fell to the ground. Wilson was arrested and charged with possession of cocaine with intent to distribute.

ISSUE: Can police order a passenger out of a car during a lawful traffic stop?

HOLDING: Yes.

RATIONALE: "We must therefore now decide whether the rule of *Mimms* applies to passengers as well as to drivers. On the public interest side of the balance, the same weighty interest in officer safety is present regardless of whether the occupant of the stopped car is a driver or passenger. Regrettably, traffic stops may be dangerous encounters. . . . In the case of passengers, the danger of the officer's standing in the path of oncoming traffic would not be present except in the case of a passenger in the left rear seat, but the fact that there is more than one occupant of the vehicle increases the possible sources of harm to the officer."

"[A]s a practical matter, the passengers are already stopped by virtue of the stop of the vehicle. The only change in their circumstances which will result from ordering them out of the car is that they will be outside of, rather than inside of, the stopped car. Outside the car, the passengers will be denied access to any possible weapon that might be concealed in the interior of the passenger compartment. . . . And the motivation of a passenger to employ violence to prevent apprehension of such a crime is every bit as great as that of the driver."

"In summary, danger to an officer from a traffic stop is likely to be greater when there are passengers in addition to the driver in the stopped car. While there is not the same basis for ordering the passengers out of the car as there is for ordering the driver out, the additional intrusion on the passenger is minimal. We therefore hold that an officer making a traffic stop may order passengers to get out of the car pending completion of the stop."

3. Asking Questions of Driver and Passenger

Berkemer v. McCarty, 468 U.S. 420 (1984)
Vote: 9-0
FACTS: Ohio State Highway Patrol Trooper Williams saw Rick McCarty driving erratically. Williams forced him to stop and asked him to get out of the vehicle. Williams noticed that McCarty was having difficulty standing and concluded that he would be charged with a traffic offense. However, McCarty was not told that he would be taken into custody. When Williams asked him to perform a "balancing test," McCarty could not do so. Williams asked him if he had been using intoxicants, and he replied that "he had consumed two beers and had smoked several joints of marijuana a short time before." His speech was slurred, and Williams placed McCarty under arrest and transported him to jail. At the jail, he was given a test to determine the amount of alcohol in his blood. The test did not detect any alcohol in McCarty's system. Williams then resumed questioning in order to obtain information for the report. McCarty answered that he had been drinking, and when then asked if he was under the influence of alcohol, he said, "I guess, barely." Williams next asked him whether the marihuana he had smoked had been treated with chemicals, and he indicated that it had not. At no point did Williams recite McCarty his rights. McCarty was charged with operating a motor vehicle while under the influence of alcohol and/or drugs and pleaded "no contest."
ISSUE: Can police ask incriminating questions of drivers during traffic stops?
HOLDING: Yes.
RATIONALE: "[T]he usual traffic stop is more analogous to a so-called '*Terry* [*v. Ohio*, 392 U.S. 1 (1968)] stop'. . . than to a formal arrest. . . . Typically, this means that the officer may ask the detainee a moderate number of questions to determine his identity

and to try to obtain information confirming or dispelling the officer's suspicions. But the detainee is not obliged to respond. And, unless the detainee's answers provide the officer with probable cause to arrest him, he must then be released. The comparatively nonthreatening character of detentions of this sort explains the absence of any suggestion in our opinions that *Terry* stops are subject to the dictates of [*Miranda v. Arizona*, 384 U.S. 436 (1966)]."

"We conclude, in short, that respondent was not taken into custody for the purposes of *Miranda* until Williams arrested him. Consequently, the statements respondent made prior to that point were admissible against him."

4. Searching Passenger's Belongings

Wyoming v. Houghton, 526 U.S. 295 (1999)
Vote: 6-3

FACTS: A Wyoming Highway Patrol officer stopped an automobile for speeding and driving with a faulty brake light. Three passengers were in the front seat: David Young (the driver), his girlfriend, and Sandra Houghton. While questioning Young, the officer noticed a syringe in his pocket. He then told Young to step out of the car and place the syringe on the hood. The officer asked him why he had the syringe, and he replied that he used it to take drugs. The backup officers ordered the female passengers out of the car and asked them for identification. Houghton falsely identified herself as "Sandra James" and stated that she did not have any identification. Meanwhile, the officer searched the passenger compartment of the car for contraband. On the backseat, he found Houghton's purse, and removed a wallet containing her license. When the officer asked her why she had lied, she replied, "In case things went bad." The officer also found a brown pouch and a container. Houghton admitted owning the container, which was also found to contain drug paraphernalia and a syringe with methamphetamine. The officer also found track marks on her arms and arrested her for felony possession of methamphetamine in a liquid amount greater than three-tenths of a gram, and a jury convicted her.

ISSUE: Can police search a passenger's belongings inside a car for contraband when they have probable cause to search the car?

HOLDING: Yes.

RATIONALE: "[N]either [*United States* v. *Ross*, 456 U.S. 798 (1982)] itself nor the historical evidence it relied upon admits of a distinction among packages or containers based on ownership. When there is probable cause to search for contraband in a car, it is reasonable for police officers—like customs officials in the Founding era—to examine packages and containers without a showing of individualized probable cause for each one. A passenger's personal belongings, just like the driver's belongings or containers attached to the car like a glove compartment, are 'in' the car, and the officer has probable cause to search for contraband *in* the car."

"[T]raumatic consequences are not to be expected when the police examine an item of personal property found in a car."

"Whereas the passenger's privacy expectations are, as we have described, considerably diminished, the governmental interests at stake are substantial. Effective law enforcement would be appreciably impaired without the ability to search a passenger's personal belongings when there is reason to believe contraband or evidence of criminal wrongdoing is hidden in the car. . . . A criminal might be able to hide contraband in a passenger's belongings as readily as in other containers in the car . . . perhaps even surreptitiously, without the passenger's knowledge or permission."

"To be sure, these factors favoring a search will not always be present, but the balancing of interests must be conducted with an eye to the generality of cases. To require that the investigating officer have positive reason to believe that the passenger and driver were engaged in a common enterprise, or positive reason to believe that the driver had time and occasion to conceal the item in the passenger's belongings, surreptitiously or with friendly permission, is to impose requirements so seldom met that a 'passenger's property' rule would dramatically reduce the ability to find and seize contraband and evidence of crime."

"We hold that police officers with probable cause to search a car may inspect passengers' belongings found in the car that are capable of concealing the object of the search."

5. Locating the Vehicle Identification Number

New York v. Class, 475 U.S. 106 (1986)
Vote: 5-4
FACTS: New York City police officers Lawrence Meyer and William McNamee observed Benigno Class speeding with a cracked windshield and pulled him over. Class then approached Meyer, and McNamee went directly to his vehicle. Class provided Meyer with registration and proof of insurance, but stated that he had no license. McNamee opened the door of the car to look for the VIN, which is located on the left doorjamb in automobiles manufactured before 1969. When the officer did not find the VIN, he reached into the car to move some papers obscuring the area where the VIN is located in later models. In doing so, McNamee saw the handle of a gun protruding from underneath the driver's seat and seized it. Class was arrested for, and convicted of, criminal possession of a weapon in the third degree.
ISSUE: Can police move papers concealing the Vehicle Identification Number?
HOLDING: Yes.
RATIONALE: "[T]he VIN plays an important part in the pervasive regulation by the government of the automobile. A motorist must surely expect that such regulation will on occasion require the State to determine the VIN of his or her vehicle, and the individual's reasonable expectation of privacy in the VIN is thereby diminished. This is especially true in the case of a driver who has committed a traffic violation. . . . In addition, it is unreasonable to have an expectation of privacy in an object required by law to be located in a place ordinarily in plain view from the exterior of the automobile. The VIN's mandated visibility makes it more similar to the exterior of the car than to

the trunk or glove compartment. The exterior of a car, of course, is thrust into the public eye, and thus to examine it does not constitute a 'search.'"

"We think it makes no difference that the papers in respondent's car obscured the VIN from the plain view of the officer. We have recently emphasized that efforts to restrict access to an area do not generate a reasonable expectation of privacy where none would otherwise exist. . . . The mere viewing of the formerly obscured VIN was not, therefore, a violation of the Fourth Amendment."

"If respondent had remained in the car, the police would have been justified in asking him to move the papers obscuring the VIN. New York law authorizes a demand by officers to see the VIN . . . and even if the state law were not explicit on this point we have no difficulty in concluding that a demand to inspect the VIN, like a demand to see license and registration papers, is within the scope of police authority pursuant to a traffic violation stop. . . . In light of the danger to the officers' safety that would have been presented by returning respondent immediately to his car, we think the search to obtain the VIN was not prohibited by the Fourth Amendment."

"All three of the factors involved in [*Pennsylvania v. Mimms*, 434 U.S. 106 (1977)] and [*Michigan v. Summers*, 452 U.S. 692 (1981)] are present in this case: the safety of the officers was served by the governmental intrusion; the intrusion was minimal; and the search stemmed from some probable cause focusing suspicion on the individual affected by the search. Indeed, here the officers' probable cause stemmed from directly observing respondent commit a violation of the law."

"When we undertake the necessary balancing of 'the nature and quality of the intrusion on the individual's Fourth Amendment interests against the importance of the governmental interests alleged to justify the intrusion . . .' the conclusion that the search here was permissible follows. As we recognized in [*Delaware v. Prouse*, 440 U.S. 648 (1979)], the search was focused in its objective and no more intrusive than necessary to fulfill that objective. The search was far less intrusive than a formal arrest, which would have been permissible for a traffic offense under New York law . . . and little more intrusive than a demand that respondent—under the eyes of the officers—move the papers himself."

C. Vehicle Searches

1. Searching the Entire Vehicle

United States v. Ross, 456 U.S. 798 (1982)
Vote: 6-3
FACTS: A reliable informant called the District of Columbia Police Department and told Detective Marcum that "Bandit" was selling narcotics kept in the trunk of a car, that he had just observed him complete a sale, and that "Bandit" had told him that more drugs were in the trunk. The informant gave Marcum a description of him and stated that the car was a "purplish maroon" Chevrolet Malibu with District of Columbia

plates. Detectives Marcum and Cassidy and Sergeant Gonzales found a parked maroon Malibu. A license check disclosed that the car was registered to Albert Ross; a computer check revealed that he fit the description and used the alias "Bandit." They pulled alongside the car, noticed that the driver matched the description, and stopped. Marcum and Cassidy told Ross to get out of the vehicle. While they searched him, Gonzales discovered a bullet on the car's front seat. He then searched the interior and found a pistol in the glove box. After Ross was arrested, Cassidy took the keys, opened the trunk, and found a paper bag that contained glassine bags containing heroin. Cassidy replaced the bag, closed the trunk, and drove the car to headquarters. At the station, Cassidy thoroughly searched the car and found a zippered red leather pouch that contained $3,200. No warrant was obtained. Ross was charged with possession of heroin with intent to distribute and convicted.

ISSUE: If the police have probable cause to search a car, can they search the entire car and open any packages or containers that may hide the object of their search without a warrant?

HOLDING: Yes.

RATIONALE: "In short, the exception to the warrant requirement established in [*Carroll v. United States*, 267 U.S. 132 (1925)]—the scope of which we consider in this case—applies only to searches of vehicles that are supported by probable cause. In this class of cases, a search is not unreasonable if based on facts that would justify the issuance of a warrant, even though a warrant has not actually been obtained."

"[I]n this case the parties have squarely addressed the question whether, in the course of a legitimate warrantless search of an automobile, police are entitled to open containers found within the vehicle. We now address that question. Its answer is determined by the scope of the search that is authorized by the exception to the warrant requirement set forth in *Carroll*."

"In its application of *Carroll*, this Court in fact has sustained warrantless searches of containers found during a lawful search of an automobile. . . ."

"It is therefore significant that the practical consequences of the *Carroll* decision would be largely nullified if the permissible scope of a warrantless search of an automobile did not include containers and packages found inside the vehicle. Contraband goods rarely are strewn across the trunk or floor of a car; since by their very nature such goods must be withheld from public view, they rarely can be placed in an automobile unless they are enclosed within some form of container. The Court in *Carroll* held that 'contraband goods *concealed* and illegally transported in an automobile or other vehicle may be searched for without a warrant. . . .' As we noted in *Henry v. United States* [361 U.S. 98 (1959)] . . . the decision in *Carroll* 'merely relaxed the requirements for a warrant on grounds of practicability.' It neither broadened nor limited the scope of a lawful search based on probable cause."

"A warrant to search a vehicle would support a search of every part of the vehicle that might contain the object of the search. When a legitimate search is under way, and when its purpose and its limits have been precisely defined, nice distinctions between closets, drawers, and containers, in the case of a home, or between glove compartments, upholstered seats, trunks, and wrapped packages, in the case of a vehicle, must give way to the interest in the prompt and efficient completion of the task at hand."

"The scope of a warrantless search of an automobile thus is not defined by the nature of the container in which the contraband is secreted. Rather, it is defined by the object of the search and the places in which there is probable cause to believe that it may be found."

"The exception recognized in *Carroll* is unquestionably one that is 'specifically established and well delineated.' We hold that the scope of the warrantless search authorized by that exception is no broader and no narrower than a magistrate could legitimately authorize by warrant. If probable cause justifies the search of a lawfully stopped vehicle, it justifies the search of every part of the vehicle and its contents that may conceal the object of the search."

2. Search of Passenger Compartment

a. First Contact While Arrestee Is in Vehicle

New York v. Belton, 453 U.S. 454 (1981)
Vote: 6-3
FACTS: A speeding automobile passed New York State trooper Douglas Nicot, who gave chase. He overtook the speeding vehicle and ordered its driver to pull over. There were four men in the car, one of whom was Roger Belton. Nicot asked to see the license and registration and discovered that none of the men owned the vehicle or was related to its owner. Meanwhile, Nicot had smelled burnt marihuana and saw on the floor of the car an envelope marked "Supergold." He directed the men to get out of the car and placed them under arrest for the unlawful possession of marihuana. He patted down each of the men and "split them up into four separate areas of the Thruway at this time so they would not be in physical touching area of each other." He then picked up the envelope and found that it contained marihuana. He also searched each of the men and then the passenger compartment of the car. On the back seat he found a black leather jacket belonging to Belton. He unzipped one of the pockets of the jacket and discovered cocaine. Placing the jacket in his automobile, he drove the four arrestees to a nearby police station. Belton was indicted for criminal possession of a controlled substance. He pleaded guilty to a lesser included offense and preserved his claim that the cocaine had been seized in violation of the Fourth and Fourteenth Amendments.
ISSUE: Can police search the passenger compartment of a car and any containers found inside as part of a valid arrest of the occupants?
HOLDING: Yes.
RATIONALE: "Our reading of the cases suggests the generalization that articles inside the relatively narrow compass of the passenger compartment of an automobile are in fact generally, even if not inevitably, within 'the area into which an arrestee might reach in order to grab a weapon or evidentiary [item]. . . .' Accordingly, we hold that when a policeman has made a lawful custodial arrest of the occupant of an automobile, he

may, as a contemporaneous incident of that arrest, search the passenger compartment of that automobile."

"It follows from this conclusion that the police may also examine the contents of any containers found within the passenger compartment, for if the passenger compartment is within reach of the arrestee, so also will containers in it be within his reach. . . . Such a container may, of course, be searched whether it is open or closed."

"'Container' here denotes any object capable of holding another object. It thus includes closed or open glove compartments, consoles, or other receptacles located anywhere within the passenger compartment, as well as luggage, boxes, bags, clothing, and the like. Our holding encompasses only the interior of the passenger compartment of an automobile and does not encompass the trunk."

"It seems to have been the theory of the Court of Appeals that the search and seizure in the present case could not have been incident to the respondent's arrest, because Trooper Nicot, by the very act of searching the respondent's jacket and seizing the contents of its pocket, had gained 'exclusive control' of them. . . . But under this fallacious theory no search or seizure incident to a lawful custodial arrest would ever be valid; by seizing an article even on the arrestee's person, an officer may be said to have reduced that article to his 'exclusive control.'"

b. First Contact after Arrestee Is outside of the Vehicle

Thornton v. United States, 541 U.S. 615 (2004)
Vote: 7-2
FACTS: Officer Deion Nichols of the Norfolk, Virginia, Police Department was driving an unmarked car and noticed Marcus Thornton driving a Lincoln Town Car. Nichols slowed down so as to avoid driving next to him, then pulled off onto a side street, and Thornton passed him. Nichols then ran a check on Thornton's license tags, which revealed that they had been issued to a 1982 Chevy, not to a Lincoln Town Car. When Thornton drove into a parking lot and got out of the vehicle, Nichols stopped him and asked him for his license, saying that his license tags did not match the vehicle. Thornton became nervous, and Nichols asked if he had any narcotics or weapons on him or in his vehicle, to which Thornton said "No." He then agreed to let Nichols pat him down, and Nichols felt a bulge in his pocket. Thornton then admitted that he had drugs on him and Nichols reached into his pocket and pulled out bags containing marijuana and crack cocaine. Nichols then arrested Thornton and searched his car, finding a handgun under the seat. Thornton was indicted for possession with intent to distribute cocaine base, possession of a firearm after having been previously convicted of a crime punishable by a term of imprisonment exceeding one year, and possession of a firearm in furtherance of a drug trafficking crime. He was convicted and argued on appeal that the seizure of the gun was a violation of the Fourth Amendment.
ISSUE: May the police search the passenger compartment of a car if the police make first contact with the arrestee only after he leaves the car?
HOLDING: Yes.

RATIONALE: "In [*New York v. Belton*, 453 U.S. 454 (1981)] we held that 'when a policeman has made a lawful custodial arrest of the occupant of an automobile, he may, as a contemporaneous incident of that arrest, search the passenger compartment of that automobile.'"

"In so holding, we placed no reliance on the fact that the officer in *Belton* ordered the occupants out of the vehicle, or initiated contact with them while they remained within it. Nor do we find such a factor persuasive in distinguishing the current situation, as it bears no logical relationship to *Belton*'s rationale. There is simply no basis to conclude that the span of the area generally within the arrestee's immediate control is determined by whether the arrestee exited the vehicle at the officer's direction, or whether the officer initiated contact with him while he remained in the car."

"The stress is no less merely because the arrestee exited his car before the officer initiated contact, nor is an arrestee less likely to attempt to lunge for a weapon or to destroy evidence if he is outside of, but still in control of, the vehicle. In either case, the officer faces a highly volatile situation. It would make little sense to apply two different rules to what is, at bottom, the same situation."

"Petitioner argues, however, that *Belton* will fail to provide a 'bright-line' rule if it applies to more than vehicle 'occupants.' But *Belton* allows police to search the passenger compartment of a vehicle incident to a lawful custodial arrest of both 'occupants' and 'recent occupants. . . .' In any event, while an arrestee's status as a 'recent occupant' may turn on his temporal or spatial relationship to the car at the time of the arrest and search, it certainly does not turn on whether he was inside or outside the car at the moment that the officer first initiated contact with him."

"Once an officer determines that there is probable cause to make an arrest, it is reasonable to allow officers to ensure their safety and to preserve evidence by searching the entire passenger compartment."

"Rather than clarifying the constitutional limits of a *Belton* search, petitioner's 'contact initiation' rule would obfuscate them. Under petitioner's proposed rule, an officer approaching a suspect who has just alighted from his vehicle would have to determine whether he actually confronted or signaled confrontation with the suspect while he remained in the car, or whether the suspect exited his vehicle unaware of, and for reasons unrelated to, the officer's presence. This determination would be inherently subjective and highly fact specific, and would require precisely the sort of ad hoc determinations on the part of officers in the field and reviewing courts that *Belton* sought to avoid. . . . So long as an arrestee is the sort of 'recent occupant' of a vehicle such as petitioner was here, officers may search that vehicle incident to the arrest."

3. Search of Containers

California v. Acevedo, 500 U.S. 565 (1991)
Vote: 6-3
FACTS: Officer Coleman of the Santa Ana, California, Police Department received a call from a drug enforcement agent in Hawaii. The agent informed Coleman that he

had seized a package containing marijuana which was to have been delivered to the Federal Express Office in Santa Ana and which was addressed to J. R. Daza. The agent arranged to send the package to Coleman instead. Coleman then was to take the package to the Federal Express office and arrest the person who arrived to claim it. Jamie Daza, arrived to claim the package, accepted it, and drove to his apartment, where he carried the package inside. Officers observed Daza come out and drop the box and paper that had contained the marijuana into a trash bin. Coleman at that point left the scene to get a search warrant. Officers then saw Richard St. George leave the apartment carrying a knapsack that appeared to be half full. The officers stopped him as he was driving off, searched the knapsack, and found one and a half pounds of marijuana.

Charles Steven Acevedo entered Daza's apartment, stayed for ten minutes, and reappeared carrying a brown bag that looked full. The officers noticed that the bag was the size of one of the wrapped marijuana packages from Hawaii. Acevedo walked to a car in the parking lot, placed the bag in the trunk, and started to drive away. Officers stopped him, opened the trunk and the bag, and found marijuana. Acevedo was charged with possession of marijuana for sale. He pleaded guilty but appealed the denial of the suppression motion.

ISSUE: Can police conduct a warrantless search of a paper bag found in the trunk of a car if they have probable cause that the bag contained marijuana?

HOLDING: Yes.

RATIONALE: "We now must decide the question deferred in [*United States v. Ross*, 456 U.S. 798 (1982)]: whether the Fourth Amendment requires the police to obtain a warrant to open the sack in a movable vehicle simply because they lack probable cause to search the entire car. We conclude that it does not."

"We now agree that a container found after a general search of the automobile and a container found in a car after a limited search for the container are equally easy for the police to store and for the suspect to hide or destroy. In fact, we see no principled distinction in terms of either the privacy expectation or the exigent circumstances between the paper bag found by the police in *Ross* and the paper bag found by the police here. Furthermore, by attempting to distinguish between a container for which the police are specifically searching and a container which they come across in a car, we have provided only minimal protection for privacy and have impeded effective law enforcement."

"At the moment when officers stop an automobile, it may be less than clear whether they suspect with a high degree of certainty that the vehicle contains drugs in a bag or simply contains drugs. If the police know that they may open a bag only if they are actually searching the entire car, they may search more extensively than they otherwise would in order to establish the general probable cause required by *Ross*."

"We cannot see the benefit of a rule that requires law enforcement officers to conduct a more intrusive search in order to justify a less intrusive one."

"'Since the police, by hypothesis, have probable cause to seize the property, we can assume that a warrant will be routinely forthcoming in the overwhelming majority of cases. . . .' And the police often will be able to search containers without a warrant, despite the [*United States v. Chadwick*, 433 U.S. 1 (1977)]-[*Arkansas v. Sanders*, 442 U.S. 753 (1979)] rule, as a search incident to a lawful arrest."

"In light of the minimal protection to privacy afforded by the *Chadwick-Sanders* rule, and our serious doubt whether that rule substantially serves privacy interests, we now hold that the Fourth Amendment does not compel separate treatment for an automobile search that extends only to a container within the vehicle."

"We conclude that it is better to adopt one clear-cut rule to govern automobile searches and eliminate the warrant requirement for closed containers set forth in *Sanders.*"

"The interpretation of the [*Carroll v. United States*, 267 U.S. 132 (1925)] doctrine set forth in *Ross* now applies to all searches of containers found in an automobile. In other words, the police may search without a warrant if their search is supported by probable cause."

"It went on to note: 'Probable cause to believe that a container placed in the trunk of a taxi contains contraband or evidence does not justify a search of the entire cab.' We reaffirm that principle. In the case before us, the police had probable cause to believe that the paper bag in the automobile's trunk contained marijuana. That probable cause now allows a warrantless search of the paper bag. The facts in the record reveal that the police did not have probable cause to believe that contraband was hidden in any other part of the automobile and a search of the entire vehicle would have been without probable cause and unreasonable under the Fourth Amendment."

"We therefore interpret *Carroll* as providing one rule to govern all automobile searches. The police may search an automobile and the containers within it where they have probable cause to believe contraband or evidence is contained."

4. Searching of Automobiles Incident to Citation

a. Full-Blown Searches and Traffic Citations

Knowles v. Iowa, 525 U.S. 113 (1998)
Vote: 9-0
FACTS: An Iowa police officer stopped Patrick Knowles for speeding and issued a citation to Knowles, although under state law he might have arrested him. The officer then conducted a full search of the car, and under the driver's seat he found a bag of marijuana and a "pot pipe." Knowles was then arrested and charged with violation of state laws dealing with controlled substances. He was found guilty; however, the officer conceded that he did not have probable cause to conduct the search. Iowa law stated that the issuance of a citation in lieu of an arrest "does not affect the officer's authority to conduct an otherwise lawful search." The Iowa Supreme Court has interpreted this provision as providing authority to officers to conduct a full-blown search of an automobile and driver incident to citation.
ISSUE: Can the police conduct a full-blown search of an automobile incident to citation?

HOLDING: No.

RATIONALE: "In [*United States v. Robinson*, 414 U.S. 218 (1973)], we noted the two historical rationales for the 'search incident to arrest' exception: (1) the need to disarm the suspect in order to take him into custody, and (2) the need to preserve evidence for later use at trial. . . . But neither of these underlying rationales for the search incident to arrest exception is sufficient to justify the search in the present case."

"We have recognized that the first rationale—officer safety—is 'both legitimate and weighty. . . .' The threat to officer safety from issuing a traffic citation, however, is a good deal less than in the case of a custodial arrest. A routine traffic stop, on the other hand, is a relatively brief encounter and 'is more analogous to a so-called "*Terry* stop" [referring to *Terry v. Ohio*, 392 U.S. 1 (1968)] . . . than to a formal arrest.'"

"But while the concern for officer safety in this context may justify the 'minimal' additional intrusion of ordering a driver and passengers out of the car, it does not by itself justify the often considerably greater intrusion attending a full field-type search." "Nor has Iowa shown the second justification for the authority to search incident to arrest—the need to discover and preserve evidence. Once Knowles was stopped for speeding and issued a citation, all the evidence necessary to prosecute that offense had been obtained. No further evidence of excessive speed was going to be found either on the person of the offender or in the passenger compartment of the car."

"Iowa nevertheless argues that a 'search incident to citation' is justified because a suspect who is subject to a routine traffic stop may attempt to hide or destroy evidence related to his identity (e.g., a driver's license or vehicle registration), or destroy evidence of another, as yet undetected crime. As for the destruction of evidence relating to identity, if a police officer is not satisfied with the identification furnished by the driver, this may be a basis for arresting him rather than merely issuing a citation. As for destroying evidence of other crimes, the possibility that an officer would stumble onto evidence wholly unrelated to the speeding offense seems remote."

b. Can Police Use Canine Dogs Incident to Citation?

Illinois v. Caballes, 543 U.S. 405 (2005)
Vote: 6-2

FACTS: Illinois State Trooper Daniel Gillette stopped Roy I. Caballes, and a second trooper, Craig Graham, a member of the Illinois State Police Drug Interdiction Team, overheard the transmission and headed for the scene with his narcotics-detection dog. When they arrived, Caballes's car was on the shoulder of the road and he was in Gillette's vehicle. While Gillette was writing a ticket, Graham walked his dog around Caballes's car and the dog alerted at the trunk. Based on the alert, the officers searched the trunk, found marijuana, and arrested Caballes. The trial judge denied his motion to suppress and to quash his arrest and Caballes was convicted of a narcotics offense, sentenced to twelve years in jail, and fined $256,136.

ISSUE: Does a "dog sniff" during a lawful traffic stop violate the Fourth Amendment?

HOLDING: No.

RATIONALE: "Here, the initial seizure of respondent when he was stopped on the highway was based on probable cause, and was concededly lawful."

"Despite this conclusion, the Illinois Supreme Court held that the initially lawful traffic stop became an unlawful seizure solely as a result of the canine sniff that occurred outside respondent's stopped car. . . . In its view, the use of the dog converted the citizen-police encounter from a lawful traffic stop into a drug investigation, and because the shift in purpose was not supported by any reasonable suspicion that respondent possessed narcotics, it was unlawful. In our view, conducting a dog sniff would not change the character of a traffic stop that is lawful at its inception and otherwise executed in a reasonable manner, unless the dog sniff itself infringed respondent's constitutionally protected interest in privacy. Our cases hold that it did not."

"Accordingly, the use of a well-trained narcotics-detection dog—one that 'does not expose noncontraband items that otherwise would remain hidden from public view . . .' during a lawful traffic stop, generally does not implicate legitimate privacy interests. In this case, the dog sniff was performed on the exterior of respondent's car while he was lawfully seized for a traffic violation. Any intrusion on respondent's privacy expectations does not rise to the level of a constitutionally cognizable infringement."

"This conclusion is entirely consistent with our recent decision that the use of a thermal-imaging device to detect the growth of marijuana in a home constituted an unlawful search. . . . Critical to that decision was the fact that the device was capable of detecting lawful activity. . . . The legitimate expectation that information about perfectly lawful activity will remain private is categorically distinguishable from respondent's hopes or expectations concerning the nondetection of contraband in the trunk of his car. A dog sniff conducted during a concededly lawful traffic stop that reveals no information other than the location of a substance that no individual has any right to possess does not violate the Fourth Amendment."

5. Motor Homes

California v. Carney, 471 U.S. 386 (1985)
Vote: 6-3
FACTS: DEA agent Robert Williams watched Charles Carney approach a youth and accompany him to a motor home parked nearby and close the shades within. Williams had information that the same motor home was used by another person who was exchanging marihuana for sex. Williams and others kept the motor home under surveillance, and when the youth left, the agents stopped him. The youth then stated that he had received marihuana for sex. At the agents' request, the youth returned to the motor home and knocked on its door. Carney stepped out. The agents identified themselves, and without a warrant or consent, one agent entered and observed marihuana, plastic bags, and a scale. Williams took Carney into custody and took possession of the motor home. A subsequent search of the motor home at the station revealed marihuana in the cupboards and refrigerator. Carney was charged with possession of marihuana for sale; he pleaded nolo contendere but appealed from the order placing him on probation.

ISSUE: Can police conduct a warrantless search of a motor home if they have probable cause?

HOLDING: Yes.

RATIONALE: "[I]t is equally clear that the vehicle falls clearly within the scope of the exception laid down in [*Carroll v. United States*, 267 U.S. 132 (1925)] and applied in succeeding cases. Like the automobile in *Carroll*, respondent's motor home was readily mobile. Absent the prompt search and seizure, it could readily have been moved beyond the reach of the police. Furthermore, the vehicle was licensed to 'operate on public streets; [was] serviced in public places; . . . and [was] subject to extensive regulation and inspection. . . .' And the vehicle was so situated that an objective observer would conclude that it was being used not as a residence, but as a vehicle."

"Respondent urges us to distinguish his vehicle from other vehicles within the exception because it was *capable of functioning as a home*. . . . To distinguish between respondent's motor home and an ordinary sedan for purposes of the vehicle exception would require that we apply the exception depending upon the size of the vehicle and the quality of its appointments. Moreover, to fail to apply the exception to vehicles such as a motor home ignores the fact that a motor home lends itself easily to use as an instrument of illicit drug traffic and other illegal activity."

"Our application of the vehicle exception has never turned on the other uses to which a vehicle might be put. The exception has historically turned on the ready mobility of the vehicle, and on the presence of the vehicle in a setting that objectively indicates that the vehicle is being used for transportation."

6. Motor Boats

United States v. Villamonte-Marquez, 462 U.S. 579 (1983)
Vote: 6-3

FACTS: Congress has provided that any customs officer may at anytime board any vessel any place in the United States and examine the documents pertaining to the vessel and use necessary force to effect such inspections. Customs officers, accompanied by Louisiana State Police, were patrolling when they sighted a sailboat. Shortly after, the officers also observed a large freighter creating a huge wake and causing the smaller vessel to rock from side to side. The patrol boat then approached and the officers asked Hamparian if the sailboat and crew were all right. Hamparian shrugged his shoulders. Officers Wilkins and Dougherty boarded and asked to see the vessel's documentation. Hamparian handed Wilkins what appeared to be a request to change the registration of a ship. While examining the document, Wilkins smelled what he thought to be burning marihuana. Looking through an open hatch, Wilkins observed burlap-wrapped bales that proved to be marihuana. Villamonte-Marquez was on a sleeping bag atop the bales. Wilkins then arrested Hamparian and Villamonte-Marquez and a search revealed 5,800 pounds of marihuana. The two men were found guilty of conspiring to import marihuana, importing marihuana, and conspiring to possess marihuana with intent to distribute.

ISSUE: May customs officials conduct warrantless searches of vessels pursuant to a statute passed by Congress?

HOLDING: Yes.

RATIONALE: "This statute appears to be the lineal ancestor of the provision of present law upon which the Government relies to sustain the boarding of the vessel in this case. Title 19 U.S.C. § 1581(a) provides that '[any] officer of the customs may at any time go on board of any vessel . . . at any place in the United States or within the customs waters . . . and examine the manifest and other documents and papers. . . .'"

"In a lineal ancestor to the statute at issue here the First Congress clearly authorized the suspicionless boarding of vessels, reflecting its view that such boardings are not contrary to the Fourth Amendment; this gives the statute before us an impressive historical pedigree. . . . The nature of waterborne commerce in waters providing ready access to the open sea is sufficiently different from the nature of vehicular traffic on highways as to make possible alternatives to the sort of 'stop' made in this case less likely to accomplish the obviously essential governmental purposes involved. . . . The nature of the governmental interest in assuring compliance with documentation requirements, particularly in waters where the need to deter or apprehend smugglers is great, is substantial; the type of intrusion made in this case, while not minimal, is limited."

"All of these factors lead us to conclude that the action of the customs officers in stopping and boarding the *Henry Morgan II* was 'reasonable,' and was therefore consistent with the Fourth Amendment."

7. Is Luggage Considered Personal Property and Protected by the Fourth Amendment?

Bond v. United States, 529 U.S. 334 (2000)

Vote: 7-2

FACTS: Steven Dewayne Bond was a passenger on a bus that left California bound for Little Rock, Arkansas. The bus stopped at a border patrol checkpoint in Sierra Blanca, Texas. Border Patrol Agent Cesar Cantu boarded the bus to check immigration status. After satisfying himself that the passengers were lawfully in the United States, Cantu began walking toward the front and squeezed luggage in the overhead storage space. Cantu squeezed a green canvas bag and noticed that it contained a "brick-like" object. Bond admitted that the bag was his and agreed to allow Cantu to open it. Upon doing so, Cantu discovered a "brick" of methamphetamine. Bond was indicted for conspiracy to possess, and possession with intent to distribute, methamphetamine and found guilty.

ISSUE: Does the physical manipulation of a bus passenger's carry-on luggage by police violate the Fourth Amendment's proscription against unreasonable searches?

HOLDING: Yes.

RATIONALE: "A traveler's personal luggage is clearly an 'effect' protected by the Amendment. . . . Indeed, it is undisputed here that petitioner possessed a privacy interest in his bag."

"But the Government asserts that by exposing his bag to the public, petitioner lost a reasonable expectation that his bag would not be physically manipulated. The Government relies on our decisions in *California v. Ciraolo* [476 U.S. 207 (1986)], and *Florida v. Riley* [488 U.S. 445 (1989)] . . . for the proposition that matters open to public observation are not protected by the Fourth Amendment."

"But *Ciraolo* and *Riley* are different from this case because they involved only visual, as opposed to tactile, observation. Physically invasive inspection is simply more intrusive than purely visual inspection. . . . Although Agent Cantu did not 'frisk' petitioner's person, he did conduct a probing tactile examination of petitioner's carry-on luggage. Obviously, petitioner's bag was not part of his person. But travelers are particularly concerned about their carry-on luggage; they generally use it to transport personal items that, for whatever reason, they prefer to keep close at hand."

"Here, petitioner sought to preserve privacy by using an opaque bag and placing that bag directly above his seat. Second, we inquire whether the individual's expectation of privacy is 'one that society is prepared to recognize as reasonable. . . .' When a bus passenger places a bag in an overhead bin, he expects that other passengers or bus employees may move it for one reason or another. Thus, a bus passenger clearly expects that his bag may be handled. He does not expect that other passengers or bus employees will, as a matter of course, feel the bag in an exploratory manner. But this is exactly what the agent did here. We therefore hold that the agent's physical manipulation of petitioner's bag violated the Fourth Amendment."

8. Checkpoints and the Fourth Amendment

a. Alcohol

Michigan Department of State Police v. Sitz, 496 U.S. 444 (1990)
Vote: 6-3
FACTS: The Michigan Department of State Police established a sobriety checkpoint program in consultation with an advisory committee. The advisory committee created guidelines setting forth procedures governing checkpoint operations, site selection, and publicity. All vehicles passing through a checkpoint would be stopped and their drivers briefly examined for signs of intoxication. In cases where an officer detected signs of intoxication, the motorist would be directed to an officer who would make further checks and possibly arrest. All other drivers would be permitted to leave.

The average delay was about twenty-five seconds. One of two drivers detained was arrested for driving under the influence of alcohol. A third driver was pulled over by an officer in an observation vehicle and arrested for driving under the influence. A group of drivers filed a complaint against the checkpoints.
ISSUE: May police stop and briefly detain drivers at an alcohol checkpoint?
HOLDING: Yes.
RATIONALE: "This case poses the question whether a State's use of highway sobriety checkpoints violates the Fourth and Fourteenth Amendments to the United States Constitution. We hold that it does not. . . ."

"No one can seriously dispute the magnitude of the drunken driving problem or the States' interest in eradicating it. Media reports of alcohol-related death and mutilation on the Nation's roads are legion."

"Conversely, the weight bearing on the other scale—the measure of the intrusion on motorists stopped briefly at sobriety checkpoints—is slight. We reached a similar conclusion as to the intrusion on motorists subjected to a brief stop at a highway checkpoint for detecting illegal aliens. . . . We see virtually no difference between the levels of intrusion on law-abiding motorists from the brief stops necessary to the effectuation of these two types of checkpoints, which to the average motorist would seem identical save for the nature of the questions the checkpoint officers might ask."

"The circumstances surrounding a checkpoint stop and search are far less intrusive than those attending a roving-patrol stop. At traffic checkpoints the motorist can see that other vehicles are being stopped, he can see visible signs of the officers' authority, and he is much less likely to be frightened or annoyed by the intrusion. . . ."

"In sum, the balance of the State's interest in preventing drunken driving, the extent to which this system can reasonably be said to advance that interest, and the degree of intrusion upon individual motorists who are briefly stopped, weighs in favor of the state program. We therefore hold that it is consistent with the Fourth Amendment."

b. Aliens

United States v. Martinez-Fuerte, 428 U.S. 543 (1976)
Vote: 7-2
FACTS: Each of the defendants in the consolidated case was arrested at a checkpoint operated by the Border Patrol away from the Mexican border, and each argued that the evidence found at the checkpoint was inadmissible under the Fourth Amendment. Amado Martinez-Fuerte approached the checkpoint driving a vehicle containing two female passengers. The women were illegal Mexican aliens who had entered the United States by using false papers and met with Martinez-Fuerte in San Diego. At the checkpoint their car was directed to the inspection area and while Martinez-Fuerte proved that he was a lawful resident, his passengers admitted their unlawful presence. He was charged with two counts of illegally transporting aliens and convicted on both.
ISSUE: May the Border Patrol stop and briefly detain drivers at an alien checkpoint?
HOLDING: Yes.
RATIONALE: "While the need to make routine checkpoint stops is great, the consequent intrusion on Fourth Amendment interests is quite limited. The stop does intrude to a limited extent on motorists' right to 'free passage without interruption . . .' and arguably on their right to personal security. But it involves only a brief detention."

"Neither the vehicle nor its occupants are searched, and visual inspection of the vehicle is limited to what can be seen without a search. This objective intrusion—the stop itself, the questioning, and the visual inspection—also existed in roving-patrol stops. But we view checkpoint stops in a different light because the subjective intrusion—the generating of concern or even fright on the part of lawful travelers—is appreciably less in the case of a checkpoint stop."

"[T]he reasonableness of the procedures followed in making these checkpoint stops makes the resulting intrusion on the interests of motorists minimal. On the other hand, the purpose of the stops is legitimate and in the public interest, and the need for this enforcement technique is demonstrated by the records in the cases before us. Accordingly, we hold that the stops and questioning at issue may be made in the absence of any individualized suspicion at reasonably located checkpoints."

"We further believe that it is constitutional to refer motorists selectively to the secondary inspection area at the San Clemente checkpoint on the basis of criteria that would not sustain a roving-patrol stop. Thus, even if it be assumed that such referrals are made largely on the basis of apparent Mexican ancestry, we perceive no constitutional violation. . . . As the intrusion here is sufficiently minimal that no particularized reason need exist to justify it, we think it follows that the Border Patrol officers must have wide discretion in selecting the motorists to be diverted for the brief questioning involved."

"Sifuentes' alternative argument is that routine stops at a checkpoint are permissible only if a warrant has given judicial authorization to the particular checkpoint location and the practice of routine stops. A warrant requirement in these circumstances draws some support from [*Camara v. Municipal Court*, 387 U.S. 523 (1967)], where the Court held that, absent consent, an 'area' warrant was required to make a building code inspection, even though the search could be conducted absent cause to believe that there were violations in the building searched."

"We do not think, however, that *Camara* is an apt model. . . . The degree of intrusion upon privacy that may be occasioned by a search of a house hardly can be compared with the minor interference with privacy resulting from the mere stop for questioning as to residence. Moreover, the warrant requirement in *Camara* served specific Fourth Amendment interests to which a warrant requirement here would make little contribution."

"In summary, we hold that stops for brief questioning routinely conducted at permanent checkpoints are consistent with the Fourth Amendment and need not be authorized by warrant. . . . '[A]ny further detention . . . must be based on consent or probable cause.'"

c. Drugs

City of Indianapolis v. Edmond, 531 U.S. 32 (2000)
Vote: 6-3
FACTS: The city of Indianapolis began to operate vehicle checkpoints to interdict drugs. The city conducted six roadblocks stopping 1,161 vehicles and arresting 104 motorists. Of the arrests, 55 were for drug-related crimes, while 49 were for others. The locations are selected in advance based on crime statistics and traffic flow. The checkpoints are usually operated during daylight hours and are identified with signs. At each checkpoint, the police stop a predetermined number of cars and at least one officer ap-

proaches the car, advises the driver that he or she is at a drug checkpoint, and asks for the license and registration. The directives stated that the officers may conduct a search only by consent or particularized suspicion. The officer also looks for signs of impairment and conducts an open-view examination of the vehicle. A narcotics dog walks around the outside of each vehicle. The officers conduct each stop the same way and cannot stop any vehicle out of sequence. The duration of each stop is five minutes or less. James Edmond and Joell Palmer were stopped separately at a narcotics checkpoint and filed a lawsuit on behalf of themselves and the class of all motorists who had been stopped or were subject to being stopped claiming that the roadblocks violated the Fourth Amendment.

ISSUE: Can police stop and briefly detain motorists at a drug checkpoint?

HOLDING: No.

RATIONALE: "We have never approved a checkpoint program whose primary purpose was to detect evidence of ordinary criminal wrongdoing. Rather, our checkpoint cases have recognized only limited exceptions to the general rule that a seizure must be accompanied by some measure of individualized suspicion. We suggested in [*Delaware* v. *Prouse*, 440 U.S. 648 (1979)] that we would not credit the 'general interest in crime control' as justification for a regime of suspicionless stops. . . . Consistent with this suggestion, each of the checkpoint programs that we have approved was designed primarily to serve purposes closely related to the problems of policing the border or the necessity of ensuring roadway safety. Because the primary purpose of the Indianapolis narcotics checkpoint program is to uncover evidence of ordinary criminal wrongdoing, the program contravenes the Fourth Amendment."

"Petitioners propose several ways in which the narcotics-detection purpose of the instant checkpoint program may instead resemble the primary purposes of the checkpoints in [*Michigan Department of State Police v. Sitz*, 496 U.S. 444 (1990)] and [*United States v. Martinez-Fuerte*, 428 U.S. 543 (1976)]. Petitioners state that the checkpoints in those cases had the same ultimate purpose of arresting those suspected of committing crimes. . . . If we were to rest the case at this high level of generality, there would be little check on the ability of the authorities to construct roadblocks for almost any conceivable law enforcement purpose."

"Petitioners argue that the Indianapolis checkpoint program is justified by its lawful secondary purposes of keeping impaired motorists off the road and verifying licenses and registrations. . . . If this were the case, however, law enforcement authorities would be able to establish checkpoints for virtually any purpose so long as they also included a license or sobriety check. . . . [O]ur special needs and administrative search cases demonstrate that purpose is often relevant when suspicionless intrusions pursuant to a general scheme are at issue."

"When law enforcement authorities pursue primarily general crime control purposes at checkpoints such as here, however, stops can only be justified by some quantum of individualized suspicion."

d. Hit and Run Accidents

Illinois v. Lidster, 540 U.S. 419 (2004)

Vote: 6-3

FACTS: An unknown motorist struck and killed a seventy-year-old bicyclist. The motorist drove off without identifying himself and one week later at about the same time and at about the same place, local police set up a highway checkpoint designed to obtain more information about the accident. Police cars with flashing lights partially blocked the highway and forced traffic to slow down. As each vehicle drew up, an officer would stop it for ten to fifteen seconds, ask the occupants whether they had seen anything, and hand each driver a flyer. Robert S. Lidster drove a van toward the checkpoint and swerved, nearly hitting one of the officers. The officer smelled alcohol and directed him to another officer who administered a sobriety test and arrested him. Lidster was convicted of driving under the influence and challenged the lawfulness of his arrest and conviction on the ground that the government used a checkpoint that violated the Fourth Amendment.

ISSUE: Are checkpoints designed to ask for information about hit-and-run accidents violations of the Fourth Amendment?

HOLDING: No.

RATIONALE: "We hold that the police stops were reasonable, hence, constitutional." "The Illinois Supreme Court basically held that our decision in [*City of Indianapolis v. Edmond,* 531 U.S. 32 (2000)] governs the outcome of this case. We do not agree."

"The checkpoint stop here differs significantly from that in *Edmond.* The stop's primary law enforcement purpose was *not* to determine whether a vehicle's occupants were committing a crime, but to ask vehicle occupants . . . for their help in providing information about a crime in all likelihood committed by others. The police expected the information elicited to help them apprehend, not the vehicle's occupants, but other individuals."

"Neither do we believe . . . that the Fourth Amendment would have us apply an *Edmond*-type rule of automatic unconstitutionality to brief, information-seeking highway stops of the kind now before us. For one thing, the fact that such stops normally lack individualized suspicion cannot by itself determine the constitutional outcome. . . . The Fourth Amendment does not treat a motorist's car as his castle. . . . And special law enforcement concerns will sometimes justify highway stops without individualized suspicion. . . ."

"For another thing, information-seeking highway stops are less likely to provoke anxiety or to prove intrusive. The stops are likely brief. The police are not likely to ask questions designed to elicit self-incriminating information. And citizens will often react positively when police simply ask for their help."

"Further, the law ordinarily permits police to seek the voluntary cooperation of members of the public in the investigation of a crime. . . . That, in part, is because voluntary requests play a vital role in police investigatory work."

"And the resulting voluntary questioning of a motorist is as likely to prove important for police investigation as is the questioning of a pedestrian. Given these considerations, it would seem anomalous were the law (1) ordinarily to allow police freely to seek the voluntary cooperation of pedestrians but (2) ordinarily to forbid police to seek similar voluntary cooperation from motorists."

"Finally, we do not believe that an *Edmond*-type rule is needed to prevent an unreasonable proliferation of police checkpoints. . . . Practical considerations—namely, limited police resources and community hostility to related traffic tie-ups—seem likely to inhibit any such proliferation. . . . And, of course, the Fourth Amendment's normal insistence that the stop be reasonable in context will still provide an important legal limitation on police use of this kind of information-seeking checkpoint."

"We hold that the stop was constitutional."

"The stop advanced this grave public concern to a significant degree. The police appropriately tailored their checkpoint stops to fit important criminal investigatory needs."

8

The Exclusionary Rule and its Exceptions

UP TO THIS POINT, THE DISCUSSION HAS FOCUSED upon the requirements that the police need to follow to obtain evidence. Since a great deal of material has been covered that pertains to obtaining evidence while following certain rules, one might ask what happens if the police fail to follow those rules. At the point where the police fail to follow the law either intentionally or sometimes even by mistake, the Supreme Court has created a remedy called the exclusionary rule. The principle laid down by the Court essentially disallows the state from using the evidence obtained by the illegal search or seizure in court. However, as we have seen so many times already, there is always an exception to a particular rule that the Court creates. The same is true with the exclusionary rule.

Beginning first with the history of the rule, its creation and application to the state and federal courts will be examined first. As one might expect, the police tried valiantly to get around the rule for some time and were successful for a period until the Court applied the rule to the states.

So, what happens to illegally obtained evidence? How do the courts refer to it? It is sometimes said that such evidence is tainted, and while it may be "tainted," sometimes the taint can be removed and the evidence may be allowed. However, this is not the only exception to the exclusionary rule. Over time, the Supreme Court has fashioned several exceptions to it.

For example, the Court has recognized the "good faith" exception whereby if the police make an innocent mistake when they reasonably believe they are following the rules governing a search or seizure, the Court has said that such evidence is allowable. In fact, a couple of different kinds of good faith exceptions exist, one that is applied to the police believing that they are following a valid state statute and another where they reasonably rely on a computer check. The "open fields" exception argues that evidence obtained in certain areas that are not part of an individual's "living space" is also exempt from the exclusionary rule. Similarly, abandoned property also is exempt from the rule. The "plain view" doctrine states that anything the police obtain via the normal use of their senses is seizable and not subject to the rule. In fact, such activity is not even classified by the Court as a search. Finally, evidence obtained during an emergency, provided the seizure itself is legally carried out, can also be used and is exempt from exclusion.

A. Foundational Concepts

1. The Exclusionary Rule

Weeks v. United States, 232 U.S. 383 (1914)
Vote: 9-0
FACTS: Fremont Weeks was arrested without a warrant at Union Station in Kansas City, Missouri, where he was employed. Police had gone to his house and were told by a neighbor where the key was kept. They entered and searched his room, taking papers and articles, which were turned over to the United States marshal. Later that day, police returned with the marshal, who thought he might find more evidence. After being admitted by someone in the house, they searched Weeks's room again and seized letters found in a drawer. None of the officers had a search warrant. Weeks filed a petition for the return of the property not directly related to the charges, which was granted. The district attorney returned part of the property taken and retained the remainder, concluding a list of the property with the statement that, "all of which last above described property is to be used in evidence in the trial of the above entitled cause, and pertains to the alleged sale of lottery tickets of the company above named."

After the jury had been sworn, Weeks again filed a petition for the return of his property, which was denied. Upon the introduction of his papers, Weeks objected on the ground that the papers had been obtained without a search warrant, the objection was overruled by the court. Among the materials admitted into evidence were a number of lottery tickets and statements with reference to the lottery and a number of letters written to Weeks with respect to the lottery, taken by the marshal. Weeks was convicted of using the mails for the purpose of transporting certain coupons or tickets representing chances in a lottery or gift enterprise.

ISSUE: Can a federal court admit evidence at trial seized by police after they have entered a home without any type of warrant?

HOLDING: No.

RATIONALE: "The maxim that 'every man's house is his castle,' is made a part of our constitutional law in the clauses prohibiting unreasonable searches and seizures, and has always been looked upon as of high value to the citizen. 'Accordingly . . . no man's house can be forcibly opened, or he or his goods be carried away after it has thus been forced, except in cases of felony, and then the sheriff must be furnished with a warrant, and take great care lest he commit a trespass. This principle is jealously insisted upon.' In *Ex parte Jackson* [96 U.S. 727 (1877)] . . . , this court recognized the principle of protection as applicable to letters and sealed packages in the mail, and held that consistently with this guaranty of the right of the people to be secure in their papers against unreasonable searches and seizures such matter could only be opened and examined upon warrants issued on oath or affirmation particularly describing the thing to be seized, 'as is required when papers are subjected to search in one's own household.'"

"The effect of the Fourth Amendment is to put the courts of the United States and Federal officials, in the exercise of their power and authority, under limitations and restraints as to the exercise of such power and authority, and to forever secure the people, their persons, houses, papers and effects against all unreasonable searches and seizures under the guise of law. This protection reaches all alike, whether accused of crime or not, and the duty of giving to it force and effect is obligatory upon all entrusted under our Federal system with the enforcement of the laws."

"The case in the aspect in which we are dealing with it involves the right of the court in a criminal prosecution to retain for the purposes of evidence the letters and correspondence of the accused, seized in his house in his absence and without his authority, by a United States Marshal holding no warrant for his arrest and none for the search of his premises. If letters and private documents can thus be seized and held and used in evidence against a citizen accused of an offense, the protection of the Fourth Amendment declaring his right to be secure against such searches and seizures is of no value, and, so far as those thus placed are concerned, might as well be stricken from the Constitution. The efforts of the courts and their officials to bring the guilty to punishment, praiseworthy as they are, are not to be aided by the sacrifice of those great principles established by years of endeavor and suffering which have resulted in their embodiment in the fundamental law of the land. . . . To sanction such proceedings would be to affirm by judicial decision a manifest neglect if not an open defiance of the prohibitions of the Constitution, intended for the protection of the people against such unauthorized action."

"'[T]he substance of the offense is the compulsory production of private papers, whether under a search warrant or a *subpoena duces tecum*, against which the person, be he individual or corporation, is entitled to protection.' If such a seizure under the authority of a warrant supposed to be legal, constitutes a violation of the constitutional protection, *a fortiori* does the attempt of an officer of the United States, the United States Marshal, acting under color of his office, without even the sanction of a warrant, constitute an invasion of the rights within the protection afforded by the Fourth Amendment."

"We therefore reach the conclusion that the letters in question were taken from the house of the accused by an official of the United States acting under color of his office in direct violation of the constitutional rights of the defendant. . . . In holding them and permitting their use upon the trial, we think prejudicial error was committed."

2. The Fruit of the Poisonous Tree Doctrine

Silverthorne Lumber v. United States, 251 U.S. 385 (1920)
Vote: 7-2
FACTS: Two of the Silverthornes were arrested at their homes and were detained for a number of hours. Federal officers and the United States marshal went to the office of Silverthorne Lumber and seized all the books, papers, and documents. An application was made for the return of the seized materials. The court ordered a return of the originals but impounded photographs and copies that were made prior to their return. A new indictment was based on the manufactured evidence from the originals. The Silverthornes refused to comply with a subpoena demanding the originals despite the fact that the court had ordered them returned. As a result of the refusal to comply, the Sil-

verthornes were charged with contempt and fined $250; Frederick W. Silverthorne was imprisoned.

ISSUE: May the police, after being ordered by a court to return illegally seized evidence, make copies and photographs of the seized material and use it to bring charges against an accused?

HOLDING: No.

RATIONALE: "It is that although of course its seizure was an outrage which the Government now regrets, it may study the papers before it returns them, copy them, and then may use the knowledge that it has gained to call upon the owners in a more regular form to produce them; that the protection of the Constitution covers the physical possession but not any advantages that the Government can gain over the object of its pursuit by doing the forbidden act. . . . In our opinion such is not the law. It reduces the Fourth Amendment to a form of words. The essence of a provision forbidding the acquisition of evidence in a certain way is that not merely evidence so acquired shall not be used before the Court but that it shall not be used at all. . . . [T]he knowledge gained by the Government's own wrong cannot be used by it in the way proposed."

3. The Silver Platter Doctrine

Elkins v. United States, 364 U.S. 206 (1960)
Vote: 5-4

FACTS: Petitioners were indicted in the United States District Court in Oregon for the offense of intercepting and divulging telephone communications and of conspiracy to do so. Before trial they filed a motion to suppress several tape and wire recordings and a tape recorder. At the hearing, the judge assumed without deciding that the articles had been obtained as the result of an unreasonable search and seizure, but denied the motion to suppress because there was no evidence that any "agent of the United States had any knowledge or information or suspicion of any kind that this search was being contemplated or was eventually made by the State officers until they read about it in the newspaper." At the trial the articles in question were admitted in evidence against the petitioners, and they were convicted.

ISSUE: May articles obtained as the result of an unreasonable search and seizure by state officers, without involvement of federal officers, be introduced in evidence against a defendant in a federal criminal trial?

HOLDING: No.

RATIONALE: "In a word, we re-examine here the validity of what has come to be called the silver platter doctrine. For the reasons that follow we conclude that this doctrine can no longer be accepted."

"[N]othing could be of greater relevance to the present inquiry than the underlying constitutional doctrine which *Wolf* [*v. Colorado*, 338 U.S. 25 (1949)] established. For there it was unequivocally determined by a unanimous Court that the Federal Constitution, by virtue of the Fourteenth Amendment, prohibits unreasonable searches and seizures by state officers."

"The foundation upon which the admissibility of state-seized evidence in a federal trial originally rested—that unreasonable state searches did not violate the Federal Constitution—thus disappeared in 1949. This removal of the doctrinal underpinning for the admissibility rule has apparently escaped the attention of most of the federal courts, which have continued to approve the admission of evidence illegally seized by state officers without so much as even discussing the impact of *Wolf*."

"If resolution of the issue were to be dictated solely by principles of logic, it is clear what our decision would have to be. For surely no distinction can logically be drawn between evidence obtained in violation of the Fourth Amendment and that obtained in violation of the Fourteenth. The Constitution is flouted equally in either case. To the victim it matters not whether his constitutional right has been invaded by a federal agent or by a state officer. It would be a curiously ambivalent rule that would require the courts of the United States to differentiate between unconstitutionally seized evidence upon so arbitrary a basis."

"Not more than half the states continue totally to adhere to the rule that evidence is freely admissible no matter how it was obtained. Most of the others have adopted the exclusionary rule in its entirety; the rest have adopted it in part. The movement towards the rule of exclusion has been halting but seemingly inexorable. Since the *Wolf* decision one state has switched its position in that direction by legislation, and two others by judicial decision. Another state, uncommitted until 1955, in that year adopted the rule of exclusion. Significantly, most of the exclusionary states which have had to consider the issue have held that evidence obtained by *federal* officers in a search and seizure unlawful under the Fourth Amendment must be suppressed in a prosecution in the *state* courts."

"Impressive as is this experience of individual states, even more is to be said for adoption of the exclusionary rule in the particular context here presented—a context which brings into focus considerations of federalism. The very essence of a healthy federalism depends upon the avoidance of needless conflict between state and federal courts. Yet when a federal court sitting in an exclusionary state admits evidence lawlessly seized by state agents, it not only frustrates state policy, but frustrates that policy in a particularly inappropriate and ironic way. For by admitting the unlawfully seized evidence the federal court serves to defeat the state's effort to assure obedience to the Federal Constitution."

"These, then, are the considerations of reason and experience which point to the rejection of a doctrine that would freely admit in a federal criminal trial evidence seized by state agents in violation of the defendant's constitutional rights. But there is another consideration—the imperative of judicial integrity. . . . '[I]f the Government becomes a lawbreaker, it breeds contempt for law; it invites every man to become a law unto himself; it invites anarchy. To declare that in the administration of the criminal law the end justifies the means—to declare that the Government may commit crimes in order to secure the conviction of a private criminal—would bring terrible retribution. Against that pernicious doctrine this Court should resolutely set its face.'"

"For these reasons we hold that evidence obtained by state officers during a search which, if conducted by federal officers, would have violated the defendant's immunity from unreasonable searches and seizures under the Fourth Amendment is inadmissible over the defendant's timely objection in a federal criminal trial."

4. Independent Source

Murray v. United States, 487 U.S. 533 (1988)
Vote: 4-3
FACTS: Based on information received from informants, federal agents had been watching Michael F. Murray and his co-conspirators and observed Murray drive a truck and James D. Carter drive a green camper into a warehouse in Boston. When they drove the vehicles out about twenty minutes later, the agents saw within the warehouse two individuals and a tractor-trailer. Murray and Carter later turned over the truck and camper to others, who were arrested, and the vehicles lawfully seized. Both vehicles contained marijuana. After receiving this information, several agents went to the warehouse and forced entry. They found it unoccupied, but observed, in plain view, burlap-wrapped bales that were later found to contain marijuana. They left without disturbing the bales, kept the warehouse under surveillance, and did not reenter it until they had a search warrant. In applying for the warrant, the agents did not mention the prior entry and did not rely on any observations made during that entry. When the warrant was issued the agents immediately reentered the warehouse and seized 270 bales of marijuana and paperwork listing customers for whom the bales were destined. Murray, Carter, and others were convicted of conspiracy to possess and distribute illegal drugs.
ISSUE: Is evidence obtained independently from an illegal search admissible in court?
HOLDING: Yes.
RATIONALE: "Almost simultaneously with our development of the exclusionary rule, in the first quarter of this century, we also announced what has come to be known as the 'independent source' doctrine."

"The Government argues that it applies also to evidence initially discovered during, or as a consequence of, an unlawful search, but later obtained independently from activities untainted by the initial illegality. We think the Government's view has better support in both precedent and policy."

"Our cases have used the concept of 'independent source' in a more general and a more specific sense. The more general sense identifies *all* evidence acquired in a fashion untainted by the illegal evidence-gathering activity. Thus, where an unlawful entry has given investigators knowledge of facts *x* and *y*, but fact *z* has been learned by other means, fact *z* can be said to be admissible because derived from an 'independent source.'"

"The original use of the term, however, and its more important use for purposes of these cases, was more specific. It was originally applied in the exclusionary rule context, by Justice Holmes, with reference to that particular category of evidence acquired by an untainted search *which is identical to the evidence unlawfully acquired. . . .*"

"As the First Circuit has observed, '[i]n the classic independent source situation, information which is received through an illegal source is considered to be cleanly obtained when it arrives through an independent source. . . .' We recently assumed this application of the independent source doctrine (in the Sixth Amendment context)."

"To determine whether the warrant was independent of the illegal entry, one must ask whether it would have been sought even if what actually happened had not occurred—not whether it would have been sought if something else had happened. That is to say, what counts is whether the actual illegal search had any effect in producing the warrant, not whether some hypothetical illegal search would have aborted the warrant. Only that much is needed to assure that what comes before the court is not the product of illegality; to go further than that would be to expand our existing exclusionary rule."

5. Attenuation

Brown v. Illinois, 422 U.S. 590 (1975)
Vote: 9-0
FACTS: Without probable cause or a warrant, Chicago detectives William Lenz and William Nolan broke into Richard Brown's apartment. They waited for him to return and arrested him as he did so. He was told to go inside the house with police, where he was searched. After the search, as he denied being Brown, police showed him a picture of himself. The police stated that he was under arrest for the murder of Roger Corpus. Brown was then driven to the police station, and on the way he gave false answers about his identity. Upon arrival, police obtained the file on the Corpus murder and gave Brown the *Miranda* warnings. Brown implicated himself in the murder and then was asked if he wanted to continue talking. He said that he did, and the discussion led Brown to admit that Jimmy Claggett had forced him to shoot Corpus. Lenz, Nolan, and Brown tried to locate Claggett and, after searching for several hours, found him and arrested him. The assistant state attorney arrived and re-Mirandized Brown, after which he repeated his statement but refused to sign it. Brown and Claggett were indicted for the murder of Corpus, and Brown's motion to suppress his statements was denied, after which, he was convicted.
ISSUE: Does issuing the *Miranda* warnings remove the taint from a confession obtained via an illegal arrest?
HOLDING: No
RATIONALE: "Thus, even if the statements in this case were found to be voluntary under the Fifth Amendment, the Fourth Amendment issue remains. *Wong Sun* [*v. United States*, 371 U.S. 471 (1963)] requires . . . that a statement . . . be 'sufficiently an act of free will to purge the primary taint.'"

"If *Miranda* [*v. Arizona*, 384 U.S. 436 (1966)] warnings . . . were held to attenuate the taint of an unconstitutional arrest . . . the effect of the exclusionary rule would be substantially diluted. . . . Arrests made without warrant or without probable cause, for questioning or 'investigation,' would be encouraged by the knowledge that evidence derived therefrom could well be made admissible at trial by the simple expedient of giving *Miranda* warnings. Any incentive to avoid Fourth Amendment violations would be eviscerated by making the warnings, in effect, a 'cure-all.'"

"It is entirely possible . . . that persons arrested illegally frequently may decide to confess, as an act of free will unaffected by the initial illegality. But the *Miranda* warnings, *alone* and *per se,* cannot always make the act sufficiently a product of free will to break."

"While we therefore reject the *per se* rule which the Illinois courts appear to have accepted, we also decline to adopt any alternative *per se* or 'but for' rule. . . . The question whether a confession is the product of a free will under *Wong Sun* must be answered on the facts of each case. No single fact is dispositive. . . . The *Miranda* warnings are an important factor, to be sure, in determining whether the confession is obtained by exploitation of an illegal arrest. But they are not the only factor to be considered. The temporal proximity of the arrest and the confession, the presence of intervening circumstances . . . and, particularly, the purpose and flagrancy of the official misconduct are all relevant. . . . The voluntariness of the statement is a threshold requirement. . . . And the burden of showing admissibility rests, of course, on the prosecution."

6. Standing

Rakas v. Illinois, 439 U.S. 128 (1978)
Vote: 5-4
FACTS: A police officer received a call about a robbery of a clothing store and the getaway car. Shortly thereafter, the officer saw a car that he thought might have been used in the robbery. After following it and after the arrival of assistance, he and several officers stopped the vehicle. The occupants of the car, Rakas and two females, were ordered out of the car while two officers searched the interior of the vehicle. A box of rifle shells were discovered in the glove compartment as was a sawed-off rifle under the front passenger seat. The officers then placed them under arrest.

At trial, the prosecution offered into evidence the sawed-off rifle and rifle shells that had been seized during the search of the automobile. Neither petitioner was the owner of the automobile and neither ever asserted that he owned the rifle or shells. The Illinois Appellate Court held that petitioners lacked standing to object to the allegedly unlawful search and seizure and denied their motion to suppress. Petitioners were convicted of armed robbery and their convictions were affirmed on appeal.
ISSUE: Must a person show that his own Fourth Amendment rights were violated during a search or seizure to have standing to object to the introduction of evidence?
HOLDING: Yes.
RATIONALE: "The proponent of a motion to suppress has the burden of establishing that his own Fourth Amendment rights were violated by the challenged search or seizure."

"The concept of standing discussed in *Jones* [*v. United States,* 362 U.S. 257 (1960)] focuses on whether the person seeking to challenge the legality of a search as a basis for suppressing evidence was himself the 'victim' of the search or seizure. Adoption of the so-called 'target' theory advanced by petitioners would in effect permit a defendant to assert that a violation of the Fourth Amendment rights of a third party entitled him to have evidence suppressed at his trial."

"There is an aspect of traditional standing doctrine that was not considered in *Jones* and which we do not question. It is the proposition that a party seeking relief must allege such a personal stake or interest in the outcome of the controversy as to assure the concrete adverseness which Art. III requires."

"We decline to extend the rule of standing in Fourth Amendment cases in the manner suggested by petitioners. As we stated. . . . 'Fourth Amendment rights are personal rights which, like some other constitutional rights, may not be vicariously asserted. . . .' A person who is aggrieved by an illegal search and seizure only through the introduction of damaging evidence secured by a search of a third person's premises or property has not had any of his Fourth Amendment rights infringed. And since the exclusionary rule is an attempt to effectuate the guarantees of the Fourth Amendment . . . , it is proper to permit only defendants whose Fourth Amendment rights have been violated to benefit from the rule's protections."

"In *Jones*, the Court set forth two alternative holdings: It established a rule of 'automatic' standing to contest an allegedly illegal search where the same possession needed to establish standing is an essential element of the offense charged; and second, it stated that 'anyone legitimately on premises where a search occurs may challenge its legality by way of a motion to suppress. . . .' Had the Court intended to adopt the target theory now put forth by petitioners, neither of the above two holdings would have been necessary since Jones was the 'target' of the police search in that case. Nor does *United States v. Jeffers* [342 U.S. 48 (1951)] or *Bumper v. North Carolina* [391 U.S. 543 (1968)] support the target theory."

"In *Alderman v. United States* [394 U.S. 165 (1969)], Mr. Justice Fortas argued that the Court should 'include within the category of those who may object to the introduction of illegal evidence "one against whom the search was directed."' The Court did not directly comment on Mr. Justice Fortas' suggestion, but it left no doubt that it rejected this theory by holding that persons who were not parties to unlawfully overheard conversations or who did not own the premises on which such conversations took place did not have standing to contest the legality of the surveillance, regardless of whether or not they were the 'targets.'"

"When we are urged to grant standing to a criminal defendant to assert a violation, not of his own constitutional rights but of someone else's, we cannot but give weight to practical difficulties. . . ."

"Conferring standing to raise vicarious Fourth Amendment claims would necessarily mean a more widespread invocation of the exclusionary rule during criminal trials. . . ."

"We would not wish to be understood as saying that legitimate presence on the premises is irrelevant to one's expectation of privacy, but it cannot be deemed controlling."

"Judged by the foregoing analysis, petitioners' claims must fail. They asserted neither a property nor a possessory interest in the automobile, nor an interest in the property seized. And as we have previously indicated, the fact that they were 'legitimately on [the] premises' in the sense that they were in the car with the permission of its owner is not determinative of whether they had a legitimate expectation of privacy in the particular areas of the automobile searched."

7. Application of the Exclusionary Rule to the States

Mapp v. Ohio, 367 U.S. 643 (1961)
Vote: 5-4

FACTS: Cleveland police arrived at Dolree Mapp's residence pursuant to information that "a person [was] hiding out in the home, who was wanted for questioning in connection with a recent bombing, and that there was a large amount of policy paraphernalia being hidden in the home." Officers knocked on the door and demanded entrance, but Mapp, after telephoning her attorney, refused to admit them without a search warrant. They advised their headquarters of the situation and undertook surveillance of the house. The officers sought entrance again later when four or more officers arrived. When Mapp did not come to the door immediately, at least one of the doors to the house was forcibly opened. Although Mapp's attorney had arrived, the officers did not allow him to see Mapp or to enter the house. Mapp was halfway down the stairs when she demanded to see the search warrant. A paper was held up by one of the officers, which she grabbed and placed in her bosom. The officers recovered the paper and handcuffed Mapp because she had been "belligerent." An officer then "grabbed" her and "twisted [her] hand," and she "yelled [and] pleaded with him" because "it was hurting." She was then forcibly taken upstairs to her bedroom where the officers searched a dresser, a chest of drawers, a closet, and some suitcases. They also looked into a photo album and through personal papers. The search spread to the rest of the second floor and the basement, where a trunk was also searched. At trial, no search warrant was produced, nor was the failure to produce one explained. Mapp was eventually convicted of knowingly having had in her possession and under her control lewd and lascivious books, pictures, and photographs.

ISSUE: Is the federal exclusionary rule applicable to the states?

HOLDING: Yes.

RATIONALE: "Today we once again examine [*Wolf v. Colorado*, 338 U.S. 25 (1949)]'s constitutional documentation of the right to privacy free from unreasonable state intrusion, and, after its dozen years on our books, are led by it to close the only courtroom door remaining open to evidence secured by official lawlessness in flagrant abuse of that basic right, reserved to all persons as a specific guarantee against that very same unlawful conduct. We hold that all evidence obtained by searches and seizures in violation of the Constitution is, by that same authority, inadmissible in a state court."

"Moreover, our holding that the exclusionary rule is an essential part of both the Fourth and Fourteenth Amendments is not only the logical dictate of prior cases, but it also makes very good sense. There is no war between the Constitution and common sense. Presently, a federal prosecutor may make no use of evidence illegally seized, but a State's attorney across the street may, although he supposedly is operating under the enforceable prohibitions of the same Amendment. Thus the State, by admitting evidence unlawfully seized, serves to encourage disobedience to the Federal Constitution which it is bound to uphold. . . . In nonexclusionary States, federal officers, being human, were by it invited to and did, as our cases indicate, step across the street to the State's attorney with their unconstitutionally seized evidence. Prosecution on the basis of that evidence was then had in a state court in utter disregard of the enforceable Fourth Amendment."

"Federal-state cooperation in the solution of crime under constitutional standards will be promoted, if only by recognition of their now mutual obligation to respect the same fundamental criteria in their approaches. 'However much in a particular case insistence upon such rules may appear as a technicality that inures to the benefit of a guilty person, the history of the criminal law proves that tolerance of shortcut methods in law enforcement impairs its enduring effectiveness.'"

"Nothing can destroy a government more quickly than its failure to observe its own laws, or worse, its disregard of the charter of its own existence. . . . Nor can it lightly be assumed that, as a practical matter, adoption of the exclusionary rule fetters law enforcement. Only last year this Court expressly considered that contention and found that 'pragmatic evidence of a sort' to the contrary was not wanting."

B. Exceptions to the Exclusionary Rule

1. Good Faith Exceptions

a. Defective Search Warrants

United States v. Leon, 468 U.S. 897 (1984)
Vote: 6-3
FACTS: An unproven informant told a Burbank police officer that "Armando" and "Patsy" were selling large quantities of cocaine and methaqualone from their home. The informant also indicated that he had witnessed a sale of methaqualone by "Patsy" at the residence and had observed a shoebox containing a large amount of cash that belonged to her. He further stated that the suspects kept only small quantities of drugs at their home and stored the rest elsewhere in Burbank.

On the basis of this information, the police initiated an investigation focusing on the suspected home and two other residences. Cars parked at the main home belonged to Armando Sanchez and Patsy Stewart. During the investigation, officers observed a car belonging to Del Castillo arrive at the first home. The driver entered the house, exited shortly thereafter carrying a small paper sack, and drove away. A check of Ricardo Del Castillo's records led police to Alberto Leon, who had previously been arrested on drug charges. A companion of his had informed the police that Leon was heavily involved in the importation of drugs. Before the investigation began, Burbank officers had learned that Leon stored a large quantity of methaqualone at his home. The officers observed several persons arrive at the Price Drive residence and leave with small packages; they observed a variety of related activities at the other residences. The officers also observed Sanchez and Stewart board separate flights for Miami. Later they returned to Los Angeles together, whereupon they consented to a search of their luggage, which revealed a small amount of marihuana.

Based on these and other observations, Officer Cyril Rombach prepared an application for a warrant to search 620 Price Drive, 716 South Sunset Canyon, 7902 Via Magdalena, and automobiles registered to each of the respondents for a list of items related to drug trafficking. Several deputy district attorneys reviewed Rombach's application, and a search warrant was issued. The searches produced large quantities of drugs at the Via Magdalena and Sunset Canyon addresses and a small quantity at the Price Drive residence. Other evidence was discovered at each of the residences and in Stewart's and Del Castillo's cars. Respondents were indicted by a grand jury and charged with conspiracy to possess and distribute cocaine and a variety of substantive counts.

ISSUE: Does the exclusionary rule bar the use of evidence seized by officers acting in reasonable reliance on a search warrant found to be unsupported by probable cause?

HOLDING: No.

RATIONALE: "We . . . conclude that suppression of evidence obtained pursuant to a warrant should be ordered only on a case-by-case basis and only in those unusual cases in which exclusion will further the purposes of the exclusionary rule."

"We have frequently questioned whether the exclusionary rule can have any deterrent effect when the offending officers acted in the objectively reasonable belief that their conduct did not violate the Fourth Amendment. 'No empirical researcher, proponent or opponent of the rule, has yet been able to establish with any assurance whether the rule has a deterrent effect. . . .' But even assuming that the rule effectively deters some police misconduct and provides incentives for the law enforcement profession as a whole to conduct itself in accord with the Fourth Amendment, it cannot be expected, and should not be applied, to deter objectively reasonable law enforcement activity."

"Where the official action was pursued in complete good faith, however, the deterrence rationale loses much of its force."

"This is particularly true, we believe, when an officer acting with objective good faith has obtained a search warrant from a judge or magistrate and acted within its scope. In most such cases, there is no police illegality and thus nothing to deter. It is the magistrate's responsibility to determine whether the officer's allegations establish probable cause and, if so, to issue a warrant comporting in form with the requirements of the Fourth Amendment. In the ordinary case, an officer cannot be expected to question the magistrate's probable-cause determination or his judgment that the form of the warrant is technically sufficient. '[Once] the warrant issues, there is literally nothing more the policeman can do in seeking to comply with the law.' Penalizing the officer for the magistrate's error, rather than his own, cannot logically contribute to the deterrence of Fourth Amendment violations."

"We conclude that the marginal or nonexistent benefits produced by suppressing evidence obtained in objectively reasonable reliance on a subsequently invalidated search warrant cannot justify the substantial costs of exclusion."

"In the absence of an allegation that the magistrate abandoned his detached and neutral role, suppression is appropriate only if the officers were dishonest or reckless in preparing their affidavit or could not have harbored an objectively reasonable belief in the existence of probable cause."

b. State Statute

Illinois v. Krull, 480 U.S. 340 (1987)
Vote: 5-4
FACTS: Krull had a license to operate Action Iron & Metal, Inc., an automobile wrecking yard in Chicago. Detective Leilan McNally of the Chicago Police Department regularly inspected the records of wrecking yards pursuant to the state statute. He entered Krull's yard and identified himself to Lucas, who was working at the yard, and asked to see the license and records of vehicle purchases. Lucas could not locate the license or records but did produce a pad on which five purchases were listed. McNally then received permission to look at the cars in the yard. Upon checking the serial numbers, McNally ascertained that three were stolen. Also, the identification number of a fourth had been removed. McNally seized the vehicles. Krull, Lucas, and Mucerino were charged with violations of the Illinois motor vehicle statutes.
ISSUE: Does the exclusionary rule bar the use of evidence seized by officers acting in reasonable reliance on a state statute later found to be unconstitutional?
HOLDING: No.
RATIONALE: "The approach used in [*United States v. Leon*, 468 U.S. 897 (1984)] is equally applicable to the present case. The application of the exclusionary rule to suppress evidence obtained by an officer acting in objectively reasonable reliance on a statute would have as little deterrent effect on the officer's actions as would the exclusion of evidence when an officer acts in objectively reasonable reliance on a warrant. Unless a statute is clearly unconstitutional, an officer cannot be expected to question the judgment of the legislature that passed the law. If the statute is subsequently declared unconstitutional, excluding evidence obtained pursuant to it prior to such a judicial declaration will not deter future Fourth Amendment violations by an officer who has simply fulfilled his responsibility to enforce the statute as written."

"Any difference between our holding in *Leon* and our holding in the instant case, therefore, must rest on a difference between the effect of the exclusion of evidence on judicial officers and the effect of the exclusion of evidence on legislators."

"There is no evidence suggesting that Congress or state legislatures have enacted a significant number of statutes permitting warrantless administrative searches violative of the Fourth Amendment. Legislatures generally have confined their efforts to authorizing administrative searches of specific categories of businesses that require regulation, and the resulting statutes usually have been held to be constitutional." Thus, we are given no basis for believing that legislators are inclined to subvert their oaths and the Fourth Amendment and that 'lawlessness among these actors requires application of the extreme sanction of exclusion.'"

"[T]he next inquiry necessitated by *Leon* is whether exclusion of evidence seized pursuant to a statute subsequently declared unconstitutional will 'have a significant deterrent effect,' on legislators enacting such statutes. Respondents have offered us no reason to believe that applying the exclusionary rule will have such an effect. Legislators enact statutes for broad, programmatic purposes, not for the purpose of procuring evidence in particular criminal investigations. There is nothing to indicate that applying the exclusionary rule to evidence seized pursuant to the statute prior to the declaration of its invalidity will act as a significant, additional deterrent. Moreover, to the extent that application of the exclusionary rule could provide some incremental deterrent, that possible benefit must be weighed against the 'substantial social costs exacted by the exclusionary rule.' When we indulge in such weighing, we are convinced that applying the exclusionary rule in this context is unjustified."

"In determining whether to apply the exclusionary rule, a court should examine whether such application will advance the deterrent objective of the rule. Although the number of individuals affected may be considered when 'weighing the costs and benefits,' of applying the exclusionary rule, the simple fact that many are affected by a statute is not sufficient to tip the balance if the deterrence of Fourth Amendment violations would not be advanced in any meaningful way."

c. Computer Error

Arizona v. Evans, 514 U.S. 1 (1995)
Vote: 7-2
FACTS: Phoenix police officer Bryan Sargent stopped Isaac Evans for driving the wrong way on a one-way street. After Evans stated that his license had been suspended, Sargent conducted a computer check and also found that there was an outstanding warrant for his arrest. Sargent then arrested Evans. While being handcuffed, Evans dropped a marijuana cigarette, and officers then found marijuana under the passenger's seat. When the police notified the court that they had arrested Evans, they found that the warrant had been quashed. However, Evans was still charged with marijuana possession.
ISSUE: Does the exclusionary rule bar the use of evidence seized by officers acting in reasonable reliance on a warrant based on a court employee clerical error?
HOLDING: No.
RATIONALE: "This case presents the question whether evidence seized in violation of the Fourth Amendment by an officer who acted in reliance on a police record indicating the existence of an outstanding arrest warrant—a record that is later determined to be erroneous—must be suppressed by virtue of the exclusionary rule regardless of the source of the error. The Supreme Court of Arizona held that the exclusionary rule required suppression of evidence even if the erroneous information resulted from an error committed by an employee of the office of the Clerk of Court. We disagree."

"In sum, respondent does not persuade us to abandon the [*United States v. Leon,* 468 U.S. 897 (1984)] framework."

"If court employees were responsible for the erroneous computer record, the exclusion of evidence at trial would not sufficiently deter future errors so as to warrant such a severe sanction. First, as we noted in *Leon,* the exclusionary rule was historically designed as a means of deterring police misconduct, not mistakes by court employees. . . . Second, respondent offers no evidence that court employees are inclined to ignore or subvert the Fourth Amendment or that lawlessness among these actors requires application of the extreme sanction of exclusion."

"Finally, and most important, there is no basis for believing that application of the exclusionary rule in these circumstances will have a significant effect on court employees responsible for informing the police that a warrant has been quashed. . . . The threat of exclusion of evidence could not be expected to deter such individuals from failing to inform police officials that a warrant had been quashed."

"If it were indeed a court clerk who was responsible for the erroneous entry on the police computer, application of the exclusionary rule also could not be expected to alter the behavior of the arresting officer. As the trial court in this case stated: 'I think the police officer [was] bound to arrest. I think he would [have been] derelict in his duty if he failed to arrest. . . .' There is no indication that the arresting officer was not acting objectively reasonably when he relied upon the police computer record. Application of the *Leon* framework supports a categorical exception to the exclusionary rule for clerical errors of court employees."

d. Consent

Illinois v. Rodriguez, 497 U.S. 177 (1990)
Vote: 6-3
FACTS: Police were summoned to the residence of Dorothy Jackson in Chicago. They were met by her daughter, Gail Fischer, who showed signs of a severe beating. She told police that she had been assaulted by Edward Rodriguez earlier that day. Fischer stated that Rodriguez was asleep, and she consented to go there with the police to unlock the door so that the officers could arrest him. During this conversation, Fischer referred to the apartment as "our" apartment, and said that she had clothes and furniture there. It is unclear whether she indicated that she currently lived there or only that she used to. The police then drove to the apartment accompanied by Fischer. They did not obtain any type of warrant prior to their departure. At the apartment, Fischer unlocked the door and gave the officers permission to enter. They entered the living room, where they observed in plain view drug paraphernalia and containers filled with white powder that they believed to be cocaine. They proceeded to the bedroom where Rodriguez was sleeping and discovered additional containers of white powder in two open cases. The officers arrested Rodriguez and seized the drugs and related paraphernalia. Rodriguez was charged with possession of a controlled substance with intent to deliver.
ISSUE: Does the exclusionary rule bar the use of evidence seized by officers acting upon the consent of a third party, whom the police, at the time of entry, reasonably believe to possess common authority of the premises but in fact, does not?
HOLDING: No.
RATIONALE: "The Fourth Amendment generally prohibits the warrantless entry of a person's home, whether to make an arrest or to search for specific objects. . . . The prohibition does not apply, however, to situations in which voluntary consent has been obtained, either from the individual whose property is searched . . . or from a third party who possesses common authority over the premises."

"The fundamental objective that alone validates all unconsented government searches is, of course, the seizure of persons who have committed or are about to commit crimes, or of evidence related to crimes. But 'reasonableness,' with respect to this necessary element, does not demand that the government be factually correct in its assessment that that is what a search will produce. Warrants need only be supported by 'probable cause,' which demands no more than a proper 'assessment of probabilities in particular factual contexts. . . .' If a magistrate, based upon seemingly reliable but factually inaccurate information, issues a warrant for the search of a house in which the sought-after felon is not present, has never been present, and was never likely to have been present, the owner of that house suffers one of the inconveniences we all expose ourselves to as the cost of living in a safe society; he does not suffer a violation of the Fourth Amendment."

"It would be superfluous to multiply these examples. It is apparent that in order to satisfy the 'reasonableness' requirement of the Fourth Amendment, what is generally demanded of the many factual determinations that must regularly be made by agents of the government—whether the magistrate issuing a warrant, the police officer executing a warrant, or the police officer conducting a search or seizure under one of the exceptions to the warrant requirement—is not that they always be correct, but that they always be reasonable."

"We see no reason to depart from this general rule with respect to facts bearing upon the authority to consent to a search. Whether the basis for such authority exists is the sort of recurring factual question to which law enforcement officials must be expected to apply their judgment; and all the Fourth Amendment requires is that they answer it reasonably. The Constitution is no more violated when officers enter without a warrant because they reasonably (though erroneously) believe that the person who has consented to their entry is a resident of the premises, than it is violated when they enter without a warrant because they reasonably (though erroneously) believe they are in pursuit of a violent felon who is about to escape."

"[W]hat we hold today does not suggest that law enforcement officers may always accept a person's invitation to enter premises. Even when the invitation is accompanied by an explicit assertion that the person lives there, the surrounding circumstances could conceivably be such that a reasonable person would doubt its truth and not act upon it without further inquiry. As with other factual determinations bearing upon search and seizure, determination of consent to enter must 'be judged against an objective standard: would the facts available to the officer at the moment . . . 'warrant a man of reasonable caution in the belief' that the consenting party had authority over the premises . . . ? If not, then warrantless entry without further inquiry is unlawful unless authority actually exists. But if so, the search is valid."

e. Particularity of Warrant Descriptions

Maryland v. Garrison, 480 U.S. 79 (1987)
Vote: 6-3
FACTS: Baltimore police executed a warrant to search the person of Lawrence McWebb and "the premises known as 2036 Park Avenue third floor apartment." When the police applied for and when they conducted the search pursuant to the warrant, they

reasonably believed that there was only one apartment on the premises. In fact, the third floor was divided into two apartments, one occupied by McWebb and one by Garrison. Before the officers executing the warrant became aware that they were in a separate apartment, they discovered the contraband that provided the basis for respondent's conviction for violating Maryland's Controlled Substances Act.

ISSUE: Can the police use evidence obtained via the execution of a search warrant that they reasonably believed particularly described the place to be searched when later it was discovered that the description was overly broad?

HOLDING: Yes.

RATIONALE: "Those items of evidence that emerge after the warrant is issued have no bearing on whether or not a warrant was validly issued. Just as the discovery of contraband cannot validate a warrant invalid when issued, so is it equally clear that the discovery of facts demonstrating that a valid warrant was unnecessarily broad does not retroactively invalidate the warrant. The validity of the warrant must be assessed on the basis of the information that the officers disclosed, or had a duty to discover and to disclose, to the issuing Magistrate. On the basis of that information, we agree with the conclusion of all three Maryland courts that the warrant, insofar as it authorized a search that turned out to be ambiguous in scope, was valid when it issued."

"[T]he record also establishes that Officer Marcus made specific inquiries to determine the identity of the occupants of the third-floor premises. The officer went to 2036 Park Avenue and found that it matched the description given by the informant: a three-story brick dwelling with the numerals 2-0-3-6 affixed to the front of the premises. The officer 'made a check with the Baltimore Gas and Electric Company and discovered that the premises of 2036 Park Ave. third floor was in the name of Lawrence McWebb. . . .' Officer Marcus testified at the suppression hearing that he inquired of the Baltimore Gas and Electric Company in whose name the third floor apartment was listed: 'I asked if there is a front or rear or middle room. They told me, one third floor was only listed to Lawrence McWebb. . . .' The officer also discovered from a check with the Baltimore Police Department that the police records of Lawrence McWebb matched the address and physical description given by the informant."

"[A]n officer's reasonable misidentification of a person does not invalidate a valid arrest is equally applicable to an officer's reasonable failure to appreciate that a valid warrant describes too broadly the premises to be searched. Under the reasoning in *Hill* [*v. California*, 401 U.S. 797 (1971)], the validity of the search of respondent's apartment pursuant to a warrant authorizing the search of the entire third floor depends on whether the officers' failure to realize the overbreadth of the warrant was objectively understandable and reasonable. Here it unquestionably was. The objective facts available to the officers at the time suggested no distinction between McWebb's apartment and the third-floor premises. . . ."

"Under either interpretation of the warrant, the officers' conduct was consistent with a reasonable effort to ascertain and identify the place intended to be searched within the meaning of the Fourth Amendment."

2. Open Fields

a. Defined

Hester v. United States, 265 U.S. 57 (1924)
Vote: 9-0

FACTS: Based on information provided to them, revenue agents went to the house of Hester's father, and as they approached they saw Henderson drive up. They concealed themselves some fifty to one hundred yards away and saw Hester come out and hand Henderson a bottle. After a signal was given, Hester went to a car and took a gallon jug from it, then he and Henderson ran. One of the officers pursued and fired a pistol, and Hester dropped his jug, which broke but kept about a quart of its contents. Henderson also threw away his bottle. The jug and bottle both contained illegal whiskey. The other officer found a jar that had been thrown out of the house that also contained whiskey. The officer entered the house. Other cars stopped at the house but were signaled by Hester's father and drove off. The officers had no warrants of any type.

ISSUE: Does the Fourth Amendment protection against unreasonable searches and seizures extend to open fields?

HOLDING: No.

RATIONALE: "It is obvious that even if there had been a trespass, the above testimony was not obtained by an illegal search or seizure. The defendant's own acts, and those of his associates, disclosed the jug, the jar and the bottle—and there was no seizure in the sense of the law when the officers examined the contents of each after it had been abandoned. This evidence was not obtained by the entry into the house and it is immaterial to discuss that. The suggestion that the defendant was compelled to give evidence against himself does not require an answer. The only shadow of a ground for bringing up the case is drawn from the hypothesis that the examination of the vessels took place upon Hester's father's land. As to that, it is enough to say that, apart from the justification, the special protection accorded by the Fourth Amendment to the people in their 'persons, houses, papers, and effects,' is not extended to the open fields. The distinction between the latter and the house is as old as the common law."

b. Curtilage

Oliver v. United States, 466 U.S. 170 (1984)
Vote: 6-3

FACTS: Acting on information that marihuana was being raised on Oliver's farm, Kentucky State Police went to investigate. After arriving, they drove to a gate with a "No Trespassing" sign. A path led around one side, so the agents walked around it and along the road for several hundred yards, passing a barn and a camper. At that point, someone shouted: "No hunting is allowed, come back up here." The officers shouted back that they were Kentucky State Police officers but found no one when they went to the camper. The officers continued and found marihuana growing a mile from Oliver's home. Oliver was arrested and indicted for "[manufacturing]" a "controlled substance."

After receiving a tip that marihuana was being grown in the woods behind Thornton's house, two officers entered the woods by a path between his residence and a neighbor's. They followed the path until they reached two fenced-in patches. The officers determined that the patches were on Thornton's property, so they obtained a search warrant and seized the marihuana. Thornton was then arrested and subsequently indicted.

ISSUE: Does the open fields doctrine extend to the curtilage of a home?

HOLDING: No.

RATIONALE: "The 'open fields' doctrine . . . permits police officers to enter and search a field without a warrant."

"Nor are the open fields 'effects' within the meaning of the Fourth Amendment. . . . [T]he term 'effects' is less inclusive than 'property' and cannot be said to encompass open fields."

"[A]n individual may not legitimately demand privacy for activities conducted out of doors in fields, except in the area immediately surrounding the home. . . . This rule is true to the conception of the right to privacy embodied in the Fourth Amendment. The Amendment reflects the recognition of the Framers that certain enclaves should be free from arbitrary government interference. For example, the Court since the enactment of the Fourth Amendment has stressed 'the overriding respect for the sanctity of the home that has been embedded in our traditions since the origins of the Republic.'"

"The historical underpinnings of the open fields doctrine also demonstrate that the doctrine is consistent with respect for 'reasonable expectations of privacy.' As Justice Holmes, writing for the Court, observed in *Hester* [*v. United States*, 265 U.S. 57 (1924)], the common law distinguished 'open fields' from the 'curtilage,' the land immediately surrounding and associated with the home. . . . The distinction implies that only the curtilage, not the neighboring open fields, warrants the Fourth Amendment protections that attach to the home. At common law, the curtilage is the area to which extends the intimate activity associated with the 'sanctity of a man's home and the privacies of life . . .' and therefore has been considered part of the home itself for Fourth Amendment purposes. Thus, courts have extended Fourth Amendment protection to the curtilage; and they have defined the curtilage, as did the common law, by reference to the factors that determine whether an individual reasonably may expect that an area immediately adjacent to the home will remain private. Conversely, the common law implies, as we reaffirm today, that no expectation of privacy legitimately attaches to open fields."

"Initially, we reject the suggestion that steps taken to protect privacy establish that expectations of privacy in an open field are legitimate. . . . The test of legitimacy is not whether the individual chooses to conceal assertedly 'private' activity. Rather, the correct inquiry is whether the government's intrusion infringes upon the personal and societal values protected by the Fourth Amendment. As we have explained, we find no basis for concluding that a police inspection of open fields accomplishes such an infringement."

"We conclude that the open fields doctrine, as enunciated in *Hester*, is consistent with the plain language of the Fourth Amendment and its historical purposes."

c. Other Buildings and Unoccupied Property

United States v. Dunn, 480 U.S. 294 (1987)
Vote: 7-2

FACTS: DEA agents discovered that Robert Lyle Carpenter had purchased large quantities of chemicals and equipment used to manufacture amphetamine and phenylacetone. The agents then obtained warrants from a Texas judge authorizing installation of "beepers" in some equipment ordered by Carpenter. After Carpenter took possession of the equipment, the agents lost the signal from one of the beepers a few days later. However, they were able to track another for about a month when Carpenter's truck arrived at Ronald Dale Dunn's ranch. The agents also began receiving signals from the beeper they had lost previously and discovered that it too was on Dunn's property.

Police made a warrantless entry onto Dunn's property, and a DEA agent accompanied by a Houston police officer crossed over the outer fence and one of the interior fences. Standing midway between the house and the barns, the DEA agent smelled what he believed to be a chemical used to make narcotics coming from the barns. The officers approached the smallest barn and, looking in, observed empty boxes. The officers then proceeded to the larger barn by crossing two fences. The officers walked to the locked wooden gates and, shining a flashlight, looked into the barn. They observed what the DEA agent thought to be a narcotics lab, but the officers did not enter. At this point the officers departed from the property, but they reentered it twice to confirm the presence of the lab. The officers then obtained a search warrant for the property and seized evidence related to the manufacture of narcotics. Dunn and Carpenter were convicted of conspiring to manufacture phenylacetone and amphetamine and to possess amphetamine with intent to distribute. Dunn was also convicted of manufacturing phenylacetone and amphetamine and possessing amphetamine with intent to distribute.

ISSUE: Is the area near a barn located approximately fifty yards from a fence surrounding a ranch house within the curtilage of the house?

HOLDING: No.

RATIONALE: "We conclude that the barn and the area around it lay outside the curtilage of the house."

"[W]e identified the central component of this inquiry as whether the area harbors the 'intimate activity associated with the 'sanctity of a man's home and the privacies of life.'"

"Drawing upon the Court's own cases and the cumulative experience of the lower courts that have grappled with the task of defining the extent of a home's curtilage, we believe that curtilage questions should be resolved with particular reference to four factors: the proximity of the area claimed to be curtilage to the home, whether the area is included within an enclosure surrounding the home, the nature of the uses to which the area is put, and the steps taken by the resident to protect the area from observation by people passing by. . . . We do not suggest that combining these factors produces a finely tuned formula that, when mechanically applied, yields a 'correct' answer to all extent-of-curtilage questions. Rather, these factors are useful analytical tools only to the degree that, in any given case, they bear upon the centrally relevant consideration—whether the area in question is so intimately tied to the home itself that it should be placed under the home's 'umbrella' of Fourth Amendment protection. Applying these factors to respondent's barn and to the area immediately surrounding it, we have little difficulty in concluding that this area lay outside the curtilage of the ranch house."

d. Overflight of Dwelling

California v. Ciraolo, 476 U.S. 207 (1986)
Vote: 5-4

FACTS: Santa Clara, California, police received a telephone tip that Ciraolo was growing marijuana in his backyard. Police were unable to observe the yard because of two fences on the property. Later that day, Officers Shutz and Rodriguez obtained a private plane and flew over Ciraolo's house at 1,000 feet. Both officers were trained in marijuana identification and easily identified marijuana plants eight to ten feet tall growing in Ciraolo's yard; they then photographed the area with a standard 35mm camera. Shutz then obtained a search warrant based on an affidavit describing the tip and their observations; a photograph of the house, the backyard, and neighboring homes was attached to the affidavit. When the warrant was executed, seventy-three plants were seized. Ciraolo pleaded guilty to a charge of cultivation of marijuana.

ISSUE: May the police take unaided aerial photographs of a backyard within the curtilage of a home while using a private plane, flying at an altitude of 1,000 feet, for the purpose of viewing marijuana plants without a warrant?

HOLDING: Yes.

RATIONALE: "It can reasonably be assumed that the 10-foot fence was placed to conceal the marijuana crop from at least street-level views. So far as the normal sidewalk traffic was concerned, this fence served that purpose."

"Yet a 10-foot fence might not shield these plants from the eyes of a citizen or a policeman perched on the top of a truck or a two-level bus. Whether respondent therefore manifested a subjective expectation of privacy from *all* observations of his backyard, or whether instead he manifested merely a hope that no one would observe his unlawful gardening pursuits, is not entirely clear in these circumstances. Respondent appears to challenge the authority of government to observe his activity from any vantage point or place if the viewing is motivated by a law enforcement purpose, and not the result of a casual, accidental observation."

"[T]he question remains whether naked-eye observation of the curtilage by police from an aircraft lawfully operating at an altitude of 1,000 feet violates an expectation of privacy that is reasonable."

"That the area is within the curtilage does not itself bar all police observation. The Fourth Amendment protection of the home has never been extended to require law enforcement officers to shield their eyes when passing by a home on public thoroughfares. Nor does the mere fact that an individual has taken measures to restrict some views of his activities preclude an officer's observations from a public vantage point where he has a right to be and which renders the activities clearly visible."

"That the observation from aircraft was directed at identifying the plants and the officers were trained to recognize marijuana is irrelevant. Such observation is precisely what a judicial officer needs to provide a basis for a warrant. Any member of the public flying in this airspace who glanced down could have seen everything that these officers observed. On this record, we readily conclude that respondent's expectation that his garden was protected from such observation is unreasonable and is not an expectation that society is prepared to honor."

"In an age where private and commercial flight in the public airways is routine, it is unreasonable for respondent to expect that his marijuana plants were constitutionally protected from being observed with the naked eye from an altitude of 1,000 feet. The Fourth Amendment simply does not require the police traveling in the public airways at this altitude to obtain a warrant in order to observe what is visible to the naked eye."

4. Plain View

a. Defined

Harris v. United States, 390 U.S. 234 (1968)
Vote: 8-0
FACTS: Harris's car had been seen leaving the site of the robbery. The car was traced and Harris was arrested as he was entering it near his home. After a brief search of the car, the officer took Harris to the station. At that point, the police decided to impound the car, and a tow was called to bring it to the precinct. It arrived about an hour after Harris. A regulation requires the officer who impounds a vehicle to thoroughly search the vehicle, to remove any valuables, and to attach a tag listing certain information about the impounding. The arresting officer, following this regulation, entered the car on the driver's side, searched the car, and tied a tag on the steering wheel. As he stepped out of the car and began to secure it, he saw the robbery victim's registration card, which had been in his stolen wallet. The officer returned to the precinct, brought Harris to the car, and showed him the card. Harris disavowed all knowledge of the card but was charged with and convicted of robbery.
ISSUE: May the police seize items within their plain view if they have the right to be in the position they are in to view the object?
HOLDING: Yes.
RATIONALE: "The sole question for our consideration is whether the officer discovered the registration card by means of an illegal search. We hold that he did not. . . . The precise and detailed findings of the District Court, accepted by the Court of Appeals, were to the effect that the discovery of the card was not the result of a search of the car, but of a measure taken to protect the car while it was in police custody. Nothing in the Fourth Amendment requires the police to obtain a warrant in these narrow circumstances."

"Once the door had lawfully been opened, the registration card, with the name of the robbery victim on it, was plainly visible. It has long been settled that objects falling in the plain view of an officer who has a right to be in the position to have that view are subject to seizure and may be introduced in evidence."

b. Movement of Objects

Arizona v. Hicks, 480 U.S. 321 (1987)
Vote: 6-3
FACTS: A bullet was fired through the floor of Hicks's apartment, injuring a man in the lower apartment. Police arrived and entered Hicks's apartment to search for the shooter, other victims, and for weapons. They found and seized three weapons and a stocking-cap mask. Officer Nelson noticed two sets of expensive stereo equipment, which seemed out of place in the apartment. Suspecting that they were stolen, he recorded their serial numbers, moving some of the components to do so, which he reported. On being advised that a turntable's serial number matched one that had been taken in a robbery, he seized it. It was later discovered that serial numbers of other components in the apartment matched those on equipment taken in the robbery, and a warrant was executed to seize that equipment as well. Hicks was indicted for the robbery. The state trial court granted Hicks's motion to suppress the evidence that had been seized. The Court of Appeals of Arizona agreed. The state appealed.
ISSUE: Does the "plain view" doctrine require police to have probable cause to move objects unrelated to the original exigency for entering a home before they can seize them?
HOLDING: Yes.
RATIONALE: "[T]aking action, unrelated to the objectives of the authorized intrusion, which exposed to view concealed portions of the apartment or its contents, did produce a new invasion of respondent's privacy unjustified by the exigent circumstance that validated the entry. This is why, contrary to Justice Powell's suggestion, the 'distinction between "looking" at a suspicious object in plain view and "moving" it even a few inches' is much more than trivial for purposes of the Fourth Amendment. It matters not that the search uncovered nothing of any great personal value to respondent—serial numbers rather than (what might conceivably have been hidden behind or under the equipment) letters or photographs. A search is a search, even if it happens to disclose nothing but the bottom of a turntable."

"We have not ruled on the question whether probable cause is required in order to invoke the 'plain view' doctrine."

"We now hold that probable cause is required. To say otherwise would be to cut the 'plain view' doctrine loose from its theoretical and practical moorings. . . . No reason is apparent why an object should routinely be seizable on lesser grounds, during an unrelated search and seizure, than would have been needed to obtain a warrant for that same object if it had been known to be on the premises."

"No special operational necessities are relied on here, however—but rather the mere fact that the items in question came lawfully within the officer's plain view. That alone cannot supplant the requirement of probable cause."

"A dwelling-place search, no less than a dwelling-place seizure, requires probable cause, and there is no reason in theory or practicality why application of the 'plain view' doctrine would supplant that requirement. . . . Indeed, to treat searches more liberally would especially erode the plurality's warning in *Coolidge* [*v. New Hampshire*, 403 U.S. 443 (1971)] that 'the "plain view" doctrine may not be used to extend a general exploratory search from one object to another until something incriminating at last emerges.' In short, whether legal authority to move the equipment could be found only as an inevitable concomitant of the authority to seize it, or also as a consequence of some independent power to search certain objects in plain view, probable cause to believe the equipment was stolen was required."

"Justice O'Connor's dissent suggests that we uphold the action here on the ground that it was a 'cursory inspection' rather than a 'full-blown search,' and could therefore be justified by reasonable suspicion instead of probable cause. . . . We are unwilling to send police and judges into a new thicket of Fourth Amendment law, to seek a creature of uncertain description that is neither a 'plain view' inspection nor yet a 'full-blown search.'"

c. Mistaken Discovery of Objects

Horton v. California, 496 U.S. 128 (1990)
Vote: 7-2
FACTS: When Erwin Wallaker returned home from the San Jose Coin Club's annual show, he entered his garage and was assaulted by two men who shocked him with a "stun gun." They then bound and handcuffed him, and robbed him of jewelry and cash. During the encounter sufficient conversation took place to allow Wallaker to identify Horton's voice. His identification was corroborated by a witness who saw the robbers leave the scene, and by evidence that Horton had attended the coin shows. Sergeant LaRault's search warrant affidavit referred to police reports that described the weapons and the proceeds, but the warrant only authorized a search for the proceeds, including three rings. LaRault searched Horton's house, but did not find the property. However, he did discover an Uzi machine gun, a .38 revolver, two stun guns, a handcuff key, a San Jose Coin Club brochure, and a few items of clothing identified by the victim. LaRault testified that while he was searching for the rings, he also was interested in finding other evidence connecting Horton to the robbery. Thus, the seized evidence was not discovered "inadvertently." Horton was convicted of armed robbery.
ISSUE: Does evidence have to be discovered inadvertently in order for it to be admissible under the plain view doctrine?
HOLDING: No.
RATIONALE: "In this case we revisit . . . [w]hether the warrantless seizure of evidence of crime in plain view is prohibited by the Fourth Amendment if the discovery of the evidence was not inadvertent. We conclude that even though inadvertence is a characteristic of most legitimate 'plain view' seizures, it is not a necessary condition."

"First, evenhanded law enforcement is best achieved by the application of objective standards of conduct, rather than standards that depend upon the subjective state of mind of the officer. The fact that an officer is interested in an item of evidence and fully expects to find it in the course of a search should not invalidate its seizure if the search is confined in area and duration by the terms of a warrant or a valid exception to the warrant requirement. If the officer has knowledge approaching certainty that the item will be found, we see no reason why he or she would deliberately omit a particular description of the item to be seized from the application for a search warrant. Specification of the additional item could only permit the officer to expand the scope of the search. On the other hand, if he or she has a valid warrant to search for one item and merely a suspicion concerning the second, whether or not it amounts to probable cause, we fail to see why that suspicion should immunize the second item from seizure if it is found during a lawful search for the first."

"Second, the suggestion that the inadvertence requirement is necessary to prevent the police from conducting general searches, or from converting specific warrants into general warrants, is not persuasive because that interest is already served by the requirements that no warrant issue unless it 'particularly describes the place to be searched and the persons or things to be seized . . .' and that a warrantless search be circumscribed by the exigencies which justify its initiation. . . . Scrupulous adherence to these requirements serves the interests in limiting the area and duration of the search that the inadvertence requirement inadequately protects. Once those commands have been satisfied and the officer has a lawful right of access, however, no additional Fourth Amendment interest is furthered by requiring that the discovery of evidence be inadvertent. If the scope of the search exceeds that permitted by the terms of a validly issued warrant or the character of the relevant exception from the warrant requirement, the subsequent seizure is unconstitutional without more."

d. Use of Devices to Improve Sight

Texas v. Brown, 460 U.S. 730 (1983)
Vote: 9-0
FACTS: Officer Tom Maples of the Fort Worth Police, assisted in setting up a license checkpoint. Around midnight, he stopped Clifford James Brown's car and asked him for his license. Maples then shined his flashlight into the car and saw Brown's hand withdraw from his pocket holding a green balloon, which Brown let fall beside his leg. Brown then reached across the passenger seat and opened the glove compartment. Maples moved so that he could get a better view of the glove box and noticed that it contained small vials, white powder, and a bag of balloons. After rummaging through the glove compartment, Brown told Maples that he did not have his license with him. Maples then instructed him to stand at the rear of the car. Brown complied and Maples reached into the car, picked up the green balloon, and noticed a powdery substance within the tied-off portion. Maples then displayed the balloon to a fellow officer, and they placed Brown under arrest. Brown was subsequently convicted of heroin possession.

ISSUE: Can evidence seized as the result of a police seizure enhanced by the use of a flashlight be admitted under the plain view doctrine?

HOLDING: Yes.

RATIONALE: "It is likewise beyond dispute that Maples's action in shining his flashlight to illuminate the interior of Brown's car trenched upon no right secured to the latter by the Fourth Amendment. The Court said in *United States v. Lee* [274 U.S. 559 (1927)] . . . '[The] use of a searchlight is comparable to the use of a marine glass or a field glass. It is not prohibited by the Constitution.' Numerous other courts have agreed that the use of artificial means to illuminate a darkened area simply does not constitute a search, and thus triggers no Fourth Amendment protection."

"Decisions by this Court since *Coolidge* [*v. New Hampshire*, 403 U.S. 443 (1971)] indicate that the use of the phrase 'immediately apparent' was very likely an unhappy choice of words, since it can be taken to imply that an unduly high degree of certainty as to the incriminatory character of evidence is necessary for an application of the 'plain view' doctrine."

"[T]he Court did not view the 'immediately apparent' language of *Coolidge* as establishing any requirement that a police officer 'know' that certain items are contraband or evidence of a crime. Indeed, *Colorado v. Bannister*, [449 U.S. 1 (1980)] was merely an application of the rule . . . that '[the] seizure of property in plain view involves no invasion of privacy and *is presumptively reasonable, assuming that there is probable cause to associate the property with criminal activity.*'"

4. Exigent Circumstances

a. Armed Suspects

Warden v. Hayden, 387 U.S. 294 (1967)

Vote: 8-1

FACTS: An armed robber entered the Diamond Cab Company in Baltimore, Maryland. He took $363 and ran. Two drivers, attracted by shouts of "Holdup," followed the man to a house. One driver described the man to the dispatcher. The dispatcher relayed the information to police, who were proceeding to the scene of the robbery. Within minutes, police arrived at the house and announced their presence. Mrs. Hayden answered, and the officers told her they believed that a robber had entered the house, and asked to search the house. She offered no objection.

The officers spread out through the first and second floors and the cellar and Hayden was found in an upstairs bedroom feigning sleep. He was arrested. Another officer was attracted to a bathroom by the noise of running water and discovered a shotgun and a pistol in a flush tank; another officer "was searching the cellar for a man or the money" and found a jacket and trousers of the type the fleeing man was said to have worn. A clip of ammunition for the pistol and a cap were found under the mattress of Hayden's bed, and ammunition for the shotgun was found in a drawer in Hayden's room. All these items of evidence were introduced against him at his trial, where he was convicted of robbery. He then initiated habeas corpus proceedings.

ISSUE: Is there an exception to the exclusionary rule that allows the police to enter a home without a warrant if exigent circumstances exist?

HOLDING: Yes.

RATIONALE: "We agree with the Court of Appeals that neither the entry without warrant to search for the robber, nor the search for him without warrant was invalid. Under the circumstances of this case, 'the exigencies of the situation made that course imperative. . . .' The police . . . acted reasonably when they entered the house and began to search for a man of the description they had been given and for weapons which he had used in the robbery or might use against them. The Fourth Amendment does not require police officers to delay in the course of an investigation if to do so would gravely endanger their lives or the lives of others. Speed here was essential, and only a thorough search of the house for persons and weapons could have insured that Hayden was the only man present and that the police had control of all weapons which could be used against them or to effect an escape."

b. Injured Home Occupants

Brigham City, Utah v. Stuart 126 S.Ct. 1943 (2006)
Vote: 9-0

FACTS: Police responded to a party at a residence. They heard shouting from inside and walked up the driveway. They then saw two juveniles drinking in the backyard and entered the yard. They saw a fight taking place inside the house between four adults trying to restrain a juvenile. An officer testified that the juvenile struck an adult in the face and that he observed blood from the injury. The fight continued, with the other adults driving the juvenile into the refrigerator which was then pushed across the floor. An officer opened the door and announced his presence twice before anyone became aware that he was there.

The officers subsequently charged the respondents. At trial, the motion to suppress was granted by the court and affirmed by the Utah Court of Appeals. The Utah Supreme Court rejected the contention that the juvenile's assault triggered the "emergency aid doctrine" because there was no justification for an "objectively reasonable belief that an unconscious, semi-conscious, or missing person feared injured or dead [was] in the home" and also because the police did not assist the injured adult but acted "exclusively in their law enforcement capacity." Finally, it also rejected the idea that the warrantless entry was justified via an exigent circumstance.

ISSUE: Is the Fourth Amendment violated when police enter a home without a warrant if they reasonably believe that an occupant is seriously injured or in imminent danger of such injury?

HOLDING: No.

RATIONALE: "'[W]arrants are generally required to search a person's home or his person unless 'the exigencies of the situation' make the needs of law enforcement so compelling that the warrantless search is objectively reasonable under the Fourth Amendment. . . .'"

"One exigency obviating the requirement of a warrant is the need to assist persons who are seriously injured or threatened with such injury. 'The need to protect or preserve life or avoid serious injury is justification for what would be otherwise illegal absent an exigency or emergency.'"

"An action is 'reasonable' under the Fourth Amendment, regardless of the individual officer's state of mind, 'as long as the circumstances, viewed *objectively*, justify [the] action. . . .' The officer's subjective motivation is irrelevant."

"'[A]n important factor to be considered when determining whether any exigency exists is the gravity of the underlying offense for which the arrest is being made. . . .' Here, the officers were confronted with *ongoing* violence occurring *within* the home."

5. Inevitable Discovery

Nix v. Williams, 467 U.S. 431 (1984)
Vote: 7-2
FACTS: In *Brewer v Williams*, [430 U.S. 387 (1977),] Robert Williams was convicted of killing Pamela Powers, who had gone with her family to a YMCA in Des Moines, Iowa, to watch a sporting event. Williams was spotted leaving the building with a bundle in his arms. Upon capture, counsel was retained. His lawyer spoke to another lawyer who was acting on his behalf in Davenport because his retained lawyer could not be there. Williams was told by both lawyers to remain silent and not talk to police, and the police grudgingly agreed not to interrogate him. In what came to be known as the "Christian Burial Speech," an officer appealed to Williams's religious views in an attempt to get him to lead police to the victim's body, for which they were searching. On appeal, evidence pertaining to the seized body and Williams's incriminating statements were suppressed, and the Supreme Court affirmed that decision, granting Williams a new trial.

At the second trial, the prosecution introduced evidence of the condition that the body was found in and related test results. It did not introduce Williams's statements or any information indicating that he led police to the body. The trial court stated that the prosecution had proved that the body would have been discovered at some point by the search teams, even without information from Williams. Williams was then convicted of the murder a second time and sentenced to life in prison. On appeal, the state again affirmed, but an appellate court reversed, holding that the state did not meet its burden that the police had not acted in bad faith.
ISSUE: Is there an inevitable discovery exception to the exclusionary rule?
HOLDING: Yes.
RATIONALE: "If the prosecution can establish by a preponderance of the evidence that the information ultimately or inevitably would have been discovered by lawful means . . . then the deterrence rationale has so little basis that the evidence should be received. Anything less would reject logic, experience, and common sense."

"The requirement that the prosecution must prove the absence of bad faith, imposed here by the Court of Appeals, would place courts in the position of withholding from juries relevant and undoubted truth that would have been available to police absent any unlawful police activity. Of course, that view would put the police in a *worse* position than they would have been in if no unlawful conduct had transpired. And, of equal importance, it wholly fails to take into account the enormous societal cost of excluding truth in the search for truth in the administration of justice. Nothing in this Court's prior holdings supports any such formalistic, pointless, and punitive approach."

"The Court of Appeals concluded, without analysis, that if an absence-of-bad-faith requirement were not imposed, 'the temptation to risk deliberate violations of the Sixth Amendment would be too great, and the deterrent effect of the Exclusionary Rule reduced too far. . . .' We reject that view. A police officer who is faced with the opportunity to obtain evidence illegally will rarely, if ever, be in a position to calculate whether the evidence sought would inevitably be discovered."

"On the other hand, when an officer is aware that the evidence will inevitably be discovered, he will try to avoid engaging in any questionable practice. In that situation, there will be little to gain from taking any dubious 'shortcuts' to obtain the evidence. Significant disincentives to obtaining evidence illegally—including the possibility of departmental discipline and civil liability—also lessen the likelihood that the ultimate or inevitable discovery exception will promote police misconduct."

"Exclusion of physical evidence that would inevitably have been discovered adds nothing to either the integrity or fairness of a criminal trial. The Sixth Amendment right to counsel protects against unfairness by preserving the adversary process in which the reliability of proffered evidence may be tested in cross-examination."

"Fairness can be assured by placing the State and the accused in the same positions they would have been in had the impermissible conduct not taken place. However, if the government can prove that the evidence would have been obtained inevitably and, therefore, would have been admitted regardless of any overreaching by the police, there is no rational basis to keep that evidence from the jury in order to ensure the fairness of the trial proceedings. In that situation, the State has gained no advantage at trial and the defendant has suffered no prejudice. Indeed, suppression of the evidence would operate to undermine the adversary system by putting the State in a *worse* position than it would have occupied without any police misconduct."

III
THE FIFTH AMENDMENT—
QUESTIONING SUSPECTS

9

Interrogation and Confessions

IN THIS CHAPTER, THE SUBJECT UNDER STUDY is what happens when the police have either identified a suspect or made an arrest. At this juncture, the questioning of suspects, or interrogation, becomes important. As one might expect, the police cannot just begin questioning or utilize any particular tactic simply because they have identified a possible suspect. There are rules to follow, and as a result some feel that the Supreme Court rulings surrounding interrogation are convoluted and unclear. As a matter of fact, it has been said that interrogation law is probably the most difficult to understand of all the areas of criminal procedure. Relatedly, the Court has also had to determine the constitutionality of the "fruit" of police interrogation: the confession. Here again, confusing rules and lack of clarity are the order of the day. Nevertheless, it is also important to note that the Court has also made some very clear "bright line" rulings in this area. As a result, some of the rules are actually quite easy to follow.

For example, over time the Supreme Court has looked at three main ways to determine the legality or admissibility of confessions obtained by the police. First among those is the voluntariness test. The question here was whether or not the confession was freely given without duress. Next in line was the "overborne will" test, that is, was the confession coerced from the suspect. If so, then the confession was excluded. In fact, the Court has ruled on several examples of such coercion. Finally, and the one used by the Court today, is the test that protects a suspect against self-incrimination. For this test, the Court stresses the right that a suspect has not to incriminate him or herself, so in effect they have the right to remain silent if they so choose. Once that right is asserted, the police must be very careful in obtaining information from the suspect. While there are exceptions to this rule, they are narrowly constructed and the police must be careful not to violate them or they run the risk of having their evidence excluded at trial.

The self-incrimination test is also complicated, as the Court has delineated several components and exceptions to it. Specifically, the Court has noted that two things must be present before the police have to give the now famous *Miranda* warnings: custody and interrogation. If one of these things is lacking, then the police do not have to worry about the *Miranda* warnings at all. These two components are sometimes referred to as the "*Miranda* triggers" because once they occur, the police must administer the warnings. The Court has ruled on what custody is and also what interrogation is (and is not) for purposes of administering the warnings, and naturally, there are exceptions to these requirements also. In fact, the Court has also ruled that where an interrogation takes place can also be factored into the equation.

Another point to remember is that the suspect has a *Fifth Amendment* right to counsel during interrogation. You may have heard about the *Sixth Amendment* right to counsel at trial. Suspects, if they choose, do not have to answer questions at all. This is important to note because the Sixth Amendment right is different from the Fifth, which applies to potential confessions. Again, the idea is to protect the suspect from incriminating himself, and the Supreme Court is involved in determining how this process takes place. For example, the Court has argued that this particular right to counsel attaches when the suspect becomes the "focus of the investigation," and naturally it has defined when that is. If a person does invoke this right, how is it expressed? The Court has also determined that the request for counsel must be clear and unequivocal. You might ask, "Can the police ask questions of the suspect after the right has been exercised?" The answer would be, "Well, sort of." The Court has stated that a suspect can waive his right to counsel and answer questions at any time, so long as the waiver is "knowing and intelligent." It is also the case that the police cannot really initiate the conversation, although the Court has decided some close calls in this area. Finally, the Court has also made some rulings in the area of police questioning suspects after they have already been charged. As you might expect, the right to have counsel present during these types of interrogations also exists.

A. Constitutional Approaches to Interrogation

1. Due Process and Voluntariness

Brown v. Mississippi, 297 U.S. 278 (1936)
Vote: 9-0
FACTS: Ed Brown, Henry Shields, and Ellington were indicted for the murder of Raymond Stewart. They pleaded not guilty. Deputy Sheriff Dial and others went to Ellington's home and requested that he accompany them to Stewart's house. Several white men accused Ellington of killing Stewart, and when he denied it, they seized him and hung him several times from a tree. After Ellington persisted in his innocence, they tied him to a tree and whipped him. Finally released, he returned home. A day or two later Dial, with another, returned and arrested Ellington taking him to a jail in a different county. On the way they stopped and again whipped Ellington, stating that they would continue until he confessed, Ellington then confessed, and was taken to jail.

Brown and Shields were also arrested and taken to the same jail, and Dial, with several white men, lashed their backs with a belt and its buckles. Told that the beating would continue until they confessed, they finally did so. The beatings continued, however, until all of the stories matched to the satisfaction of the accusers.

Members of the mob then warned the defendants that if they changed their story, they would return and beat them again. The next day, two sheriffs and several others came to hear their confessions. One of the sheriffs admitted that he had heard about the whipping but asserted that he had no knowledge of it and stated that one of the defendants was limping and did not sit down. The defendant told him that he had been strapped so severely that he could not sit. Rope burns were also visible on one of the defendants' neck. Testimony as to the confessions was objected to by their counsel, and the defendants then stated that the confessions had been procured by torture. The two sheriffs and one other person were witnesses as to the confessions, which were admitted by the court. The accused were found guilty two days after the trial began and sentenced to death. The appellate court affirmed the convictions, and the state supreme court heard their additional appeal but denied their contention that the confessions were coerced and that they did not have the opportunity to speak to their lawyers in a reasonable way.

ISSUE: Can confessions obtained by torture be considered voluntary and consistent with due process?

HOLDING: No.

RATIONALE: "It is sufficient to say that in pertinent respects the transcript reads more like pages torn from some medieval account, than a record made within the confines of a modern civilization which aspires to an enlightened constitutional government."

"There was thus enough before the court when these confessions were first offered to make known to the court that they were not, beyond all reasonable doubt, free and voluntary; and the failure of the court then to exclude the confessions is sufficient to reverse the judgment, under every rule of procedure that has heretofore been prescribed."

"The evidence upon which the conviction was obtained was the so-called confessions. Without this evidence a peremptory instruction to find for the defendants would have been inescapable. The defendants were put on the stand, and by their testimony the facts and the details thereof as to the manner by which the confessions were extorted from them were fully developed. . . . The facts are not only undisputed, they are admitted, and admitted to have been done by officers of the state, in conjunction with other participants, and all this was definitely well known to everybody connected with the trial, and during the trial, including the state's prosecuting attorney and the trial judge presiding."

"[T]he freedom of the State in establishing its policy is the freedom of constitutional government and is limited by the requirement of due process of law. Because a State may dispense with a jury trial, it does not follow that it may substitute trial by ordeal. The rack and torture chamber may not be substituted for the witness stand. The State may not permit an accused to be hurried to conviction under mob domination— where the whole proceeding is but a mask—without supplying corrective process. . . . Nor may a State, through the action of its officers, contrive a conviction through the pretense of a trial which in truth is 'but used as a means of depriving a defendant of liberty through a deliberate deception of court and jury by the presentation of testimony known to be perjured. . . .' It would be difficult to conceive of methods more revolting to the sense of justice than those taken to procure the confessions of these petitioners, and the use of the confessions thus obtained as the basis for conviction and sentence was a clear denial of due process."

"In *Fisher v State* [145 Miss. 116], the court said: 'Coercing the supposed state's criminals into confessions and using such confessions so coerced from them against them in trials has been the curse of all countries. It was the chief inequity, the crowning infamy of the Star Chamber, and the Inquisition, and other similar institutions. The constitution recognized the evils that lay behind these practices and prohibited them in this country. . . . The duty of maintaining constitutional rights of a person on trial for his life rises above mere rules of procedure and wherever the court is clearly satisfied that such violations exist, it will refuse to sanction such violations and will apply the corrective.'"

a. Injured Suspects or Witnesses

Mincey v. Arizona, 437 U.S. 385 (1978)
Vote: 8-1
FACTS: Officer Barry Headricks knocked on the door of an apartment occupied by Rufus Mincey. Headricks arranged to buy heroin from him and left to obtain money. He returned with nine other plainclothes officers and a deputy county attorney. John Hodgman opened the door. Headricks moved into the bedroom while Hodgman tried to keep the other officers from entering. As the police entered, shots were heard from the bedroom and Headricks collapsed and later died in the hospital. Other officers

found Mincey lying on the floor, wounded, and semiconscious. He was taken to the emergency room where he was treated.

After the shooting, the officers looked around for other victims and found a woman wounded in the bedroom closet and Mincey's three acquaintances in the living room. The agents did not investigate any further but only guarded the suspects and the premises. Homicide detectives then proceeded to open drawers, closets, and cupboards. They emptied pockets; dug bullet fragments out of the walls and floors; pulled up carpet and every item in the apartment was inventoried. The search lasted four days and 200 to 300 objects were seized. No warrant was ever obtained.

The evening of the shooting, Detective Hust interrogated Mincey at the hospital, but Mincey was unable to talk. He was only able to respond to questions by writing answers on pieces of paper. Hust placed Mincey under arrest for Headricks's murder and gave Mincey the *Miranda* warnings. Although Mincey asked frequently to speak to a lawyer, Hust continued until almost midnight. Mincey was convicted for murder, assault, and three drug offenses.

ISSUE: Can a confession obtained via constant questioning of a critically injured suspect be admissible?

HOLDING: No.

RATIONALE: "In light of our holding that Mincey's hospital statements were not voluntarily given, it is unnecessary to reach his alternative contention that their use against him was impermissible."

"But *any* criminal trial use against a defendant of his *involuntary* statement is a denial of due process of law 'even though there is ample evidence aside from the confession to support the conviction.'"

"It is hard to imagine a situation less conducive to the exercise of 'a rational intellect and a free will' than Mincey's. . . . He was . . . unable to escape or resist the . . . interrogation."

"But despite Mincey's entreaties to be let alone, Hust ceased the interrogation only during intervals when Mincey lost consciousness or received medical treatment, and after each such interruption returned relentlessly to his task. The statements at issue were thus the result of virtually continuous questioning of a seriously and painfully wounded man on the edge of consciousness."

"There were not present in this case some of the gross abuses that have led the Court in other cases to find confessions involuntary, such as beatings . . . or 'truth serums. . . .' But 'the blood of the accused is not the only hallmark of an unconstitutional inquisition. . . .' Determination of whether a statement is involuntary . . . requires careful evaluation of all the circumstances of the interrogation."

"It is apparent from the record in this case that Mincey's statements were not 'the product of his free and rational choice. . . .' Due process of law requires that statements obtained as these were cannot be used in any way against a defendant at his trial."

b. Involuntariness and Non-Criminal Cases

Chavez v. Martinez, 538 U.S. 760 (2003)
Vote: 6-3
FACTS: Police officers Maria Peña and Andrew Salinas were investigating suspected drug activity. While questioning an individual, they heard a bicycle approaching on a darkened path. They ordered the rider, Oliverio Martinez, to get off the bike, spread his legs, and place his hands behind his head. He complied. Salinas then frisked Martinez and discovered a knife. An altercation ensued. The officers claimed that Martinez drew Salinas's gun and pointed it at them. Martinez denies this version, but both sides agree that Salinas yelled, "He's got my gun!" Peña then shot Martinez several times, causing severe injuries that left him permanently blinded and paralyzed from the waist down. The officers then arrested Martinez.

Ben Chavez, a patrol supervisor, arrived with paramedics and accompanied Martinez to the hospital and then questioned him while he was receiving treatment. The interview lasted about ten minutes, but took place over a forty-five-minute period, with Chavez leaving the room to permit treatment. Initially, Martinez answered "I don't know," "I am dying," and "I am choking." However, he later stated that he took the gun from Salinas's holster and pointed it at the police, and that he used heroin. At one point, Martinez said, "I am not telling you anything until they treat me," but Chavez continued. Martinez was never read his *Miranda* rights. He was not charged with a crime. His responses to Chavez's questioning were never used against him in a prosecution. However, Martinez sued Chavez, arguing that his actions violated his Fifth Amendment right not to be compelled to be a witness against himself, as well as his Fourteenth Amendment due process right to be free from coercive questioning.

ISSUE: Does the protection against coercive questioning apply to noncriminal cases?
HOLDING: No.
RATIONALE: "We conclude that Martinez's allegations fail to state a violation of his constitutional rights. The Fifth Amendment . . . requires that 'no person . . . shall be compelled *in any criminal case* to be a *witness* against himself. . . .' We fail to see how, based on the text of the Fifth Amendment, Martinez can allege a violation of this right, since Martinez was never prosecuted for a crime, let alone compelled to be a witness against himself in a criminal case."

"In our view, a 'criminal case' at the very least requires the initiation of legal proceedings. . . . We need not decide today the precise moment when a 'criminal case' commences; it is enough to say that police questioning does not constitute a 'case.'"

"Here, Martinez was never made to be a 'witness' against himself in violation of the Fifth Amendment's Self-Incrimination Clause because his statements were never admitted as testimony against him in a criminal case. Nor was he ever placed under oath and exposed to '"the cruel trilemma of self-accusation, perjury or contempt. . . ."' The text of the Self-Incrimination Clause simply cannot support the Ninth Circuit's view that the mere use of compulsive questioning, without more, violates the Constitution."

"Nor can the Ninth Circuit's approach be reconciled with our case law. It is well established that the government may compel witnesses to testify at trial or before a grand jury, on pain of contempt. . . . Our holdings in these cases demonstrate that, contrary to the Ninth Circuit's view, mere coercion does not violate the text of the Self-Incrimination Clause absent use of the compelled statements in a criminal case against the witness."

"We fail to see how Martinez was any more 'compelled in any criminal case to be a witness against himself' than an immunized witness forced to testify on pain of contempt. . . . The fact that Martinez did not *know* his statements could not be used against him does not change our view that no violation of Fifth Amendment's Self-Incrimination Clause occurred here."

"Our views on the proper scope of the Fifth Amendment's Self-Incrimination Clause do not mean that police torture or other abuse that results in a confession is constitutionally permissible so long as the statements are not used at trial; it simply means that the Fourteenth Amendment's Due Process Clause, rather than the Fifth Amendment's Self-Incrimination Clause, would govern the inquiry in those cases and provide relief in appropriate circumstances."

c. Test for Involuntariness

Townsend v. Sain, 372 U.S. 293 (1963)
Vote: 5-4
FACTS: Chicago police arrested Charles Townsend after they received information from Campbell that Townsend was connected with the robbery and murder of Jack Boone. Townsend was under the influence of heroin before his arrest, and it was his practice to take injections three to five hours apart. At about 2:30 a.m. he was taken to the police station and questioned for about two hours. He denied committing any crimes and was taken to another station, where he remained until that evening. He was then returned to the first station and placed in a lineup so that he could be viewed by the victim of a different robbery. When Anagnost, a victim of another robbery, identified someone other than Townsend, a scuffle ensued, and Townsend was again questioned for about an hour. He complained before the arrival of an assistant state's attorney that he had stomach pains, that he was suffering from withdrawal, that he wanted a doctor, and that he was in need of heroin. Officer Cagney called a police doctor who Townsend claims gave him something like "truth serum" and left some tablets for the pain. The medication helped with the pain, and he again began to respond to questions. After the doctor left, Officer Fitzgerald and the assistant state's attorney joined Cagney and questioned Townsend for about twenty-five minutes. They all then moved to a different room, where a court reporter took down Townsend's statements. Shortly thereafter, Townsend confessed and questioning ceased.

The following day, Townsend read transcripts of his confessions and signed them. He again experienced withdrawal, and the doctor brought additional pills. Townsend again confessed at a hearing while on the witness stand.

However, at the later hearing on Townsend's motion to suppress, Townsend disputed this series of events. He claimed that Cagney punched him in the stomach after Anagnost identified someone else in the lineup, and that Cagney said that Townsend knew he had committed the robbery. Townsend then stated that he fell and vomited blood and water and that he was sick from the drugs. Cagney then said that he would get a doctor if he would "cooperate" about Boone's murder. A few minutes later Cagney said that he thought him innocent and would call the doctor to help him. Townsend claimed that the doctor gave him an injection and several pills. He stated that he felt dizzy and sleepy when Anagnost was brought into the room, and he was told to tell him that he had committed the robbery.

He then stated that he was at a desk, given a pen, and he signed his name believing that he was going to be released. He said that he was then taken to a room with flickering lights, where he was told to keep his head up, and finally returned to his cell. Townsend said that the next morning he felt much better but could not remember anything that happened after the injection, but an officer told him that he had confessed. He was then taken to a room where he was asked about several robberies, and he confessed to all of them but complained of feeling sleepy. He then took the rest of the pills that the doctor provided and was taken to the state attorney's office, where he signed an additional form. The doctor gave him different color pills, some of which he took immediately. They kept him awake all night, and in the morning he was taken to the hearing, where he testified on the stand because he said the police told him to. He was convicted of murder at trial and sentenced to death.

ISSUE: Is a confession obtained from a person whose will is overborne by drugs admissible?

HOLDING: No.

RATIONALE: "Numerous decisions of this Court have established the standards governing the admissibility of confessions into evidence. If an individual's 'will was overborne' or if his confession was not 'the product of a rational intellect and a free will' his confession is inadmissible because coerced. These standards are applicable whether a confession is the product of physical intimidation or psychological pressure and, of course, are equally applicable to a drug-induced statement. It is difficult to imagine a situation in which a confession would be less the product of a free intellect, less voluntary, than when brought about by a drug having the effect of a 'truth serum. . . .' Any questioning by police officers which *in fact* produces a confession which is not the product of a free intellect renders that confession inadmissible. The Court has usually so stated the test. . . . 'If the confession which petitioner made . . . was in fact involuntary, the conviction cannot stand. . . .'"

"It is at least generally recognized that the administration of sufficient doses of scopolamine will break down the will. . . . The early literature on the subject designated scopolamine as a 'truth serum.'"

"Furthermore, a crucial fact was not disclosed at the state-court hearing: that the substance injected into Townsend before he confessed has properties which may trigger statements in a legal sense involuntary. This fact was vital to whether his confession was the product of a free will and therefore admissible."

2. Right to Counsel (Focus of the Investigation)

Escobedo v. Illinois, 378 U.S. 478 (1964)

Vote: 5-4

FACTS: Danny Escobedo's brother-in-law was shot, and Escobedo was arrested without a warrant and interrogated early the next morning. He made no statement and obtained release through his lawyer. However, Benedict DiGerlando, who was in custody, told police that Escobedo had fired the shots. That evening, Escobedo and his sister, the widow, were arrested and taken to the police station and while en route, the police handcuffed Escobedo and told him that DiGerlando had identified him as the shooter. Escobedo testified that the police told him that they should admit to the crime but that he requested a lawyer in response. Police stated that he would not have been allowed to leave even though he had not been charged. Shortly after Escobedo arrived at the station, so did his lawyer. The lawyer testified that when he arrived he asked several different officers to be permitted to see Escobedo, and each time he was denied. At one point, he and Escobedo saw each other and waved to one another, but police closed the door. He continued to wait and again asked to see Escobedo but was denied permission. During the course of the interrogation, Escobedo testified that he repeatedly requested to speak to his lawyer but was denied permission. Escobedo also said that he heard an officer tell his lawyer that they could not speak until the police were finished, which police confirmed. Escobedo further testified that officer Montejano told him that he and his sister could leave if he implicated DiGerlando, which he then did. Montejano denied making such statements.

Another officer stated that during the interrogation he told Escobedo that DiGerlando had identified him as the shooter and Escobedo said that he was lying and that he would tell him that himself. Escobedo was then allowed to confront DiGerlando, to whom he said that it was he (DiGerlando) who had shot the victim. After this he made further inculpatory statements. Assistant State's Attorney Theodore J. Cooper then took Escobedo's statement. Cooper testified that he did not advise Escobedo of his rights. Escobedo's statements were admitted over his objection, and he was convicted of murder.

ISSUE: Can a statement made by a person that the police have focused on as a suspect be admitted if the police have denied a request to speak with an attorney?

HOLDING: No.

RATIONALE: "We . . . consider whether the petitioner's statement was constitutionally admissible at his trial. . . . We conclude, for the reasons stated below, that it was not."

"The interrogation here was conducted before petitioner was formally indicted. But in the context of this case, that fact should make no difference. When petitioner requested, and was denied, an opportunity to consult with his lawyer, the investigation had ceased to be a general investigation of 'an unsolved crime. . . .' Petitioner had become the accused, and the purpose of the interrogation was to 'get him' to confess his guilt despite his constitutional right not to do so."

"It cannot be doubted that, placed in the position in which the accused was when the statement was made to him that the other suspected person had charged him with crime, the result was to produce upon his mind the fear that if he remained silent it would be considered an admission of guilt, and therefore render certain his being committed for trial as the guilty person."

"We hold, therefore, that where, as here, the investigation is no longer a general inquiry into an unsolved crime but has begun to focus on a particular suspect, the suspect has been taken into police custody, the police carry out a process of interrogations that lends itself to eliciting incriminating statements, the suspect has requested and been denied an opportunity to consult with his lawyer, and the police have not effectively warned him of his absolute constitutional right to remain silent, the accused has been denied 'the Assistance of Counsel' in violation of the Sixth Amendment to the Constitution as 'made obligatory upon the States by the Fourteenth Amendment . . .' and that no statement elicited by the police during the interrogation may be used against him at a criminal trial."

"State refusal of a request to engage counsel violates due process not only if the accused is deprived of counsel at trial on the merits, . . . *but also if he is deprived of counsel for any part of the pretrial proceedings,* provided that he is so prejudiced thereby as to infect his subsequent trial with an absence of 'that fundamental fairness essential to the very concept of justice. . . .' The latter determination necessarily depends upon all the circumstances of the case."

3. Self-Incrimination

a. Application to the States

Malloy v. Hogan, 378 U.S. 1 (1964)
Vote: 5-4
FACTS: Hartford, Connecticut, police arrested William Malloy during a gambling raid. He pleaded guilty to pool selling and was sentenced to one year in jail and fined $500. The sentence was suspended after ninety days, at which time he was to be given two years probation. About sixteen months later, Malloy was ordered to testify before the Superior Court of Hartford County, which was conducting an inquiry into gambling and other criminal activity. During his testimony, he was asked several questions about his arrest and conviction, and he refused to answer due to their incriminating nature. The court found him in contempt and committed him to prison until he was willing to answer the questions. Malloy's application for a writ of habeas corpus was denied by both the Superior and the Connecticut Supreme Courts. The Connecticut Supreme Court held that the privilege against self-incrimination was not available to a witness in a state proceeding, that the Fourteenth Amendment gave no privilege to him, and that he had not properly invoked the privilege available under the state constitution.
ISSUE: Is the Fifth Amendment privilege against self-incrimination applicable to the states?
HOLDING: Yes.

RATIONALE: "We hold today that the Fifth Amendment's exception from compulsory self-incrimination is also protected by the Fourteenth Amendment against abridgment by the States."

"The marked shift to the federal standard in state cases began with *Lisenba v. California* [314 U.S. 219 (1941)] . . . where the Court spoke of the accused's 'free choice to admit, to deny, or to refuse to answer. . . .' The shift reflects recognition that the American system of criminal prosecution is accusatorial, not inquisitorial, and that the Fifth Amendment privilege is its essential mainstay. . . . Governments, state and federal, are thus constitutionally compelled to establish guilt by evidence independently and freely secured, and may not use coercion to prove a charge against an accused out of his own mouth. Since the Fourteenth Amendment prohibits the States from inducing a person to confess through 'sympathy falsely aroused . . .' or other like inducement far short of 'compulsion by torture . . .' it follows a fortiori that it also forbids the States to resort to imprisonment, as here, to compel him to answer questions that might incriminate him. The Fourteenth Amendment secures against state invasion the same privilege that the Fifth Amendment guarantees against federal infringement—the right of a person to remain silent unless he chooses to speak in the unfettered exercise of his own will, and to suffer no penalty."

"Mapp [*v. Ohio*, 367 U.S. 643 (1961)] held that the Fifth Amendment privilege against self-incrimination implemented the Fourth Amendment in such cases, and that the two guarantees of personal security conjoined in the Fourteenth Amendment to make the exclusionary rule obligatory upon the States. We relied upon . . . *Boyd* [*v. United States*, 116 U.S. 616 (1886)] . . . , and . . . held that . . . any forcible and compulsory extortion of a man's own testimony, or of his private papers to be used as evidence to convict him of crime, or to forfeit his goods, is within the condemnation of (those Amendments). . . ."

"The Court thus has rejected the notion that the Fourteenth Amendment applies to the States only a 'watered-down, subjective version of the individual guarantees of the Bill of Rights. . . .' What is accorded is a privilege of refusing to incriminate one's self, and the feared prosecution may be by either federal or state authorities. . . . It would be incongruous to have different standards determine the validity of a claim of privilege based on the same feared prosecution, depending on whether the claim was asserted in a state or federal court. Therefore, the same standards must determine whether an accused's silence in either a federal or state proceeding is justified."

b. Protecting the Privilege against Self-Incrimination

Miranda v. Arizona, 384 U.S. 436 (1966)
Vote: 5-4
FACTS: Ernesto Miranda was arrested for kidnapping and rape and taken to a Phoenix police station. The complaining witness identified him. He was then taken to an interrogation room, where he was questioned by two police officers. The officers admitted that Miranda was not advised that he had a right to have an attorney, and after two hours, they had a signed, written confession from him. The confession stated that

Miranda had made it voluntarily, without threats or promises of immunity and with full knowledge of his legal rights. Miranda was convicted in a different trial for an unrelated robbery charge. A statement introduced at that trial was obtained from Miranda during the same interrogation. At the robbery trial, an officer testified that during the questioning he did not tell Miranda that his statements would be held against him or that he could consult with a lawyer. Another officer stated that Miranda was told that anything he said would be used against him and that he was not required to speak to them. The written confession was admitted over his objection, and Miranda was convicted of the charges.

ISSUE: Do the police, prior to questioning, have to warn a suspect that he has a right to remain silent, that any statement he makes may be used as against him, and that he has a right to the presence of an attorney?

HOLDING: Yes.

RATIONALE: "Our holding . . . briefly stated it is this: the prosecution may not use statements, whether exculpatory or inculpatory, stemming from custodial interrogation of the defendant unless it demonstrates the use of procedural safeguards effective to secure the privilege against self-incrimination. By custodial interrogation, we mean questioning initiated by law enforcement officers after a person has been taken into custody or otherwise deprived of his freedom of action in any significant way. As for the procedural safeguards to be employed, unless other fully effective means are devised to inform accused persons of their right of silence and to assure a continuous opportunity to exercise it, the following measures are required. Prior to any questioning, the person must be warned that he has a right to remain silent, that any statement he does make may be used as evidence against him, and that he has a right to the presence of an attorney, either retained or appointed. The defendant may waive effectuation of these rights, provided the waiver is made voluntarily, knowingly and intelligently. If, however, he indicates in any manner and at any stage of the process that he wishes to consult with an attorney before speaking there can be no questioning. Likewise, if the individual is alone and indicates in any manner that he does not wish to be interrogated, the police may not question him."

"Unless a proper limitation upon custodial interrogation is achieved . . . there can be no assurance that practices of this nature will be eradicated in the foreseeable future."

"The current practice of incommunicado interrogation is at odds with one of our Nation's most cherished principles—that the individual may not be compelled to incriminate himself. Unless adequate protective devices are employed to dispel the compulsion inherent in custodial surroundings, no statement obtained from the defendant can truly be the product of his free choice."

"The question in these cases is whether the privilege is fully applicable during a period of custodial interrogation. . . . We are satisfied that all the principles embodied in the privilege apply to informal compulsion exerted by law-enforcement officers during in-custody questioning. An individual swept from familiar surroundings into police custody, surrounded by antagonistic forces, and subjected to the techniques of persuasion described above cannot be otherwise than under compulsion to speak."

"But a confession obtained by compulsion must be excluded whatever may have been the character of the compulsion, and whether the compulsion was applied in a judicial proceeding or otherwise."

"In addition to the expansive historical development of the privilege and the sound policies which have nurtured its evolution, judicial precedent thus clearly establishes its application to incommunicado interrogation."

"[A] warning at the time of the interrogation is indispensable to overcome its pressures and to insure that the individual knows he is free to exercise the privilege at that point in time."

"The warning of the right to remain silent must be accompanied by the explanation that anything said can and will be used against the individual in court. This warning is needed in order to make him aware not only of the privilege, but also of the consequences of forgoing it. It is only through an awareness of these consequences that there can be any assurance of real understanding and intelligent exercise of the privilege."

"The circumstances surrounding in-custody interrogation can operate very quickly to overbear the will of one merely made aware of his privilege by his interrogators. Therefore, the right to have counsel present at the interrogation is indispensable to the protection of the Fifth Amendment privilege under the system we delineate today. Our aim is to assure that the individual's right to choose between silence and speech remains unfettered throughout the interrogation process."

"The presence of counsel at the interrogation may serve several significant subsidiary functions as well. If the accused decides to talk to his interrogators, the assistance of counsel can mitigate the dangers of untrustworthiness. With a lawyer present the likelihood that the police will practice coercion is reduced, and if coercion is nevertheless exercised the lawyer can testify to it in court. The presence of a lawyer can also help to guarantee that the accused gives a fully accurate statement to the police and that the statement is rightly reported by the prosecution at trial."

"Accordingly we hold that an individual held for interrogation must be clearly informed that he has the right to consult with a lawyer and to have the lawyer with him during interrogation under the system for protecting the privilege we delineate today. As with the warnings of the right to remain silent and that anything stated can be used in evidence against him, this warning is an absolute prerequisite to interrogation. No amount of circumstantial evidence that the person may have been aware of this right will suffice to stand in its stead. Only through such a warning is there ascertainable assurance that the accused was aware of this right."

"In order fully to apprise a person . . . of his rights . . . it is necessary to warn him not only that he has the right to consult with an attorney, but also that if he is indigent a lawyer will be appointed to represent him. Without this additional warning, the admonition of the right to consult with counsel would often be understood as meaning only that he can consult with a lawyer if he has one or has the funds to obtain one. The warning of a right to counsel would be hollow if not couched in terms that would convey to the indigent . . . the knowledge that he too has a right to have counsel present. As with the warnings of the right to remain silent and of the general right to counsel, only by effective and express explanation to the indigent of this right can there be assurance that he was truly in a position to exercise it."

"[W]hen the individual is first subjected to police interrogation while in custody at the station or otherwise deprived of his freedom of action in any significant way. It is at this point that our adversary system of criminal proceedings commences. . . . Under the system of warnings we delineate today or under any other system which may be devised and found effective, the safeguards to be erected about the privilege must come into play at this point."

"In dealing with custodial interrogation, we will not presume that a defendant has been effectively apprised of his rights and that his privilege against self-incrimination has been adequately safeguarded on a record that does not show that any warnings have been given or that any effective alternative has been employed."

c. Miranda Triggers

1. Custody

Stansbury v. California, 511 U.S. 318 (1994)
Vote: 9-0
FACTS: Robyn Jackson disappeared from a playground in Baldwin Park, California. The next morning, in Pasadena, Andrew Zimmerman observed a large man emerge from a car and throw something into a nearby flood control channel. He called the police, who arrived and discovered Robyn Jackson's body. Officer Thomas Johnston investigated and discovered that the young girl had talked to two ice cream truck drivers, one of whom was Robert Edward Stansbury, prior to her disappearance. Johnston considered only the other driver to be a suspect, and after he was interrogated, Johnston asked Baldwin Park officer Lee to contact Stansbury to see if he would come in for questioning.

Lee and other officers arrived at Stansbury's trailer at 11:00 that evening. When Stansbury answered, Lee told him they were investigating a homicide to which he was a possible witness and asked if he would go to the police station to answer questions, and he agreed. At the station, Johnston questioned Stansbury about his activities, and neither Johnston nor the other officer issued *Miranda* warnings. Stansbury told the officers that he spoke with the victim at about 6:00, returned to his trailer at 9:00, and left the trailer at about midnight in his housemate's car. This fact about the car aroused Johnston's suspicions, and when Stansbury admitted to prior convictions for rape, kidnaping, and child molestation, Johnston terminated the interview and another officer read him his *Miranda* rights. Stansbury made no further statements, requested an attorney, and was arrested. Stansbury was convicted of first-degree murder, rape, kidnapping, and lewd acts on a child under the age of fourteen and sentenced to death.
ISSUE: Is custody for the purposes of the police having to administer the *Miranda* warnings a "formal restraint on the freedom of movement associated with a formal arrest?"
HOLDING: Yes.
RATIONALE: "We hold, not for the first time, that an officer's subjective and undisclosed view concerning whether the person being interrogated is a suspect is irrelevant to the assessment whether the person is in custody."

"An officer's obligation to administer *Miranda* [*v. Arizona*, 384 U.S. 436 (1966)] warnings attaches, however, 'only where there has been such a restriction on a person's freedom as to render him "in custody. . . .".'" In determining whether an individual was in custody, a court must examine all of the circumstances surrounding the interrogation, but 'the ultimate inquiry is simply whether there [was] a "formal arrest or restraint on freedom of movement" of the degree associated with a formal arrest.'"

"Our decisions make clear that the initial determination of custody depends on the objective circumstances of the interrogation, not on the subjective views harbored by either the interrogating officers or the person being questioned."

"'[A] policeman's unarticulated plan has no bearing on the question whether a suspect was "in custody" at a particular time'; rather, 'the only relevant inquiry is how a reasonable man in the suspect's position would have understood his situation.' Other cases of ours have been consistent in adhering to this understanding of the custody element of *Miranda*."

"The same principle obtains if an officer's undisclosed assessment is that the person being questioned is not a suspect. In either instance, one cannot expect the person under interrogation to probe the officer's innermost thoughts. Save as they are communicated or otherwise manifested to the person being questioned, an officer's evolving but unarticulated suspicions do not affect the objective circumstances of an interrogation or interview, and thus cannot affect the *Miranda* custody inquiry."

"An officer's knowledge or beliefs may bear upon the custody issue if they are conveyed, by word or deed, to the individual being questioned. . . . Those beliefs are relevant only to the extent they would affect how a reasonable person in the position of the individual being questioned would gauge the breadth of his or her 'freedom of action. . . .'"

2. Place of Interrogation
A. POLICE STATIONS
1. Voluntary Questioning
Oregon v. Mathiason, 429 U.S. 492 (1977)
Vote: 7-2
FACTS: During the course of a house burglary investigation an officer asked the victim if she suspected anyone. She replied that Carl Mathiason was the only one she could think of, as he was a parolee and her son's friend. The officer tried on different occasions to contact Mathiason but was unsuccessful. When the officer left his card at Mathiason's apartment with a note asking him to call, Mathiason did. Since Mathiason had no preference about where they should meet the officer asked if he could meet at the state patrol office. The officer met Mathiason in the hall and told him that he was not under arrest, but the door was closed. The two sat across a desk and the police radio could be heard. The officer told Mathiason he wanted to talk about a burglary and that his truthfulness would possibly be considered by the authorities. The officer also stated that he believed that he was involved in the burglary and falsely stated that his prints were found at the scene. Mathiason was quiet and then admitted the theft. The officer

then read Mathiason his *Miranda* rights. He then took a taped confession. At the end of the taped confession, the officer released him and said that he was referring the case to determine whether criminal charges would be filed. Mathiason was eventually convicted of first-degree burglary.

ISSUE: Do the police have to administer the *Miranda* warnings prior to questioning a suspect if he voluntarily comes to the police station and is told that he is not under arrest?

HOLDING: No.

RATIONALE: "[T]here is no indication that the questioning took place in a context where respondent's freedom to depart was restricted in any way. He came voluntarily to the police station, where he was immediately informed that he was not under arrest. At the close of a one half-hour interview respondent did in fact leave the police station without hindrance. It is clear from these facts that Mathiason was not in custody 'or otherwise deprived of his freedom of action in any significant way.'"

"Such a noncustodial situation is not converted to one in which *Miranda* [*v. Arizona*, 384 U.S. 436 (1966)] applies simply because a reviewing court concludes that, even in the absence of any formal arrest or restraint on freedom of movement, the questioning took place in a 'coercive environment.' Any interview of one suspected of a crime by a police officer will have coercive aspects to it, simply by virtue of the fact that the police officer is part of a law enforcement system which may ultimately cause the suspect to be charged with a crime. But police officers are not required to administer *Miranda* warnings to everyone whom they question. Nor is the requirement of warnings to be imposed simply because the questioning takes place in the station house, or because the questioned person is one whom the police suspect."

"The officer's false statement about having discovered Mathiason's fingerprints at the scene was found by the Supreme Court of Oregon to be another circumstance contributing to the coercive environment which makes the *Miranda* rationale applicable. Whatever relevance this fact may have to other issues in the case, it has nothing to do with whether respondent was in custody for purposes of the *Miranda* rule.'"

2. Age of Suspect and Experience with Authorities
Yarborough v. Alvarado, 541 U.S. 652 (2004)
Vote: 5-4

FACTS: Paul Soto and Michael Alvarado attempted to steal a truck in the parking lot of a mall. Soto pulled out a .357 Magnum and approached Francisco Castaneda, who was standing near the truck emptying trash into a dumpster. Soto then demanded money and the keys. Alvarado approached the passenger side and crouched down. When Castaneda refused to comply, Soto shot and killed him. Alvarado then helped hide the gun. Los Angeles County Sheriff Cheryl Comstock led the investigation. She left word at Alvarado's house and also contacted his mother with the message that she wished to speak with Alvarado. His parents brought him to the station to be interviewed and waited while Alvarado went with Comstock. Alvarado later contended that his parents had asked to be present during the interview but were not allowed. Comstock brought Alvarado to a room and began interviewing for about two hours. The interview was recorded by Comstock without Alvarado's knowledge, and only she and Alvarado were present. Alvarado was not given a *Miranda* warning. Comstock asked Alvarado to recount the events on the night of the shooting. He explained that he had been drinking and after a few hours, part of the group went to a nearby mall. Then he went to bed. Comstock confronted him by stating that witnesses said that he was involved in the shooting, but he denied it.

Alvarado slowly began to change his story and admitted being present but claimed that he did not know what happened or who had a gun. When he hesitated, Comstock tried to encourage him to discuss what happened by appealing to his sense of honesty and the need to bring in the man who shot Castaneda. Alvarado then admitted he had helped the other man try to steal the truck, that the other man was Soto, that he knew Soto was armed, and that he had helped hide the gun. Alvarado explained that he did not expect Soto to kill anyone. Toward the end of the interview, Comstock twice asked Alvarado if he needed to take a break, but he declined. Comstock returned with Alvarado to the lobby of the sheriff's station, where he met his parents, who then drove him home.

Soto and Alvarado were later charged with first-degree murder and attempted robbery, and Alvarado moved to suppress the statements he had made in the interview. Alvarado testified that he happened to be standing in the parking lot when a gun went off. The government's cross-examination relied on Alvarado's statement to Comstock, and Alvarado admitted having made some statements but denied others. When Alvarado denied statements, the prosecution played excerpts from the recording of the interview. Alvarado agreed that he did not 'feel coerced or threatened in any way' during the interview. The jury convicted Soto and Alvarado of first-degree murder and attempted robbery.

ISSUE: Are age and experience with police relevant to the *Miranda* custody analysis?

HOLDING: No.

RATIONALE: "The Court of Appeals reached the opposite result by placing considerable reliance on Alvarado's age and inexperience with law enforcement. Our Court has not stated that a suspect's age or experience is relevant to the *Miranda* [*v. Arizona*, 384 U.S. 436 (1966)] custody analysis."

"Our opinions applying the *Miranda* custody test have not mentioned the suspect's age, much less mandated its consideration. The only indications in the Court's opinions relevant to a suspect's experience with law enforcement have rejected reliance on such factors."

"The *Miranda* custody inquiry is an objective test. . . . The objective test furthers 'the clarity of [Miranda's] rule . . .' ensuring that the police do not need 'to make guesses as to [the circumstances] at issue before deciding how they may interrogate the suspect.'"

"At the same time, the objective *Miranda* custody inquiry could reasonably be viewed as different from doctrinal tests that depend on the actual mindset of a particular suspect, where we do consider a suspect's age and experience. For example, the voluntariness of a statement is often said to depend on whether 'the defendant's will was overborne . . .' a question that logically can depend on 'the characteristics of the accused . . .' In concluding that there was 'no principled reason' why such factors should not also apply to the *Miranda* custody inquiry . . . the Court of Appeals ignored the argument that the custody inquiry states an objective rule designed to give clear guidance to the police, while consideration of a suspect's individual characteristics—including his age—could be viewed as creating a subjective inquiry."

"Indeed, reliance on Alvarado's prior history with law enforcement was improper not only under the deferential standard . . . but also as a *de novo* matter. In most cases, police officers will not know a suspect's interrogation history. . . . Even if they do, the relationship between a suspect's past experiences and the likelihood a reasonable person with that experience would feel free to leave often will be speculative. True, suspects with prior law enforcement experience may understand police procedures and reasonably feel free to leave unless told otherwise. . . . We do not ask police officers to consider these contingent psychological factors when deciding when suspects should be advised of their *Miranda* rights. . . . The inquiry turns too much on the suspect's subjective state of mind and not enough on the 'objective circumstances of the interrogation.'"

B. PRISONS AND JAILS
Mathis v. United States, 391 U.S. 1 (1968)
Vote: 5-3
FACTS: Mathis was convicted on two counts of knowingly filing false claims against the Government. The fraud charges were claims for tax refunds from tax returns and the returns' asserted income from two different companies that the government was unable to locate. Part of the evidence consisted of documents and statements obtained from Mathis by an agent while he was in prison serving a state sentence. The agent never warned Mathis that any evidence he gave could be used against him and that he had a right to remain silent as well as a right to counsel and that if he was unable to afford counsel, one would be appointed for him.
ISSUE: Does a known agent who questions an inmate have to administer *Miranda* warnings prior to questioning even if no charges have been filed?
HOLDING: Yes.
RATIONALE: "There can be no doubt that the documents and oral statements given by petitioner to the government agent and used against him were strongly incriminating. In the *Miranda* [*v. Arizona*, 384 U.S. 436 (1966)] case this Court's opinion stated at some length the constitutional reasons why one in custody who is interrogated by officers about matters that might tend to incriminate him is entitled to be warned 'that he has the right to remain silent, that anything he says can be used against him in a court of law, that he has the right to the presence of an attorney, and that if he cannot afford an attorney one will be appointed for him prior to any questioning if he so desires. . . .' The Government here seeks to escape application of the *Miranda* warnings on two arguments: (1) that these questions were asked as a part of a routine tax investigation where no criminal proceedings might even be brought, and (2) that the peti-

tioner had not been put in jail by the officers questioning him, but was there for an entirely separate offense. These differences are too minor and shadowy to justify a departure from the well-considered conclusions of *Miranda* with reference to warnings to be given to a person held in custody."

"[T]ax investigations frequently lead to criminal prosecutions, just as the one here did. . . . We reject the contention that tax investigations are immune from the *Miranda* requirements for warnings to be given a person in custody."

"The Government also seeks to narrow the scope of the *Miranda* holding by making it applicable only to questioning one who is 'in custody' in connection with the very case under investigation. There is no substance to such a distinction, and in effect it goes against the whole purpose of the *Miranda* decision which was designed to give meaningful protection to Fifth Amendment rights."

c. Homes
Baltimore Department of Social Services v. Bouknight, 493 U.S. 549 (1990)
Vote: 7-2

FACTS: After observing Jacqueline Bouknight abuse her infant son, Maurice M., in a hospital after treatment for serious injuries, personnel notified the Baltimore City Department of Social Services (BCDSS), which obtained an order removing him from her control. Several months later, the order directed that he be temporarily returned to his mother. Bouknight was allowed to remain custodian of Maurice provided that she agree to several conditions of BCDSS and the court, which she did. Months later, caseworkers argued that Bouknight would not cooperate with them and that she could not provide for the child. The court ordered that Maurice be removed, but Bouknight would not indicate where he was when caseworkers went to her home. Evidence further showed that while Bouknight claimed that her son was staying with a relative, none of her relatives said they had seen him. BCDSS then asked the police to issue a missing persons report and referred the case for investigation. The juvenile court then cited Bouknight for violating the custody order and, expressing concern that Maurice was endangered or dead, the court issued a warrant for Bouknight. She failed to provide her son at subsequent hearings, and again relatives stated that they had not seen him. After another hearing, she was found in contempt for failure to produce Maurice as directed, and the court had her incarcerated until she told where he was. Bouknight claimed that the contempt order violated her right against self-incrimination, while the court stated the contempt charge was for her direct refusal to obey the court, not for her refusal to testify in a proceeding. She was eventually convicted of theft while she appealed the order.

ISSUE: Can a mother refuse an order of the juvenile court to produce her child by invoking the Fifth Amendment privilege against self-incrimination?

HOLDING: No.

RATIONALE: "In this action, we must decide whether a mother . . . may invoke the Fifth Amendment privilege against self-incrimination to resist an order of the juvenile court to produce the child. We hold that she may not."

"The Fifth Amendment's protection 'applies only when the accused is compelled to make a *testimonial* communication that is incriminating.'"

"But a person may not claim the Amendment's protections based upon the incrimination that may result from the contents or nature of the thing demanded."

"The possibility that a production order will compel testimonial assertions that may prove incriminating does not, in all contexts, justify invoking the privilege to resist production. . . . Even assuming that this limited testimonial assertion is sufficiently incriminating and 'sufficiently testimonial for purposes of the privilege . . .' Bouknight may not invoke the privilege to resist the production order because she has assumed custodial duties related to production and because production is required as part of a noncriminal regulatory regime."

"When a person assumes control over items that are the legitimate object of the government's noncriminal regulatory powers, the ability to invoke the privilege is reduced. . . . The principle . . . is: '[W]here, by virtue of their character and the rules of law applicable to them . . . custodian has no privilege to refuse production although their contents tend to incriminate him. In assuming their custody he has accepted the incident obligation to permit inspection.'"

"The juvenile court may place a child within its jurisdiction with social service officials or 'under supervision in his own home or in the custody or under the guardianship of a relative or other fit person, upon terms the court deems appropriate. . . .' The provision that authorized the juvenile court's efforts to gain production of Maurice reflects this broad applicability."

"Many orders will arise in circumstances entirely devoid of criminal conduct. Even when criminal conduct may exist, the court may properly request production and return of the child, and enforce that request through exercise of the contempt power, for reasons related entirely to the child's well-being and through measures unrelated to criminal law enforcement or investigation. . . . Finally, production in the vast majority of cases will embody no incriminating testimony, even if in particular cases the act of production may incriminate the custodian through an assertion of possession or the existence, or the identity, of the child. . . . These orders to produce children cannot be characterized as efforts to gain some testimonial component of the act of production. The government demands production of the very public charge entrusted to a custodian, and makes the demand for compelling reasons unrelated to criminal law enforcement and as part of a broadly applied regulatory regime."

D. OFFICE OF A PROBATION OFFICER

Minnesota v. Murphy, 465 U.S. 420 (1984)

Vote: 6-3

FACTS: In 1974, Minneapolis police twice questioned Marshall Murphy concerning the rape and murder of a girl, but no charges were filed. In 1980, Murphy pleaded guilty to a charge of false imprisonment and was given probation. The terms of the agreement required that he participate in a treatment program for sex offenders, report to his probation officer, and be truthful with the probation officer. He was told that failure to comply could result in a probation revocation hearing. Murphy met with his probation officer at her office once a month. When she learned that he had abandoned treatment, she wrote to him explaining that failure to see her would result in a request for a warrant. She agreed not to seek revocation because he was doing well in other areas. A counselor from the program later informed the officer that Murphy had admitted to a rape and murder in 1974. After discussions with her superior, she determined that the police should know about the offense. She then wrote to Murphy and asked him to contact her to discuss a treatment plan.

The officer began by telling Murphy about the information she had received, and he became angry and stated that he 'felt like calling a lawyer.' The probation officer replied that he would have to deal with that on his own. He then denied the false imprisonment charge, admitted that he had committed the rape and murder, and attempted to persuade the officer that further extenuating circumstances explained the crimes. She then told Murphy that she had to relay the information to the police and encouraged him to turn himself in. He then left and later told her that he had been told by his lawyer not to surrender. She then obtained a warrant, and he was eventually indicted for the murder.

ISSUE: Can a statement made by a probationer to his probation officer without prior warnings be admitted at trial?

HOLDING: Yes.

RATIONALE: "Murphy was in no better position than the ordinary witness at a trial or before a grand jury who is subpoenaed, sworn to tell the truth, and obligated to answer on the pain of contempt, unless he invokes the privilege and shows that he faces a realistic threat of self-incrimination. The answers of such a witness to questions put to him are not compelled within the meaning of the Fifth Amendment unless the witness is required to answer over his valid claim of the privilege. This much is reasonably clear from our cases."

"These cases, taken together, 'stand for the proposition that, in the ordinary case, if a witness under compulsion to testify makes disclosures instead of claiming the privilege, the government has not "compelled" him to incriminate himself.'"

"It has long been recognized that '[the] Constitution does not forbid the asking of criminative questions . . .' and nothing in our prior cases suggests that the incriminating nature of a question, by itself, excuses a timely assertion of the privilege. . . . If a witness—even one under a general compulsion to testify—answers a question that both he and the government should reasonably expect to incriminate him, the Court need ask only whether the particular disclosure was 'compelled' within the meaning of the Fifth Amendment."

"[T]he first case squarely to hold that a witness under compulsion to make disclosures must assert the privilege in a timely manner, is illustrative. . . . The Court concluded without hesitation that '[his] failure at any time to assert the constitutional privilege leaves him in no position to complain now that he was compelled to give testimony against himself.'"

"Thus it is that a witness confronted with questions that the government should reasonably expect to elicit incriminating evidence ordinarily must assert the privilege rather than answer if he desires not to incriminate himself. . . . But if he chooses to answer, his choice is considered to be voluntary since he was free to claim the privilege and would suffer no penalty as the result of his decision to do so."

"[T]he Minnesota Supreme Court held that the probation officer's failure to inform Murphy of the Fifth Amendment privilege barred use of his confession at trial. Four factors have been advanced in support of this conclusion, but we find them, alone or in combination, insufficient to excuse Murphy's failure to claim the privilege in a timely manner."

"First, the probation officer could compel Murphy's attendance and truthful answers. The Minnesota Supreme Court failed to explain how this transformed a routine interview into an inherently coercive setting."

"Second . . . [we] have already explained that this factor does not give rise to a self-executing privilege. . . . The mere fact that an investigation has focused on a suspect does not trigger the need for *Miranda* [*v. Arizona*, 384 U.S. 436 (1966)] warnings in noncustodial settings. . . ."

"Third . . . the nature of probation is such that probationers should expect to be questioned on a wide range of topics relating to their past criminality. . . . Murphy's situation was in this regard indistinguishable from that facing suspects who are questioned in noncustodial settings and grand jury witnesses who are unaware of the scope of an investigation or that they are considered potential defendants."

"Custodial arrest is said to convey to the suspect a message that he has no choice but to submit to the officers' will and to confess. . . . It is unlikely that a probation interview, arranged by appointment at a mutually convenient time, would give rise to a similar impression. Moreover, custodial arrest thrusts an individual into 'an unfamiliar atmosphere' or 'an interrogation environment . . . created for no purpose other than to subjugate the individual to the will of his examiner.' Many of the psychological ploys discussed in *Miranda* capitalize on the suspect's unfamiliarity with the officers and the environment. Murphy's regular meetings with his probation officer should have served to familiarize him with her."

"We conclude . . . that since Murphy revealed incriminating information instead of timely asserting his Fifth Amendment privilege, his disclosures were not compelled incriminations. Because he had not been compelled to incriminate himself, Murphy could not successfully invoke the privilege to prevent the information he volunteered to his probation officer from being used against him in a criminal prosecution."

E. GRAND JURY

Hoffman v. United States, 341 U.S. 479 (1951)

Vote: 8-1

FACTS: A special grand jury was empanelled in Philadelphia to investigate various criminal activities committed against the government. Hoffman appeared as directed by subpoena but refused to answer several questions pertaining to his activities with a fugitive witness, asserting his right to be free from self-incrimination. His assertion was challenged by the government in federal court. It held that no danger of incrimination existed and ordered him to return to the grand jury and answer the questions about the fugitive. Hoffman stated that he would not obey and was found to be in contempt and sentenced to five months.

ISSUE: Can a grand jury witness assert the Fifth Amendment right to be free from self-incrimination?

HOLDING: Yes.

RATIONALE: "The privilege afforded not only extends to answers that would in themselves support a conviction under a federal criminal statute but likewise embraces those which would furnish a link in the chain of evidence needed to prosecute the claimant for a federal crime. . . . But this protection must be confined to instances where the witness has reasonable cause to apprehend danger from a direct answer. . . . The witness is not exonerated from answering merely because he declares that in so doing he would incriminate himself—his say-so does not of itself establish the hazard of incrimination. It is for the court to say whether his silence is justified . . . and to require him to answer if 'it clearly appears to the court that he is mistaken . . .' However, if the witness, upon interposing his claim, were required to prove the hazard in the sense in which a claim is usually required to be established in court, he would be compelled to surrender the very protection which the privilege is designed to guarantee. To sustain the privilege, it need only be evident from the implications of the question, in the setting in which it is asked, that a responsive answer to the question or an explanation of why it cannot be answered might be dangerous because injurious disclosure could result. The trial judge in appraising the claim 'must be governed as much by his personal perception of the peculiarities of the case as by the facts actually in evidence.'"

3. Interrogation
a. Defined
Rhode Island v. Innis, 446 U.S. 291 (1980)
Vote: 6-3

FACTS: John Mulvaney, taxicab driver, disappeared after being dispatched, and his body was discovered four days later in a shallow grave. He died from a shotgun blast to the back of his head. Providence police received a call from Gerald Aubin, also a taxi-cab driver, who reported that a man with a sawed-off shotgun had just robbed him and that he had dropped the man off near Mount Pleasant. While at the police station, Aubin noticed a picture of Thomas Innis on a bulletin board and identified him as the man who had robbed him. He again identified him in a photo array. Officer Lovell spotted Innis standing in the street and stopped his car. After Innis walked over, Lovell arrested him and advised him of his *Miranda* rights. Lovell did not converse with Innis other than to give him a cigarette. Sergeant Sears and Captain Leyden arrived and each gave him the warnings. Innis then stated that he understood and wanted to speak with a lawyer. Leyden then directed that Innis be driven to the station. Gleckman, Williams, and McKenna, were assigned to accompany him, and Leyden instructed them not to question, intimidate, or coerce him in any way. While en route, Gleckman spoke with McKenna about the missing shotgun and expressed concern that local children might find it and injure themselves. Williams said nothing, but overheard the conversation.

Innis then interrupted the conversation, stating the he wanted to show the officers where the gun was. McKenna then told Leyden that they were returning to the scene, and that Innis would show them where the gun was. Leyden again advised Innis of his *Miranda* rights and Innis stated that he understood but that he "wanted to get the gun out of the way because of the kids in the area in the school." He then led the police to a field, where he pointed out the shotgun under some rocks. Innis was eventually convicted of kidnapping, robbery, and murder.

ISSUE: Is interrogation for the purposes of requiring the administration of the *Miranda* warnings defined as express questioning or its functional equivalent?

HOLDING: Yes.

RATIONALE: "[W]e first define the term 'interrogation' under *Miranda* [*v. Arizona*, 384 U.S. 436 (1966)]."

"The starting point for defining 'interrogation' in this context is, of course, the Court's *Miranda* opinion. There the Court observed that '[by] custodial interrogation, we mean *questioning* initiated by law enforcement officers after a person has been taken into custody or otherwise deprived of his freedom of action in any significant way. . . .' This passage and other references throughout the opinion to 'questioning' might suggest that the *Miranda* rules were to apply only to those police interrogation practices that involve express questioning of a defendant while in custody."

"We do not, however, construe the *Miranda* opinion so narrowly. . . . The concern of the Court in *Miranda* was that the 'interrogation environment. . .' would . . . undermine the privilege against compulsory self-incrimination. . . . The police practices that evoked this concern included several that did not involve express questioning."

"We conclude that the *Miranda* safeguards come into play whenever a person in custody is subjected to either express questioning or its functional equivalent. That is to say, the term 'interrogation' under *Miranda* refers not only to express questioning, but also to any words or actions on the part of the police (other than those normally attendant to arrest and custody) that the police should know are reasonably likely to elicit an incriminating response from the suspect."

"By 'incriminating response' we refer to any response—whether inculpatory or exculpatory that the *prosecution* may seek to introduce at trial."

"It must also be established that a suspect's incriminating response was the product of words or actions on the part of the police that they should have known were reasonably likely to elicit an incriminating response."

b. Routine Questioning
South Dakota v. Neville, 459 U.S. 553 (1983)
Vote: 7-2

FACTS: Two South Dakota officers stopped Neville after he went through a stop sign. They asked him for his license and asked him to get out of the car. As he did, he fell against it to support himself. The officers smelled alcohol on his breath; he did not have a license and told the officers that it was revoked after a D.W.I. conviction. When Neville failed field sobriety tests, he was arrested and read his *Miranda* rights. He stated that he understood his rights and agreed to talk without a lawyer. The officers then asked him to submit to a blood-alcohol test and warned him that he could lose his license if he refused. Neville refused stating, "I'm too drunk, I won't pass the test." The officers asked him a second time and then took him to the police station, where they read the request a third time. Neville continued to refuse, saying he was too drunk to pass it. South Dakota law specifically stated that refusal to submit to a blood-alcohol test may be admissible into evidence.

ISSUE: Does the admission into evidence a defendant's refusal to take a blood test violate the Fifth Amendment protection against self-incrimination?

HOLDING: No.

RATIONALE: "*Schmerber* [*v. California*, 384 U.S. 757 (1966)], then, clearly allows a State to force a person suspected of driving while intoxicated to submit to a blood-alcohol test. . . . South Dakota law authorizes the Department of Public Safety, after providing the person who has refused the test an opportunity for a hearing, to revoke for one year both the person's license to drive and any nonresident operating privileges he may possess. Such a penalty for refusing to take a blood-alcohol test is unquestionably legitimate, assuming appropriate procedural protections."

"South Dakota further discourages the choice of refusal by allowing the refusal to be used against the defendant at trial."

"Most courts applying general Fifth Amendment principles to the refusal to take a blood test have found no violation of the privilege against self-incrimination. Many courts . . . have reasoned that refusal to submit is a physical act rather than a communication and for this reason is not protected by the privilege. Evidence of refusal to take a potentially incriminating test is similar to other circumstantial evidence of consciousness of guilt, such as escape from custody and suppression of evidence."

"Since no impermissible coercion is involved when the suspect refuses to submit to take the test, regardless of the form of refusal, we prefer to rest our decision on this ground, and draw possible distinctions when necessary for decision in other circumstances."

"In contrast to these prohibited choices, the values behind the Fifth Amendment are not hindered when the State offers a suspect the choice of submitting to the blood-alcohol test or having his refusal used against him. The simple blood-alcohol test is so safe, painless, and commonplace . . . that respondent concedes, as he must, that the State could legitimately compel the suspect, against his will, to accede to the test. Given, then, that the offer of taking a blood-alcohol test is clearly legitimate, the action becomes no *less* legitimate when the State offers a second option of refusing the test, with the attendant penalties for making that choice."

"[W]e do not think it fundamentally unfair for South Dakota to use the refusal to take the test as evidence of guilt, even though respondent was not specifically warned that his refusal could be used against him at trial."

"Moreover, the *Miranda* [*v. Arizona*, 384 U.S. 436 (1966)] warnings emphasize the dangers of choosing to speak ('whatever you say can and will be used as evidence against you in court'), but give no warning of adverse consequences from choosing to remain silent. This imbalance in the delivery of *Miranda* warnings, we recognized in

Doyle [*v. Ohio*, 426 U.S. 610 (1976)], implicitly assures the suspect that his silence will not be used against him. The warnings challenged here, by contrast, contained no such misleading implicit assurances as to the relative consequences of his choice."

"While the State did not actually warn respondent that the test results could be used against him, we hold that such a failure to warn was not the sort of implicit promise to forgo use of evidence that would unfairly 'trick' respondent if the evidence were later offered against him at trial. We therefore conclude that the use of evidence of refusal after these warnings comported with the fundamental fairness required by due process."

c. Assorted Attempts to Continue Interrogation
1. After Silence Invoked
Michigan v. Mosley, 423 U.S. 96 (1975)
Vote: 6-2
FACTS: Richard Bert Mosley was arrested in Detroit in connection with robberies at the Blue Goose Bar and a White Tower Restaurant. Detective James Cowie was acting on a tip implicating Mosley and three other men. Cowie brought Mosley to the station and advised him of his *Miranda* rights and had him read and sign a departmental rights notification form. After filling out the arrest papers, Cowie questioned Mosley about the robbery of the restaurant. When Mosley said he did not want to answer any questions, Cowie stopped the interrogation. At no time did Mosley indicate a desire to consult with a lawyer. He was then taken to a cell. Later that evening, Detective Hill brought Mosley to the Homicide Bureau for questioning about the fatal shooting of Leroy Williams, who had died during a holdup attempt. Mosley had not been arrested for or questioned on this charge by Cowie. Before questioning began, Hill advised Mosley of his *Miranda* rights. Mosley read the form silently and aloud, and Hill then read and explained the warnings and had him sign the form. Mosley at first denied involvement in the murder, but after Hill told him that Smith had confessed and had named him as the "shooter," Mosley implicated himself, and again, at no time did Mosley ask to speak with a lawyer or say that he did not want to answer questions. He was then charged with first-degree murder and convicted.
ISSUE: May the police initiate questioning of an accused on an unrelated charge to the one for which he has invoked his right to silence, but not asserted his right to speak to a lawyer, and where he was properly given the *Miranda* warnings for both periods of questioning?
HOLDING: Yes.
RATIONALE: "This passage states that 'the interrogation must cease' when the person in custody indicates that 'he wishes to remain silent.' It does not state under what circumstances, if any, a resumption of questioning is permissible. The passage could be literally read to mean that a person who has invoked his 'right to silence' can never again be subjected to custodial interrogation by any police officer at any time or place on any subject. Another possible construction of the passage would characterize 'any statement taken after the person invokes his privilege' as 'the product of compulsion'

and would therefore mandate its exclusion from evidence. . . . Or the passage could be interpreted to require only the immediate cessation of questioning, and to permit a resumption of interrogation after a momentary respite."

"It is evident that any of these possible literal interpretations would lead to absurd and unintended results. At the other extreme, a blanket prohibition against the taking of voluntary statements or a permanent immunity from further interrogation, regardless of the circumstances, would transform the *Miranda* [*v. Arizona*, 384 U.S. 436 (1966)] safeguards into wholly irrational obstacles to legitimate police investigative activity, and deprive suspects of an opportunity to make informed and intelligent assessments of their interests. Clearly, therefore, neither this passage nor any other passage in the *Miranda* opinion can sensibly be read to create a *per se* proscription of indefinite duration upon any further questioning by any police officer on any subject, once the person in custody has indicated a desire to remain silent."

"Through the exercise of his option to terminate questioning he can control the time at which questioning occurs, the subjects discussed, and the duration of the interrogation. The requirement that law enforcement authorities must respect a person's exercise of that option counteracts the coercive pressures of the custodial setting. We therefore conclude that the admissibility of statements obtained after the person in custody has decided to remain silent depends under *Miranda* on whether his 'right to cut off questioning' was 'scrupulously honored.'"

"This is not a case, therefore, where the police failed to honor a decision of a person in custody to cut off questioning, either by refusing to discontinue the interrogation upon request or by persisting in repeated efforts to wear down his resistance and make him change his mind."

"For these reasons, we conclude that the admission in evidence of Mosley's incriminating statement did not violate the principles of *Miranda* v. *Arizona*."

2. After Unclear Assertion of Right to Have Counsel Present
Davis v. United States, 512 U.S. 452 (1994)
Vote: 9-0
FACTS: Robert L. Davis, a member of the U.S. Navy, spent the evening shooting pool on the base. When Keith Shackleton lost a thirty-dollar bet, he refused to pay, and after the club closed, Shackleton was found beaten to death with a pool cue behind the commissary. The investigation by the Naval Investigative Service (NIS) gradually focused on Davis when agents discovered that he was at the club, and that he was absent without authorization the next morning. The agents also learned that only privately owned cues could be removed from the club and that Davis owned two, one of which had a bloodstain on it. The agents were told by different people that Davis had admitted the crime or had given details that indicated his involvement.

NIS agents interviewed Davis at the their office and advised him that he was a suspect, that he did not have to make a statement, that any statement could be used against him at a court-martial, and that he could speak to an attorney and have an attorney present during questioning. Davis waived his rights to remain silent and to counsel, both orally and in writing. During questioning, Davis said, "Maybe I should talk to a lawyer," whereupon the agents asked him if he was asking for a lawyer or just making a comment about one. Davis then replied that he did not want a lawyer, and after a break, the agents again reminded him of his rights. However, Davis later said, "I think I want a lawyer before I say anything else," and at that point the agents ceased their questioning. Davis was later convicted of one count of unpremeditated murder.

ISSUE: Is the statement, "Maybe I should talk to a lawyer?" sufficient to assert the claim to have counsel present during interrogation?

HOLDING: No.

RATIONALE: "[The applicability of the] '"rigid" prophylactic rule' of *Edwards* [v. Arizona, 451 U.S. 477 (1981)] requires courts to 'determine whether the accused *actually invoked* his right to counsel. . . .' To avoid difficulties of proof and to provide guidance to officers conducting interrogations, this is an objective inquiry. . . . Invocation of the *Miranda* [v. Arizona, 384 U.S. 436 (1966)] right to counsel 'requires, at a minimum, some statement that can reasonably be construed to be an expression of a desire for the assistance of an attorney. . . .' But if a suspect makes a reference to an attorney that is ambiguous or equivocal in that a reasonable officer in light of the circumstances would have understood only that the suspect *might* be invoking the right to counsel, our precedents do not require the cessation of questioning."

"Rather, the suspect must unambiguously request counsel. As we have observed, 'a statement either is such an assertion of the right to counsel or it is not. . . .' [A] suspect . . . must articulate his desire to have counsel present sufficiently clearly that a reasonable police officer in the circumstances would understand the statement to be a request for an attorney. If the statement fails to meet the requisite level of clarity, *Edwards* does not require that the officers stop questioning the suspect."

"We decline petitioner's invitation to extend *Edwards* and require law enforcement officers to cease questioning immediately upon the making of an ambiguous or equivocal reference to an attorney. . . . [I]t would needlessly prevent the police from questioning a suspect in the absence of counsel even if the suspect did not wish to have a lawyer present. Nothing in *Edwards* requires the provision of counsel to a suspect who consents to answer questions without the assistance of a lawyer."

"We recognize that requiring a clear assertion of the right to counsel might disadvantage some suspects who—because of fear, intimidation, lack of linguistic skills, or a variety of other reasons—will not clearly articulate their right to counsel although they actually want to have a lawyer present. But the primary protection afforded suspects subject to custodial interrogation is the *Miranda* warnings themselves. . . . A suspect who knowingly and voluntarily waives his right to counsel after having that right explained to him has indicated his willingness to deal with the police unassisted. Although *Edwards* provides an additional protection—if a suspect subsequently requests an attorney, questioning must cease—it is one that must be affirmatively invoked by the suspect."

"[I]f we were to require questioning to cease if a suspect makes a statement that *might* be a request for an attorney, this clarity and ease of application would be lost. Police officers would be forced to make difficult judgment calls about whether the suspect in fact wants a lawyer even though he has not said so, with the threat of suppression if they guess wrong. We therefore hold that, after a knowing and voluntary waiver of the *Miranda* rights, law enforcement officers may continue questioning until and unless the suspect clearly requests an attorney."

"The courts below found that petitioner's remark to the NIS agents—'Maybe I should talk to a lawyer'—was not a request for counsel, and we see no reason to disturb that conclusion."

3. After Right to Counsel Invoked
a. *Second Interrogation of Post-Arrestee*
Edwards v. Arizona, 451 U.S. 477 (1981)
Vote: 9-0

FACTS: Edwards was arrested pursuant to a warrant for robbery, burglary, and first-degree murder. At the police station, when he was given the *Miranda* warnings, he stated that he understood them and was willing to be questioned. After being told that another suspect had implicated him, he denied involvement and gave a taped statement of his alibi and then tried to make a deal. The officer told him that he wanted a statement but that he could not negotiate; however, he gave him the number of an attorney. Edwards made the call, but hung up and said, "I want an attorney before making a deal." At that point, questioning ceased, and Edwards was taken to jail. The next morning, two officers came to the jail and asked to see Edwards. When the detention officer informed Edwards that they wished to speak with him, he stated that he did not want to talk to anyone. The guard then told him that "he had to" and then took him to the officers. The officers then identified themselves, stated they wanted to talk to him, and administered the *Miranda* warnings. Edwards was willing to talk, but he first wanted to hear the statement of the accomplice who implicated him. After listening to the tape, he said that he would make a nonrecorded statement, but the officers replied that it did not matter since they could testify in court about whatever he said. Edwards then stated: "I'll tell you anything you want to know, but I don't want it on tape." He then implicated himself and was convicted at trial.

ISSUE: Is the Fifth Amendment right to have counsel present during interrogation violated when the police obtain a post-arrest confession from a suspect in a second interrogation after he has invoked his right to have counsel present during questioning?

HOLDING: Yes.

RATIONALE: "Edwards asserted his right to counsel and his right to remain silent . . . but that the police, without furnishing him counsel, returned the next morning to confront him and, as a result of the meeting, secured incriminating oral admissions. . . . Edwards insists that having exercised his right on the 19th to have counsel present during interrogation, he did not validly waive that right on the 20th. For the following reasons, we agree."

"[T]he Court has strongly indicated that additional safeguards are necessary when the accused asks for counsel; and we now hold that when an accused has invoked his right to have counsel present during custodial interrogation, a valid waiver of that right cannot be established by showing only that he responded to further police-initiated custodial interrogation even if he has been advised of his rights. We further hold that an accused, such as Edwards, having expressed his desire to deal with the police only through counsel, is not subject to further interrogation by the authorities until counsel has been made available to him, unless the accused himself initiates further communication, exchanges, or conversations with the police."

"*Miranda* [*v. Arizona*, 384 U.S. 436 (1966)] itself indicated that the assertion of the right to counsel was a significant event and that once exercised by the accused, 'the interrogation must cease until an attorney is present. . . .' Our later cases have not abandoned that view. . . . And just last Term, in a case where a suspect in custody had invoked his *Miranda* right to counsel, the Court again referred to the 'undisputed right' under *Miranda* to remain silent and to be free of interrogation 'until he had consulted with a lawyer. . . .' We . . . emphasize that it is inconsistent with *Miranda* and its progeny for the authorities, at their instance, to reinterrogate an accused in custody if he has clearly asserted his right to counsel."

"The Fifth Amendment right identified in *Miranda* is the right to have counsel present at any custodial interrogation."

b. Interrogations Unrelated to Arrested Offense
Arizona v. Roberson, 486 U.S. 675 (1988)
Vote: 6-2
FACTS: Roberson was arrested at the scene of a burglary and officers advised him that he had a right to remain silent and also the right to have an attorney present during interrogation. Roberson replied that he "wanted a lawyer before answering any questions." After several days, while Roberson was still in custody for this burglary arrest, a different officer interrogated him about a different burglary that happened just prior to the one for which he was arrested, and that officer was not aware of the fact that he had requested a lawyer. After administering Roberson his rights, the officer obtained an incriminating statement about the first burglary. In the prosecution for that offense, the trial court suppressed that statement, but Roberson was eventually convicted for the burglary for which he was caught at the scene.
ISSUE: Can the police question a suspect who has asserted his right to counsel during interrogation about an offense unrelated to the subject of their initial investigation?
HOLDING: No.
RATIONALE: "Petitioner contends that the bright-line, prophylactic *Edwards* [*v. Arizona*, 451 U.S. 477 (1981)] rule should not apply when the police-initiated interrogation following a suspect's request for counsel occurs in the context of a separate investigation. According to petitioner, both our cases and the nature of the factual setting compel this distinction. We are unpersuaded."

"[T]he presumption raised by a suspect's request for counsel—that he considers himself unable to deal with the pressures of custodial interrogation without legal assistance—does not disappear simply because the police have approached the suspect, still in custody, still without counsel, about a separate investigation."

"This discomfort is precisely the state of mind that *Edwards* presumes to persist unless the suspect himself initiates further conversation about the investigation; unless he otherwise states . . . there is no reason to assume that a suspect's state of mind is in any way investigation-specific."

"Our recognition of that fact, however, surely lends no support to petitioner's argument that in the Fifth Amendment context, 'statements about different offenses, developed at different times, by different investigators, in the course of two wholly independent investigations, should not be treated the same. . . .' This argument overlooks the difference between the Sixth Amendment right to counsel and the Fifth Amendment right against self incrimination. The former arises from the fact that the suspect has been formally charged with a particular crime and thus is facing a state apparatus that has been geared up to prosecute him. The latter is protected by the prophylaxis of having an attorney present to counteract the inherent pressures of custodial interrogation, which arise from the fact of such interrogation and exist regardless of the number of crimes under investigation or whether those crimes have resulted in formal charges."

"Petitioner's attempts at distinguishing the factual setting here from that in *Edwards* are equally unavailing. Petitioner first relies on the plurality opinion in *Oregon v. Bradshaw* [462 U.S. 1039 (1983)] which stated that *Edwards* laid down 'a prophylactic rule, designed to protect an accused in police custody from being badgered by police officers in the manner in which the defendant in *Edwards* was.' Petitioner reasons that 'the chances that an accused will be questioned so repeatedly and in such quick succession that it will "undermine the will" of the person questioned, or will constitute "badger[ing]," are so minute as not to warrant consideration, if the officers are truly pursuing separate investigations. . . .' It is by no means clear, though, that police engaged in separate investigations will be any less eager than police involved in only one inquiry to question a suspect in custody. Further, to a suspect who has indicated his inability to cope with the pressures of custodial interrogation by requesting counsel, any further interrogation without counsel having been provided will surely exacerbate whatever compulsion to speak the suspect may be feeling. Thus, we also disagree with petitioner's contention that fresh sets of *Miranda* [*v. Arizona*, 384 U.S. 436 (1966)] warnings will 'reassure' a suspect."

"[C]ustodial interrogation must be conducted pursuant to established procedures, and those procedures in turn must enable an officer who proposes to initiate an interrogation to determine whether the suspect has previously requested counsel. . . . Whether a contemplated reinterrogation concerns the same or a different offense, or whether the same or different law enforcement authorities are involved in the second investigation, the same need to determine whether the suspect has requested counsel exists. The police department's failure to honor that request cannot be justified by the lack of diligence of a particular officer."

c. Is the Sixth Amendment Assertion of Counsel the Same as the Fifth?

McNeil v. Wisconsin, 501 U.S. 171 (1991)

Vote: 6-3

FACTS: Paul McNeil was arrested in Omaha, Nebraska, pursuant to a warrant charging him with armed robbery in Wisconsin. Shortly after his arrest, two sheriffs arrived and asked to question him after they gave him the *Miranda* warnings, but he refused. However, he did not ask to see an attorney. He was brought back to Wisconsin and brought before a court official for the robbery charge. An attorney was appointed for him at this initial appearance. Later that evening, Deputy Sheriff Joseph Butts visited McNeil in jail in conjunction with a murder, attempted murder, and armed burglary in Caledonia, because he was a suspect. Butts administered the *Miranda* warnings and McNeil waived them. McNeil then denied any knowledge of the crimes but did not deny involvement in them. Butts returned in two days with detectives and again Mirandized McNeil, who again waived his rights by initialing a form. McNeil then implicated himself and two others in the offenses that Butts was investigating. McNeil also initialed references to himself in a typed confession. McNeil admitted at a later Mirandized interview that he lied about another person's involvement to minimize his own. He again initialized another statement. He was then charged with and convicted of second-degree murder, attempted first-degree murder, and armed robbery, despite his attempts at suppression his statements.

ISSUE: Does an invocation of the Sixth Amendment right to counsel during a hearing constitute an invocation of the Fifth Amendment right to have counsel present during questioning?

HOLDING: No.

RATIONALE: "The Sixth Amendment right, however, is offense specific. It cannot be invoked once for all future prosecutions, for it does not attach until a prosecution is commenced . . . 'at or after the initiation of adversary judicial criminal proceedings—whether by way of formal charge, preliminary hearing, indictment, information, or arraignment. . . .'"

"Because petitioner provided the statements at issue here before his Sixth Amendment right to counsel with respect to the *Caledonia offenses* had been (or even could have been) invoked, that right poses no bar to the admission of the statements in this case."

"[W]e come at last to the issue here: Petitioner seeks to prevail by combining the two of them. He contends that, although he expressly waived his *Miranda* [*v. Arizona,* 384 U.S. 436 (1966)] right to counsel on every occasion he was interrogated, those waivers were the invalid product of impermissible approaches, because his prior invocation of the offense-specific Sixth Amendment right with regard to the West Allis burglary was also an invocation of the nonoffense-specific *Miranda-Edwards* [*v. Arizona,* 451 U.S. 477 (1981)] right. We think that is false as a matter of fact."

"As to the former: The purpose of the Sixth Amendment counsel guarantee—and hence the purpose of invoking it—is to 'protect the unaided layman at critical confrontations' with his 'expert adversary,' the government. . . . The purpose of the *Miranda-Edwards* guarantee, on the other hand—and hence the purpose of invoking it—is to protect a quite different interest: the suspect's 'desire to deal with the police only through counsel. . . .' To invoke the Sixth Amendment interest is, as a matter of *fact, not* to invoke the *Miranda-Edwards* interest. One might be quite willing to speak to the police without counsel present concerning many matters, but not the matter under prosecution. It can be said, perhaps, that it is *likely* that one who has asked for counsel's assistance in defending against a prosecution would want counsel present for all custodial interrogation, even interrogation unrelated to the charge. That is not necessarily true, since suspects often believe that they can avoid the laying of charges by demonstrating an assurance of innocence through frank and unassisted answers to questions. But even if it were true, the *likelihood* that a suspect would wish counsel to be present is not the test for applicability of *Edwards*. The rule of that case . . . requires . . . some statement that can reasonably be construed to be an expression of a desire for the assistance of an attorney *in dealing with custodial interrogation by the police*. Requesting the assistance of an attorney at a bail hearing does not bear that construction."

"Our holding in *Michigan v. Jackson* [475 U.S. 625 (1986)] . . . implicitly rejects any equivalence in fact between invocation of the Sixth Amendment right to counsel and the expression necessary to trigger *Edwards*."

"There remains to be considered the possibility that, even though the assertion of the Sixth Amendment right to counsel does not *in fact* imply an assertion of the *Miranda* 'Fifth Amendment' right, we should declare it to be such as a matter of sound policy."

"Petitioner urges upon us the desirability of providing a 'clear and unequivocal' guideline for the police: no police-initiated questioning of any person in custody who has requested counsel to assist him in defense or in interrogation. . . . Petitioner's proposal . . . is not contained within, or even in furtherance of, the Sixth Amendment's right to counsel or the Fifth Amendment's right against compelled self-incrimination."

4. Initiation of Further Communication

Oregon v. Bradshaw, 462 U.S. 1039 (1983)
Vote: 5-4

FACTS: Oregon police were investigating the death of Lowell Reynolds, as his body had been found in his wrecked truck, in which he appeared to have been a passenger. He died from traumatic injury and asphyxia by drowning. During the investigation, the police asked James Edward Bradshaw to accompany them to the station for questioning. Upon arrival Bradshaw was advised of his rights, and he repeated his earlier account, wherein he admitted that he had provided Reynolds and others with liquor for a party at Reynolds' house, but denied involvement in the accident that killed him. Bradshaw suggested that Reynolds might have been killed by the person that had assaulted him at the party. Bradshaw was then arrested for furnishing liquor to Reynolds and advised of his *Miranda* rights. An officer then told Bradshaw his theory: that he thought that Bradshaw had been driving during the accident. Again Bradshaw denied involvement and said, "I do want an attorney before it goes very much further," and the officer terminated the discussion.

Sometime during his transfer to a different jail Bradshaw asked an officer, "Well, what is going to happen to me now?" The officer replied by saying, "You do not have to talk to me. You have requested an attorney and I don't want you talking to me unless you so desire because anything you say—because—since you have requested an attorney, you know, it has to be at your own free will. . . ." Bradshaw said that he understood, and the two spoke about where he was being taken and the offense with which he would be charged. The officer then suggested that Bradshaw might help himself by taking a polygraph, and he agreed. Bradshaw was given the warnings again and then waived them before the exam. After the polygraph examiner stated that he believed that Bradshaw was lying during the exam, Bradshaw recanted his earlier story and confessed to driving and being drunk during the accident that killed Reynolds. Bradshaw was found guilty after a bench trial of first-degree manslaughter, driving while under the influence of intoxicants, and driving while his license was revoked.

ISSUE: Does an accused that initiates a conversation with police after his request to speak to a lawyer qualify as a waiver of his right to have counsel present during interrogation?

HOLDING: Yes.

RATIONALE: "Respondent's question in the present case, 'Well, what is going to happen to me now?', admittedly was asked prior to respondent's being '[subjected] to further interrogation by the authorities.' The Court of Appeals, after quoting relevant language from *Edwards* [*v. Arizona*, 451 U.S. 477 (1981)], concluded that 'under the reasoning enunciated in *Edwards*, defendant did not make a valid waiver of his Fifth Amendment rights, and his statements were inadmissible.'"

"We think the Oregon Court of Appeals misapprehended the test laid down in *Edwards*. . . . [W]e held that after the right to counsel had been asserted by an accused, further interrogation of the accused should not take place 'unless the accused himself initiates further communication, exchanges, or conversations with the police.'"

"There can be no doubt in this case that in asking, 'Well, what is going to happen to me now?', respondent 'initiated' further conversation in the ordinary dictionary sense of that word."

"Although ambiguous, the respondent's question in this case as to what was going to happen to him evinced a willingness and a desire for a generalized discussion about the investigation; it was not merely a necessary inquiry arising out of the incidents of the custodial relationship. It could reasonably have been interpreted by the officer as relating generally to the investigation. That the police officer so understood it is apparent from the fact that he immediately reminded the accused that '[you] do not have to talk to me,' and only after the accused told him that he 'understood' did they have a generalized conversation. . . . On these facts we believe that there was not a violation of the *Edwards* rule."

5. Attempts to Interrogate after Unwarned Admission
Oregon v. Elstad, 470 U.S. 298 (1985)
Vote: 6-3
FACTS: The home of Mr. and Mrs. Gilbert Gross was burglarized, and missing were assets valued at $150,000. A witness contacted the sheriffs and implicated Michael Elstad, the Gross's neighbor and friend of their son. Officers Burke and McAllister went to Elstad's home with an arrest warrant, and when his mother answered the door, she led them to her son's room where he was listening to his stereo. The officers asked him to get dressed and come to the living room. McAllister asked Elstad's mother to go into the kitchen, where he told her that they had an arrest warrant for her son. Burke remained with Elstad in the living room and testified that Elstad stated that he did not know why the police were there but later said, "Yes, I was there" when Burke said that he felt that he was involved with the Gross burglary. As the officers escorted Elstad, his father arrived and was told that his son was a burglary suspect. The father then said to Elstad, "I told you that you were going to get into trouble. You wouldn't listen to me. You never learn."

Elstad was then taken to the Sheriff's department office and joined by Burke and McAllister in McAllister's office. McAllister then advised Elstad of his Miranda rights, which he waived. Elstad then confessed, explaining that he had known that the Gross family was out of town and that he had been paid to lead others to the house and show them how to enter. The confession was typed out, reviewed by Elstad, read back to him, and then initialed and signed by Elstad and both officers. As an aside, Elstad added and initialed, "After leaving the house Robby & I went back to [the] van & Robby handed me a small bag of grass." Elstad concedes that the officers made no threats or promises at any time and Elstad was found guilty of first-degree burglary.

ISSUE: Does the failure by police to initially administer *Miranda* require that subsequent statements, obtained after the administration of the warnings, be excluded?
HOLDING: No.
RATIONALE: "[R]espondent here contends that a failure to administer *Miranda* [*v. Arizona*, 384 U.S. 436 (1966)] warnings necessarily breeds the same consequences as police infringement of a constitutional right, so that evidence uncovered following an unwarned statement must be suppressed as 'fruit of the poisonous tree.' We believe this view misconstrues the nature of the protections afforded by *Miranda* warnings."

"Voluntary statements 'remain a proper element in law enforcement. . . .' 'Indeed, far from being prohibited by the Constitution, admissions of guilt by wrongdoers, if not coerced, are inherently desirable. . . . Absent some officially coerced self-accusation, the Fifth Amendment privilege is not violated by even the most damning admissions.'"

"Respondent's contention that his confession was tainted by the earlier failure of the police to provide *Miranda* warnings and must be excluded as 'fruit of the poisonous tree' assumes the existence of a constitutional violation."

"If errors are made by law enforcement officers in administering the prophylactic *Miranda* procedures, they should not breed the same irremediable consequences as police infringement of the Fifth Amendment itself. It is an unwarranted extension of

Miranda to hold that a simple failure to administer the warnings, unaccompanied by any actual coercion or other circumstances calculated to undermine the suspect's ability to exercise his free will, so taints the investigatory process that a subsequent voluntary and informed waiver is ineffective for some indeterminate period. Though *Miranda* requires that the unwarned admission must be suppressed, the admissibility of any subsequent statement should turn in these circumstances solely on whether it is knowingly and voluntarily made."

"The failure of police to administer *Miranda* warnings does not mean that the statements received have actually been coerced, but only that courts will presume the privilege against compulsory self-incrimination has not been intelligently exercised. . . . In these circumstances, a careful and thorough administration of *Miranda* warnings serves to cure the condition that rendered the unwarned statement inadmissible. The warning conveys the relevant information and thereafter the suspect's choice whether to exercise his privilege to remain silent should ordinarily be viewed as an 'act of free will.'"

"The Oregon court nevertheless identified a subtle form of lingering compulsion, the psychological impact of the suspect's conviction that he has let the cat out of the bag and, in so doing, has sealed his own fate. But endowing the psychological effects of *voluntary* unwarned admissions with constitutional implications would, practically speaking, disable the police from obtaining the suspect's informed cooperation even when the official coercion proscribed by the Fifth Amendment played no part in either his warned or unwarned confessions."

"This Court has never held that the psychological impact of voluntary disclosure of a guilty secret qualifies as state compulsion or compromises the voluntariness of a subsequent informed waiver. The Oregon court, by adopting this expansive view of Fifth Amendment compulsion, effectively immunizes a suspect who responds to pre-*Miranda* warning questions from the consequences of his subsequent informed waiver of the privilege of remaining silent. . . . When neither the initial nor the subsequent admission is coerced, little justification exists for permitting the highly probative evidence of a voluntary confession to be irretrievably lost to the factfinder."

"There is a vast difference between the direct consequences flowing from coercion of a confession by physical violence or other deliberate means calculated to break the suspect's will and the uncertain consequences of disclosure of a 'guilty secret' freely given in response to an unwarned but noncoercive question, as in this case."

"The relevant inquiry is whether, in fact, the second statement was also voluntarily made. As in any such inquiry, the finder of fact must examine the surrounding circumstances and the entire course of police conduct with respect to the suspect in evaluating the voluntariness of his statements. The fact that a suspect chooses to speak after being informed of his rights is, of course, highly probative. We find that the dictates of *Miranda* and the goals of the Fifth Amendment proscription against use of compelled testimony are fully satisfied in the circumstances of this case by barring use of the unwarned statement in the case in chief. . . . We hold today that a suspect who has once responded to unwarned yet uncoercive questioning is not thereby disabled from waiving his rights and confessing after he has been given the requisite *Miranda* warnings."

6. Interrogation after the Defendant Is Formally Charged
a. *Noncustodial Interrogation after Retention of Counsel*

Massiah v. United States, 377 U.S. 201 (1964)

Vote: 6-3

FACTS: Winston Massiah was a member of the crew of the SS *Santa Maria.* Federal customs officials in New York received information that he was going to transport narcotics aboard that ship from South America. As a result, the agents searched the *Santa Maria* upon its arrival and discovered several packages of cocaine. Massiah was arrested, arraigned, and indicted for possession of narcotics aboard a United States vessel. In July a superseding indictment was returned, charging Massiah and Jesse Colson with the same substantive offense and with having conspired to possess narcotics aboard a United States vessel and to import, conceal, and facilitate the sale of narcotics. Massiah, who had retained a lawyer, pleaded not guilty and was released on bail, along with Colson. A few days later, Colson decided to cooperate with the investigation and permitted an agent to install a transmitter under the front seat of his car. Colson and Massiah held a lengthy conversation while in Colson's car, and by prearrangement the agent sat in a car parked out of sight. Massiah made several incriminating statements, which were admitted at trial, and Massiah was convicted.

ISSUE: Does a noncustodial interrogation, obtained after the accused has been charged and retained a lawyer, violate the Sixth Amendment right to have counsel present during interrogation?

HOLDING: Yes.

RATIONALE: "In *Spano v. New York* [360 U.S. 315 (1959)] . . . this Court reversed a state criminal conviction because a confession had been wrongly admitted into evidence against the defendant at his trial. In that case the defendant had already been indicted for first-degree murder at the time he confessed. . . . [F]our concurring Justices pointed out that the Constitution required reversal of the conviction upon the sole and specific ground that the confession had been deliberately elicited by the police after the defendant had been indicted, and therefore at a time when he was clearly entitled to a lawyer's help. . . . It was said that a Constitution which guarantees a defendant the aid of counsel at such a trial could surely vouchsafe no less to an indicted defendant under interrogation by the police in a completely extrajudicial proceeding. Anything less, it was said, might deny a defendant 'effective representation by counsel at the only stage when legal aid and advice would help him.'"

"And since the *Spano* decision the same basic constitutional principle has been broadly reaffirmed by this Court."

"We hold that the petitioner was denied the basic protections of that guarantee when there was used against him at his trial evidence of his own incriminating words, which federal agents had deliberately elicited from him after he had been indicted and in the absence of his counsel."

"All that we hold is that the defendant's own incriminating statements, obtained by federal agents under the circumstances here disclosed, could not constitutionally be used by the prosecution as evidence against *him* at his trial."

b. The "Christian Burial Speech" and Interrogation

Brewer v. Williams, 430 U.S. 387 (1977)

Vote: 5-4

FACTS: Pamela Powers went with her family to the YMCA in Des Moines, Iowa, to watch her brother's wrestling tournament. When she did not return from the bathroom, a search for her proved unsuccessful. Robert Williams, who had escaped from a mental hospital, was a resident of the YMCA, and soon after Pamela's disappearance he was seen in the lobby carrying clothes and a large bundle. A young boy helped him open the street door and the door to his car. When Williams placed the bundle in the front seat the boy "saw two legs in it and they were skinny and white" but Williams drove away. His car was found in Davenport the next day and an arrest warrant was issued for him.

Henry McKnight, an attorney, went to Des Moines and informed the police that he had received a call from Williams and that he had advised Williams to turn himself in. Williams surrendered and officers gave him the *Miranda* warnings. The Davenport police then called police in Des Moines to inform them that Williams had surrendered. McKnight was still at the Des Moines headquarters, and Williams conversed with McKnight on the phone. In the presence of police, McKnight told Williams that police would be driving to Davenport to pick him up, that the officers would not interrogate or mistreat him, and that Williams was not to talk to them about Pamela Powers. It was then agreed that Detective Leaming and another officer would pick up Williams, that they would bring him directly back, and that they would not question him. Williams was arraigned in Davenport on the arrest warrant, and the judge advised him of his rights and committed him to jail. Before leaving the room, Williams spoke to a lawyer named Kelly, who advised him not to make any statements until consulting with McKnight. The officers arrived to pick up Williams and soon after met with Williams and Kelly, who, they understood, was acting as Williams's lawyer. Leaming again repeated the *Miranda* warnings and stated that he and Williams would be visiting on the trip. Williams then conferred with Kelly, and Kelly reiterated to Leaming that Williams was not to be questioned about the girl. Kelly firmly stated that the agreement with McKnight was to be carried out, but he was denied permission to ride in the police car back to Des Moines.

At no time during the trip did Williams express a desire to talk, but he did state, "When I get to Des Moines and see Mr. McKnight, I am going to tell you the whole story." Leaming knew that Williams was a former mental patient and that he was deeply religious. Leaming and Williams began a conversation, and Leaming then addressed Williams as Reverend and delivered what has come to be known as the "Christian burial speech," stating that the weather would prevent the finding of the body and that the parents should have closure and be able to give their daughter a Christian burial. Leaming then stated that he did not want to discuss it anymore but that Williams should think about it. Williams then directed Leaming to tell other officers where articles of Pamela's belongings were on two occasions, but they were not recovered. He then directed them to Pamela's body. Williams was indicted and convicted of first-degree murder.

ISSUE: Is the Fifth Amendment right to have counsel present during questioning violated when police engage in conversation designed to elicit an incriminating response after a defendant has asserted his right to have counsel present during questioning and after he has been charged?

HOLDING: Yes.

RATIONALE: "Williams was deprived of a different constitutional right—the right to the assistance of counsel."

"There can be no serious doubt, either, that Detective Leaming deliberately and designedly set out to elicit information from Williams just as surely as—and perhaps more effectively than—if he had formally interrogated him."

"Williams's consistent reliance upon the advice of counsel in dealing with the authorities refutes any suggestion that he waived that right. . . . Williams had effectively asserted his right to counsel by having secured attorneys at both ends of the automobile trip, both of whom, acting as his agents, had made clear to the police that no interrogation was to occur during the journey. Williams knew of that agreement and, particularly in view of his consistent reliance on counsel, there is no basis for concluding that he disavowed it."

"The circumstances of record in this case thus provide no reasonable basis for finding that Williams waived his right to the assistance of counsel."

"The crime of which Williams was convicted was senseless and brutal, calling for swift and energetic action by the police to apprehend the perpetrator and gather evidence with which he could be convicted. No mission of law enforcement officials is more important. Yet '[d]isinterested zeal for the public good does not assure either wisdom or right in the methods it pursues. . . . Although we do not lightly affirm the issuance of a writ of habeas corpus in this case, so clear a violation of the Sixth and Fourteenth Amendments as here occurred cannot be condoned. The pressures on state executive and judicial officers charged with the administration of the criminal law are great, especially when the crime is murder and the victim a small child. But it is precisely the predictability of those pressures that makes imperative a resolute loyalty to the guarantees that the Constitution extends to us all."

c. Interrogation by an Informant after Indictment in Jail
United States v. Henry, 447 U.S. 264 (1980)

Vote: 6-3

FACTS: The United Virginia Bank/Seaboard National in Norfolk, Virginia, was robbed. Witnesses saw two men in masks and carrying guns enter while a third waited in the car. None were able to identify Billy Gale Henry as one of the robbers. About an hour after the robbery, the car was discovered, and inside was found a receipt signed by Allen R. Norris and a lease, also signed by Norris. Two men, who were convicted of the robbery, were arrested at the address that was on the lease and discovered with them were the proceeds of the robbery and the guns and masks used. Agents traced the rent receipt to Henry, and he was arrested in Atlanta. Shortly after Henry was incarcerated, agents working on the robbery contacted Nichols, an inmate at the jail, who for some time had been an FBI informant. No information existed as to whether the agent contacted Nichols specifically to acquire information about Henry.

Nichols informed the agent that he was housed in the same cellblock as Henry, and the agent told him to be alert to any statements but not to initiate any conversation with or question Henry regarding the robbery. After Nichols was released, the agent again contacted him. Nichols reported that Henry had told him about the robbery, and Nichols was then paid for the information. When Henry was tried, an FBI agent testified about the rental slip and the evidence at the house. Other witnesses connected Henry to the house, including the rental agent, who identified Henry as the 'Allen R. Norris,' the man who had rented the house and had taken the rental receipt. A neighbor testified that prior to the robbery she saw Henry at the house with Luck, one of the two men who had been convicted for the robbery. In addition, palm prints on the lease matched Henry's. Nichols testified that he had conversations with Henry while in the jail and that Henry admitted his involvement in the robbery. Henry was eventually convicted of the bank robbery.

ISSUE: Is the Sixth Amendment right to counsel violated when a government informant obtains incriminating statements from a defendant who has been indicted?

HOLDING: Yes.

RATIONALE: "The question here is whether under the facts of this case a Government agent 'deliberately elicited' incriminating statements from Henry within the meaning of *Massiah* [*v. United States*, 377 U.S. 201 (1964)]. Three factors are important. First, Nichols was acting under the instructions as a paid informant for the Government; second, Nichols was ostensibly no more than a fellow inmate of Henry; and third, Henry was in custody and under indictment at the time he was engaged in conversation by Nichols."

"The Court of Appeals viewed the record as showing that Nichols deliberately used his position to secure incriminating information from Henry when counsel was not present and held that conduct attributable to the Government. . . . This combination of circumstances is sufficient to support the Court of Appeals' determination. Even if the agent's statement that he did not intend that Nichols would take affirmative steps to secure incriminating information is accepted, he must have known that such propinquity likely would lead to that result."

"While affirmative interrogation, absent waiver, would certainly satisfy *Massiah*, we are not persuaded, as the Government contends, that *Brewer v. Williams* [430 U.S. 387 (1977)] . . . modified *Massiah*'s 'deliberately elicited' test."

"In both *Massiah* and this case, the informant was charged with the task of obtaining information from an accused. Whether *Massiah*'s codefendant questioned Massiah about the crime or merely engaged in general conversation about it was a matter of no concern to the *Massiah* Court. Moreover, we deem it irrelevant that in *Massiah* the agent had to arrange the meeting between Massiah and his codefendant while here the agents were fortunate enough to have an undercover informant already in close proximity to the accused."

"The Government argues that this Court should apply a less rigorous standard under the Sixth Amendment where the accused is prompted by an undisclosed undercover informant than where the accused is speaking in the hearing of persons he knows to be Government officers. That line of argument, however, seeks to infuse Fifth Amendment concerns against compelled self-incrimination into the Sixth Amendment protection of the right to the assistance of counsel. An accused speaking to a known Government agent is typically aware that his statements may be used against him. The adversary positions at that stage are well established; the parties are then 'arm's-length' adversaries."

"When the accused is in the company of a fellow inmate who is acting by pre-arrangement as a Government agent, the same cannot be said. Conversation stimulated in such circumstances may elicit information that an accused would not intentionally reveal to persons known to be Government agents."

"As a ground for imposing the prophylactic requirements in *Miranda v. Arizona*, 384 U.S. 436 (1966), this Court noted the powerful psychological inducements to reach for aid when a person is in confinement. . . . While the concern in *Miranda* was limited to custodial police interrogation, the mere fact of custody imposes pressures on the accused; confinement may bring into play subtle influences that will make him particularly susceptible to the ploys of undercover Government agents."

d. Admitting Statements at Trial Made outside Presence of Counsel
Fellers v. United States, 540 U.S. 519 (2004)

Vote: 9-0

FACTS: After a grand jury indicted John J. Fellers for conspiracy to distribute methamphetamine, Lincoln Police Sergeant Michael Garnett and Lancaster County Deputy Sheriff Jeff Bliemeister went to his home in Lincoln, Nebraska, to arrest him. They knocked on his door, and when he answered, they identified themselves and asked if they could come in. Fellers then invited them into his living room. The officers stated they had come to discuss his involvement in methamphetamine distribution, that they had an arrest warrant for him, and that he had been indicted. The officers told Fellers that it involved several others, and he admitted that he knew the individuals mentioned. They then transported Fellers to jail and advised him of his *Miranda* rights. Fellers and the officers then signed a waiver form, and Fellers again inculpated himself. Fellers moved to suppress the statements he made at his home and at the jail, arguing that they were taken in violation of his Sixth Amendment right to counsel. He was eventually convicted of conspiring to possess with intent to distribute methamphetamine.

ISSUE: Is the use of statements from an accused after he has been indicted but while he is being arrested a violation of his Sixth Amendment right to counsel?

HOLDING: Yes.

RATIONALE: "The Sixth Amendment right to counsel is triggered 'at or after the time that judicial proceedings have been initiated . . . "whether by way of formal charge, preliminary hearing, indictment, information, or arraignment. . . ."' We have held that an accused is denied 'the basic protections' of the Sixth Amendment 'when there [is] used against him at his trial evidence of his own incriminating words, which federal agents . . . deliberately elicited from him after he had been indicted and in the absence of his counsel.'"

"We have consistently applied the deliberate-elicitation standard in subsequent Sixth Amendment cases . . . and we have expressly distinguished this standard from the Fifth Amendment custodial-interrogation standard."

"The Court of Appeals erred in holding that the absence of an 'interrogation' foreclosed petitioner's claim that the jailhouse statements should have been suppressed as fruits of the statements taken from petitioner at his home. First, there is no question that the officers in this case 'deliberately elicited' information from petitioner. . . . Because the ensuing discussion took place after petitioner had been indicted, outside the presence of counsel, and in the absence of any waiver of petitioner's Sixth Amendment rights, the Court of Appeals erred in holding that the officers' actions did not violate the Sixth Amendment standards."

e. Post Request Responses and Clarity of the Right to Counsel

Smith v. Illinois, 469 U.S. 91 (1984)

Vote: 6-3

FACTS: Shortly after his arrest, Steven Smith was taken by two detectives to an interrogation room for questioning about a robbery. The session began with one of them beginning to read him his rights and with Smith making the assertion that a relative told him that the police would try to "railroad him." When the police got to the point in the warnings where they told Smith that he had the right to consult with a lawyer, he stated that he would like to do so. Instead of stopping the interrogation, the police continued to finish the warnings and then asked again if Smith wanted to talk, even though he said he was confused. Smith then told the police that he knew in advance about the robbery, but that he did not participate. After further questioning, Smith admitted that he committed the robbery but then recanted and claimed again that he only knew about the planning of it. Smith then insisted that he wanted a lawyer. This time the detectives terminated the interrogation. Smith was later convicted of armed robbery.

ISSUE: Can an accused's responses after his request for counsel be used to cast doubt on the clarity of the initial request?

HOLDING: No.

RATIONALE: "The conflict among courts is addressed to the relevance of alleged ambiguities or equivocations that either (1) *precede* an accused's purported request for counsel, or (2) are part of the request *itself*. Neither circumstance pertains here, however. . . . As Justice Simon noted in his dissent below, 'with the possible exception of the word "uh" the defendant's statement in this case was neither indecisive nor ambiguous.'"

"As Justice Simon emphasized below, '[a] statement either is such an assertion [of the right to counsel] or it is not. . . .' Where nothing about the request for counsel or the circumstances leading up to the request would render it ambiguous, all questioning must cease. In these circumstances, an accused's subsequent statements are relevant only to the question whether the accused waived the right he had invoked. Invocation and waiver are entirely distinct inquiries, and the two must not be blurred by merging them together."

"Our decision is a narrow one. . . . We hold only that, under the clear logical force of settled precedent, an accused's *postrequest* responses to further interrogation may not be used to cast retrospective doubt on the clarity of the initial request itself. Such subsequent statements are relevant only to the distinct question of waiver."

f. Initiation of Interrogation and Waiver of the Right to Counsel

Wyrick v. Fields, 459 U.S. 42 (1982)

Vote: 8-1

FACTS: Edwards Fields, then a soldier, was charged with raping an eighty-one-year-old woman. After his arrest, he was released on his own recognizance and retained a lawyer. After consulting with his counsel and with a military attorney provided for him, Fields requested a polygraph, which was conducted by the Army's Criminal Investigation Division (CID) at the fort. Fields was given a consent form, which he signed, informing him of his rights. The CID agent read to Fields a statement summarizing the charge and stating that he had the right to a lawyer and that he could stop questioning at any time. He concluded by asking Fields if he wanted a lawyer at that time, and Fields said that he did not. At the end of the polygraph, the agent told Fields that he had been lying, and asked him if he could explain why his answers were bothering him. Fields then admitted having sex with the victim but said that she had initiated and consented to it. The agent then asked Fields if he wished to discuss the matter further with another agent and the police chief, and he agreed. The police chief also read Fields the *Miranda* warnings, and he repeated that he had had sex with the victim, but that it had been consensual. Fields was convicted of rape.

ISSUE: Does a request by an accused to submit to a polygraph amount to initiating interrogation?

HOLDING: Yes.

RATIONALE: "We have concluded that the Court of Appeals' majority misconstrued this Court's recent decision in *Edwards v. Arizona*, 451 U.S. 477 (1981), and imposed a new and unjustified limit on police questioning of a suspect who voluntarily, knowingly, and intelligently waives his right to have counsel present."

"When the suspect has initiated the dialogue, *Edwards* makes clear that the right to have a lawyer present can be waived. . . ."

"The Eighth Circuit acknowledged—as it had to—that '[there] is no question that Fields waived his right to have counsel present while the [polygraph] examination itself was being conducted.'"

"Fields did not merely initiate a 'meeting.' By requesting a polygraph examination, he initiated interrogation. That is, Fields waived not only his right to be free of contact with the authorities in the absence of an attorney, but also his right to be free of interrogation about the crime of which he was suspected. Fields validly waived his right to have counsel present at 'post-test' questioning, unless the circumstances changed so seriously that his answers no longer were voluntary, or unless he no longer was making a 'knowing and intelligent relinquishment or abandonment' of his rights."

"The Court of Appeals relied on two facts indicating the need for a new set of warnings: the polygraph examination had been discontinued, and Fields was asked if he could explain the test's unfavorable results. To require new warnings because of these two facts is unreasonable."

"The only plausible explanation for the court's holding is that, encouraged by what it regarded as a *per se* rule established in *Edwards*, it fashioned another rule of its own: that, notwithstanding a voluntary, knowing, and intelligent waiver of the right to have counsel present at a polygraph examination, and notwithstanding clear evidence that the suspect understood that right and was aware of his power to stop questioning at any time or to speak to an attorney at any time, the police again must advise the suspect of his rights before questioning him at the same interrogation about the results of the polygraph. The court indicated that this rule was needed because it thought that the use of polygraph 'results' in questioning . . . is inherently coercive. But Courts of Appeals . . . and state courts, have rejected such a rule. . . . The Eighth Circuit's rule certainly finds no support in *Edwards*, which emphasizes that the totality of the circumstances, including the fact that the suspect initiated the questioning, is controlling. Nor is the rule logical. . . . The rule is simply an unjustifiable restriction on reasonable police questioning."

10

The *Miranda* Warnings

IN THE LAST CHAPTER INTERROGATION and confessions were both discussed at length. This chapter makes a departure from that material by examining the right against self-incrimination and examining how the state must act to protect it. Today, the Supreme Court follows the self-incrimination test to determine whether or not an interrogation has been properly conducted. As a general rule to determine if the interrogation is fair, the police must administer the "*Miranda* warnings" once a custodial arrest has been made. However, beyond this basic requirement, several rules, exceptions, and issues have arisen that the Court has been called upon to address over the years.

For example, the Supreme Court has been asked to determine what kinds of evidence is protected by the Fifth Amendment. In response, the Court has ruled that primarily *testimonial* evidence is covered. Further, the Court has been asked to decide so many cases dealing with the *Miranda v. Arizona*, 384 U.S. 436 (1966) holding that it has recently ruled on the constitutionality of the original case. The Court has also been involved in determining when, and consequently how, a suspect can waive his or her *Miranda* rights altogether. More specifically, the Court has determined that a waiver must be voluntary, and it has gotten involved in determining what kinds of actions and evidence indicate such a waiver.

While these issues are closely related to one another, the Court has also decided many cases whose decisions, although considered part of *Miranda* law, are a bit more narrowly drawn. Some examples of such rulings include whether or not inmates must be Mirandized if an informant has been placed in a suspect's cell and listens to the suspect tell a story. The Court has also stated that a violation of the *Miranda* rule cannot be cured by a subsequent administration of the warnings. The issue of whether or not Sixth Amendment trial rights are violated if police statements are admitted has also been addressed. The Court has also stated that unwarned statements aren't always completely excluded, sometimes such statements can be used for very specific and narrowly drawn purposes. Additionally, the Court has stated that finding physical evidence via an unwarned statement is constitutional. Finally, as is so often the case with legal rulings, there are several exceptions to the *Miranda* rule, where police are not required to give the warnings at all. These are rare occurrences but as an example, when the public safety is at risk, police do not have to administer the *Miranda* warnings.

A. Constitutionality

Dickerson v. United States, 530 U.S. 428 (2000)
Vote: 7-2
FACTS: Charles Thomas Dickerson was indicted for bank robbery, conspiracy to commit bank robbery, and using a firearm in the course of committing a crime of violence. Before trial, he moved to suppress a statement he had made to the FBI because he had not been given the *Miranda* warnings before being questioned. The district court suppressed the statement and the Government appealed to the U.S. Court of Appeals for the Fourth Circuit, which held that a federal law that was passed shortly after *Miranda v. Arizona* was decided, which made the admissibility of statements turn solely on whether they were voluntarily, was satisfied in Dickerson's case. The Court also held that the original *Miranda* decision was unconstitutional and that Congress had the authority to determine the admissibility of suspect statements.
ISSUE: Is the *Miranda* decision constitutional?
HOLDING: Yes.
RATIONALE: "In *Miranda v. Arizona* [384 U.S. 436 (1966)] . . . we held that certain warnings must be given before a suspect's statement made during custodial interrogation could be admitted in evidence. In the wake of that decision, Congress enacted 18 U.S.C. §3501, which in essence laid down a rule that the admissibility of such statements should turn only on whether or not they were voluntarily made. We hold that *Miranda*, being a constitutional decision of this Court, may not be in effect overruled by an Act of Congress, and we decline to overrule *Miranda* ourselves. We therefore hold that *Miranda* and its progeny in this Court govern the admissibility of statements made during custodial interrogation in both state and federal courts."

"But first and foremost of the factors on the other side—that *Miranda* is a constitutional decision—is that both *Miranda* and two of its companion cases applied the rule to proceedings in state courts. . . ."

"Our conclusion regarding *Miranda*'s constitutional basis is further buttressed by the fact that we have allowed prisoners to bring alleged *Miranda* violations before the federal courts in habeas corpus proceedings. . . ."

"The *Miranda* opinion itself begins by stating that the Court granted certiorari 'to explore some facets of the problems . . . of applying the privilege against self-incrimination to in-custody interrogation, *and to give concrete constitutional guidelines for law enforcement agencies and courts to follow.* . . .' In fact, the majority opinion is replete with statements indicating that the majority thought it was announcing a constitutional rule. Indeed, the Court's ultimate conclusion was that the unwarned confessions obtained in the four cases before the Court in *Miranda* 'were obtained from the defendant under circumstances that did not meet constitutional standards for protection of the privilege.'"

"Additional support for our conclusion that *Miranda* is constitutionally based is found in the *Miranda* Court's invitation for legislative action to protect the constitutional right against coerced self-incrimination. . . . However, the Court . . . opined that the Constitution would not preclude legislative solutions that differed from the prescribed *Miranda* warnings but which were 'at least as effective in apprising accused persons of their right of silence and in assuring a continuous opportunity to exercise it.'"

"[W]e have also broadened the application of the *Miranda* doctrine. . . . These decisions illustrate the principle—not that *Miranda* is not a constitutional rule—but that no constitutional rule is immutable. No court laying down a general rule can possibly foresee the various circumstances in which counsel will seek to apply it, and the sort of modifications represented by these cases are as much a normal part of constitutional law as the original decision."

"The principles of *stare decisis* weigh heavily against overruling it now . . . the doctrine carries such persuasive force that we have always required a departure from precedent to be supported by some 'special justification.'"

"*Miranda* has become embedded in routine police practice to the point where the warnings have become part of our national culture. . . . While we have overruled our precedents when subsequent cases have undermined their doctrinal underpinnings . . . we do not believe that this has happened to the *Miranda* decision."

"In sum, we conclude that *Miranda* announced a constitutional rule that Congress may not supersede legislatively. Following the rule of *stare decisis*, we decline to overrule *Miranda* ourselves."

B. Waiver

1. Defined

Moran v. Burbine, 475 U.S. 412 (1986)
Vote: 6-3
FACTS: Mary Jo Hickey was found unconscious in a parking lot in Providence, Rhode Island, suffering from head injuries inflicted by a pipe found at the scene. She died three weeks later. Police arrested Brian Burbine and two others in connection with a burglary, but shortly before, Detective Ferranti learned that the man responsible for Hickey's death lived at a certain place and was called "Butch." Ferranti informed Burbine of his *Miranda* rights. Burbine refused to sign a waiver, and Ferranti then spoke with the other suspects and obtained statements implicating Burbine in the murder. Ferranti called police to convey the information, and an hour later, officers arrived to question Burbine about the murder.

Burbine's sister called the public defender to obtain counsel for her brother. Her concern was the burglary, and she was unaware that he was under suspicion for murder. She asked for Richard Casparian to discuss a different charge, and as soon as the conversation ended, the attorney she spoke to tried to get Casparian. She then called another attorney, Allegra Munson, and told her about Burbine's arrest. Munson then called the police and was told that Burbine was being held but he was finished for the night. She was not told that he was a suspect in the murder, and at no time did Burbine know that his sister was trying to retain counsel for him. The police then conducted a series of interviews concerning the murder, but prior to each, Burbine was informed of his *Miranda* rights. On three separate occasions he signed a form acknowledging that he understood his right to have an attorney present and explicitly indicated that he "[did] not want an attorney called or appointed for [him]" before he gave a statement. Evidence at the suppression hearing indicated that he was left in a room where he had a phone, which he declined to use. Eventually, he signed three statements and the jury found him guilty of first-degree murder.

ISSUE: Is a waiver of *Miranda* rights valid if the police fail to tell a suspect that others are trying to obtain counsel for him as long as the waiver is made voluntarily and intelligently?

HOLDING: Yes.

RATIONALE: "*Miranda* [*v. Arizona*, 384 U.S. 436 (1966)] holds that '[t]he defendant may waive effectuation' of the rights conveyed in the warnings 'provided the waiver is made voluntarily, knowingly and intelligently. . . .' The inquiry has two distinct dimensions. . . . First, the relinquishment of the right must have been voluntary in the sense that it was the product of a free and deliberate choice rather than intimidation, coercion, or deception. Second, the waiver must have been made with a full awareness of both the nature of the right being abandoned and the consequences of the decision to abandon it. Only if the 'totality of the circumstances surrounding the interrogation' reveal both an uncoerced choice and the requisite level of comprehension may a court properly conclude that the *Miranda* rights have been waived."

"Under this standard, we have no doubt that respondent validly waived his right to remain silent and to the presence of counsel."

"[W]e have never read the Constitution to require that the police supply a suspect with a flow of information to help him calibrate his self-interest in deciding whether to speak or stand by his rights. Once it is determined that a suspect's decision not to rely on his rights was uncoerced, that he at all times knew he could stand mute and request a lawyer, and that he was aware of the State's intention to use his statements to secure a conviction, the analysis is complete and the waiver is valid as a matter of law."

"But whether intentional or inadvertent, the state of mind of the police is irrelevant to the question of the intelligence and voluntariness of respondent's election to abandon his rights."

"Moreover, problems of clarity to one side, reading *Miranda* to require the police in each instance to inform a suspect of an attorney's efforts to reach him would work a substantial and, we think, inappropriate shift in the subtle balance struck in that decision."

a. Is Miranda a per se Rule that Requires Exclusion of All Unwarned Statements?

North Carolina v. Butler, 441 U.S. 369 (1979)

Vote: 5-3

FACTS: William Thomas Butler was convicted of kidnapping, armed robbery, and felonious assault. Evidence indicated that he and Elmer Lee had robbed a gas station and had shot the attendant. The attendant was paralyzed, but survived to testify, and the prosecution produced statements made by Butler after his arrest. Outside the presence of the jury, FBI Agent Martinez testified that he had advised Butler of his *Miranda* rights and that the agents had then taken him to the FBI office. After determining that he was literate, he was given a waiver form, which he stated that he understood. Butler refused to sign the waiver but was told that the agents would like him to talk. Butler said: "I will talk to you but I am not signing any form." He then made incriminating statements and said nothing when advised of his right to a lawyer. At no time did he request counsel or attempt to terminate questioning.

ISSUE: Is the *Miranda* decision a per se rule that excludes the statement of a person under custodial interrogation unless, at the time the statement was made, he explicitly waived the right to the presence of a lawyer?

HOLDING: No.

RATIONALE: "An express written or oral statement of waiver of the right to remain silent or of the right to counsel is usually strong proof of the validity of that waiver, but is not inevitably either necessary or sufficient to establish waiver. The question is not one of form, but rather whether the defendant in fact knowingly and voluntarily waived the rights delineated in the *Miranda* case. As was unequivocally said in *Miranda* [*v. Arizona*, 384 U.S. (1966)], mere silence is not enough. That does not mean that the defendant's silence, coupled with an understanding of his rights and a course of conduct indicating waiver, may never support a conclusion that a defendant has waived his rights. The courts must presume that a defendant did not waive his rights; the prosecution's burden is great; but in at least some cases waiver can be clearly inferred from the actions and words of the person interrogated."

"The *per se* rule that the North Carolina Supreme Court has found in *Miranda* does not speak to these concerns. . . . This is not the first criminal case to question whether a defendant waived his constitutional rights. It is an issue with which courts must repeatedly deal. Even when a right so fundamental as that to counsel at trial is involved, the question of waiver must be determined on 'the particular facts and circumstances surrounding that case, including the background, experience, and conduct of the accused.'"

b. Mental Illness, Compulsion, and Miranda

Colorado v. Connelly, 479 U.S. 157 (1986)
Vote: 6-3

FACTS: Francis Connelly approached Denver police officer Patrick Anderson and stated that he had murdered someone and wanted to talk. Anderson Mirandized him, but he stated that he still wanted to talk. Anderson then asked Connelly if he had been drinking or taking drugs, and Connelly stated that he had been a mental patient. Anderson again told Connelly that he did not have to speak, but Connelly said that it was "all right," and that he would talk because his conscience was upsetting him. Detective

Stephen Antuna then arrived, and Connelly was again advised of his rights and asked "what he had on his mind." Connelly stated that he had come to confess to killing Mary Ann Junta. He was then taken to the station where a records search revealed that an unidentified female body had been found. Connelly further spoke to the officers and agreed to take them to the scene.

During an interview with an attorney, Connelly became disoriented and gave confused answers, stating that "voices" had told him to come to Denver and confess. He was then evaluated and was initially found incompetent but later found competent to proceed. At a preliminary hearing, Connelly moved to suppress his statements. A doctor testified that Connelly had chronic schizophrenia and was psychotic. He found that Connelly was instructed to either confess to the killing or commit suicide and that his illness interfered with his ability to make rational choices.

ISSUE: Does a confession made by a suspect who claims that it was compelled by his mental illness, not police coercion, violate the *Miranda* rule?

HOLDING: No.

RATIONALE: "Thus the cases considered by this Court over the 50 years since *Brown v. Mississippi* [297 U.S. 278 (1936)] have focused upon the crucial element of police overreaching. While each confession case has turned on its own set of factors justifying the conclusion that police conduct was oppressive, all have contained a substantial element of coercive police conduct. Absent police conduct causally related to the confession, there is simply no basis for concluding that any state actor has deprived a criminal defendant of due process of law."

"Respondent would now have us require sweeping inquiries into the state of mind of a criminal defendant who has confessed, inquiries quite divorced from any coercion brought to bear on the defendant by the State. We think the Constitution rightly leaves this sort of inquiry to be resolved by state laws governing the admission of evidence and erects no standard of its own in this area."

"We hold that coercive police activity is a necessary predicate to the finding that a confession is not 'voluntary' within the meaning of the Due Process Clause of the Fourteenth Amendment."

"The sole concern of the Fifth Amendment, on which *Miranda* [*v.* Arizona, 384 U.S. 436 (1966)] was based, is governmental coercion. . . . Indeed, the Fifth Amendment privilege is not concerned 'with moral and psychological pressures to confess emanating from sources other than official coercion. . . .' The voluntariness of a waiver of this privilege has always depended on the absence of police overreaching. . . ."

"Respondent urges this Court to adopt his 'free will' rationale, and to find an attempted waiver invalid whenever the defendant feels compelled to waive his rights by reason of any compulsion, even if the compulsion does not flow from the police. . . . *Miranda* protects defendants against government coercion leading them to surrender rights protected by the Fifth Amendment; it goes no further than that. Respondent's perception of coercion . . . from the 'voice of God . . .' is a matter to which the United States Constitution does not speak."

2. Evidence Indicating a Waiver

a. Invocation of the Right to Counsel by a Juvenile

Fare v. Michael C., 442 U.S. 707 (1979)
Vote: 5-4
FACTS: Michael C. was implicated in the murder of Robert Yeager with the crime oc-curring during a robbery of Yeager's home. A truck registered under Michael C.'s mother's name was seen near Yeager's home at the time of the killing, and a man matching Michael's description was seen by the truck and near the home. Van Nuys, California, police took Michael into custody when he was sixteen and a half years old and on probation. He had also served time in a youth camp and had a record of sev-eral previous offenses. Upon Michael's arrival at the police station, officers interrogated him and recorded the conversation. One officer stated that he had been brought in for questioning about a murder. The officer then fully advised Michael of his rights, upon which he stated that he understood. At some point, he asked for his probation officer but was denied the opportunity to speak with him. However, he was again notified that he did not have to speak if he did not wish to. He then made incriminating statements and drawings pertaining to the murder. Michael C. moved to suppress this evidence at a juvenile hearing initiated to make him a ward of the court.
ISSUE: Is the request to see a probation officer by a juvenile a per se invocation of the right to counsel under the *Miranda* rule?
HOLDING: No.
RATIONALE: "The Court in *Miranda* [*v.* Arizona, 384 U.S. 436 (1966)] recognized that 'the attorney plays a vital role in the administration of criminal justice under our Consti-tution. . . .' It is this pivotal role of legal counsel that justifies the *per se* rule established in *Miranda*, and that distinguishes the request for counsel from the request for a probation officer, a clergyman, or a close friend. A probation officer simply is not necessary, in the way an attorney is, for the protection of the legal rights of the accused, juvenile or adult. He is significantly handicapped by the position he occupies in the juvenile system from serving as an effective protector of the rights of a juvenile suspected of a crime."

"The fact that a relationship of trust and cooperation between a probation officer and a juvenile might exist, however, does not indicate that the probation officer is ca-pable of rendering effective legal advice sufficient to protect the juvenile's rights during interrogation by the police, or of providing the other services rendered by a lawyer. . . . Such an extension would impose the burdens associated with the rule of *Miranda* on the juvenile justice system and the police without serving the interests that rule was de-signed simultaneously to protect. If it were otherwise, a juvenile's request for almost anyone he considered trustworthy enough to give him reliable advice would trigger the rigid rule of *Miranda*."

"Similarly, the fact that the State has created a statutory duty on the part of the pro-bation officer to protect the interests of the juvenile does not render the probation of-ficer any more capable of rendering legal assistance to the juvenile or of protecting his legal rights, especially in light of the fact that the State has also legislated a duty on the part of the officer to report wrongdoing by the juvenile and serve the ends of the juvenile court system. . . . Though such a statutory duty might serve to distinguish to some degree the probation officer from the coach and the clergyman, it does not justify the extension of *Miranda* to requests to see probation officers."

"[W]e decline to find that the request for the probation officer is tantamount to the request for an attorney."

"We hold, therefore, that it was error to find that the request by respondent to speak with his probation officer *per se* constituted an invocation of respondent's Fifth Amendment right to be free from compelled self-incrimination."

b. Refusing to Sign Form but Agreeing to Talk

Connecticut v. Barrett, 479 U.S. 523 (1987)
Vote: 7-2
FACTS: William Barrett was transported from New Haven to Wallingford, where he was a suspect in a sexual assault. Upon arriving, Officer Peter Cameron advised him of his rights, and he signed an acknowledgment. Barrett stated that "he would not give the police any written statements but he had no problem in talking about the incident." About thirty minutes later, officers Cameron and John Genovese questioned him. He was again advised of his rights and signed another acknowledgment and then gave a statement admitting his involvement in the sexual assault. Since the tape recorder malfunctioned, police conducted another interview. Barrett was advised of his rights and again stated that "he was willing to talk about [the incident] verbally but he did not want to put anything in writing until his attorney came." He then repeated his confession, but when officers discovered that the recorder again had malfunctioned, Cameron wrote out Barrett's statement. Barrett was convicted of sexual assault, unlawful restraint, and possession of a controlled substance.
ISSUE: Is the admission of an oral confession a violation of the *Miranda* protection against self-incrimination if the suspect states he does not want to make any written statements but will talk?
HOLDING: No.
RATIONALE: "The Connecticut Supreme Court nevertheless held as a matter of law that respondent's limited invocation of his right to counsel prohibited all interrogation absent initiation of further discussion by Barrett. Nothing in our decisions, however, or in the rationale of *Miranda* [*v. Arizona,* 384 U.S. 436 (1966)], requires authorities to ignore the tenor or sense of a defendant's response to these warnings."

"But we know of no constitutional objective that would be served by suppression in this case. . . . The fact that officials took the opportunity provided by Barrett to obtain an oral confession is quite consistent with the Fifth Amendment. *Miranda* gives the defendant a right to choose between speech and silence, and Barrett chose to speak."

"To conclude that respondent invoked his right to counsel for all purposes requires not a broad interpretation of an ambiguous statement, but a disregard of the ordinary meaning of respondent's statement."

"We also reject the contention that the distinction drawn by Barrett between oral and written statements indicates an understanding of the consequences so incomplete that we should deem his limited invocation of the right to counsel effective for all purposes."

3. Voluntariness of the Waiver

a. Awareness of Possible Subjects of Interrogation

Colorado v. Spring, 479 U.S. 564 (1987)
Vote: 7-2
FACTS: John Leroy Spring and a companion shot and killed Donald Walker during a hunting trip. An informant told ATF agents that Spring was selling firearms and that he had discussed Walker's killing. The agents then set up a "buy" from Spring and arrested him. An agent advised Spring of his rights, and he was advised again after he was transported to the ATF office. At the office, he was also advised that he could stop the questioning at any time. Spring then signed a form stating that he understood and waived his rights and that he wanted to talk. The agents asked Spring about the firearms transactions and then asked him if he had a record. He admitted that he had a juvenile record for shooting his aunt. The agents then asked if he had ever shot anyone else. Spring said, "I shot another guy once." The agents asked him if he had ever been to Colorado, and he said no. The agents then asked if he had shot Walker and Spring said no. The interview then terminated.

Colorado police visited Spring while he was in jail for the firearms offenses. The officers gave him the *Miranda* warnings, and he again signed a form indicating that he understood his rights and wanted to waive them. The officers informed him that they wanted to question him about Walker's killing, and Spring stated that he "wanted to get it off his chest." He confessed and never terminated the questioning nor requested counsel. The officers prepared a statement summarizing the interview, which he read, edited, and signed. Spring was convicted of first-degree murder.
ISSUE: Is the suspect's awareness of all the crimes about which he may be questioned relevant to determining the validity of his decision to waive the privilege against self-incrimination?
HOLDING: No.
RATIONALE: "There is no doubt that Spring's decision to waive his Fifth Amendment privilege was voluntary. He alleges no 'coercion of a confession by physical violence or other deliberate means calculated to break [his] will . . . ,' and the trial court found none. . . . Absent evidence that Spring's 'will [was] overborne and his capacity for self-determination critically impaired' because of coercive police conduct . . . , his waiver of his Fifth Amendment privilege was voluntary under this Court's decision in *Miranda* [*v. Arizona*, 384 U.S. 436 (1966)]."

"The Constitution does not require that a criminal suspect know and understand every possible consequence of a waiver of the Fifth Amendment privilege."

"In sum, we think that the trial court was indisputably correct in finding that Spring's waiver was made knowingly and intelligently within the meaning of *Miranda*."

"He contends that the failure to inform him of the potential subjects of interrogation constitutes the police trickery and deception condemned in *Miranda*, thus rendering his waiver of *Miranda* rights invalid. Spring, however, reads this statement in *Miranda* out of context and without due regard to the constitutional privilege the *Miranda* warnings were designed to protect."

"This Court has never held that mere silence by law enforcement officials as to the subject matter of an interrogation is 'trickery' sufficient to invalidate a suspect's waiver of *Miranda* rights, and we expressly decline so to hold today."

"Once *Miranda* warnings are given, it is difficult to see how official silence could cause a suspect to misunderstand the nature of his constitutional right. . . . 'Indeed, it seems self-evident that one who is told he is free to refuse to answer questions is in a curious posture to later complain that his answers were compelled.'"

"This Court's holding in *Miranda* specifically required that the police inform a criminal suspect that he has the right to remain silent and that *anything* he says may be used against him. There is no qualification of this broad and explicit warning. . . . Accordingly, we hold that a suspect's awareness of all the possible subjects of questioning in advance of interrogation is not relevant to determining whether the suspect voluntarily, knowingly, and intelligently waived his Fifth Amendment privilege."

b. Postindictment Waiver and Interrogation

Patterson v. Illinois, 487 U.S. 285 (1988)
Vote: 5-4

FACTS: Patterson and other members of the "Vice Lords" gang became involved in a fight with a rival gang, the "Black Mobsters." After the fight, a former member of the Mobsters, James Jackson, went to where the Vice Lords had fled. A second fight broke out, with Patterson and other Vice Lords beating Jackson. The Vice Lords then put him in a car, drove to a nearby street, and left him face down in a puddle of water. Later, police discovered Jackson dead and obtained warrants for the Vice Lords on charges of battery and mob action, in connection with the first fight. One of the members gave a statement concerning the first fight and implicated the Vice Lords and Patterson in Jackson's murder. Patterson was arrested and informed of his rights, and he volunteered to answer questions. Patterson gave a statement concerning the initial fight but denied knowing anything about Jackson's death. Patterson and two other gang members were then indicted for Jackson's murder.

Officer Michael Gresham, told Patterson that because he had been indicted he was being transferred to jail. Patterson then asked Gresham which of the gang members had been charged with the murder, and after learning that one had been omitted, asked, "[W]hy wasn't he indicted, he did everything." Patterson also explained that a witness would support his account. Gresham then interrupted and handed him a *Miranda* form and read the warnings aloud. Patterson initialed each of the warnings and signed the waiver. Patterson then gave a statement concerning the murder, describing in detail the role of the Vice Lords and himself. Later that day, he again confessed to Smith. At the interview, Smith reviewed the waiver and Patterson confirmed that he had signed and understood it. Smith went through the waiver again and Patterson signed the form. Smith also mentioned that he was a lawyer working with the police on the Jackson case. Patterson then gave another incriminating statement and he was later convicted of murder.

ISSUE: Does a suspect who is given the *Miranda* warnings during postindictment questioning make a valid waiver of his Sixth-Amendment right to counsel if he chooses to speak to police?

HOLDING: Yes.

RATIONALE: "[T]he key inquiry in a case such as this one must be: Was the accused, who waived his Sixth Amendment rights during postindictment questioning, made sufficiently aware of his right to have counsel present during the questioning, and of the possible consequences of a decision to forgo the aid of counsel? In this case, we are convinced that by admonishing petitioner with the *Miranda* [*v. Arizona*, 384 U.S. 436 (1966)] warnings, respondent has met this burden and that petitioner's waiver of his right to counsel at the questioning was valid."

"There is little more petitioner could have possibly been told in an effort to satisfy this portion of the waiver inquiry."

"Second, the *Miranda* warnings also served to make petitioner aware of the consequences of a decision by him to waive his Sixth Amendment rights during postindictment questioning. Petitioner knew that any statement that he made could be used against him in subsequent criminal proceedings. This is the ultimate adverse consequence petitioner could have suffered by virtue of his choice to make uncounseled admissions to the authorities. This warning also sufficed—contrary to petitioner's claim here . . . to let petitioner know what a lawyer could 'do for him' during the postindictment questioning: namely, advise petitioner to refrain from making any such statements."

"Our conclusion is supported by petitioner's inability, in the proceedings before this Court, to articulate with precision what additional information should have been provided to him before he would have been competent to waive his right to counsel."

"As a general matter, then, an accused who is admonished with the warnings prescribed by this Court . . . has been sufficiently apprised of the nature of his Sixth Amendment rights, and of the consequences of abandoning those rights, so that his waiver on this basis will be considered a knowing and intelligent one."

"We consequently reject petitioner's argument . . . , that since 'the Sixth Amendment right [to counsel] is far superior to that of the Fifth Amendment right . . .' waiver of an accused's Sixth Amendment right to counsel should be 'more difficult' to effectuate than waiver of a suspect's Fifth Amendment rights. . . . [W]e have never suggested that one right is 'superior' or 'greater' than the other, nor is there any support in our cases for the notion that because a Sixth Amendment right may be involved, it is more difficult to waive than the Fifth Amendment counterpart."

"Applying this approach, it is our view that whatever warnings suffice for *Miranda's* purposes will also be sufficient in the context of postindictment questioning. . . . With respect to this inquiry, we do not discern a substantial difference between the usefulness of a lawyer to a suspect during custodial interrogation, and his value to an accused at postindictment questioning."

C. Nontestimonial Evidence

Schmerber v. California, 384 U.S. 757 (1966)
Vote: 5-4
FACTS: Schmerber was arrested at a hospital while being treated for injuries suffered in a car accident. A police officer directed that a blood sample be withdrawn by a physician, and the analysis of the sample indicated intoxication. As a result, the analysis was admitted in evidence at the trial. Schmerber objected because the blood had been withdrawn without his consent. He argued several constitutional violations, one of which was a violation of the privilege against self-incrimination. Schmerber was convicted of driving under the influence.
ISSUE: Does the privilege against self-incrimination protect an accused from being compelled to provide a blood sample?
HOLDING: No.
RATIONALE: "We therefore must now decide whether the withdrawal of the blood and admission in evidence of the analysis involved in this case violated petitioner's privilege. We hold that the privilege protects an accused only from being compelled to testify against himself, or otherwise provide the State with evidence of a testimonial or communicative nature, and that the withdrawal of blood and use of the analysis in question in this case did not involve compulsion to these ends."

"As the passage in *Miranda* [*v. Arizona*, 384 U.S. 436 (1966)] implicitly recognizes, however, the privilege has never been given the full scope which the values it helps to protect suggest. History and a long line of authorities in lower courts have consistently limited its protection to situations in which the State seeks to submerge those values by obtaining the evidence against an accused through 'the cruel, simple expedient of compelling it from his own mouth. In sum, the privilege is fulfilled only when the person is guaranteed the right to remain silent unless he chooses to speak in the unfettered exercise of his own will.'"

D. Undercover Agents and the Miranda Warnings

Illinois v. Perkins, 496 U.S. 292 (1990)
Vote: 8-1
FACTS: In 1984, Richard Stephenson was murdered in a suburb of St. Louis. Donald Charlton told police that he had learned about a homicide from another inmate at the Graham Correctional Facility. Charlton told police that he had befriended Lloyd Perkins, who told him about a murder that he had committed. On hearing his account, the police treated Charlton's story as credible.

Police traced Perkins to a jail in Montgomery County, Illinois, where he was being held on a charge of aggravated battery, unrelated to the murder. The police decided to place an agent and Charlton in the cellblock with Perkins. The plan was for Charlton and Agent John Parisi to pose as escapees from a work release program. Parisi and Charlton were supposed to engage Perkins in conversation and report anything he said about the Stephenson murder.

Charlton introduced Parisi by his alias and told Perkins that he "wasn't going to do any more time" and suggested that they escape. Perkins stated that the jail was "rinky-dink" and that they could "break out." The trio met in Perkins's cell later that evening to make a plan. Perkins said that his girlfriend could smuggle in a pistol, and Charlton replied, "Hey, I'm not a murderer, I'm a burglar. That's your guys' profession." After telling Charlton that he would be responsible for any murder, Parisi asked Perkins if he had ever "done" anybody. He said that he had and described the Stephenson murder. Parisi did not give Perkins *Miranda* warnings before the conversation. Parisi and Perkins then engaged in some casual conversation before Perkins retired for the night. Perkins was charged with the Stephenson murder.

ISSUE: Does an undercover officer have to give *Miranda* warnings to an incarcerated suspect before asking him questions that may elicit an incriminating response?
HOLDING: No.
RATIONALE: "Conversations between suspects and undercover agents do not implicate the concerns underlying *Miranda* [*v. Arizona*, 384 U.S. 436 (1966)]. The essential ingredients of a 'police-dominated atmosphere' and compulsion are not present when an incarcerated person speaks freely to someone whom he believes to be a fellow inmate. Coercion is determined from the perspective of the suspect. . . . When a suspect considers himself in the company of cellmates and not officers, the coercive atmosphere is lacking."

"It is the premise of *Miranda* that the danger of coercion results from the interaction of custody and official interrogation. We reject the argument that *Miranda* warnings are required whenever a suspect is in custody in a technical sense and converses with someone who happens to be a government agent. Questioning by captors, who appear to control the suspect's fate, may create mutually reinforcing pressures that the Court has assumed will weaken the suspect's will, but where a suspect does not know that he is conversing with a government agent, these pressures do not exist. The state court here mistakenly assumed that because the suspect was in custody, no undercover questioning could take place. When the suspect has no reason to think that the listeners have official power over him, it should not be assumed that his words are motivated by the reaction he expects from his listeners."

"Ploys to mislead a suspect or lull him into a false sense of security that do not rise to the level of compulsion or coercion to speak are not within *Miranda*'s concerns."

"*Miranda* was not meant to protect suspects from boasting about their criminal activities in front of persons whom they believe to be their cellmates. . . . He spoke at his own peril."

"The tactic employed here to elicit a voluntary confession from a suspect does not violate the Self-Incrimination Clause. We held in *Hoffa v. United States*, 385 U.S. 293 (1966), that placing an undercover agent near a suspect in order to gather incriminating information was permissible under the Fifth Amendment."

"Where the suspect does not know that he is speaking to a government agent there is no reason to assume the possibility that the suspect might feel coerced."

"The use of undercover agents is a recognized law enforcement technique, often employed in the prison context to detect violence against correctional officials or inmates, as well as for the purposes served here. The interests protected by *Miranda* are not implicated in these cases, and the warnings are not required to safeguard the constitutional rights of inmates who make voluntary statements to undercover agents."

"We hold that an undercover law enforcement officer posing as a fellow inmate need not give *Miranda* warnings to an incarcerated suspect before asking questions that may elicit an incriminating response."

E. Can Giving *Miranda* Warnings Break the Chain between the Illegality and the Confession?

Kaupp v. Texas, 538 U.S. 626 (2003)
Vote: 9-0
FACTS: After a fourteen-year-old girl disappeared, Harris County Sheriffs learned that she had had a sexual relationship with her half brother, who was with Robert Kaupp on the day she disappeared. After sheriffs questioned Kaupp and the girl's brother, Kaupp was allowed to leave. Eventually the brother confessed that he had stabbed his half sister and dumped her body in a ditch, but he also implicated Kaupp. Detectives failed to obtain a warrant for Kaupp, but Officer Gregory Pinkins decided to "get [Kaupp] in and confront him with what [the brother] had said." With several other officers, Pinkins went to Kaupp's house at 3 a.m. After being let in, Pinkins, awakened Kaupp with a flashlight, identified himself, and said, "We need to go and talk." Kaupp said "Okay," and the officers handcuffed him and led him, shoeless and dressed only in shorts and a T-shirt, into a patrol car. Nothing indicates that Kaupp was told that he was free to

decline to go with the officers. They took him to the scene of the crime and then to the station, where they gave him the *Miranda* warnings. After a few minutes of questioning, he confessed to his involvement in the girl's murder. He was later indicted and convicted of murder.

ISSUE: Can the giving of the *Miranda* warnings alone after an illegal arrest be sufficient to purge the taint of a subsequent confession?

HOLDING: No.

RATIONALE: "Since Kaupp was arrested before he was questioned, and because the state does not even claim that the sheriff's department had probable cause to detain him at that point, well-established precedent requires suppression of the confession unless that confession was 'an act of free will [sufficient] to purge the primary taint. . . .' Demonstrating such purgation is, of course, a function of circumstantial evidence, with the burden of persuasion on the state. Relevant considerations include observance of *Miranda* [*v. Arizona*, 384 U.S. 436 (1966)], '[t]he temporal proximity of the arrest and the confession, the presence of intervening circumstances, and, particularly, the purpose and flagrancy of the official misconduct.'"

"The record before us shows that only one of these considerations, the giving of *Miranda* warnings, supports the state, and we held in *Brown* that '*Miranda* warnings, *alone* and *per se*, cannot always . . . break, for Fourth Amendment purposes, the causal connection between the illegality and the confession. . . .' In fact, the state has not even alleged 'any meaningful intervening event' between the illegal arrest and Kaupp's confession. . . . Unless, on remand, the state can point to testimony undisclosed on the record before us, and weighty enough to carry the state's burden despite the clear force of the evidence shown here, the confession must be suppressed."

F. Are Sixth Amendment Rights at Trial Violated When a Nontestifying Accomplice's Statements to Police Are Admitted?

Lilly v. Virginia, 527 U.S. 116 (1999)
Vote: 9-0
FACTS: Benjamin Lee Lilly, his brother Mark, and Mark's roommate Gary Wayne Barker broke into a home and stole liquor, guns, and a safe. The next day, they abducted Alex DeFilippis, and one of them shot him at a deserted location. The men then committed two more robberies before they were arrested. The police questioned each of them, but Lilly did not mention the murder and stated that the others forced him to participate in the robberies. Mark and Barker stated that Lilly planned the robberies and killed DeFilippis. A recording of Mark's statement indicated that he was questioned from 1:35 a.m. until 2:53 a.m., and Mark said that he was drunk the entire time. When asked about his participation, Mark admitted that he stole liquor from the house and beer from the store. He also stated that he was

present during the killing. He was told that he would be charged with robbery and that, unless he broke "family ties," Lilly "may be dragging you right into a life sentence." Mark stated that while he was drinking, Lilly and Barker had "got some guns or something" during the burglary. Mark said that Barker had pulled a gun in a robbery and stated that Lilly had planned the carjacking and that he "didn't have nothing to do with the shooting."

When the Commonwealth called Mark as a witness, he invoked his privilege against self-incrimination. The Commonwealth then introduced statements that Mark had made to police after his arrest, but Lilly objected on the ground that the statements shifted responsibility for the crimes to himself and that their admission would violate the Sixth Amendment's Confrontation Clause. Lilly was found guilty of robbery, abduction, carjacking, possession of a firearm by a felon, and four charges of illegal use of a firearm, in addition to murder, for which he was sentenced to death.

ISSUE: Is it a Confrontation Clause violation when a nontestifying accomplice's confession is admitted that incriminated the accused in a murder?

HOLDING: Yes.

RATIONALE: "The decisive fact, which we make explicit today, is that accomplices' confessions that inculpate a criminal defendant are not within a firmly rooted exception to the hearsay rule as that concept has been defined in our Confrontation Clause jurisprudence."

"Nonetheless, the historical underpinnings of the Confrontation Clause and the sweep of our prior confrontation cases offer one cogent reminder: It is highly unlikely that the presumptive unreliability that attaches to accomplices' confessions that shift or spread blame can be effectively rebutted when the . . . government is involved in the statements' production, and when the statements describe past events and have not been subjected to adversarial testing."

"Applying these principles, the Commonwealth's asserted guarantees of trustworthiness fail to convince us that Mark's confession was sufficiently reliable as to be admissible without allowing petitioner to cross-examine him. That other evidence at trial corroborated portions of Mark's statements is irrelevant. . . . In [*Idaho v. Wright*, 497 U.S. 805 (1990)], we concluded that the admission of hearsay statements by a child declarant violated the Confrontation Clause even though the statements were admissible under an exception to the hearsay rule recognized in Idaho, and even though they were corroborated by other evidence."

"[A]s we have explained, such statements are suspect insofar as they inculpate other persons. '[T]hat a person is making a broadly self-inculpatory confession does not make more credible the confession's non-self-inculpatory parts. . . .' Similarly, the absence of an express promise of leniency to Mark does not enhance his statements' reliability to the level necessary for their untested admission."

"The admission of the untested confession of Mark Lilly violated petitioner's Confrontation Clause rights."

G. Do Witnesses Who Deny Culpability
Have Valid Fifth Amendment Privileges?

Ohio v. Reiner, 532 U.S. 17 (2001)
Vote: 9-0
FACTS: Matthew Reiner was charged with involuntary manslaughter in connection with the death of his two-month-old son, Alex. The coroner testified that Alex had died from "shaken baby syndrome." He estimated that the injury occurred just before he stopped breathing. The child died two days later when life support was removed and evidence revealed that he had a broken rib and leg at the time of death. His twin brother, Derek, had several broken ribs. Reiner had been with Alex for half an hour just before Alex stopped breathing. His experts testified that Alex could have been injured several hours before his death when he was in the care of the family babysitter, Susan Batt. Batt informed the court that she intended to assert her Fifth Amendment privilege and was given transactional immunity. She then testified that she had refused to testify without immunity although she had done nothing wrong. She denied any involvement in Alex's death and testified that she had never shaken Alex or his brother. She said she had nothing to do with the other injuries to both children. The jury found Reiner guilty. On appeal, the conviction was reversed, and the Supreme Court of Ohio affirmed the reversal on the ground that Batt had no valid Fifth Amendment privilege and that the grant of immunity was unlawful and prejudiced Reiner, because it effectively told the jury that Batt did not cause the injuries.
ISSUE: Does a witness, who denies all culpability in a crime, have a Fifth Amendment privilege against self-incrimination?
HOLDING: Yes.
RATIONALE: "[T]his privilege not only extends 'to answers that would in themselves support a conviction . . . but likewise embraces those which would furnish a link in the chain of evidence needed to prosecute the claimant. . . .' '[I]t need only be evident from the implications of the question, in the setting in which it is asked, that a responsive answer to the question or an explanation of why it cannot be answered might be dangerous because injurious disclosure could result.'"

"But we have never held . . . that the privilege is unavailable to those who claim innocence. To the contrary, we have emphasized that one of the Fifth Amendment's 'basic functions . . . is to protect *innocent* men . . . "who otherwise might be ensnared by ambiguous circumstances. . . ."'" In *Grunewald* [*v. United States*, 353 U.S. 391 (1957)], we recognized that truthful responses of an innocent witness, as well as those of a wrongdoer, may provide the government with incriminating evidence from the speaker's own mouth."

"The Supreme Court of Ohio's determination that Batt did not have a valid Fifth Amendment privilege because she denied any involvement in the abuse of the children clearly conflicts with *Hoffman* [*v. United States*, 341 U.S. 479 (1951)] and *Grunewald*. Batt had 'reasonable cause' to apprehend danger from her answers if questioned at respondent's trial."

H. Are Notes Taken by a Therapist Protected for Self-Incrimination Purposes?

Jaffee v. Redmond, 518 U.S. 1 (1996)
Vote: 7-2

FACTS: Police officer Mary Lu Redmond was the first to respond to a call at an apartment complex. As she arrived, two of Ricky Allen Sr.'s sisters ran toward her, shouting that there had been a stabbing in an apartment. Redmond requested an ambulance and then exited her car and walked toward the building. Before she reached the building, several men ran out, one of whom was waving a pipe. When the men ignored her order to get on the ground, she drew her revolver, and then two other men came out of the building—one, Allen, chasing the other. According to Redmond, Allen had a butcher knife and ignored her orders drop it. Redmond then shot Allen when she felt that he was going to stab the other man. Allen died at the scene. Redmond testified that before other officers arrived "people came pouring out of the buildings," and a confrontation between her and the crowd ensued.

Carrie Jaffee, as special administrator for the deceased Allen, filed suit alleging that Redmond had violated Allen's constitutional rights by using excessive force during the encounter. During discovery Jaffee learned that Redmond had about fifty counseling sessions with a licensed social worker employed by the complex. Jaffee sought access to the notes from the sessions for use in cross-examining Redmond, which she resisted.

ISSUE: Are statements made by an officer to a social worker during counseling sessions protected from compelled disclosure?

HOLDING: Yes.

RATIONALE: "The Senate Report accompanying the 1975 adoption of the Rules indicates that Rule 501 'should be understood as reflecting the view that the recognition of a privilege based on a confidential relationship . . . should be determined on a case-by-case basis. . . .' The Rule thus did not freeze the law governing the privileges of witnesses in federal trials at a particular point in our history, but rather directed federal courts to 'continue the evolutionary development of testimonial privileges.'"

"Guided by these principles, the question we address today is whether a privilege protecting confidential communications between a psychotherapist and her patient 'promotes sufficiently important interests to outweigh the need for probative evidence. . . .' Both 'reason and experience' persuade us that it does."

"Like the spousal and attorney-client privileges, the psychotherapist-patient privilege is 'rooted in the imperative need for confidence and trust. . . .' Effective psychotherapy, by contrast, depends upon an atmosphere of confidence and trust in which the patient is willing to make a frank and complete disclosure of facts, emotions, memories, and fears. Because of the sensitive nature of the problems for which individuals consult psychotherapists, disclosure of confidential communications made during counseling sessions may cause embarrassment or disgrace. For this reason, the mere possibility of disclosure may impede development of the confidential relationship necessary for successful treatment."

"In contrast to the significant public and private interests supporting recognition of the privilege, the likely evidentiary benefit that would result from the denial of the privilege is modest. If the privilege were rejected, confidential conversations between psychotherapists and their patients would surely be chilled, particularly when it is obvious that the circumstances that give rise to the need for treatment will probably result in litigation."

"That it is appropriate for the federal courts to recognize a psychotherapist privilege under Rule 501 is confirmed by the fact that all 50 States and the District of Columbia have enacted into law some form of psychotherapist privilege."

"[W]e hold that confidential communications between a licensed psychotherapist and her patients in the course of diagnosis or treatment are protected from compelled disclosure under Rule 501 of the Federal Rules of Evidence."

I. Can Miranda Be Delayed for Purposes of Obtaining a Confession?

Missouri v. Seibert, 542 U.S. 600 (2004)
Vote: 5-4
FACTS: Patrice Seibert's son Jonathan had cerebral palsy, and when he died in his sleep she feared charges of neglect because he had bedsores. In her presence, two of her other sons and two of their friends devised a plan to conceal Jonathan's death by incinerating his body in the course of burning their mobile home, in which they planned to leave Donald Rector, a mentally ill teenager living with the family, to avoid the appearance that Jonathan had been unattended. Seibert's son Darian and a friend set the fire, and Rector died. A few days later, the police awakened Seibert at 3 a.m. at a hospital where Darian was being treated for burns. In arresting her, Officer Kevin Clinton followed instructions from Officer Richard Hanrahan that he refrain from giving her *Miranda* warnings. After she had been taken to the station and left alone for fifteen to twenty minutes, Hanrahan questioned her without *Miranda* warnings for about thirty minutes, repeating "Donald was also to die in his sleep." After Seibert admitted that Donald was meant to die, she was given a break. Hanrahan then turned on a recorder, gave Seibert the *Miranda* warnings, and obtained a signed waiver. He resumed the questioning with "Ok, 'Trice, we've been talking for a little while about what happened on Wednesday the twelfth, haven't we?" and confronted her with her prewarning statements. She was convicted of second-degree murder.
ISSUE: Is an accused's confession, given after the *Miranda* warnings were intentionally delayed for the purpose of obtaining a prewarned confession, admissible in court?
HOLDING: No.
RATIONALE: "By any objective measure, applied to circumstances exemplified here, it is likely that if the interrogators employ the technique of withholding warnings until after interrogation succeeds in eliciting a confession, the warnings will be ineffective in preparing the suspect for successive interrogation, close in time and similar in content. After all, the reason that question-first is catching on is as obvious as its manifest purpose, which is to get a confession the suspect would not make if he understood his rights at the outset; the sensible underlying assumption is that with one confession in

hand before the warnings, the interrogator can count on getting its duplicate, with trifling additional trouble. Upon hearing warnings only in the aftermath of interrogation and just after making a confession, a suspect would hardly think he had a genuine right to remain silent, let alone persist in so believing once the police began to lead him over the same ground again. A more likely reaction on a suspect's part would be perplexity about the reason for discussing rights at that point, bewilderment being an unpromising frame of mind for knowledgeable decision. What is worse, telling a suspect that 'anything you say can and will be used against you,' without expressly excepting the statement just given, could lead to an entirely reasonable inference that what he has just said will be used, with subsequent silence being of no avail. Thus, when *Miranda* [*v. Arizona*, 384 U.S 436 (1966)] warnings are inserted in the midst of coordinated and continuing interrogation, they are likely to mislead and 'depriv[e] a defendant of knowledge essential to his ability to understand the nature of his rights and the consequences of abandoning them. . . .'"

"Missouri argues that a confession repeated at the end of an interrogation sequence envisioned in a question-first strategy is admissible on the authority of *Oregon v. Elstad*, 470 U.S. 298 (1985) but the argument disfigures that case."

"The contrast between [*Oregon v. Elstad*, 470 U.S. 298 (1985)] and this case reveals a series of relevant facts that bear on whether *Miranda* warnings delivered midstream could be effective enough to accomplish their object: the completeness and detail of the questions and answers in the first round of interrogation, the overlapping content of the two statements, the timing and setting of the first and the second, the continuity of police personnel, and the degree to which the interrogator's questions treated the second round as continuous with the first."

"Because the question-first tactic effectively threatens to thwart *Miranda*'s purpose of reducing the risk that a coerced confession would be admitted. . . . Seibert's post-warning statements are inadmissible."

J. Exceptions to *Miranda*

1. Public Safety

New York v. Quarles, 467 U.S. 649 (1984)
Vote: 5-4
FACTS: Officers Frank Kraft and Sal Scarring were approached in their car by a young woman who told them that she had just been raped. She described her assailant as a black male, about six feet tall, and wearing a black jacket with the name "Big Ben" printed on the back. She told the officers that the man entered a nearby supermarket and that he had a gun. The officers drove her to the market, and Kraft entered while Scarring called for backup. Kraft spotted Benjamin Quarles who matched the description. Quarles then ran toward the back of the store while Kraft, with his gun drawn, followed. Upon regaining sight of Quarles, Kraft ordered him to stop and put his hands

over his head. Quarles did so, and and Kraft then discovered that Quarels was wearing an empty shoulder holster. After handcuffing him, Kraft asked him where the gun was. Quarles nodded in the direction of some boxes and said, "the gun is over there." Kraft retrieved a loaded revolver from one of the cartons, placed Quarles under arrest, and read him the *Miranda* warnings. Quarles stated that he would answer questions without an attorney. Kraft then asked Quarles if he owned the gun and where he had bought it. He replied that he owned it and that he had purchased it in Miami. Quarles was charged with criminal possession of a weapon.

ISSUE: Are the police required to administer the *Miranda* warnings before asking questions of a suspect if the public safety is in danger?

HOLDING: No.

RATIONALE: "We hold that on these facts there is a 'public safety' exception to the requirement that *Miranda* [*v. Arizona*, 384 U.S. 436 (1966)] warnings be given before a suspect's answers may be admitted into evidence, and that the availability of that exception does not depend upon the motivation of the individual officers involved. In a kaleidoscopic situation such as the one confronting these officers, where spontaneity rather than adherence to a police manual is necessarily the order of the day, the application of the exception which we recognize today should not be made to depend on post hoc findings at a suppression hearing concerning the subjective motivation of the arresting officer."

"Whatever the motivation of individual officers in such a situation, we do not believe that the doctrinal underpinnings of *Miranda* require that it be applied in all its rigor to a situation in which police officers ask questions reasonably prompted by a concern for the public safety."

"In such a situation, if the police are required to recite the familiar *Miranda* warnings before asking the whereabouts of the gun, suspects in Quarles's position might well be deterred from responding."

"We conclude that the need for answers to questions in a situation posing a threat to the public safety outweighs the need for the prophylactic rule protecting the Fifth Amendment's privilege against self-incrimination. We decline to place officers such as Officer Kraft in the untenable position of having to consider, often in a matter of seconds, whether it best serves society for them to ask the necessary questions without the *Miranda* warnings and render whatever probative evidence they uncover inadmissible, or for them to give the warnings in order to preserve the admissibility of evidence they might uncover but possibly damage or destroy their ability to obtain that evidence and neutralize the volatile situation confronting them."

"The exception will not be difficult for police officers to apply because in each case it will be circumscribed by the exigency which justifies it. We think police officers can and will distinguish almost instinctively between questions necessary to secure their own safety or the safety of the public and questions designed solely to elicit testimonial evidence from a suspect."

2. Impeachment

Harris v. New York, 401 U.S. 222 (1971)
Vote: 5-4

FACTS: Harris was charged with selling heroin to an undercover officer. At trial, the officer testified as to details of the sales, a second officer verified some facts, and a third testified about the chemical analysis of the heroin. Harris took the stand and admitted knowing the officer but only admitted making a sale of the contents of a glassine bag to the officer while claiming that it was baking powder and part of a scheme to defraud the buyer. On cross-examination, Harris was asked whether he had made statements to police after his arrest, statements that partially contradicted his testimony. Harris testified that he could remember almost none of the questions recited by the prosecutor. The prosecutor made no attempt to use these statements against Harris, conceding that they were inadmissible under *Miranda*. At the request of Harris's counsel, the written statement from which the prosecutor had read in his impeaching process was placed in the record but not shown to the jury. The trial judge instructed the jury that the statements attributed to Harris could be considered only in passing on his credibility and not as evidence of guilt. In closing, both counsel argued the substance of the impeaching statements. The jury then found Harris guilty on the second count of the indictment.

ISSUE: Can statements rendered inadmissible by *Miranda* be used to impeach the credibility of the accused?

HOLDING: Yes.

RATIONALE: "It does not follow from *Miranda* [*v. Arizona*, 384 U.S. 436 (1966)] that evidence inadmissible against an accused in the prosecution's case in chief is barred for all purposes, provided of course that the trustworthiness of the evidence satisfies legal standards."

"In *Walder v. United States*, 347 U.S. 62 (1954), the Court permitted physical evidence, inadmissible in the case in chief, to be used for impeachment purposes."

"It is true that *Walder* was impeached as to collateral matters included in his direct examination, whereas petitioner here was impeached as to testimony bearing more directly on the crimes charged. We are not persuaded that there is a difference in principle that warrants a result different from that reached by the Court in *Walder*."

"Every criminal defendant is privileged to testify in his own defense, or to refuse to do so. But that privilege cannot be construed to include the right to commit perjury. . . . Having voluntarily taken the stand, petitioner was under an obligation to speak truthfully and accurately, and the prosecution here did no more than utilize the traditional truth-testing devices of the adversary process."

"The shield provided by *Miranda* cannot be perverted into a license to use perjury by way of a defense, free from the risk of confrontation with prior inconsistent utterances. We hold, therefore, that petitioner's credibility was appropriately impeached by use of his earlier conflicting statements."

3. *Miranda* Violations and Finding a Witness

Michigan v. Tucker, 417 U.S. 433 (1974)
Vote: 8-1
FACTS: A woman in Pontiac, Michigan, was found in her home by a friend, Luther White, in serious condition. She was tied, gagged, and partially disrobed, and she had been raped, and beaten. She was unable to tell White anything about the assault. While White was trying to get help, he saw a dog in the house. This attracted his attention because he knew that the woman did not own a dog. Later, when talking with police, White observed the dog a second time, and police followed the dog to Tucker's house. Neighbors also connected the dog with Tucker. Police then arrested Tucker and brought him in for questioning. Prior to the interrogation the police asked Tucker whether he knew for what crime he had been arrested, whether he wanted an attorney, and whether he understood his rights. He replied that he did understand the crime, that he did not want an attorney, and that he understood his rights. The police further advised him that any statements he might make could be used against him in court. However, they did not tell him that he would be provided with counsel if he could not pay.

The police then questioned Tucker about his activities on the night of the attack. He replied that he had first been with Robert Henderson and then later at home, alone, asleep. The police contacted Henderson, but his story discredited Tucker's. Henderson acknowledged that he had been with Tucker on the night of the crime but said that he had left early. Henderson also told police that he saw Tucker the next day and asked him about some scratches on his face, "asked him if he got hold of a wild one or something." He stated that Tucker responded by stating: "(S)omething like that." Then, Henderson said, he asked Tucker "who it was," and respondent said: "(S)ome woman lived the next block over," adding: "She is a widow woman," or words to that effect. Henderson testified at trial, and Tucker was convicted of rape.

ISSUE: Does the *Miranda* rule require that a witness's testimony be excluded if the witness was discovered based on questioning of the suspect that did not include the full set of warnings?
HOLDING: No.
RATIONALE: "Here we deal, not with the offer of respondent's own statements in evidence, but only with the testimony of a witness whom the police discovered as a result of respondent's statements. This recourse to respondent's voluntary statements does no violence to such elements of the adversary system as may be embodied in the Fifth, Sixth, and Fourteenth Amendments."

"In summary, we do not think that any single reason supporting exclusion of this witness' testimony, or all of them together, are very persuasive. By contrast, we find the arguments in favor of admitting the testimony quite strong. For, when balancing the interests involved, we must weigh the strong interest under any system of justice of making available to the trier of fact all concededly relevant and trustworthy evidence which either party seeks to adduce. In this particular case we also "must consider society's interest in the effective prosecution of criminals in light of the protection our pre-*Miranda* [*v. Arizona*, 384 U.S. 436 (1966)] standards afford criminal defendants. . . .

These interests may be outweighed by the need to provide an effective sanction to a constitutional right . . . but they must in any event be valued. Here respondent's own statement, which might have helped the prosecution show respondent's guilty conscience at trial, had already been excised from the prosecution's case. . . ."

"This Court has already recognized that a failure to give interrogated suspects full *Miranda* warnings does not entitle the suspect to insist that statements made by him be excluded in every conceivable context."

4. Harmless Error

Arizona v. Fulminante, 499 U.S. 279 (1991)
Vote: 5-4

FACTS: Oreste Fulminante called the Mesa, Arizona, police to report that his eleven-year-old stepdaughter, Jeneane Michelle Hunt, was missing. He had been caring for her while her mother was in the hospital. Two days later, her body was found in the desert with two gunshot wounds to the head with a ligature around her neck. Due to decomposition, it was impossible to tell whether she had been sexually assaulted. Fulminante's statements to police concerning Jeneane's disappearance and his relationship with her were inconsistent, and he became a suspect. When no charges were filed against him, he left Arizona for New Jersey, where he was later convicted on federal charges of possession of a firearm by a felon.

Fulminante was incarcerated in the Ray Brook Federal Correctional Institution in New York where he became friends with Anthony Sarivola, then serving a sixty-day sentence for extortion. Sarivola, a former police officer, had been involved in loan-sharking for organized crime but then became an informant for the FBI. After befriending Fulminante, he heard that Fulminante was suspected of killing a child in Arizona. Sarivola then raised the subject with Fulminante, but he denied any involvement. On one occasion, he told Sarivola that Jeneane had been killed by bikers; on another, he said he did not know what had happened. Sarivola passed this information to the FBI, who instructed him to find out more.

Sarivola said that he knew Fulminante was "starting to get some tough treatment and whatnot" from other inmates because of the rumor, and he offered to protect Fulminante from his fellow inmates, but he said that he told him, "'You have to tell me about it, you know. I mean, in other words, for me to give you any help.'" Fulminante then admitted that he had driven Jeneane to the desert on his motorcycle, choked her, sexually assaulted her, and made her beg for her life, before shooting her twice in the head. Sarivola was released from prison, and Fulminante was released six months later, only to be arrested again for another weapons violation. Prior to trial, Fulminante moved to suppress the statement he had given Sarivola in prison, as well as a second confession he had given to Donna Sarivola, following his release from prison. He asserted that the confession to Sarivola was coerced, and that the second confession was the "fruit" of the first. Fulminante was convicted of Jeneane's murder and was sentenced to death.

ISSUE: Are coerced confessions trial errors in the sense that they can be subjected to the harmless error analysis to determine their admissibility?

HOLDING: Yes.

RATIONALE: "Since this Court's landmark decision in *Chapman* [*v. California,* 386 U.S. 18 (1967)] in which we adopted the general rule that a constitutional error does not automatically require reversal of a conviction, the Court has applied harmless-error analysis to a wide range of errors and has recognized that most constitutional errors can be harmless."

"The common thread connecting these cases is that each involved 'trial error' error which occurred during the presentation of the case to the jury. . . ."

"It is evident from a comparison of the constitutional violations which we have held subject to harmless error, and those which we have held not, that involuntary statements or confessions belong in the former category. The admission of an involuntary confession is a 'trial error,' similar in both degree and kind to the erroneous admission of other types of evidence. . . . When reviewing the erroneous admission of an involuntary confession, the appellate court, as it does with the admission of other forms of improperly admitted evidence, simply reviews the remainder of the evidence against the defendant to determine whether the admission of the confession was harmless beyond a reasonable doubt."

"Nor can it be said that the admission of an involuntary confession is the type of error which 'transcends the criminal process.' This Court has applied harmless-error analysis to the violation of other constitutional rights similar in magnitude and importance and involving the same level of police misconduct. . . . This is especially true in a case such as this one where there are no allegations of physical violence on behalf of the police."

"Of course an involuntary confession may have a more dramatic effect on the course of a trial than do other trial errors—in particular cases it may be devastating to a defendant—but this simply means that a reviewing court will conclude in such a case that its admission was not harmless error; it is not a reason for eschewing the harmless-error test entirely."

K. Invocation of Right to Silence and Impeachment

1. Prosecution Cross-Examination and Silence

Doyle v. Ohio, 426 U.S. 610 (1976)
Vote: 6-3
FACTS: William Bonnell offered to assist the local police department in setting up drug "pushers" in return for support in his efforts to receive lenient treatment with his latest legal problems, and the narcotics agents agreed. Bonnell advised the unit that he had arranged a "buy" of ten pounds of marihuana and needed $1,750 to pay for it; however, the agents were only able to collect $1,320. Bonnell took the money and left while agents in two cars followed. He met Jefferson Doyle in Dover, Ohio, and then Bonnell and Richard Wood drove in Bonnell's truck to New Philadelphia while Doyle was to go

and obtain the marihuana and then meet them at a prearranged location. When Doyle arrived at Bonnell's truck in New Philadelphia, the two vehicles proceeded to a parking lot. Then Bonnell drove off in his truck. Doyle and Wood left in Doyle's car, and they quickly found that they had been paid $430 less than the agreed upon price. They began looking for Bonnell and were stopped by New Philadelphia police acting on instructions from the narcotics agents. Agent Beamer arrived and made the arrests and administered the *Miranda* warnings. A search of the car uncovered the $1,320.

At both trials, defense counsel's cross-examination of the narcotics agents were designed to show that none of them had actually seen the transaction but had seen only Bonnell standing next to Doyle's car with a package under his arm. Both Doyle and Wood admitted to everything except who was selling marihuana to whom. According to them, Bonnell had framed them. The arrangement had been for Bonnell to sell Doyle ten pounds of marihuana, but Doyle had changed his mind at the last minute concerning the price. Doyle tried to explain, but Bonnell got angry and threw the money into Doyle's car and took the marihuana back to his truck. The chase was Wood and Doyle trying to ask Bonnell what the money was for. As part of a cross-examination for impeachment at trial, the prosecutor asked Doyle and Wood why they had not told the story to the agent when they were arrested. Both men were convicted of selling ten pounds of marijuana.

ISSUE: Can the prosecution cross-examine a defendant as to postarrest silence for the purpose of impeachment?

HOLDING: No.

RATIONALE: "We conclude that use of the defendant's post-arrest silence in this manner violates due process. . . ."

"Despite the importance of cross-examination, we have concluded that the *Miranda* decision compels rejection of the State's position. . . . Silence in the wake of these warnings may be nothing more than the arrestee's exercise of these *Miranda* [*v. Arizona*, 384 U.S. 436 (1966)] rights. Thus, every post-arrest silence is insolubly ambiguous because of what the State is required to advise the person arrested. . . . Moreover, while it is true that the *Miranda* warnings contain no express assurance that silence will carry no penalty, such assurance is implicit to any person who receives the warnings. In such circumstances, it would be fundamentally unfair and a deprivation of due process to allow the arrested person's silence to be used to impeach an explanation subsequently offered at trial."

"We hold that the use for impeachment purposes of petitioners' silence, at the time of arrest and after receiving *Miranda* warnings, violated the Due Process Clause of the Fourteenth Amendment."

2. Postarrest Silence and Harmless Error

Brecht v. Abrahamson, 507 U.S. 619 (1993)

Vote: 5-4

FACTS: Todd A. Brecht was serving a prison sentence in Georgia when his sister Molly and her husband Roger Hartman paid the restitution for his crime and assumed custody of him. This caused tension because Roger, a local district attorney, disapproved of Brecht's drinking and homosexuality. The Hartmans told Brecht, that he was not to drink alcohol or engage in homosexual activities in their home, but he quickly violated the rule. While the Hartmans were away, he broke into their liquor cabinet, found a rifle in a room, and began shooting cans in the backyard. When Roger returned from work, Brecht shot him in the back and sped off. Hartman was able to summon help, but his wound was fatal. Brecht drove the car into a ditch and told police that he had called a tow truck. Brecht then hitched a ride to Minnesota, where he was stopped by police and was arrested. When he was told that he was being held for the shooting, he stated, "it was a big mistake," and asked to talk with "somebody that would understand [him]." He was then taken to Wisconsin, Mirandized, and charged with first-degree murder. At trial, he admitted shooting Hartman, but claimed it was an accident. The State argued that Brecht failed to get help and failed to mention anything about the accidental shooting to anyone. Over objections, the State also asked Brecht whether he had told anyone at any time before trial that the shooting was an accident, to which Brecht replied "No," and made several references to petitioner's pretrial silence during closing argument. Brecht was convicted.

ISSUE: Is the use of postarrest silence for impeachment a harmless error under the habeas corpus substantial effect test?

HOLDING: Yes.

RATIONALE: "In this case we must decide whether the *Chapman* [*v. California*, 386 U.S. 18 (1967)] harmless-error standard applies in determining whether the prosecution's use for impeachment purposes of petitioner's post-*Miranda* [*v. Arizona*, 384 U.S. 436 (1966)] silence, in violation of due process under *Doyle* [*v. Ohio*, 426 U.S. 610 (1976)] . . . entitles petitioner to habeas corpus relief. We hold that it does not. Instead, the standard for determining whether habeas relief must be granted is whether the *Doyle* error 'had substantial and injurious effect or influence in determining the jury's verdict. . . .' The *Kotteakos* [*v. United States*, 328 U.S. 750 (1946)] harmless-error standard is better tailored to the nature and purpose of collateral review than the *Chapman* standard, and application of a less onerous harmless-error standard on habeas promotes the considerations underlying our habeas jurisprudence. Applying this standard, we conclude that petitioner is not entitled to habeas relief."

"The first time petitioner claimed that the shooting was an accident was when he took the stand at trial. It was entirely proper—and probative—for the State to impeach his testimony by pointing out that petitioner had failed to tell anyone before the time he received his *Miranda* warnings at his arraignment about the shooting being an accident. . . . On the other hand, the State's references to petitioner's silence after that point in time . . . crossed the *Doyle* line. For it is conceivable that, once petitioner had been given his *Miranda* warnings, he decided to stand on his right to remain silent because he believed his silence would not be used against him at trial."

"*Doyle* . . . is rooted in fundamental fairness and due process concerns. However real these concerns, *Doyle* does not 'overprotec[t]' them. . . . Under the rationale of

Doyle, due process is violated whenever the prosecution uses for impeachment purposes a defendant's post-*Miranda* silence."

"Instead, we think *Doyle* error fits squarely into the category of constitutional violations which we have characterized as 'trial error.'"

"In light of these considerations, we must decide whether the same harmless-error standard that the state courts applied on direct review of petitioner's *Doyle* claim also applies in this habeas proceeding. . . . For these reasons, it scarcely seems logical to require federal habeas courts to engage in the identical approach to harmless-error review that *Chapman* requires state courts to engage in on direct review."

"Absent affirmative evidence that state-court judges are ignoring their oath, we discount petitioner's argument that courts will respond to our ruling by violating their Article VI duty to uphold the Constitution. . . . In any event, we think the costs of applying the *Chapman* standard on federal habeas outweigh the additional deterrent effect, if any, that would be derived from its application on collateral review."

"Overturning final and presumptively correct convictions on collateral review because the State cannot prove that an error is harmless under *Chapman* undermines the States' interest in finality and infringes upon their sovereignty over criminal matters. Moreover, granting habeas relief merely because there is a 'reasonable possibility' that trial error contributed to the verdict . . . is at odds with the historic meaning of habeas corpus—to afford relief to those whom society has 'grievously wronged.' Retrying defendants whose convictions are set aside also imposes significant 'social costs,' including the expenditure of additional time and resources for all the parties involved, the 'erosion of memory' and 'dispersion of witnesses' that accompany the passage of time and make obtaining convictions on retrial more difficult, and the frustration of 'society's interest in the prompt administration of justice.'"

"The imbalance of the costs and benefits of applying the *Chapman* harmless-error standard on collateral review counsels in favor of applying a less onerous standard on habeas review of constitutional error. . . . The test under *Kotteakos* is whether the error 'had substantial and injurious effect or influence in determining the jury's verdict. . . .' The *Kotteakos* standard is thus better tailored to the nature and purpose of collateral review and more likely to promote the considerations underlying our recent habeas cases. Moreover, because the *Kotteakos* standard is grounded in the federal harmless-error rule, federal courts may turn to an existing body of case law in applying it."

"For the foregoing reasons, then, we hold that the *Kotteakos* harmless-error standard applies in determining whether habeas relief must be granted because of constitutional error of the trial type. . . . Our inquiry here is whether, in light of the record as a whole, the State's improper use for impeachment purposes of petitioner's post-*Miranda* silence, 'had substantial and injurious effect or influence in determining the jury's verdict.' We think it clear that it did not."

L. Is Physical Evidence Found as a Result of an Unwarned Statement Admissible?

United States v. Patane, 542 U.S. 630 (2004)
Vote: 5-4

FACTS: Samuel Francis Patane, was arrested for harassing his ex-girlfriend, Linda O'Donnell. He was released on bond, subject to a restraining order. Patane violated the order by attempting to call O'Donnell. Colorado Springs police officer Tracy Fox began to investigate. A probation officer informed an agent at the Bureau of Alcohol, Tobacco, and Firearms (ATF), that Patane, a convicted felon, illegally possessed a pistol. The ATF contacted Detective Josh Benner, and he and Fox proceeded to Patane's house. Fox arrested Patane for violating the restraining order. Detective Benner attempted to advise Patane of his *Miranda* rights but Patane asserted that he knew his rights so neither officer bothered to complete them.

Benner then asked Patane about the pistol. He was initially reluctant to discuss it, stating, "I am not sure I should tell you anything about the Glock because I don't want you to take it away from me." Benner persisted, and Patane told him that it was in his bedroom and allowed Benner to get it. Patane was indicted for possession of a firearm by a convicted felon.

ISSUE: Does the failure to give *Miranda* warnings require the exclusion of the physical fruit of the unwarned, though voluntary statement?

HOLDING: No.

RATIONALE: "Because the *Miranda* [*v. Arizona*, 384 U.S. 436 (1966)] rule protects against violations of the Self-Incrimination Clause, which, in turn, is not implicated by the introduction at trial of physical evidence resulting from voluntary statements, we answer the question presented in the negative."

"The Self-Incrimination Clause, however, is not implicated by the admission into evidence of the physical fruit of a voluntary statement. Accordingly, there is no justification for extending the *Miranda* rule to this context. And just as the Self-Incrimination Clause primarily focuses on the criminal trial, so too does the *Miranda* rule. The *Miranda* rule is not a code of police conduct, and police do not violate the Constitution (or even the *Miranda* rule, for that matter) by mere failures to warn. For this reason, the exclusionary rule articulated in cases such as *Wong Sun* [*v. United States*, 371 U.S. 471 (1963)] does not apply."

"For present purposes, it suffices to note that the core protection afforded by the Self-Incrimination Clause is a prohibition on compelling a criminal defendant to testify against himself at trial. . . . The Clause cannot be violated by the introduction of non-testimonial evidence obtained as a result of voluntary statements."

"More generally, the *Miranda* rule 'does not require that the statements [taken without complying with the rule] and their fruits be discarded as inherently tainted. . . .' Such a blanket suppression rule could not be justified by reference to the 'Fifth Amendment goal of assuring trustworthy evidence' or by any deterrence rationale."

"Furthermore, the Self-Incrimination Clause contains its own exclusionary rule. . . . We have repeatedly explained 'that those subjected to coercive police interrogations have an *automatic* protection from the use of their involuntary statements (or evidence derived from their statements) in any subsequent criminal trial. . . .' This explicit textual protection supports a strong presumption against expanding the *Miranda* rule any further."

IV

PRETRIAL, TRIAL, AND POSTTRIAL PROCEDURES

11

Identification

CONTINUING WITH THE ACCUSED and the right to counsel, this chapter departs from the *Fifth Amendment right* to have a lawyer present during *interrogation* and examines the *Sixth Amendment right* to have counsel present for *trial preparations*. This right has been interpreted broadly and includes the right to have a lawyer acting on your behalf at all stages of the trial process. This has historically been understood to mean that once the state begins proceedings against an accused, he or she has the right to have an attorney basically rebut the state. In other words, once the state begins to initiate formal proceedings such as arraignments, the filing of charges, preliminary hearings, and so forth, the accused has the right to be represented by a lawyer.

The Supreme Court has spoken a bit more clearly in this area than it has in others, so the rules with regard to right to counsel associated with the adjudication process are easier to understand. For example, if the police seek to identify a suspect via a lineup or showup and that person has been charged, that person has the right to have a lawyer present. Further, the Court has also stated that in-court identifications of an accused who was not represented by counsel at a lineup also violates the Sixth Amendment right to counsel. However, the Court's rule with regard to identification procedures is narrow: the right attaches when a suspect has been charged. In other words, the Supreme Court has also ruled that if adversarial proceedings have not begun, then the Sixth Amendment right to have counsel present at a lineup does not exist. Further, the Court has also ruled on the suggestibility of a one-person showup. Like it has in so many other contexts, the Court has elected to look at each of these cases individually and base its decisions on the "totality of the circumstances," if the witness can make a reliable identification, courts are allowed to admit them. The Court has also held that like the right to waive the assistance of counsel in the Fifth Amendment context for interrogation, a suspect can also waive their right to have counsel present for the identification process. Finally, the Court has held that no Sixth Amendment right to have counsel present exists if a suspect is placed in a photographic lineup, even if the suspect has already been charged.

A. Is Counsel Required at Postindictment Identification Proceedings?

1. Postindictment Identification Proceedings

United States v. Wade, 388 U.S. 218 (1967)
Vote: 5-4

FACTS: A man with a strip of tape on each side of his face entered a federal bank in Eustace, Texas, pointed a pistol at the cashier and vice president and forced them to fill a pillowcase with money. The man then drove away with an accomplice who had been waiting in a stolen car. A few months later, Wade and two others were indicted for conspiring to rob the bank. Wade was arrested and counsel was appointed. An FBI agent, without notice to Wade's lawyer, arranged for the two bank employees to observe a lineup, conducted in a courtroom, of Wade and several others. Each person in the line wore strips of tape, and each said in turn, "Put the money in the bag," the words spoken by the robber. As a result, both employees identified Wade as the robber. At trial, the employees, when asked if the robber was present, pointed to Wade. They both later testified to the lineup identification in the courtroom. Wade's counsel moved for an acquittal or to strike the courtroom identifications on the ground that the lineup, without notice to and in the absence of counsel, violated Wade's privilege against self-incrimination and his right to the assistance of counsel. The motion was denied and Wade was convicted.

ISSUE: Does an accused have a Sixth Amendment right to have counsel present at a postindictment lineup?

HOLDING: Yes.

RATIONALE: "[T]oday's law enforcement machinery involves critical confrontations of the accused by the prosecution at pretrial proceedings where the results might well settle the accused's fate and reduce the trial itself to a mere formality. In recognition of these realities of modern criminal prosecution, our cases have construed the Sixth Amendment guarantee to apply to 'critical' stages of the proceedings. The guarantee reads: 'In all criminal prosecutions, the accused shall enjoy the right . . . to have the Assistance of Counsel *for his defence.* . . .' (emphasis supplied.) The plain wording of this guarantee thus encompasses counsel's assistance whenever necessary to assure a meaningful 'defence.'"

"It is central to that principle that in addition to counsel's presence at trial, the accused is guaranteed that he need not stand alone against the State at any stage of the prosecution, formal or informal, in court or out, where counsel's absence might derogate from the accused's right to a fair trial."

"Since it appears that there is grave potential for prejudice, intentional or not, in the pretrial lineup, which may not be capable of reconstruction at trial, and since presence of counsel itself can often avert prejudice and assure a meaningful confrontation at trial, there can be little doubt that for Wade the postindictment lineup was a critical stage of the prosecution at which he was 'as much entitled to such aid (of counsel) . . . as at the trial itself. . . .' No substantial countervailing policy considerations have been advanced against the requirement of the presence of counsel. Concern is expressed that the requirement will forestall prompt identifications and result in obstruction of the confrontations. . . . And to refuse to recognize the right to counsel for fear that counsel will obstruct the course of justice is contrary to the basic assumptions upon which this Court has operated in Sixth Amendment cases."

"[F]or the reasons expressed, law enforcement may be assisted by preventing the infiltration of taint in the prosecution's identification evidence. That result cannot help the guilty avoid conviction but can only help assure that the right man has been brought to justice."

2. Testimony Obtained from an Illegal Lineup

Gilbert v. California, 388 U.S. 263 (1967)
Vote: 5-4
FACTS: The FBI arrested Gilbert in Philadelphia for the robbery of the Alhambra Mutual Savings and Loan Association and for the murder of a police officer at the scene. Several witnesses identified Gilbert in court based on a lineup conducted in an auditorium about two weeks after he was indicted. At that point, Gilbert had appointed counsel but his representative was never notified of the lineup, which took place on a stage with about 100 people in the audience. Bright lights focused on the suspects so that they could not see any of the alleged witnesses. Gilbert argued that the testimony of some of the witnesses that identified him at the lineup was improperly admitted against him. Gilbert was convicted of the robbery and the murder of a police officer and sentenced to death.
ISSUE: Can testimony obtained from a witness who identified a suspect in a postindictment, uncounseled lineup be admitted at trial?
HOLDING: No.
RATIONALE: "The admission of the in-court identifications without first determining that they were not tainted by the illegal lineup but were of independent origin was constitutional error. . . ."

"Quite different considerations are involved as to the admission of the testimony of the manager of the apartment house at the guilt phase and of the eight witnesses at the penalty stage that they identified Gilbert at the lineup. That testimony is the direct result of the illegal lineup 'come at by exploitation of (the primary) illegality. . . .' Only a per se exclusionary rule as to such testimony can be an effective sanction to assure that law enforcement authorities will respect the accused's constitutional right to the presence of his counsel at the critical lineup. In the absence of legislative regulations adequate to avoid the hazards to a fair trial which inhere in lineups as presently conducted, the desirability of deterring the constitutionally objectionable practice must prevail over the undesirability of excluding relevant evidence. . . . That conclusion is buttressed by the consideration that the witness' testimony of his lineup identification will enhance the impact of his in-court identification on the jury and seriously aggravate whatever derogation exists of the accused's right to a fair trial."

3. Showups and Due Process

Stovall v. Denno, 388 U.S. 293 (1967)

Vote: 5-4

FACTS: Dr. Paul Behrendt was stabbed to death in the kitchen of his home in Garden City, Long Island, and his wife, also a physician, jumped at the assailant. He knocked her to the floor and stabbed her eleven times. The police found a shirt on the floor and keys in its pocket that were traced to Stovall. He was arrested, but an arraignment was postponed until he could retain counsel. As a result of the attack, Mrs. Behrendt underwent major surgery to save her life. The police, without affording Stovall time to retain counsel, arranged with her surgeon to permit them to bring him to her hospital room the day after the surgery. Stovall was handcuffed to one of several officers who, with two members of the district attorney's office, brought him to the room. Stovall was the only black in the room, and Mrs. Behrendt identified him from her hospital bed after being asked by an officer whether he "was the man" and after he spoke a few words for voice identification. Mrs. Behrendt and the officers testified at the trial as to her identification of Stovall in the hospital room, and she also made an in-court identification. Stovall was convicted and sentenced to death.

ISSUE: Should the *Wade-Gilbert* rule be applied to cases retroactively?

HOLDING: No.

RATIONALE: "We hold that [*United States v. Wade,* 388 U.S. 218 (1967)] and *Gilbert* [*v. California,* 388 U.S. 263 (1967)] affect only those cases and all future cases which involve confrontations for identification purposes conducted in the absence of counsel after this date. The rulings of *Wade* and *Gilbert* are therefore inapplicable in the present case. We think also that on the facts of this case petitioner was not deprived of due process of law in violation of the Fourteenth Amendment."

"A conviction which rests on a mistaken identification is a gross miscarriage of justice. The *Wade* and *Gilbert* rules are aimed at minimizing that possibility by preventing the unfairness at the pretrial confrontation that experience has proved can occur and assuring meaningful examination of the identification witness' testimony at trial. Does it follow that the rules should be applied retroactively? We do not think so."

"The unusual force of the countervailing considerations strengthens our conclusion in favor of prospective application. The law enforcement officials of the Federal Government and of all 50 States have heretofore proceeded on the premise that the Constitution did not require the presence of counsel at pretrial confrontations for identification. Today's rulings were not foreshadowed in our cases; no court announced such a requirement until Wade was decided. . . . It is, therefore, very clear that retroactive application of *Wade* and *Gilbert* 'would seriously disrupt the administration of our criminal laws.' We said, 'To require all of those States now to void the conviction of every person who did not testify at his trial would have an impact upon the administration of their criminal law so devastating as to need no elaboration.' We conclude, therefore, that the *Wade* and *Gilbert* rules should not be made retroactive."

B. Exceptions to the Wade-Gilbert Rule

1. Identifications before Adversarial Judicial Proceedings

Kirby v. Illinois, 406 U.S. 682 (1972)

Vote: 5-4

FACTS: Willie Shard reported to Chicago police that two men robbed him of traveler's checks and a Social Security card. Two officers stopped Kirby and Ralph Bean, and when asked for identification, Kirby produced a wallet that contained Shard's checks and Social Security card. Shard's papers were also found in Bean's possession. When asked to explain why he had Shard's property, Kirby first said that the checks were "play money," and then that he had won them in a crap game. The officers then arrested Kirby and Bean and took them to a police station. After checking the records, the officers learned of the Shard robbery. Police brought Shard to the station, and he identified Kirby and Bean, but no lawyer was present. Kirby and Bean never asserted, nor were advised of, their right to counsel. The two men were subsequently indicted for robbery and given counsel. Shard testified for the prosecution. He described his identification of the two men at the police station and identified them again in the courtroom. Both men were convicted.

ISSUE: Is the *Wade-Gilbert* exclusionary rule applicable to identifications made before the suspect is formally charged?

HOLDING: No.

RATIONALE: "[I]t has been firmly established that a person's Sixth and Fourteenth Amendment right to counsel attaches only at or after the time that adversary judicial proceedings have been initiated against him."

"The *Powell* [*v. Alabama,* 287 U.S. 45 (1932)] case makes clear that the right attaches at the time of arraignment, and the Court has recently held that it exists also at the time of a preliminary hearing. . . . But the point is that, while members of the Court have differed as to existence of the right to counsel in the contexts of some of the above cases, all of those cases have involved points of time at or after the initiation of adversary judicial criminal proceedings—whether by way of formal charge, preliminary hearing, indictment, information, or arraignment."

"The initiation of judicial criminal proceedings is far from a mere formalism. It is the starting point of our whole system of adversary criminal justice. For it is only then that the government has committed itself to prosecute, and only then that the adverse positions of government and defendant have solidified. It is then that a defendant finds himself faced with the prosecutorial forces of organized society, and immersed in the intricacies of substantive and procedural criminal law. It is this point, therefore, that marks the commencement of the 'criminal prosecutions' to which alone the explicit guarantees of the Sixth Amendment are applicable."

"In this case we are asked to import into a routine police investigation an absolute constitutional guarantee historically and rationally applicable only after the onset of formal prosecutorial proceedings. We decline to do so. . . . We decline to depart from that rationale today by imposing a per se exclusionary rule upon testimony concerning an identification that took place long before the commencement of any prosecution whatever."

2. Suggestivity v. Accuracy

Neil v. Biggers, 409 U.S. 188 (1972)
Vote: 5-3
FACTS: Margaret Beamer testified that a youth with a butcher knife grabbed her in the doorway to her kitchen and that she could see his face in the light from the bedroom. When she screamed, her daughter also began to scream and the assailant told the victim to "tell her to shut up, or I'll kill you both." She was then walked at knifepoint along a railroad track, taken into the woods, and raped. She testified that "the moon was shining brightly, full moon." After the rape, the attacker ran off, and Beamer went home, the whole incident having taken between fifteen minutes and half an hour. She then gave the police "only a very general description," describing him as "being fat and flabby with smooth skin, bushy hair and a youthful voice." She also testified at the habeas corpus hearing that she had described her assailant as being between sixteen and eighteen years old and between five feet ten inches and six feet tall, as weighing between 180 and 200 pounds, and as having a dark brown complexion, which was corroborated by an officer testifying from his notes.

On several occasions, Beamer viewed suspects in her home or at the station, some in lineups and others in showups, and was shown between thirty and forty photographs. She told police that a man pictured in one of the photographs had features similar to those of her attacker, but did not identify anyone. The police then called her to the station to view Archie Nathaniel Biggers, who was being detained on another charge. The police checked the jail and juvenile home and, finding no one fitting Biggers's description, they conducted a showup, which consisted of two detectives walking Biggers past the victim. At her request, the police directed him to say "shut up or I'll kill you." The testimony was not clear as to whether Beamer first identified him and then asked that he repeat the words or made her identification after he had spoken. The victim testified that she had "no doubt" about her identification. Biggers was eventually convicted of rape.
ISSUE: Does a suggestive identification have to be excluded if, under the "totality of the circumstances," no substantial likelihood of misidentifying the suspect exists?
HOLDING: No.
RATIONALE: "We have considered on four occasions the scope of due process protection against the admission of evidence deriving from suggestive identification procedures."

"Some general guidelines emerge from these cases as to the relationship between suggestiveness and misidentification. It is, first of all, apparent that the primary evil to be avoided is 'a very substantial likelihood of irreparable misidentification. . . .' Suggestive confrontations are disapproved because they increase the likelihood of misidentification, and unnecessarily suggestive ones are condemned for the further reason that the increased chance of misidentification is gratuitous. But as *Stovall* [*v. Denno*, 388 U.S. 293 (1967)] makes clear, the admission of evidence of a showup without more does not violate due process."

"What is less clear from our cases is whether . . . unnecessary suggestiveness alone requires the exclusion of evidence. . . . The purpose of a strict rule barring evidence of unnecessarily suggestive confrontations would be to deter the police from using a less reliable procedure where a more reliable one may be available, and would not be based on the assumption that in every instance the admission of evidence of such a confrontation offends due process. . . . Such a rule would have no place in the present case, since both the confrontation and the trial preceded *Stovall*, when we first gave notice that the suggestiveness of confrontation procedures was anything other than a matter to be argued to the jury."

"As indicated by our cases, the factors to be considered in evaluating the likelihood of misidentification include the opportunity of the witness to view the criminal at the time of the crime, the witness' degree of attention, the accuracy of the witness' prior description of the criminal, the level of certainty demonstrated by the witness at the confrontation, and the length of time between the crime and the confrontation. Applying these factors, we disagree with the District Court's conclusion."

3. Reliability and Corrupting Influence of Suggestibility

Manson v. Braithwaite, 432 U.S. 98 (1977)
Vote: 7-2
FACTS: Jimmy D. Glover, a Connecticut trooper, and Henry Alton Brown, an informant, went to an apartment for the purpose of purchasing drugs from "Dickie Boy" Cicero. Glover and Brown knocked at the door of one of the two apartments served by the stairway. The area was illuminated by natural light from a window in the third floor hallway and the door was opened twelve to eighteen inches in response to the knock. Glover observed a man and a woman standing at the door and Brown identified himself. Glover then asked for "two things" of narcotics and the man held out his hand, and Glover gave him two $10 bills. The man returned and handed Glover two glassine bags, and while the door was open, Glover observed his face. Only a few minutes elapsed from the time the door first opened until it closed the second time. Glover and Brown then left and drove to headquarters where he described the seller to Hartford police officer Michael D'Onofrio. Glover at that time did not know the identity of the seller but described him as being "a colored man, approximately five feet eleven inches tall, dark complexion, black hair, short Afro style, and having high cheekbones, and of heavy build. He was wearing at the time blue pants and a plaid shirt." D'Onofrio, suspecting that Nowell Braithwaite might be the seller, obtained a photograph and left it at Glover's office. D'Onofrio was not acquainted with Braithwaite but did know him by sight and had seen him "(s)everal times." Glover viewed the photograph and identified the person shown as the one from whom he had purchased the drugs. Glover also made an identification in court.

Braithwaite testified that on the day in question, he had "a lot of back pains, muscle spasms . . . a bad heart . . . high blood pressure . . . neuralgia in my face, and sinus," and that at no time on that day had he been at the disputed address. His wife testified that after her husband had refreshed her memory, she recalled that he was home all day on May 5. Doctor Vietzke, whom Braithwaite had consulted on a different date, heard his complaints and discovered that he had high blood pressure. In fact, he underwent surgery for a herniated disc. The court felt that the photograph should have been excluded, regardless of reliability, because the examination of the single photograph was unnecessary and suggestive and, in the court's view, the evidence was unreliable. Braithwaite was charged with and convicted of both possession and sale of heroin.

ISSUE: Does the Fourteenth Amendment require exclusion of an identification made by an unnecessary and suggestive procedure so long as, under the "totality of the circumstances," the identification is reliable?

HOLDING: No.

RATIONALE: "The respondent . . . proposes a per se rule of exclusion that he claims is dictated by the demands of the Fourteenth Amendment's guarantee of due process."

"Thus, [*United States v. Wade*, 388 U.S. 218 (1967)] and its companion cases reflect the concern that the jury not hear eyewitness testimony unless that evidence has aspects of reliability. It must be observed that both approaches before us are responsive to this concern. The per se rule, however, goes too far since its application automatically and peremptorily, and without consideration of alleviating factors, keeps evidence from the jury that is reliable and relevant."

"The second factor is deterrence. Although the per se approach has the more significant deterrent effect, the totality approach also has an influence on police behavior. The police will guard against unnecessarily suggestive procedures under the totality rule, as well as the per se one, for fear that their actions will lead to the exclusion of identifications as unreliable."

"The third factor is the effect on the administration of justice. Here the per se approach suffers serious drawbacks. Since it denies the trier reliable evidence, it may result, on occasion, in the guilty going free. Also, because of its rigidity, the per se approach may make error by the trial judge more likely than the totality approach. And in those cases in which the admission of identification evidence is error under the per se approach but not under the totality approach cases in which the identification is reliable despite an unnecessarily suggestive identification procedure—reversal is a Draconian sanction. Certainly, inflexible rules of exclusion that may frustrate rather than promote justice have not been viewed recently by this Court with unlimited enthusiasm."

"*Stovall* [*v. Denno*, 388 U.S. 293 (1967)], with its reference to 'the totality of the circumstances . . . and Biggers, with its continuing stress on the same totality . . . did not, singly or together, establish a strict exclusionary rule or new standard of due process."

"We therefore conclude that reliability is the linchpin in determining the admissibility of identification testimony for both pre- and post-*Stovall* confrontations."

C. Multiple Lineups with the Same Suspect and Witness

Foster v. California, 394 U.S. 440 (1969)
Vote: 5-4
FACTS: The day after the robbery of a Western Union office, Clay surrendered and implicated Foster and Grice. Apparently, Foster and Clay entered the office while Grice waited in a car. The only witness to the crime was Joseph David, the manager. After Foster had been arrested, David was called to the police station to view a lineup, and one of the three men was Foster. He is close to six feet in height, while the others were short. Foster wore a leather jacket, which David said was similar to the one he had seen worn by the robber. After the lineup, David could not positively identify Foster but "thought" he was the man. David then asked to speak to Foster, and he was brought into an office and sat across from David. Except for prosecuting officials there was no one else present. David still was uncertain, and a week or so later, the police arranged for David to view a five-person lineup. Foster was the only person in the second lineup who had appeared in the first. This time David was "convinced" Foster was the man. At trial, David testified to his identification of Foster and also repeated his identification in the courtroom. Foster was charged with the robbery of the Western Union office and convicted.
ISSUE: Do identification procedures that cause suspects to stand out against all other participants and allow for one-to-one confrontations violate due process?
HOLDING: Yes.
RATIONALE: "But in declaring the rule of [*United States v. Wade*, 388 U.S. 218 (1967)] and *Gilbert* [*v. California*, 388 U.S. 263 (1967)] to be applicable only to lineups conducted after those cases were decided, we recognized that, judged by the 'totality of the circumstances,' the conduct of identification procedures may be 'so unnecessarily suggestive and conducive to irreparable mistaken identification' as to be a denial of due process of law."

"Judged by that standard, this case presents a compelling example of unfair lineup procedures. . . . This Court pointed out in *Stovall* [*v. Denno*, 388 U.S. 293 (1967)] that '(t)he practice of showing suspects singly to persons for the purpose of identification, and not as part of a lineup, has been widely condemned.'"

"The suggestive elements in this identification procedure made it all but inevitable that David would identify petitioner whether or not he was in fact 'the man.' In effect, the police repeatedly said to the witness, 'This is the man. . . .' This procedure so undermined the reliability of the eyewitness identification as to violate due process."

"In a decision handed down since the Supreme Court of California declined to consider petitioner's case, it reversed a conviction because of the unfair makeup of a lineup. In that case, the California court said: '(W)e do no more than recognize . . . that unfairly constituted lineups have in the past too often brought about the conviction of the innocent. . . .' In the present case the pretrial confrontations clearly were so arranged as to make the resulting identifications virtually inevitable."

D. Photographic Identification

1. Is Photographic Identification Permissible?

Simmons v. United States, 390 U.S. 377 (1968)
Vote: 6-2

FACTS: Two men entered a Chicago bank and one pointed a gun at a teller and ordered her to put money into a sack. After they left, an employee saw one of the men sitting on the passenger side of a car with a large scrape on the right door. Police found the car and discovered that it belonged to Mrs. Rey, sister-in-law of Simmons. She told police that she had loaned the car to her brother, Andrews. FBI agents came to the house of Mrs. Mahon, Andrews's mother, without a warrant, but she allegedly gave them permission to search. They found two suitcases, one of which contained a holster, a sack similar to the one in the robbery, coin cards, and bill wrappers from the bank. The next morning, the FBI obtained from another of Andrews's sisters snapshots of Andrews and Simmons, who was said by the sister to have been with Andrews the previous afternoon. These snapshots were shown to the bank employees who had witnessed the robbery. Each witness identified Simmons as representing one of the robbers. Later, three employees identified photographs of Garrett as depicting the other; the other two witnesses stated that they did not have a clear view of the second robber. The three men were indicted and convicted of robbery. Simmons argued that his pretrial identification by means of the photographs was so unnecessarily suggestive and conducive to misidentification as to deny him due process of law.

ISSUE: Is an identification obtained from photographs so impermissibly suggestive so as to give rise to a very substantial likelihood of irreparable misidentification that violates due process?

HOLDING: No.

RATIONALE: "Despite the hazards of initial identification by photograph, this procedure has been used widely and effectively in criminal law enforcement, from the standpoint both of apprehending offenders and of sparing innocent suspects the ignominy of arrest by allowing eyewitnesses to exonerate them through scrutiny of photographs. The danger that use of the technique may result in convictions based on misidentification may be substantially lessened by a course of cross-examination at trial which exposes to the jury the method's potential for error. We are unwilling to prohibit its employment, either in the exercise of our supervisory power or, still less, as a matter of constitutional requirement. Instead, we hold that each case must be considered on its own facts, and that convictions based on eyewitness identification at trial following a pretrial identification by photograph will be set aside on that ground only if the photographic identification procedure was so impermissibly suggestive as to give rise to a very substantial likelihood of irreparable misidentification."

"[T]he identification of Simmons was correct, even though the identification procedure employed may have in some respects fallen short of the ideal. We hold that in the factual surroundings of this case the identification procedure used was not such as to deny Simmons due process of law or to call for reversal under our supervisory authority."

2. Right to Counsel and Postindictment Photographic Display Identifications

United States v. Ash, 413 U.S. 300 (1973)
Vote: 6-3
FACTS: A man with a stocking mask entered a bank in Washington, D.C., and began waving a pistol. He ordered an employee to hang up the phone and instructed all others not to move. A second man, also wearing a mask, entered, scooped up money, and left. The gunman followed, and both men escaped. Charles McFarland, a government informer, told authorities that he had discussed the robbery with Charles L. Ash Jr.

An FBI agent showed witnesses black-and-white mug shots of five black males of generally the same description, one of which was of Ash. All the witnesses made uncertain identifications of Ash. However, Ash and codefendant John L. Bailey were indicted on five counts related to the robbery.

Three years later at the trial, the prosecutor used a photographic display to determine whether his witnesses would be able to make in-court identifications. Shortly before the trial, an FBI agent and the prosecutor showed five color photographs to the four witnesses, three of them selected the picture of Ash, but one was unable to make any selection. None of the witnesses selected Bailey. At trial, three witnesses who had been inside the bank identified Ash, but they were unwilling to state that they were certain and none of them made an in-court identification of Bailey. The fourth witness, made positive in-court identifications of both Ash and Bailey but Bailey's counsel sought to impeach the identification by calling the FBI agent who had shown the color photographs to the witnesses before the trial. Bailey's counsel demonstrated that the witness who had identified Bailey in court had failed to identify a color photograph of Bailey previously. Bailey's counsel also brought out the fact that this witness had selected another man as a robber. The prosecutor then became concerned that the jury might believe that the witness had selected a third person when, in fact, the witness had selected Ash. After a conference, the judge ruled that all five color photographs would be admitted. The court of appeals held that this constituted the introduction of a postindictment identification at the prosecutor's request and over the objection of defense counsel. Ash was convicted on all counts.
ISSUE: Does an accused have a Sixth Amendment right to have counsel present when the Government conducts a postindictment photographic display for the purpose of obtaining an identification?
HOLDING: No.

RATIONALE: "We conclude that the dangers of mistaken identification, mentioned in [*United States v. Wade*, 388 U.S. 218 (1967)], were removed from context by the Court of Appeals and were incorrectly utilized as a sufficient basis for requiring counsel. Although Wade did discuss possibilities for suggestion and the difficulty for reconstructing suggestivity, this discussion occurred only after the Court had concluded that the lineup constituted a trial-like confrontation, requiring the 'Assistance of Counsel' to preserve the adversary process. . . ."

"[C]ounsel is rather to be provided to prevent the defendant himself from falling into traps devised by a lawyer on the other side and to see to it that all available defenses are proffered."

"Since the accused himself is not present at the time of the photographic display, and asserts no right to be present . . . no possibility arises that the accused might be misled by his lack of familiarity with the law or overpowered by his professional adversary."

"Even if we were willing to view the counsel guarantee in broad terms as a generalized protection of the adversary process, we would be unwilling to go so far as to extend the right to a portion of the prosecutor's trial-preparation interviews with witnesses. Although photography is relatively new, the interviewing of witnesses before trial is a procedure that predates the Sixth Amendment. . . . The traditional counterbalance in the American adversary system for these interviews arises from the equal ability of defense counsel to seek and interview witnesses himself."

"No greater limitations are placed on defense counsel in constructing displays, seeking witnesses, and conducting photographic identifications than those applicable to the prosecution. Selection of the picture of a person other than the accused, or the inability of a witness to make any selection, will be useful to the defense in precisely the same manner that the selection of a picture of the defendant would be useful to the prosecution."

"Pretrial photographic identifications, however, are hardly unique in offering possibilities for the actions of the prosecutor unfairly to prejudice the accused. Evidence favorable to the accused may be withheld; testimony of witnesses may be manipulated; the results of laboratory tests may be contrived. In many ways the prosecutor, by accident or by design, may improperly subvert the trial. The primary safeguard against abuses of this kind is the ethical responsibility of the prosecutor. . . . If that safeguard fails, review remains available under due process standards. . . . These same safeguards apply to misuse of photographs."

"We are not persuaded that the risks inherent in the use of photographic displays are so pernicious that an extraordinary system of safeguards is required."

"We hold, then, that the Sixth Amendment does not grant the right to counsel at photographic displays conducted by the Government for the purpose of allowing a witness to attempt an identification of the offender."

12

Prosecutorial Procedures

MUCH OF THE PRIOR MATERIAL that we have examined has focused on the kinds of activities that the police must undertake and rules that they must adhere to when admitting a particular person to the criminal justice system. However, in this chapter we begin to depart from that area and to focus on another: the courtroom work group. More particularly, the prosecutor, the defense, and ultimate arbiter of their actions, the jury. In this chapter, we will focus on the role of the prosecutor and what he or she must do to ensure that the suspect is properly accused, defended, and adjudicated. The prosecutor serves "the people" in the sense that he is the representative of the jurisdiction that wishes to punish the accused. As such, this individual is, like the police, also bound by certain regulations that ensure that the accused is fairly treated as the state seeks to have a particular punishment or status imposed. As one might expect, prosecutors have a great many tasks to complete and represent their jurisdictions at many different stages of the process.

Naturally, because these individuals do wield a great deal of authority, the Supreme Court has been involved in determining what they can and cannot do, and in so doing, has set some parameters for the scope of their power. Some of these decisions focus on the nature of filing charges against a suspect. For example, the Court has acknowledged that the prosecutor has the right to determine whether or not to file charges against someone and the accused is also formally notified of those charges at an initial appearance. At this point, the prosecution can also make statements with regard to bail (allowing the accused to possibly be released prior to trial) or to keep the person detained in jail. Depending on the jurisdiction, the formal statement of charges for the court will come in the form of an information, which is written up by the prosecutor after a preliminary hearing, or an indictment, which is handed down by a grand jury. The Court has also stated that the grand jury is a secret proceeding and that it has powers that a normal trial jury does not have. The preliminary hearing is also unique in that it is what some people have referred to as a "mini trial" because the accused has some of the same rights available at that proceeding that he or she would have at a full-blown trial.

The Supreme Court has also weighed in on other pretrial procedures influenced by the prosecutor: plea bargaining, according to the Court, is a valued institution. However, it has also said that the prosecution should play fair and hold to its agreements if they are adhered to by the accused. Following this general theme of fairness, the Court has also held that the prosecution must turn over its case-related material to the defense so that it can fairly contest the charges that the state has brought. Finally, while it is sometimes brought up by the judge or the defense, the issue of the accused's competency to stand trial sometimes comes up, and with that, the prosecution must deal with the competency hearing.

A. Decision to Charge

Wayte v. United States, 470 U.S. 598 (1985)

Vote: 7-2

FACTS: The president issued a proclamation directing certain males to register with the military during the week of July 21, 1980. Wayte did not register but did write letters to officials stating that he did not intend to register, and his correspondence was placed in a file that included letters similar to his. The Selective Service had a policy of prosecuting only those in this particular file. Wayte did not respond to a letter sent to him detailing his obligation to register and stating that violation could result in criminal prosecution. The Selective Service referred Wayte and others to the Department of Justice, which then referred his case and the others to the FBI and U.S. Attorneys. The U.S. Attorney for the Central District of California sent Wayte another letter urging him to register, and again he failed to respond. A grace period of over a year was instituted for nonregistrants, and Wayte still failed to comply. Shortly thereafter, the Department of Justice began to seek indictments, and after an FBI interview, Wayte again refused to register and was indicted.

ISSUE: Does the decision to prosecute rest with the authority of the prosecutor?

HOLDING: Yes.

RATIONALE: "In our criminal justice system, the Government retains 'broad discretion' as to whom to prosecute. . . . '[S]o long as the prosecutor has probable cause to believe that the accused committed an offense defined by statute, the decision whether or not to prosecute, and what charge to file or bring before a grand jury, generally rests entirely in his discretion. . . .' This broad discretion rests largely on the recognition that the decision to prosecute is particularly ill-suited to judicial review. Such factors as the strength of the case, the prosecution's general deterrence value, the Government's enforcement priorities, and the case's relationship to the Government's overall enforcement plan are not readily susceptible to the kind of analysis the courts are competent to undertake. Judicial supervision in this area, moreover, entails systemic costs of particular concern. Examining the basis of a prosecution delays the criminal proceeding, threatens to chill law enforcement by subjecting the prosecutor's motives and decisionmaking to outside inquiry, and may undermine prosecutorial effectiveness by revealing the Government's enforcement policy. All these are substantial concerns that make the courts properly hesitant to examine the decision whether to prosecute."

"[A]lthough prosecutorial discretion is broad, it is not '"unfettered." Selectivity in the enforcement of criminal laws is . . . subject to constitutional constraints. . . .' In particular, the decision to prosecute may not be 'deliberately based upon an unjustifiable standard such as race, religion, or other arbitrary classification . . .' including the exercise of protected statutory and constitutional protections."

B. Pretrial Detention

United States v. Salerno, 481 U.S. 739 (1987)
Vote: 6-3
FACTS: Congress passed the Bail Reform Act of 1984 to address "the alarming problem of crimes committed by persons on release." The Act requires a judicial officer to determine whether an arrestee shall be detained by providing that if the judicial officer finds that nothing will reasonably assure the appearance of the person and the safety of others by clear and convincing evidence, he shall order the detention of the person prior to trial in writing. The Act provides for several procedural safeguards. The judicial officer is not given complete discretion but may consider relevant factors such as seriousness of the charges, prior record, and so on.

Anthony Salerno and Vincent Cafaro were arrested after being charged in a twenty-nine-count indictment alleging Racketeer Influenced and Corrupt Organizations Act (RICO) violations, mail and wire fraud offenses, extortion, and various gambling violations. The RICO counts alleged thirty-five acts of racketeering, including fraud, extortion, gambling, and conspiracy to commit murder. At their arraignment, the Government moved to have them detained pursuant to the Bail Reform Act on the ground that no condition of release would assure the safety of the community or any person. The Government showed that Salerno was the "boss" and that Cafaro was a "captain" in the Genovese family. According to the Government, they participated in violent conspiracies.

ISSUE: Does the provision of the Bail Reform Act of 1984 that allows for the pretrial detention of an accused on the ground of dangerousness violate the excessive bail clause of the Eighth Amendment or Due Process?
HOLDING: No.
RATIONALE: "We hold that, as against the facial attack mounted by these respondents, the Act fully comports with constitutional requirements."

"[W]e have found that sufficiently compelling governmental interests can justify detention of dangerous persons. Thus, we have found no absolute constitutional barrier to detention of potentially dangerous resident aliens pending deportation proceedings. We have also held that the government may detain mentally unstable individuals who present a danger to the public . . . and dangerous defendants who become incompetent to stand trial. . . . We have approved of postarrest regulatory detention of juveniles when they present a continuing danger to the community. . . . Even competent adults may face substantial liberty restrictions as a result of the operation of our criminal justice system. If the police suspect an individual of a crime, they may arrest and hold him until a neutral magistrate determines whether probable cause exists. . . . Finally, respondents concede . . . that an arrestee may be incarcerated until trial if he presents a risk of flight . . . or a danger to witnesses."

"[W]e think that these cases show a sufficient number of exceptions to the rule that the congressional action challenged here can hardly be characterized as totally novel."

"The government's interest in preventing crime by arrestees is both legitimate and compelling. . . . The Bail Reform Act . . . operates only on individuals who have been arrested for a specific category of extremely serious offenses. . . . Congress specifically found that these individuals are far more likely to be responsible for dangerous acts in the community after arrest. . . . While the Government's general interest in preventing crime is compelling, even this interest is heightened when the Government musters convincing proof that the arrestee, already indicted or held to answer for a serious crime, presents a demonstrable danger to the community. Under these narrow circumstances, society's interest in crime prevention is at its greatest."

"On the other side of the scale, of course, is the individual's strong interest in liberty. We do not minimize the importance and fundamental nature of this right. But, as our cases hold, this right may, in circumstances where the government's interest is sufficiently weighty, be subordinated to the greater needs of society. We think that Congress' careful delineation of the circumstances under which detention will be permitted satisfies this standard."

"The Act authorizes the detention prior to trial of arrestees charged with serious felonies who are found after an adversary hearing to pose a threat to the safety of individuals or to the community which no condition of release can dispel. The numerous procedural safeguards detailed above must attend this adversary hearing. We are unwilling to say that this . . . concern . . . on its face violates either the Due Process Clause of the Fifth Amendment or the Excessive Bail Clause of the Eighth Amendment."

C. Grand Jury

1. Uniqueness

United States v. Williams, 504 U.S. 36 (1992)
Vote: 5-4
FACTS: John H. Williams Jr., an investor, was indicted by a federal grand jury for "knowingly mak[ing] [a] false statement or report . . . for the purpose of influencing . . . the action [of a federally insured financial institution]." According to the indictment, Williams gave several banks statements that overstated the value of his assets and interest income in order to influence the banks' actions on his loan requests. The misrepresentation was effected through two statements one of which included "current assets" of $6 million from three companies. The Government asserted that listing them as assets that could be reduced to cash was misleading, since Williams knew that none of the companies could afford to satisfy the notes. The second document allegedly misrepresented Williams's interest income, since it failed to reflect that the interest payments received were funded entirely by his own loans to those companies. The statement falsely implied that Williams was deriving interest income from an independent source. After his arraignment, the district court granted the motion for disclosure of all exculpatory portions of the grand jury transcripts. Upon review, Williams argued for the dismissal of the indictment, alleging that the Government had failed to present substantial exculpatory evidence to the grand jury.

ISSUE: Do courts have the supervisory authority over grand juries to demand the dismissal of indictments if prosecutors do not present exculpatory evidence?

HOLDING: No.

RATIONALE: "Respondent . . . argues that imposition of the Tenth Circuit's disclosure rule is supported by the courts' 'supervisory power.' We think not. [*United States v. Hasting*, 461 U.S. 499 (1983)], and the cases that rely upon the principle it expresses, deal strictly with the courts' power to control their *own* procedures."

"Because the grand jury is an institution separate from the courts, over whose functioning the courts do not preside, we think it clear that, as a general matter at least, no such 'supervisory' judicial authority exists."

"[T]he grand jury is mentioned in the Bill of Rights, but not in the body of the Constitution. It has not been textually assigned, therefore, to any of the branches described in the first three Articles. It 'is a constitutional fixture in its own right. . . .' Although the grand jury normally operates, of course, in the courthouse and under judicial auspices, its institutional relationship with the Judicial Branch has traditionally been, so to speak, at arm's length. Judges' direct involvement in the functioning of the grand jury has generally been confined to the constitutive one of calling the grand jurors together and administering their oaths of office."

"These authorities suggest that any power federal courts may have to fashion, on their own initiative, rules of grand jury procedure is a very limited one, not remotely comparable to the power they maintain over their own proceedings."

"[R]equiring the prosecutor to present exculpatory as well as inculpatory evidence would alter the grand jury's historical role, transforming it from an accusatory to an adjudicatory body."

"It is axiomatic that the grand jury sits not to determine guilt or innocence, but to assess whether there is adequate basis for bringing a criminal charge. . . . That has always been so; and to make the assessment it has always been thought sufficient to hear only the prosecutor's side. . . . Neither in this country nor in England has the suspect under investigation by the grand jury ever been thought to have a right to testify or to have exculpatory evidence presented."

"Imposing upon the prosecutor a legal obligation to present exculpatory evidence in his possession would be incompatible with this system."

2. Indictment

Hamling v. United States, 418 U.S. 87 (1974)

Vote: 5-4

FACTS: A grand jury in the United States District Court for the Southern District of California indicted several people, including William L. Hamling, on twenty-one counts of use of the mails to carry an obscene book, *The Illustrated Presidential Report of the Commission on Obscenity and Pornography,* and an obscene advertisement brochure. The mailing of the brochures was accomplished by using other businesses. Approximately 55,000–58,000 of the brochures were mailed and those that responded

would be sent the *Illustrated Report.* The evidence indicated that the individual petitioners were officers in the businesses and that they were involved with selling the *Illustrated Report.* Prior to trial, petitioners moved to dismiss the indictment on the
grounds that it failed to inform them of the charges, that the grand jury had insufficient evidence to indict, and that it was improperly instructed on the law. The Court
denied the motions and petitioners were convicted on twelve counts of mailing and
conspiring to mail the obscene advertisement. The jury was unable to reach a verdict
on the counts that charged the mailing of the allegedly obscene report.

ISSUE: Is an indictment sufficient if it only contains the elements of the offense and allows the accused to enter a plea?

HOLDING: Yes.

RATIONALE: "Petitioners attack the sufficiency of the indictment under which they
were charged for two reasons: first, that it charged them only in the statutory language
. . . which they contend was unconstitutionally vague as applied to them; and, second,
that the indictment failed to give them adequate notice of the charges against them."

"Our prior cases indicate that an indictment is sufficient if it, first, contains the elements of the offense charged and fairly informs a defendant of the charge against which
he must defend, and, second, enables him to plead an acquittal or conviction in bar of
future prosecutions for the same offense. . . . It is generally sufficient that an indictment set forth the offense in the words of the statute itself, as long as 'those words of
themselves fully, directly, and expressly, without any uncertainty or ambiguity, set forth
all the elements necessary to constitute the offence intended to be punished. . . .' 'Undoubtedly the language of the statute may be used in the general description of an offence, but it must be accompanied with such a statement of the facts and circumstances
as will inform the accused of the specific offence, coming under the general description, with which he is charged.'"

3. Selection Bias

Rose v. Mitchell, 443 U.S. 545 (1979)
Vote: 7-2

FACTS: James E. Mitchell, James Nichols Jr., and two other men were jointly indicted
in Tipton County, Tennessee, with two counts of first-degree murder in connection
with the shootings of patrons during the robbery of White's Cafe. Prior to trial, respondents moved to dismiss the indictment on the grounds that the grand jury and the
foreman had been selected in a racially discriminatory fashion. At a hearing, testimony
was taken from the three county jury commissioners, from two former Tipton County
grand jury foremen, from the foreman of the grand jury serving at the time respondents were indicted, and from eleven of the twelve other members of their grand jury.
Some of those deposed at the hearing testified that they did not think that a black had
ever served as a foreman of a grand jury. The court denied the motion and a jury convicted the defendants on both counts. The objection to the compilation of the grand
jury was raised again in a petition for habeas corpus.

ISSUE: Is racial discrimination in the selection of the members of a grand jury a valid ground for overturning a conviction?

HOLDING: Yes.

RATIONALE: "For nearly a century, this Court in an unbroken line of cases has held that 'a criminal conviction of a Negro cannot stand under the Equal Protection Clause of the Fourteenth Amendment if it is based on an indictment of a grand jury from which Negroes were excluded by reason of their race.' A criminal defendant 'is entitled to require that the State not deliberately and systematically deny to members of his race the right to participate as jurors in the administration of justice. . . .' Accordingly, where sufficient proof of discrimination in violation of the Fourteenth Amendment has been made out and not rebutted, this Court uniformly has required that the conviction be set aside and the indictment returned by the unconstitutionally constituted grand jury be quashed."

"We decline now to depart from this longstanding consistent practice, and we adhere to the Court's previous decisions."

"Discrimination on account of race was the primary evil at which the Amendments adopted after the War Between the States, including the Fourteenth Amendment, were aimed. It is clear from the earliest cases applying the Equal Protection Clause in the context of racial discrimination in the selection of a grand jury, that the Court from the first was concerned with the broad aspects of racial discrimination that the Equal Protection Clause was designed to eradicate, and with the fundamental social values the Fourteenth Amendment was adopted to protect, even though it addressed the issue in the context of reviewing an individual criminal conviction."

"Discrimination on the basis of race, odious in all aspects, is especially pernicious in the administration of justice. Selection of members of a grand jury because they are of one race and not another destroys the appearance of justice and thereby casts doubt on the integrity of the judicial process. The exclusion from grand jury service of Negroes, or any group otherwise qualified to serve, impairs the confidence of the public in the administration of justice. As this Court repeatedly has emphasized, such discrimination 'not only violates our Constitution and the laws enacted under it but is at war with our basic concepts of a democratic society and a representative government. . . .' The harm is not only to the accused, indicted as he is by a jury from which a segment of the community has been excluded. It is to society as a whole."

"Because discrimination on the basis of race in the selection of members of a grand jury thus strikes at the fundamental values of our judicial system and our society as a whole, the Court has recognized that a criminal defendant's right to equal protection of the laws has been denied when he is indicted by a grand jury from which members of a racial group purposefully have been excluded. . . . For this same reason, the Court also has reversed the conviction and ordered the indictment quashed in such cases without inquiry into whether the defendant was prejudiced in fact by the discrimination at the grand jury stage."

"[W]e adhere to our position that discrimination in the selection of the grand jury remains a valid ground for setting aside a criminal conviction."

4. Authority

United States v. Calandra, 414 U.S. 338 (1974)
Vote: 6-3
FACTS: Federal agents obtained a search warrant for John Calandra's business in Cleveland in connection with a gambling operation. The warrant specified the seizure of bookmaking records and a master affidavit contained information from FBI informants, surveillance conducted by FBI agents, and electronic surveillance ordered by a court. Federal agents executing the warrant found a card referring to Dr. Walter Loveland, who was known to have been the victim in a "loansharking" investigation. The agent had the card seized along with the other items. The grand jury subpoenaed Calandra in order to ask him questions about the evidence that was seized, but he refused to testify by invoking his Fifth Amendment protection against self-incrimination. He later tried to have the evidence suppressed on the grounds that the warrant was insufficient and that the search exceeded its scope.
ISSUE: Can a grand jury compel testimony from a witness who claims that evidence was obtained against him from an illegal search and seizure?
HOLDING: Yes.
RATIONALE: "Traditionally the grand jury has been accorded wide latitude to inquire into violations of criminal law. No judge presides to monitor its proceedings. It deliberates in secret and may determine alone the course of its inquiry. The grand jury may compel the production of evidence or the testimony of witnesses as it considers appropriate, and its operation generally is unrestrained by the technical procedural and evidentiary rules governing the conduct of criminal trials."

"A grand jury proceeding is not an adversary hearing in which the guilt or innocence of the accused is adjudicated. Rather, it is an ex parte investigation to determine whether a crime has been committed and whether criminal proceedings should be instituted against any person. The grand jury's investigative power must be broad if its public responsibility is adequately to be discharged."

"Yet the duty to testify has been regarded as 'so necessary to the administration of justice' that the witness' personal interest in privacy must yield to the public's overriding interest in full disclosure. . . . Furthermore, a witness may not interfere with the course of the grand jury's inquiry. He 'is not entitled to urge objections of incompetency or irrelevancy, such as a party might raise, for this is no concern of his. . . .' Nor is he entitled 'to challenge the authority of the court or of the grand jury' or 'to set limits to the investigation that the grand jury may conduct.'"

D. Preliminary Hearing

1. Prompt Appearance before a Judge after Arrest to Determine Probable Cause

Gerstein v. Pugh, 420 U.S. 103 (1975)

Vote: 9-0

FACTS: Pugh was arrested and an information charging him with robbery, carrying a concealed weapon, and possession of a firearm during a felony was filed. Henderson was arrested and charged with breaking and entering and assault and battery. At the time Pugh and Henderson were arrested, a Florida rule authorized preliminary hearings to test probable cause for detention. But the courts held that the filling of an information removed a suspect's right to a preliminary hearing and the only methods for obtaining a determination of probable cause were a special statute allowing a hearing after thirty days and arraignment. As a result, a person charged by information could be detained for a substantial period solely on the decision of a prosecutor. Pugh and Henderson filed a class action against Dade County claiming a constitutional right to a judicial hearing on the issue of probable cause.

ISSUE: Does a suspect have a constitutional right to a judicial determination of probable cause for pretrial detention?

HOLDING: Yes.

RATIONALE: "Once the suspect is in custody, however, the reasons that justify dispensing with the magistrate's neutral judgment evaporate. There no longer is any danger that the suspect will escape or commit further crimes while the police submit their evidence to a magistrate. And, while the State's reasons for taking summary action subside, the suspect's need for a neutral determination of probable cause increases significantly. The consequences of prolonged detention may be more serious than the interference occasioned by arrest. Pretrial confinement may imperil the suspect's job, interrupt his source of income, and impair his family relationships. . . . When the stakes are this high, the detached judgment of a neutral magistrate is essential if the Fourth Amendment is to furnish meaningful protection from unfounded interference with liberty. Accordingly, we hold that the Fourth Amendment requires a judicial determination of probable cause as a prerequisite to extended restraint of liberty following arrest."

"This result has historical support in the common law that has guided interpretation of the Fourth Amendment. . . . At common law it was customary, if not obligatory, for an arrested person to be brought before a justice of the peace shortly after arrest. . . . The justice of the peace would 'examine' the prisoner and the witnesses to determine whether there was reason to believe the prisoner had committed a crime. If there was, the suspect would be committed to jail or bailed pending trial. If not, he would be discharged from custody."

"Although a conscientious decision that the evidence warrants prosecution affords a measure of protection against unfounded detention, we do not think prosecutorial judgment standing alone meets the requirements of the Fourth Amendment. More recently . . . the Court held that a prosecutor's responsibility to law enforcement is inconsistent with the constitutional role of a neutral and detached magistrate. We reaffirmed that principle in [*Shadwick v. City of Tampa*, 407 U.S. 345 (1972)], and held that probable cause for the issuance of an arrest warrant must be determined by someone independent of police and prosecution."

"Whatever procedure a State may adopt, it must provide a fair and reliable determination of probable cause as a condition for any significant pretrial restraint of liberty, and this determination must be made by a judicial officer either before or promptly after arrest."

2. Right to Counsel

Coleman v. Alabama, 399 U.S. 1 (1970)
Vote: 5-3
FACTS: Casey Reynolds testified at trial that he was changing a tire when three men approached him from across the road. One of them shot him and then the three ran up to him as he was holding on to his wife. Reynolds testified that John Henry Coleman put his hand on Mrs. Reynolds's shoulder. As the men fled across the street from an oncoming car, Reynolds was shot again and Otis Stephens was the shooter, stating that he saw him "in the car lights" while "looking straight at him." Reynolds also stated that he saw Coleman "face to face" and "got a real good look at him." Additionally, the suspects were not provided with counsel at their preliminary hearing. However, Detective Fordham testified at the suppression hearing that he had spoken to Reynolds at the hospital after the assault and about two weeks later, and that on neither occasion was Reynolds able to provide much about the men above a vague description. However, Detective Fordham also testified that at the time Reynolds gave the description he was in pain. Fordham also stated that Reynolds did not identify any of his attackers from pictures, although it is not clear if he was shown any of the suspects. Detective Hart testified that a lineup was held and that Reynolds identified Stephens. Reynolds stated that he identified Coleman at the lineup before Coleman could respond to a request that he speak certain words used by the attackers. Petitioners were convicted of assault with intent to murder.
ISSUE: Is the preliminary hearing a "critical stage" of the prosecution that requires a lawyer?
HOLDING: Yes.
RATIONALE: "It does not follow that the Alabama preliminary hearing is not a 'critical stage' of the State's criminal process. The determination whether the hearing is a 'critical stage' requiring the provision of counsel depends, as noted, upon an analysis 'whether potential substantial prejudice to defendant's rights inheres in the . . . confrontation and the ability of counsel to help avoid that prejudice. . . .' Plainly the guiding hand of counsel at the preliminary hearing is essential to protect the indigent accused against an erroneous or improper prosecution. First, the lawyer's skilled

examination and cross-examination of witnesses may expose fatal weaknesses in the State's case that may lead the magistrate to refuse to bind the accused over. Second, in any event, the skilled interrogation of witnesses by an experienced lawyer can fashion a vital impeachment tool for use in cross-examination of the State's witnesses at the trial, or preserve testimony favorable to the accused of a witness who does not appear at the trial. Third, trained counsel can more effectively discover the case the State has against his client and make possible the preparation of a proper defense to meet that case at the trial. Fourth, counsel can also be influential at the preliminary hearing in making effective arguments for the accused on such matters as the necessity for an early psychiatric examination or bail."

"The inability of the indigent accused on his own to realize these advantages of a lawyer's assistance compels the conclusion that the Alabama preliminary hearing is a 'critical stage' of the State's criminal process at which the accused is 'as much entitled to such aid (of counsel) . . . as at the trial itself.'"

E. Plea Bargaining

1. Importance

Santobello v. New York, 404 U.S. 257 (1971)
Vote: 4-3
FACTS: Santobello was indicted on two gambling-related charges and during negotiations agreed to plead guilty to a lesser charge without making a recommendation as to the sentence. However, several delays took place, and Santobello's new attorney recommended that he withdraw his plea stating that damaging evidence against him had been obtained via an illegal search. In addition to withdrawing his guilty plea, he also renewed his motion to suppress the evidence discovered by the search. At the sentencing, all of Santobello's motions were denied, and he found out that the original judge had retired. He renewed the motions before the new judge, which were rejected. Further, a new prosecutor had taken the case and recommended the maximum sentence after citing Santobello's criminal history. Santobello's lawyer objected, saying that the original prosecutor promised no recommendation. But the new prosecutor argued that he had no information about not making a recommendation in his files. The judge then ended the debate and sentenced Santobello to the maximum one-year sentence.
ISSUE: Is plea bargaining an important part of the criminal justice process?
HOLDING: Yes.
RATIONALE: "The disposition of criminal charges by agreement between the prosecutor and the accused, sometimes loosely called 'plea bargaining,' is an essential component of the administration of justice. Properly administered, it is to be encouraged. If every criminal charge were subjected to a full-scale trial, the States and the Federal Government would need to multiply by many times the number of judges and court facilities."

"Disposition of charges after plea discussions is not only an essential part of the process but a highly desirable part for many reasons. It leads to prompt and largely final disposition of most criminal cases; it avoids much of the corrosive impact of enforced idleness during pretrial confinement for those who are denied release pending trial; it protects the public from those accused persons who are prone to continue criminal conduct even while on pretrial release; and, by shortening the time between charge and disposition, it enhances whatever may be the rehabilitative prospects of the guilty when they are ultimately imprisoned."

2. Prosecutorial Charging Practices

Bordenkircher v. Hayes, 434 U.S. 357 (1978)
Vote: 5-4
FACTS: Paul Lewis Hayes, was indicted by a grand jury for uttering a forged instrument. After his arraignment, Hayes, his lawyer, and the prosecutor met to discuss a possible plea bargain. The prosecutor offered to recommend a sentence of five years if Hayes would plead guilty. He also said that if Hayes did not plead guilty and 'save[d] the court the inconvenience and necessity of a trial,' he would seek an indictment under the Kentucky Habitual Criminal Act, which would subject Hayes to a life sentence. While the prosecutor did not actually obtain the recidivist indictment until after the plea negotiations had ended, his intention to do so was expressed at the outset, and Hayes was thus fully informed of the terms of the offer when he chose not to plead guilty. The prosecutor subsequently obtained an indictment charging him under the Act. Hayes never contested that the habitual crime charge was justified, that the prosecutor had evidence to support the charge, and that Hayes's refusal to plead guilty to the original charge was what led to his indictment under the habitual criminal statute. Hayes was found guilty on the charge of uttering a forged instrument and further found that he had twice before been convicted of felonies. As required by the Act, he was sentenced to life. The appellate court found that the prosecutor's decision to indict Hayes as a habitual offender was a legitimate use of authority in the plea-bargaining process.
ISSUE: Does the threat to reindict an accused on more serious charges if he does not plead guilty violate the Due Process Clause of the Fourteenth Amendment?
HOLDING: No.
RATIONALE: "[T]he Court of Appeals in the present case . . . held that the substance of the plea offer itself violated the limitations imposed by the Due Process Clause of the Fourteenth Amendment. . . . [W]e have concluded that the Court of Appeals was mistaken in so ruling."

"[I]n the 'give-and-take' of plea bargaining, there is no such element of punishment or retaliation so long as the accused is free to accept or reject the prosecution's offer."

"While confronting a defendant with the risk of more severe punishment clearly may have a 'discouraging effect on the defendant's assertion of his trial rights . . .' by tolerating and encouraging the negotiation of pleas, this Court has necessarily accepted as constitutionally legitimate the simple reality that the prosecutor's interest at the bargaining table is to persuade the defendant to forgo his right to plead not guilty."

"In our system, so long as the prosecutor has probable cause to believe that the accused committed an offense defined by statute, the decision whether or not to prosecute, and what charge to file or bring before a grand jury, generally rests entirely in his discretion. . . . To hold that the prosecutor's desire to induce a guilty plea is an 'unjustifiable standard,' which, like race or religion, may play no part in his charging decision, would contradict the very premises that underlie the concept of plea bargaining itself. Moreover, a rigid constitutional rule that would prohibit a prosecutor from acting forthrightly in his dealings with the defense could only invite unhealthy subterfuge that would drive the practice of plea bargaining back into the shadows from which it has so recently emerged."

"We hold only that the course of conduct engaged in by the prosecutor in this case, which no more than openly presented the defendant with the unpleasant alternatives of forgoing trial or facing charges on which he was plainly subject to prosecution, did not violate the Due Process Clause of the Fourteenth Amendment."

3. Accusations of Prosecutorial Breach of the Plea Agreement

Blackledge v. Allison, 431 U.S. 63 (1977)
Vote: 8-0
FACTS: Gary Darrell Allison was indicted by a grand jury in North Carolina for breaking and entering, attempted safe robbery, and possession of burglary tools. At his arraignment, he initially pleaded not guilty, but after learning that his codefendant planned to plead guilty, he entered a guilty plea to one charge of attempted safe robbery. Allison answered several questions by the judge concerning the plea, its consequences, and whether or not it was voluntary. Allison stated that he knew the sentence possibilities, that he understood that his sentence could be up to ten years imprisonment, and that no one had threatened him concerning the plea. He also stated where and by whom the promise concerning the sentence was made. The judge then accepted the plea, but three days later, he was sentenced to 17–21 years in prison. Allison subsequently filed a writ of habeas corpus challenging the sentence, which was denied.
ISSUE: If a prisoner can show clear facts that a plea agreement was violated by the state, is he entitled to a hearing to present those facts?
HOLDING: Yes.
RATIONALE: "[T]he barrier of the plea or sentencing proceeding record, although imposing, is not invariably insurmountable. In administering the writ of habeas corpus and its counterpart, the federal courts cannot fairly adopt a per se rule excluding all possibility that a defendant's representations at the time his guilty plea was accepted were so much the product of such factors as misunderstanding, duress, or misrepresentation by others. . . ."

"The allegations in this case were not in themselves so 'vague (or) conclusory . . .' as to warrant dismissal for that reason alone. . . ." The critical question is whether these allegations, when viewed against the record of the plea hearing, were so 'palpably incredible,' so 'patently frivolous or false . . .' as to warrant summary dismissal. In the light of the nature of the record . . . we conclude that Allison's petition should not have been summarily dismissed."

"Although '(l)ogically the general inquiry should elicit information about plea bargaining, . . . it seldom has in the past. . . .' Particularly if, as Allison alleged, he was advised by counsel to conceal any plea bargain, his denial that any promises had been made might have been a courtroom ritual more sham than real. We thus cannot conclude that the allegations in Allison's habeas corpus petition, when measured against the 'record' of the arraignment, were so 'patently false or frivolous' as to warrant summary dismissal."

"In short, it may turn out upon remand that a full evidentiary hearing is not required. But Allison is 'entitled to careful consideration and plenary processing of [his claim], including full opportunity for presentation of the relevant facts.'"

4. Voluntariness of the Plea

Boykin v. Alabama, 395 U.S. 238 (1969)
Vote: 7-2
FACTS: Within a two-week period, a series of robberies occurred in Mobile, Alabama. The victims were shopkeepers who were forced to hand over money. While robbing one store, the assailant fired his gun, sending a bullet into the ceiling. A few days earlier, the robber had allowed his gun to discharge, which struck a customer in the leg. A grand jury indicted Boykin for robbery—an offense punishable by death. Shortly after a lawyer was appointed, Boykin pleaded guilty to all charges. The judge did not ask Boykin about the pleas nor did he have the opportunity to address the court. Boykin's lawyer engaged in a brief cross-examination at a sentencing hearing, and again Boykin never addressed the court, nor did he testify. The judge instructed the jury and stressed that Boykin had pleaded guilty to all five charges of robbery, defined as "the felonious taking of money . . . from another against his will . . . by violence or by putting him in fear . . . (carrying) from ten years minimum in the penitentiary to the supreme penalty of death by electrocution." The jury, upon deliberation, found petitioner guilty and sentenced him to death on each of the five charges.
ISSUE: Does a trial record that does not disclose that a defendant made a voluntary plea violate due process?
HOLDING: Yes.
RATIONALE: "Admissibility of a confession must be based on a 'reliable determination on the voluntariness issue which satisfies the constitutional rights of the defendant.'"

"We think that the same standard must be applied to determining whether a guilty plea is voluntarily made. For, as we have said, a plea of guilty is more than an admission of conduct; it is a conviction. Ignorance, incomprehension, coercion, terror, inducements, subtle or blatant threats might be a perfect cover-up of unconstitutionality."

"'Consequently, if a defendant's guilty plea is not equally voluntary and knowing, it has been obtained in violation of due process and is therefore void. Moreover, because a guilty plea is an admission of all the elements of a formal criminal charge, it cannot be truly voluntary unless the defendant possesses an understanding of the law in relation to the facts.'"

"The three dissenting justices in the Alabama Supreme Court stated the law accurately when they concluded that there was reversible error 'because the record does not disclose that the defendant voluntarily and understandingly entered his pleas of guilty.'"

5. Validity of the Plea and the Death Penalty

Brady v. United States, 397 U.S. 742 (1970)
Vote: 9-0
FACTS: Robert M. Brady was charged with kidnapping, and since the victim was harmed, he faced a maximum penalty of death. Brady decided to plead not guilty initially because the judge was unwilling to try the case without a jury, also Brady made no real attempt to reduce the possibility of a death penalty by waiving a jury trial. His lawyer informed him of the possibility that he could receive a death sentence. However, upon learning that his codefendant, who had confessed, would plead guilty and testify against him, Brady pleaded guilty. After the judge examined him as to voluntariness of his decision, the new plea was accepted. Brady was subsequently sentenced to fifty years, which was later reduced to thirty. Brady argued that his plea was involuntary because the death penalty statute coerced his plea, because his lawyer pressured him, and because his plea was induced by promises of a reduced sentence and clemency. However, all of the appellate courts involved held that his plea was voluntarily made.
ISSUE: Is a guilty plea to a charge to avoid the death penalty involuntary?
HOLDING: No.
RATIONALE: "The trial judge in 1959 found the plea voluntary before accepting it; the District Court in 1968, after an evidentiary hearing, found that the plea was voluntarily made; the Court of Appeals specifically approved the finding of voluntariness. We see no reason on this record to disturb the judgment of those courts. Petitioner, advised by competent counsel, tendered his plea after his codefendant, who had already given a confession, determined to plead guilty and became available to testify against petitioner. It was this development that the District Court found to have triggered Brady's guilty plea."

"The voluntariness of Brady's plea can be determined only by considering all of the relevant circumstances surrounding it. . . . But even if we assume that Brady would not have pleaded guilty except for the death penalty provision of § 1201(a), this assumption merely identifies the penalty provision as a 'but for' cause of his plea. That the statute caused the plea in this sense does not necessarily prove that the plea was coerced and invalid as an involuntary act."

"[W]e are convinced that his plea was voluntarily and intelligently made and we have no reason to doubt that his solemn admission of guilt was truthful."

F. Discovery

1. Is There a Constitutional Right to Discovery of an Undercover Agent?

Weatherford v. Bursey, 429 U.S. 545 (1977)
Vote: 7-2

FACTS: Bursey, Weatherford, and two others, vandalized a Selective Service office in Columbia, South Carolina. The police were notified by Weatherford, who was working undercover and was released on bond and continuing his ruse. Prior to trial, Weatherford met with Bursey and his counsel, Wise, and discussed the defense. At no time did Weatherford seek information or ask for a meeting. He was asked to participate in an effort to help Bursey. During the meetings, Bursey and Wise suspected that an informer might be involved but never asked Weatherford if he was one. At no time did Weatherford provide the State with information about Bursey's defense. Until the day of the trial, Weatherford had not expected to be a witness because he had been seen in the company of police, but he was called for the State. He testified as to his undercover work and gave an eyewitness account of how the building was vandalized. Bursey was convicted but disappeared and did not begin serving his sentence until he was arrested eighteen months later. Bursey then alleged in a 1983 suit that Weatherford had passed defense information to the State depriving him of his Sixth and Fourteenth Amendment rights to the assistance of counsel and to a fair trial.

ISSUE: Does the presence of an undercover agent at a defense conference, who was invited by the accused's attorney, and who provides no information to the State about the conference, violate the Sixth Amendment right to assistance of counsel?

HOLDING: No.

RATIONALE: "[A]s the Court of Appeals applied the rule in this case, it would appear that if an undercover agent meets with a criminal defendant who is awaiting trial and with his attorney and if the forthcoming trial is discussed without the agent's revealing his identity, a violation of the defendant's constitutional rights has occurred, whatever was the purpose of the agent in attending the meeting, whether or not he reported on the meeting to his superiors, and whether or not any specific prejudice to the defendant's preparation for or conduct of the trial is demonstrated or otherwise threatened."

"We cannot agree that these cases, individually or together, either require or suggest the rule announced by the Court of Appeals and now urged by Bursey."

"If anything is to be inferred from these two cases with respect to the right to counsel, it is that when conversations with counsel have been overheard, the constitutionality of the conviction depends on whether the overheard conversations have produced, directly or indirectly, any of the evidence offered at trial. This is a far cry from the per se rule announced by the Court of Appeals below. . . . [T]here is nothing in their findings or in the record to indicate any 'use of evidence that might be otherwise inadmissible.'"

"[T]he Court did not hold that the Sixth Amendment right to counsel subsumes a right to be free from intrusion by informers into counsel-client consultations. Nor did it purport to describe the contours of any such right."

"Nor do we believe that federal or state prosecutors will be so prone to lie or the difficulties of proof will be so great that we must always assume not only that an informant communicates what he learns from an encounter with the defendant and his counsel but also that what he communicates has the potential for detriment to the defendant or benefit to the prosecutor's case."

"Moreover, this is not a situation where the State's purpose was to learn what it could about the defendant's defense plans and the informant was instructed to intrude on the lawyer-client relationship or where the informant has assumed for himself that task and acted accordingly."

"[T]he per se rule . . . would require the informant to refuse to participate in attorney-client meetings, even though invited, and thus for all practical purposes to unmask himself. Our cases, however, have recognized the unfortunate necessity of undercover work. . . ."

2. Requirements of Discovery

a. Suppression of Exculpatory Evidence by the Prosecution

Brady v. Maryland, 373 U.S. 83 (1963)
Vote: 7-2
FACTS: John Brady and Donald Boblit were found guilty of first-degree murder and were sentenced to die. At trial, Brady testified and admitted his participation in the crime, but stated that Boblit did the killing. In his summation to the jury, Brady's lawyer conceded that Brady was guilty of murder in the first degree, and only asked that the jury spare his life. Prior to trial, Brady's lawyer requested that the prosecution allow him to examine Boblit's statements. The lawyer was given access to the statements, but one that indicated Boblit's guilt in the actual killing was withheld from him and was not discovered until after the trial and Brady had been convicted. Brady moved for a new trial based upon these findings but was denied.
ISSUE: Does the suppression by the prosecution of evidence favorable to an accused upon request violate due process where the evidence is material either to guilt or to punishment?
HOLDING: Yes.
RATIONALE: "We agree with the Court of Appeals that suppression of this confession was a violation of the Due Process Clause of the Fourteenth Amendment."

"This ruling is an extension of *Mooney v. Holohan,* 294 U.S. 103 [(1935)], where the Court ruled on what nondisclosure by a prosecutor violates due process: 'It is a requirement that cannot be deemed to be satisfied by mere notice and hearing if a state has contrived a conviction through the pretense of a trial which in truth is but used as a means of depriving a defendant of liberty through a deliberate deception of court and jury by the presentation of testimony known to be perjured. Such a contrivance by a state to procure the conviction and imprisonment of a defendant is as inconsistent with the rudimentary demands of justice as is the obtaining of a like result by intimidation.'"

"The Third Circuit in the [*United States ex rel. Almeida v. Baldi*, 195 F.2d 815] case construed that statement in *Pyle* [*v. Kansas*, 317 U.S. 213 (1942)] . . . to mean that the 'suppression of evidence favorable' to the accused was itself sufficient to amount to a denial of due process. . . . In *Napue v. Illinois*, 360 U.S. 264 [(1959)] . . . we extended the test formulated in *Mooney* . . . when we said: 'The same result obtains when the State, although not soliciting false evidence, allows it to go uncorrected when it appears.'"

"We now hold that the suppression by the prosecution of evidence favorable to an accused upon request violates due process where the evidence is material either to guilt or to punishment. . . ."

"The principle of *Mooney* . . . is not punishment of society for misdeeds of a prosecutor but avoidance of an unfair trial to the accused. Society wins not only when the guilty are convicted but when criminal trials are fair. . . . A prosecution that withholds evidence on demand of an accused which, if made available, would tend to exculpate him or reduce the penalty helps shape a trial that bears heavily on the defendant."

b. Voluntary Disclosure of Evidence By the Prosecution

United States v. Agurs, 427 U.S. 97 (1976)
Vote: 7-2
FACTS: Linda Agurs and James Sewell registered in a motel as man and wife. Sewell was wearing knives on his person and had about $360. About fifteen minutes later, employees heard Agurs scream for help. Sewell was on top of Agurs struggling for a bowie knife that she was holding. A witness stated that as his hand grasped the blade he was trying to force it into her chest. The employees separated them and called the police, but Agurs left before they arrived. Sewell died of his wounds a short time later. Evidence indicated that the two had sex, that Sewell had gone to the bathroom down the hall, and that the struggle occurred when he returned. None of his money was found, and the jury may have inferred that Agurs took Sewell's money and that the fight started when Sewell reentered the room. The following morning Agurs surrendered to the police and was given a physical exam, which revealed no cuts of any kind except needle marks on her arm. An autopsy of Sewell disclosed that he had several stab wounds in his chest and abdomen, and defensive wounds on his arms and hands. Agurs's defense was the argument that Sewell had attacked her with the knife and that her actions were in self-defense. It took the jury about twenty-five minutes to return a guilty verdict of second-degree murder.

Three months later Agurs's lawyer argued for a new trial asserting that he had discovered that Sewell had a prior record that indicated his violent personality and that the prosecutor had failed to disclose this information. The Government argued that there was no duty to provide the information on Sewell's record because it was readily available. The district court denied the motion and rejected the Government's argument that there was no duty to disclose the evidence.

ISSUE: Does the prosecutor have a duty to volunteer exculpatory evidence to the defense?

HOLDING: Yes.

RATIONALE: "[I]f the subject matter of such a request is material, or indeed if a substantial basis for claiming materiality exists, it is reasonable to require the prosecutor to respond either by furnishing the information or by submitting the problem to the trial judge. When the prosecutor receives a specific and relevant request, the failure to make any response is seldom, if ever, excusable."

"If there is a duty to respond to a general request of that kind, it must derive from the obviously exculpatory character of certain evidence in the hands of the prosecutor. But if the evidence is so clearly supportive of a claim of innocence that it gives the prosecution notice of a duty to produce, that duty should equally arise even if no request is made."

"Because we are dealing with an inevitably imprecise standard, and because the significance of an item of evidence can seldom be predicted accurately until the entire record is complete, the prudent prosecutor will resolve doubtful questions in favor of disclosure. But to reiterate a critical point, the prosecutor will not have violated his constitutional duty of disclosure unless his omission is of sufficient significance to result in the denial of the defendant's right to a fair trial."

"Whether or not procedural rules authorizing such broad discovery might be desirable, the Constitution surely does not demand that much. . . . The mere possibility that an item of undisclosed information might have helped the defense, or might have affected the outcome of the trial, does not establish 'materiality' in the constitutional sense."

"[T]here are situations in which evidence is obviously of such substantial value to the defense that elementary fairness requires it to be disclosed even without a specific request. For though the attorney for the sovereign must prosecute the accused with earnestness and vigor, he must always be faithful to his client's overriding interest that 'justice shall be done.' He is the 'servant of the law, the twofold aim of which is that guilt shall not escape or innocence suffer.'"

"It necessarily follows that if the omitted evidence creates a reasonable doubt that did not otherwise exist, constitutional error has been committed. This means that the omission must be evaluated in the context of the entire record. If there is no reasonable doubt about guilt whether or not the additional evidence is considered, there is no justification for a new trial. On the other hand, if the verdict is already of questionable validity, additional evidence of relatively minor importance might be sufficient to create a reasonable doubt."

c. Impeachment Information and Plea Bargaining

United States v. Ruiz, 536 U.S. 622 (2002)

Vote: 9-0

FACTS: After immigration agents found thirty kilograms of marijuana in Angela Ruiz's luggage, prosecutors offered her a plea bargain that asks a defendant to waive indictment, trial, and appeal. In return, the Government recommends a downward departure from the sentencing guidelines. The proposed agreement states that any information pertaining to the innocence of the accused was to be turned over to the defense. However, it requires that the defendant "waive the right" to receive impeachment information about the prosecution's witnesses and any information that would support a defense at trial. Because Ruiz would not agree, the prosecutors withdrew their offer. The Government then indicted her for drug possession and Ruiz pleaded guilty. At sentencing, Ruiz asked for the downward departure that the Government would have recommended had she accepted the agreement. The Court denied it, and imposed a standard sentence instead. The sentence was vacated on appeal, as the court held that prosecutors are required to make impeachment information available to a defendant before trial and before they enter into a plea agreement.

ISSUE: Does the Sixth Amendment require that federal prosecutors disclose impeachment information about their witnesses before entering into a plea agreement?

HOLDING: No.

RATIONALE: "In this case, the Ninth Circuit in effect held that a guilty plea is not 'voluntary . . .' unless the prosecutors first made the same disclosure of material impeachment information that the prosecutors would have had to make had the defendant insisted upon a trial. We must decide whether the Constitution requires that preguilty plea disclosure of impeachment information. We conclude that it does not."

"First, impeachment information is special in relation to the *fairness of a trial,* not in respect to whether a plea is *voluntary.* . . . But the Constitution does not require the prosecutor to share all useful information with the defendant."

"It is particularly difficult to characterize impeachment information as critical information of which the defendant must always be aware prior to pleading guilty given the random way in which such information may, or may not, help a particular defendant. The degree of help that impeachment information can provide will depend upon the defendant's own independent knowledge of the prosecution's potential case—a matter that the Constitution does not require prosecutors to disclose."

"Second, we have found no legal authority embodied either in this Court's past cases or in cases from other circuits that provide significant support for the Ninth Circuit's decision. To the contrary, this Court has found that the Constitution, in respect to a defendant's awareness of relevant circumstances, does not require complete knowledge of the relevant circumstances, but permits a court to accept a guilty plea . . . despite various forms of misapprehension under which a defendant might labor."

"Third, due process considerations, the very considerations that led this Court to find trial-related rights to exculpatory and impeachment information in *Brady* [*v. Maryland,* 373 U.S. 83 (1963)] and *Giglio* [*v. United States,* 405 U.S. 150 (1972)], argue against the existence of the 'right' that the Ninth Circuit found here."

"At the same time, a constitutional obligation to provide impeachment information during plea bargaining, prior to entry of a guilty plea, could seriously interfere with the Government's interest in securing those guilty pleas that are factually justified, desired by defendants, and help to secure the efficient administration of justice. The Ninth Circuit's rule risks premature disclosure of Government . . . information, which . . . could 'disrupt ongoing investigations.'"

"It could require the Government to devote substantially more resources to trial preparation prior to plea bargaining, thereby depriving the plea-bargaining process of its main resource-saving advantages. Or it could lead the Government instead to abandon its heavy reliance upon plea bargaining in a vast number—90% or more—of federal criminal cases. We cannot say that the Constitution's due process requirement demands so radical a change in the criminal justice process in order to achieve so comparatively small a constitutional benefit."

"These considerations, taken together, lead us to conclude that the Constitution does not require the Government to disclose material impeachment evidence prior to entering a plea agreement with a criminal defendant."

d. Disclosure of Impeachment Evidence and Death Cases

Banks v. Dretke, 540 U.S. 668 (2004)
Vote: 7-2
FACTS: Police found the corpse of sixteen-year-old Richard Whitehead in Pocket Park, Texas, and an autopsy revealed that he had been shot three times. Bowie County Sheriff Willie Huff learned that Whitehead had been in the company of Delma Banks Jr. Huff received a call from an informant reporting that Banks was going to Dallas to get a weapon. That evening, Huff and other officers followed Banks to Dallas, where Banks visited a residence from April 12 to 14. Police stopped Banks's vehicle en route from Dallas, found a handgun in it, and arrested the car's occupants. Returning to the Dallas residence Banks had visited, Huff interviewed Charles Cook and recovered a second gun that Cook said Banks had left with him. Tests later identified the second gun as the Whitehead murder weapon.

In a pretrial hearing, Banks's lawyer sought information from Huff concerning the informant who told Huff that Banks would be driving to Dallas. The prosecution argued that such information was privileged; however, in a letter, the prosecution advised Banks's lawyer that the State would provide him with all the information to which he was entitled. Witnesses at trial said they saw Banks and Whitehead together and that they heard gunshots in the park where Whitehead was found.

Cook testified at the guilt phase of the death penalty trial, that Banks had blood on his leg when he arrived in Dallas on April 12 and stated that Banks told him that he got it from someone that he had killed. He also said that shortly before the police questioned him, Banks came back and requested the gun. On cross-examination, Cook three times represented that he had not talked to anyone about his testimony even though he had been coached by Huff and prosecutors. The prosecution stated at the guilt phase that Cook had been completely truthful.

At the penalty phase the next day, Vetrano Jefferson testified to a violent encounter with Banks, and informant Robert Farr testified about the visit with Banks in Dallas. Farr perjured himself twice on cross-examination by stating that he did not speak to police and that he had not tried to illegally obtain prescription drugs in the past. He also implied that Banks was willing to commit violence in conjunction with other crimes. Friends and relatives testified on Banks's behalf, and Banks took the stand and admitted to obtaining a gun and the encounter with Jefferson, but he denied planning other crimes with Farr. The jury convicted Banks and the judge then sentenced him to death. Banks alleged on appeal that that the prosecution knowingly failed to turn over exculpatory evidence that would identify Farr as an informant. The state denied Banks's charges and the court rejected his claim.

ISSUE: Does the failure by prosecutors to turn over exculpatory impeachment evidence qualify as a violation of due process?

HOLDING: Yes.

RATIONALE: "We set out in *Strickler* v. *Greene*, 527 U.S. 263 (1999), the three components or essential elements of a *Brady* [v. *Maryland*, 373 U.S. 83 (1963)] prosecutorial misconduct claim: 'The evidence at issue must be favorable to the accused, either because it is exculpatory, or because it is impeaching; that evidence must have been suppressed by the State, either willfully or inadvertently; and prejudice must have ensued. . . .' Corresponding to the second *Brady* component (evidence suppressed by the State), a petitioner shows 'cause' when the reason for his failure to develop facts in state-court proceedings was the State's suppression of the relevant evidence; coincident with the third *Brady* component (prejudice), prejudice within the compass of the 'cause and prejudice' requirement exists when the suppressed evidence is 'material' for *Brady* purposes. . . . As to the first *Brady* component (evidence favorable to the accused), beyond genuine debate, the suppressed evidence relevant here, Farr's paid informant status, qualifies as evidence advantageous to Banks."

"Our decisions lend no support to the notion that defendants must scavenge for hints of undisclosed *Brady* material when the prosecution represents that all such material has been disclosed."

"A rule thus declaring 'prosecutor may hide, defendant must seek,' is not tenable in a system constitutionally bound to accord defendants due process. 'Ordinarily, we presume that public officials have properly discharged their official duties. . . .' Courts, litigants, and juries properly anticipate that obligations [to refrain from improper methods to secure a conviction] . . . plainly rest[ing] upon the prosecuting attorney, will be faithfully observed. . . . Prosecutors' dishonest conduct or unwarranted concealment should attract no judicial approbation."

"As the State acknowledged at oral argument, Farr was 'paid for a critical role in the scenario that led to the indictment.'"

"Because Banks had no criminal record, Farr's testimony about Banks's propensity to commit violent acts was crucial to the prosecution. . . . What Farr told the jury, the prosecution urged, was 'of the utmost significance' to show '[Banks] is a danger to friends and strangers, alike.'"

"Farr's declaration supporting Banks's federal habeas petition, however, vividly contradicts that denial: 'I assumed that if I did not help [Huff] . . . he would have me arrested for drug charges.' Had jurors known of Farr's continuing interest in obtaining Deputy Sheriff Huff's favor, in addition to his receipt of funds to 'set [Banks] up,' they might well have distrusted Farr's testimony, and, insofar as it was uncorroborated, disregarded it."

"At least as to the penalty phase . . . one can hardly be confident that Banks received a fair trial, given the jury's ignorance of Farr's true role in the investigation and trial of the case. . . . On the record before us, one could not plausibly deny the existence of the requisite 'reasonable probability of a different result' had the suppressed information been disclosed to the defense. . . ."

3. Relevance of Evidence

United States v. Bagley, 473 U.S. 667 (1985)
Vote: 5-3
FACTS: Hughes Anderson Bagley was indicted on fifteen charges of violating federal drug and firearms statutes. About a month prior to trial, his lawyer filed a discovery motion that requested information about government witnesses that were going to be called. James O'Connor and Donald Mitchell were state police officers but were privately employed as security guards and also helped in an investigation of Bagley. The prosecution provided materials that indicated that no promises were made to them for their cooperation in the investigation. With the help of the officers' testimony, Bagley was convicted of the drugs charges but acquitted of the firearms charges in a bench trial. Bagley filed Freedom of Information Act requests and obtained documents detailing contracts for information with the ATF and that the agents were paid for the information that they provided after the trial. The prosecution did not provide the contracts as part of the discovery request, and Bagley moved to vacate his sentence, claiming that his discovery rights under *Brady* were violated. The district court found that because no amounts were promised to the agents prior to the trial that no violation occurred by not providing the initial agreement to the defense. However, the court of appeals held that failing to provide the information impeded Bagley's defense.
ISSUE: Does the failure to provide requested information require reversal if the accused does not show that the failure resulted in prejudice to his defense?
HOLDING: No.
RATIONALE: "Thus, the Court of Appeals' holding is inconsistent with our precedents."

"Moreover, the court's reliance on *Davis v. Alaska* [415 U.S. 308 (1974)] for its 'automatic reversal' rule is misplaced. In *Davis*, the defense sought to cross-examine a crucial prosecution witness concerning his probationary status as a juvenile delinquent. . . . Pursuant to a state rule of procedure and a state statute making juvenile adjudications inadmissible, the trial judge prohibited the defense from conducting the cross-examination."

"The present case, in contrast, does not involve any direct restriction on the scope of cross-examination. The defense was free to cross-examine the witnesses on any relevant subject, including possible bias or interest resulting from inducements made by the Government. The constitutional error, if any, in this case was the Government's failure to assist the defense by disclosing information that might have been helpful in conducting the cross-examination. As discussed above, such suppression of evidence amounts to a constitutional violation only if it deprives the defendant of a fair trial. Consistent with 'our overriding concern with the justice of the finding of guilt . . .' a constitutional error occurs, and the conviction must be reversed, only if the evidence is material in the sense that its suppression undermines confidence in the outcome of the trial."

4. Cumulative Evidence and the Failure to Disclose

Kyles v. Whitley, 514 U.S. 419 (1995)
Vote: 5-4
FACTS: Dolores Dye left the Schwegmann's store in New Orleans after shopping. A man shot her in the head, took her keys, and drove away. Police took statements from six witnesses, who all stated that he was a black, and most said that he had braided hair. However, their further descriptions were markedly different. Police believed the attacker might have driven his car to the scene, so they recorded the plate numbers of the cars in the lots around the store but obtained no leads. However, a man calling himself James Joseph called and reported that on the day of the murder he had bought a red Thunderbird from Curtis Lee Kyles. He said that he had read about Dye's murder and feared that he had the victim's car. He agreed to meet with police. The informant met Detective John Miller, who was wearing a microphone. He now said he was Joseph Banks and that he was called Beanie, and his story changed since his call. Beanie now told Miller that he bought a red LTD and led Miller to a nearby bar, where he had left the car, later identified as Dye's. Beanie told Miller that he lived with Kyles's brother-in-law (Johnny Burns), and when asked if Kyles ever wore his hair in plaits, Beanie said that he did but that he "had a bush" when he bought the car.

Beanie was concerned that he was a suspect and explained that he had been seen driving Dye's car and had changed its plates. Miller acknowledged that possession of the car was suspicious, but told him that he "didn't do anything wrong." Beanie implicated Kyles and stated that Kyles carried a .38 and a .32, and if the police "set him up good," they could "get that same gun" used to kill Dye. Beanie rode with Miller and Sgt. James Eaton, in an unmarked car and pointed out Kyles's apartment building. Beanie told the officers that after he bought the car, he and Burns drove Kyles to Schwegmann's to pick up his car, described as an orange four-door Ford. When asked where the car was, Beanie stated that it had been "[o]n the same side [of the lot] where the woman was killed at." The officers later drove Beanie to Schwegmann's, where he pointed out the space where Kyles's car had been parked. Beanie also said that when he and Burns brought Kyles to the lot, he had gone to some bushes to get a brown purse, which he hid in a closet at his apartment. Beanie said that Kyles had "a lot of groceries" in Schwegmann's bags and a baby's potty "in the car." Beanie told Eaton that Kyles's garbage would go out the next day and that if Kyles was "smart" he would "put [the purse] in [the] garbage." Beanie made it clear that he expected a reward, saying that he was not "doing all of this for nothing." The police assured Beanie that he would not lose the $400 he paid for the car.

After the visit to Schwegmann's, Eaton and Miller took Beanie to a police station where Miller interviewed him on the record, and Beanie signed it, using "Joseph Banks." Beanie repeated some material from the recorded statement, but portions were contradictory. He did not explain the inconsistencies, and the police did not question him about them. According to a statement given to the prosecutor, Beanie went to Kyles's apartment after a phone conversation with an officer who asked whether Kyles had the murder weapon. Beanie later left the apartment to call Miller, after which he returned and then left to meet Miller, who asked about the gun as he "rode around" with Miller.

Kyles was arrested as he left the apartment, which was then searched. Behind the kitchen stove, the police found a .32 caliber revolver containing five live and one spent cartridge, and ballistics showed that it was the pistol used to murder Dye. In a wardrobe, the officers found a holster that fit the gun. In a drawer, they discovered several .32 caliber rounds of the same brand as those found in the pistol. In the kitchen, they found cans of cat and dog food, some of them the brands Dye had purchased and in Schwegmann's sacks. Police opened the garbage bags and found Dye's purse, identification, and other belongings wrapped in a Schwegmann's sack. Kyles's prints were only found on a Schwegmann's sales slip and Beanie's fingerprints were not compared to any of the fingerprints found. The lead detective, Dillman, put together a photo lineup of Kyles (but not of Beanie) and showed it to five of the six witnesses who had given statements. Three of them picked Kyles; the other two could not identify Kyles as the assailant.

Kyles was indicted for first-degree murder, and before trial, his lawyer filed a motion for disclosure of any exculpatory or impeachment evidence. The prosecution responded that there was none, despite the six eyewitness statements taken by police; Beanie's contradictory statements; the printout of license numbers of cars parked at Schwegmann's on the night of the murder, which did not identify Kyles's car; the police memorandum calling for the seizure of the garbage after Beanie had suggested that the purse might be there; and evidence linking Beanie to other crimes at Schwegmann's and to the murder of Patricia Leidenheimer, committed before the Dye murder.

At the first trial, the State's case was testimony from four people who were at the scene (three of whom had picked Kyles from the photo lineup). Kyles maintained his innocence and supported his alibi that he had been picking up his children from school. The defense argued that Kyles was framed by Beanie, who had planted evidence in Kyles's apartment and his garbage in order to remove an obstacle to romance with Pinky Burns and to obtain reward money. Beanie did not testify.

After four hours, a mistrial was declared and the prosecutor interviewed Beanie. The notes to this interview showed that Beanie again changed his story. Neither chief prosecutor Strider's notes nor any of the other notes and transcripts were given to the defense. Kyles was tried again. The State's case was again the testimony of the four witnesses who identified Kyles for the jury. The prosecution also offered a blown-up photograph taken at the crime scene, which they argued showed a two-toned car that was Kyles's. They suggested that Kyles had left his car at Schwegmann's on the day of the murder and retrieved it later, a theory for which they offered no evidence. Once again, Beanie did not testify. The defense argued that the witnesses were mistaken, and other witnesses testified to seeing Beanie, with his hair in plaits, driving a red car similar to the victim's or trying to sell them the car. Burns testified that he had seen Beanie at Kyles's apartment, stooping down near the stove where the gun was found. To explain the pet food, the defense stated that Kyles's family had a dog and cat and often fed stray animals. Kyles again took the stand and denied any involvement. He explained his fingerprints on a receipt in Dye's car by stating that Beanie had picked him up in a red car and had taken him to Schwegmann's, where he bought transmission fluid and cigarettes. He thought that the receipt might have fallen from the bag when he removed the cigarettes. The prosecutor had Beanie brought into the courtroom, and all witnesses, after viewing Beanie standing next to Kyles, reaffirmed their previous identifications of Kyles as the murderer. Kyles was convicted of first-degree murder and sentenced to death, and Beanie received a total of $1,600 in reward money. It was revealed in the course of review that the State had failed to disclose evidence favorable to the defense.

ISSUE: Is the prosecution required to measure the net effect of evidence withheld pursuant to a discovery request if the suppression raises the reasonable probability that its disclosure would have produced a different result?

HOLDING: Yes.

RATIONALE: "[W]e follow the established rule that the state's obligation under *Brady* [*v. Maryland*, 373 U.S. 83 (1963)] . . . to disclose evidence favorable to the defense, turns on the cumulative effect of all such evidence suppressed by the government, and we hold that the prosecutor remains responsible for gauging that effect regardless of any failure by the police to bring favorable evidence to the prosecutor's attention. Because the net effect of the evidence withheld by the State in this case raises a reasonable probability that its disclosure would have produced a different result, Kyles is entitled to a new trial."

"The result reached by the Fifth Circuit majority is compatible with a series of independent materiality evaluations, rather than the cumulative evaluation required by [*United States v. Bagley*, 473 U.S. 667 (1985)]. . . ."

"[T]he effective impeachment of one eyewitness can call for a new trial even though the attack does not extend directly to others, as we have said before."

"In assessing the significance of the evidence withheld, one must of course bear in mind that not every item of the State's case would have been directly undercut if the *Brady* evidence had been disclosed. It is significant, however, that the physical evidence remaining unscathed would, by the State's own admission, hardly have amounted to overwhelming proof that Kyles was the murderer."

"Similarly undispositive is the small Schwegmann's receipt on the front passenger floorboard of the LTD, the only physical evidence that bore a fingerprint identified as Kyles's. Kyles explained that Beanie had driven him to Schwegmann's on Friday to buy cigarettes and transmission fluid, and he theorized that the slip must have fallen out of the bag when he removed the cigarettes. This explanation is consistent with the location of the slip when found and with its small size."

"[T]he question is not whether the State would have had a case to go to the jury if it had disclosed the favorable evidence, but whether we can be confident that the jury's verdict would have been the same. Confidence that it would have been cannot survive a recap of the suppressed evidence . . . (a) that the investigation was limited by the police's uncritical readiness to accept the story and suggestions of an informant whose accounts were inconsistent . . . and whose own behavior was enough to raise suspicions of guilt; (b) that the lead police detective who testified was either less than wholly candid or less than fully informed; (c) that the informant's behavior raised suspicions that he had planted both the murder weapon and the victim's purse in the places they were found; (d) that one of the four eyewitnesses . . . had given a description that . . . better described the informant; (e) that another eyewitness had been coached, since he had first stated that he had not seen the killer outside the getaway car, or the killing itself, whereas at trial he claimed to have seen the shooting, described the murder weapon exactly, and omitted portions of his initial description that would have been troublesome for the case; (f) that there was no consistency to eyewitness descriptions of the killer's height, build, age, facial hair, or hair length."

"Since all of these possible findings were precluded by the prosecution's failure to disclose the evidence that would have supported them, 'fairness' cannot be stretched to the point of calling this a fair trial."

5. Polygraph Information

Wood v. Bartholomew, 516 U.S. 1 (1995)
Vote: 5-4
FACTS: Dwayne Earl Bartholomew robbed a coin-operated laundry in Tacoma, Washington, and killed the attendant. He confessed to the robbery and said that the shots came from his gun but argued that his single-action revolver discharged by accident. Testimony was also obtained from Bartholomew's brother, Rodney, and his girlfriend, Tracy Dormady. Rodney and Tracy testified that they had gone to the laundry and that Bartholomew was in his car in the lot when they arrived. Rodney testified that Bartholomew told him that he intended to rob the store and "leave no witnesses." Rodney and Tracy then left and went to her house. Bartholomew arrived a short time later, and when Tracy asked if he had killed the attendant he replied that "he had put two bullets in the kid's head." Tracy also testified that she had heard him say that he intended to leave no witnesses. Bartholomew testified in his own behalf and admitted threatening the victim and forcing him to lie down on the floor but that while he was removing the money, the gun accidentally fired. He also claimed that it went off again as he was leaving and denied telling anyone that he intended to leave no witnesses. He also stated that Rodney had helped by convincing the attendant to open the door after it had been locked, although he left before the robbery. The prosecution requested that Rodney and Tracy submit to polygraphs, which Tracy passed but which indicated that Rodney was lying. Neither examination was disclosed to the defense.
ISSUE: Does the prosecution have to provide polygraph examinations of their witnesses to the defense as part of its disclosure requirements?

HOLDING: No.

RATIONALE: "The decision below is a misapplication of our *Brady* [*v. Maryland*, 373 U.S. 83 (1963)] jurisprudence."

"To begin with, on the Court of Appeals' own assumption, the polygraph results were inadmissible under state law, even for impeachment purposes, absent a stipulation by the parties . . . and the parties do not contend otherwise. The information at issue here, then—the results of a polygraph examination of one of the witnesses—is not 'evidence' at all. Disclosure of the polygraph results, then, could have had no direct effect on the outcome of trial, because respondent could have made no mention of them either during argument or while questioning witnesses."

"In speculating that the undisclosed polygraph results might have affected trial counsel's preparation, and hence the result at trial, the Ninth Circuit disagreed with, or disregarded, the view of respondent's own trial counsel."

"Trial counsel's strategic decision to limit his questioning of Rodney undermines the suggestion by the Court of Appeals that counsel might have chosen to depose Rodney had the polygraph results been disclosed. But of even greater importance was counsel's candid acknowledgment that disclosure would not have affected the scope of his cross-examination."

"In short, it is not 'reasonably likely' that disclosure of the polygraph results—inadmissible under state law—would have resulted in a different outcome at trial."

"Whenever a federal court grants habeas relief to a state prisoner the issuance of the writ exacts great costs to the State's legitimate interest in finality. And where, as here, retrial would occur 13 years later, those costs and burdens are compounded many times. Those costs may be justified where serious doubts about the reliability of a trial infested with constitutional error exist. But where, as in this case, a federal appellate court, second-guessing a convict's own trial counsel, grants habeas relief on the basis of little more than speculation with slight support, the proper delicate balance between the federal courts and the States is upset to a degree that requires correction."

G. Competency

1. Information Useable to Determine Competency

Drope v. Missouri, 420 U.S. 162 (1975)
Vote: 9-0
FACTS: James E. Drope and two others were indicted for the rape of his wife. A psychiatrist who had examined Drope at his counsel's request and whose report was attached to the motion suggested treatment. The continuance was granted, but at the next hearing Drope's lawyer objected to proceeding to trial on the ground that he had understood the case would be continued until a later date and was not prepared. He also stated that Drope was not a person of sound mind and should have a further psychiatric examination before trial. The trial judge noted that the motion was not in

proper form and that he had had failed to file another, so the objection was overruled and the case proceed to trial.

The prosecution called Drope's wife as its first witness and she testified that he participated with four of his friends in raping her and subjecting her to abuse and indignities, but that she had resumed living with him on the advice of his psychiatrist and so that their children would be taken care of. She also testified that she had told Drope's attorney of her belief that her husband was sick and needed psychiatric care and that she had signed a statement disavowing a desire to prosecute. However, she also stated that after talking to his psychiatrist she was not convinced he was sick and that she had changed her mind about not wanting to prosecute because, she said, he had "tried to choke me, tried to kill me." Drope did not appear for the trial the following morning, and when the judge directed counsel to proceed, Drope's attorney moved for a mistrial because Drope had shot himself. The trial judge denied the motion, and the prosecution then called more witnesses and, after producing proof of a prior conviction, rested its case. The jury returned a verdict of guilty. Drope then filed a motion for a new trial, stating that he had been in the hospital but did not remember the shooting. However, he told several different witnesses that he shot himself due to his legal problems. The trial judge denied the motion stating that his absence was due to his desire to avoid the trial.

ISSUE: Is an accused's due process rights violated when the court fails to order a psychiatric exam to determine competency to stand trial in light of evidence that suggests incompetency?

HOLDING: Yes.

RATIONALE: "However, we are constrained to disagree with the sentencing judge that counsel's pretrial contention that 'the defendant is not a person of sound mind and should have a further psychiatric examination before the case should be forced to trial,' did not raise the issue of petitioner's competence to stand trial. This statement also may have tended to blur the aspect of petitioner's mental condition which would bear on his criminal responsibility and that which would bear on his competence to stand trial. However, at that stage, and with the obvious advantages of hindsight, it seems to us that it would have been, at the very least, the better practice to order an immediate examination."

"Although we do not . . . suggest that courts must accept without question a lawyer's representations concerning the competence of his client . . . an expressed doubt in that regard by one with 'the closest contact with the defendant . . .' is unquestionably a factor which should be considered. Moreover, resolution of the issue of competence to stand trial at an early date best serves both the interests of fairness . . . and of sound judicial administration."

"Notwithstanding the difficulty of making evaluations of the kind required in these circumstances, we conclude that the record reveals a failure to give proper weight to the information suggesting incompetence which came to light during trial. . . . Although a defendant's demeanor during trial may be such as to obviate 'the need for extensive reliance on psychiatric prediction concerning his capabilities . . .' that 'this reasoning offers no justification for ignoring the uncontradicted testimony of . . . (a) history of pronounced irrational behavior.'"

"The import of our decision in *Pate* [*v. Robinson*, 383 U.S. 375 (1966)] . . . is that evidence of a defendant's irrational behavior, his demeanor at trial, and any prior medical opinion on competence to stand trial are all relevant in determining whether further inquiry is required, but that even one of these factors standing alone may, in some circumstances, be sufficient. There are, of course, no fixed or immutable signs which invariably indicate the need for further inquiry. . . ."

3. What Must Government Do If an Accused Is Found Incompetent?

Jackson v. Indiana, 406 U.S. 715 (1972)

Vote: 7-0

FACTS: Theon Jackson, a deaf mute with a mental capacity of a preschool child, could not read, write, or communicate except through sign language. He was charged in the separate robberies of two women, which involved taking their purses and a few dollars. The record sheds no light on the charges since, upon receipt of not guilty pleas, the court set in motion the Indiana procedures for determining his competency to stand trial. The court appointed two psychiatrists to examine Jackson, and a competency hearing was held. The court received the examining doctors' report and testimony and from an interpreter through whom they had attempted to communicate with Jackson. The report stated that Jackson was unable to understand the charges or to participate in his defense. One doctor testified that it was doubtful that he could ever learn to read or write. The other doctor also doubted whether Jackson could develop communication skills. The interpreter testified that Indiana had no facilities that could help someone like Jackson to learn such skills. The trial court ordered him committed to the Indiana Department of Mental Health until such time as that Department should certify to the court that "the defendant is sane." Jackson's lawyer then moved for a new trial, arguing that there was no evidence that he was "insane," or that he would ever attain a status that the court might regard as "sane." Counsel argued that Jackson's commitment amounted to a "life sentence" without his ever having been convicted and that the commitment deprived Jackson of his Fourteenth Amendment rights to due process and equal protection, and constituted cruel and unusual punishment under the Eighth Amendment. The trial court denied the motion.

ISSUE: Is a defendant's due process rights violated if he is confined solely because of his incompetency?

HOLDING: Yes.

RATIONALE: "[W]e also hold that Indiana's indefinite commitment of a criminal defendant solely on account of his incompetency to stand trial does not square with the Fourteenth Amendment's guarantee of due process."

"Since *Greenwood* [*v. United States*, 350 U.S. 366 (1956)], federal courts without exception have found improper any straightforward application of §§ 4244 and 4246 to a defendant . . . an indefinite commitment on the ground of incompetency alone."

"Without a finding of dangerousness, one committed thereunder can be held only for a 'reasonable period of time' necessary to determine whether there is a substantial chance of his attaining the capacity to stand trial in the foreseeable future. If the chances are slight, or if the defendant does not in fact improve, then he must be released or granted a §§ 4247–4248 hearing."

"*Greenwood*. . . justified the commitment by treating it as if accomplished under allied statutory provisions relating directly to the individual's 'insanity' and society's interest in his indefinite commitment. . . . And it sustained commitment only upon the finding of dangerousness. As Part A, shows, all these elements subsequently have been held not simply sufficient, but necessary, to sustain a commitment like the one involved here."

"It is clear that Jackson's commitment rests on proceedings that did not purport to bring into play, indeed did not even consider relevant, any of the articulated bases for exercise of Indiana's power of indefinite commitment. The state statutes contain at least two alternative methods for invoking this power. But Jackson was not afforded any 'formal commitment proceedings addressed to (his) ability to function in society,' or to society's interest in his restraint, or to the State's ability to aid him in attaining competency through custodial care or compulsory treatment, the ostensible purpose of the commitment. At the least, due process requires that the nature and duration of commitment bear some reasonable relation to the purpose for which the individual is committed."

"We hold, consequently, that a person charged by a State with a criminal offense who is committed solely on account of his incapacity to proceed to trial cannot be held more than the reasonable period of time necessary to determine whether there is a substantial probability that he will attain that capacity in the foreseeable future. If it is determined that this is not the case, then the State must either institute the customary civil commitment proceeding that would be required to commit indefinitely any other citizen, or release the defendant. Furthermore, even if it is determined that the defendant probably soon will be able to stand trial, his continued commitment must be justified by progress toward that goal."

13

Right to Counsel

I N THIS CHAPTER, WE CONTINUE THE EXAMINATION of the rules and procedures that court officials must follow during the criminal process. However, instead of focusing on the prosecution as we did in chapter 12, here the majority of the material centers on the Sixth Amendment right to counsel and the defense attorney. It is the accused that enjoys the right to have a lawyer at different parts of the criminal process, and this right is designed to protect an individual from being treated unfairly by the police and the state. To avoid confusion, the Sixth Amendment right to counsel is different from the earlier cases that address the right to be free from self-incrimination. That right is grounded in the *Fifth Amendment,* and it protects a suspect primarily against illegal or coercive interrogation tactics. The *Sixth Amendment* right is designed to ensure that the accused is treated fairly during the trial process.

For example, the Supreme Court has stated that the accused has several rights at trial that are exercised through a lawyer. For example, the Court has stated that an accused has a right to a speedy and public trial, where he may, if he chooses to, confront the witnesses against him or waive his right to be present. The accused also has a right to compulsory process; that is, a defendant may force others involved in the case to testify if their information has a bearing on his innocence or guilt.

Additionally, the Sixth Amendment right to counsel for the trial process is important by itself because the Court has ruled on several issues directly related to how and when the right attaches. More specifically, while the Court has forcefully stated that an indigent defendant has the right to have a lawyer appointed for him, that same defendant *does not* have the right to determine *which* lawyer will be appointed. The Court has also ruled that an accused has the right to confer with their lawyer. In fact, the right has even been extended to juveniles in delinquency hearings. The Court has also spoken very clearly, although it took some time, on which jurisdictions were required to provide counsel for indigents. Death penalty cases were the first where the Court stated that lawyers must be provided, and then it gradually applied the right to the states for different types of offenses. The Court's construction of the right to counsel for this process is quite a liberal one because it has stated that even the accused can act as his or her own lawyer.

A related issue to the right to have a lawyer act on one's behalf in the first place is the effectiveness of the assistance that they provide. As one might expect, the Court has also made a determination as to what effective assistance of counsel is and how that standard has developed. Further, the Court has also stated that an accused that has been convicted also has a right to appeal and with that, the right to have counsel appointed. However, that right is limited by the fact that it has also held that someone who has suffered a conviction only has a constitutional right to one appeal and that the state's responsibility in providing counsel stops after that appeal has been acted upon.

A. Right to a Speedy Trial

1. Test for Determining Violation of Right

Barker v. Wingo, 407 U.S. 514 (1972)
Vote: 9-0
FACTS: An elderly couple was beaten to death by assailants wielding a tire iron, and Silas Manning and Willie Barker were arrested and indicted. The trial was set for a few months later, but the State of Kentucky believed that Barker could not be convicted unless Manning testified against him. Beginning on the day of Manning's trial, the prosecution sought and obtained the first of a series of sixteen continuances of Barker's trial, and Barker made no objection. Unfortunately, the prosecution encountered a great deal of difficulty, and after several trials, finally convicted Manning a few years after the crime had taken place.

The court that was responsible for trying Barker held three terms per year. The first continuance postponed the trial until the September 1959 term, the second was only for one month. However, every subsequent continuance was moved until the next term. After some time, Barker was released on bail and remained free until his trial. He made no objection to the first eleven continuances. After the twelfth, Barker's attorney moved to have the indictment dismissed, which was denied. Barker did not object to two subsequent continuances, and on the day of the trial the court postponed the start until the June term due to the illness of the investigator involved in the case. Barker's lawyer again objected but was unsuccessful, and the trial was postponed due to the investigator's illness. At this point, the court, announced that the case would be dismissed for lack of prosecution if it were not tried during the next term. The final trial date was set for October 9, 1963, and on that date, Barker moved to dismiss the indictment, specifying that his right to a speedy trial had been violated, but the motion was denied. The trial then proceeded with Manning as the chief witness, and Barker was convicted and given a life sentence. Barker appealed, relying on his speedy trial claim.

ISSUE: Is the means for determining a violation of the right to speedy trial a balancing test in which the conduct of the prosecution and the defendant are weighed?
HOLDING: Yes.
RATIONALE: "Finally, and perhaps most importantly, the right to speedy trial is a more vague concept than other procedural rights. It is, for example, impossible to determine with precision when the right has been denied. We cannot definitely say how long is too long in a system where justice is supposed to be swift but deliberate. . . . Thus, as we recognized in *Beavers v. Haubert* [198 U.S. 77 (1905)] any inquiry into a speedy trial claim necessitates a functional analysis of the right in the particular context of the case. . . ."

"The approach we accept is a balancing test, in which the conduct of both the prosecution and the defendant are weighed."

"A balancing test necessarily compels courts to approach speedy trial cases on an ad hoc basis. We can do little more than identify some of the factors which courts should assess in determining whether a particular defendant has been deprived of his right. . . . [W]e identify four such factors: Length of delay, the reason for the delay, the defendant's assertion of his right, and prejudice to the defendant."

"Closely related to length of delay is the reason the government assigns to justify the delay. Here, too, different weights should be assigned to different reasons. A deliberate attempt to delay the trial in order to hamper the defense should be weighted heavily against the government. A more neutral reason such as negligence or overcrowded courts should be weighted less heavily. . . . Finally, a valid reason, such as a missing witness, should serve to justify appropriate delay."

"Whether and how a defendant asserts his right is closely related to the other factors we have mentioned. The strength of his efforts will be affected by the length of the delay, to some extent by the reason for the delay, and most particularly by the personal prejudice, which is not always readily identifiable, that he experiences. The more serious the deprivation, the more likely a defendant is to complain. The defendant's assertion of his speedy trial right, then, is entitled to strong evidentiary weight in determining whether the defendant is being deprived of the right. We emphasize that failure to assert the right will make it difficult for a defendant to prove that he was denied a speedy trial."

"We regard none of the four factors identified above as either a necessary or sufficient condition to the finding of a deprivation of the right of speedy trial. Rather, they are related factors and must be considered together with such other circumstances as may be relevant."

2. Length of the Delay and Speedy Trial

Doggett v. United States, 505 U.S. 647 (1992)
Vote: 5-4
FACTS: Marc Doggett was indicted in 1980 for conspiring with others to import and distribute cocaine. Douglas Driver, the principal agent investigating the case, told the United States Marshal's Service that the DEA would oversee Doggett's arrest. Officers that arrived at his parents' house to arrest him found that he had left for Colombia four days earlier. To catch Doggett on his return to the United States, Driver sent word of his arrest warrant to all customs stations and to several law enforcement organizations and added his name to the Treasury Enforcement Communication System (TECS), and the National Crime Information Center computer system. The TECS entry expired that September, however, and Doggett's name vanished from the system.

In 1981, Driver found out that Doggett was under arrest on drug charges in Panama and, assuming that an extradition request would be useless, asked Panama to "expel" Doggett to the United States. Although the Panamanian authorities promised to comply, they instead let him go to Colombia, where he stayed with an aunt. In 1982, he passed through customs in New York City and settled in Virginia. After his return, he married, earned a degree, found a job as a computer manager, lived openly under his name, and obeyed the law. Doggett's travels abroad had not wholly escaped the Government's notice, however. Driver was never told that Doggett went to Columbia and assumed that Doggett was still serving time in a Panama. He never checked on Doggett and did not find out until 1985 that Doggett had gone to Columbia. Driver then assumed that Doggett had settled there, and he made no effort to track Doggett down. It was not until 1988, when the Marshal's Service ran a credit check on people subject to arrest warrants that the Government found out where Doggett was. Finally, six years after his return and eight and a half years after his indictment, he was arrested. He moved to dismiss the indictment, arguing that the Government's failure to prosecute him earlier violated his right to a speedy trial.

ISSUE: Does a delay of eight and a half years between an accused's indictment and arrest violate the right to a speedy trial?

HOLDING: Yes.

RATIONALE: "[A]s we discuss below, the presumption that pretrial delay has prejudiced the accused intensifies over time."

"As for *Barker* [*v. Wingo*, 407 U.S. 514 (1972)]'s second criterion, the Government claims to have sought Doggett with diligence. The findings of the courts below are to the contrary. . . . While the Government's lethargy may have reflected no more than Doggett's relative unimportance in the world of drug trafficking, it was still findable negligence, and the finding stands."

"[W]e generally have to recognize that excessive delay presumptively compromises the reliability of a trial in ways that neither party can prove or, for that matter, identify. While such presumptive prejudice cannot alone carry a Sixth Amendment claim without regard to the other *Barker* criteria . . . it is part of the mix of relevant facts, and its importance increases with the length of delay."

"*Barker* stressed that official bad faith in causing delay will be weighed heavily against the government, and a bad-faith delay the length of this negligent one would present an overwhelming case for dismissal."

"While not compelling relief in every case where bad-faith delay would make relief virtually automatic, neither is negligence automatically tolerable simply because the accused cannot demonstrate exactly how it has prejudiced him. It was on this point that the Court of Appeals erred, and on the facts before us, it was reversible error."

"When the Government's negligence thus causes delay six times as long as that generally sufficient to trigger judicial review . . . and when the presumption of prejudice, albeit unspecified, is neither extenuated, as by the defendant's acquiescence . . . nor persuasively rebutted, the defendant is entitled to relief."

3. Waiver of Speedy Trail Act Application

Zedner v. United States 126 S.Ct. 1976 (2006)
Vote: 9-0
FACTS: In 1996, Zedner tried to defraud several financial institutions in New York State with several poorly made $10,000,000 U.S. Bond notes. He was indicted for seven counts of attempting to defraud a financial institution and one count of possessing

counterfeit instruments. After two continuances, the defense requested another longer one, to which the court requested "waiver of all time" of the application of the Speedy Trial Act, to which the defense agreed. The court provided a form that both Zedner and the defense counsel signed. Zedner continued to request continuances, and the following four years resulted in different hearings but no trial. One of the hearings determined that Zedner was incompetent to stand trial. He moved to dismiss the indictment, arguing that a violation of the Speedy Trial Act had taken place. The court denied the motion, pointing out his waiver. Zedner was eventually found guilty of six counts of trying to defraud a financial institution. The Court of Appeals affirmed the conviction.

ISSUE: Can an accused waive the application of the Speedy Trial Act "for all time?"

HOLDING: No.

RATIONALE: "[T]he Speedy Trial Act comprehensively regulates the time within which a trial must begin. . . . Conspicuously, §3161(h) has no provision excluding periods of delay during which a defendant waives the application of the Act, and it is apparent from the terms of the Act that this omission was a considered one. Instead of simply allowing defendants to opt out of the Act, the Act demands that defense continuance requests fit within one of the specific exclusions set out."

"This interpretation is entirely in accord with the Act's legislative history."

"Because defendants may be content to remain on pretrial release, and indeed may welcome delay, it is unsurprising that Congress refrained from empowering defendants to make prospective waivers of the Act's application."

"It is significant that §3162(a)(2) makes no mention of prospective waivers, and there is no reason to think that Congress wanted to treat prospective and retrospective waivers similarly. Allowing prospective waivers would seriously undermine the Act because there are many cases—like the case at hand—in which the prosecution, the defense, and the court would all be happy to opt out of the Act, to the detriment of the public interest."

B. Witness Confrontation

Maryland v. Craig, 497 U.S. 836 (1990)
Vote: 5-4
FACTS: A grand jury charged Sandra Craig with child abuse, sexual offenses, perverted sexual practice, assault, and battery. The victim was a six-year-old girl who had attended a kindergarten center owned and operated by Craig. Before trial, the State sought to invoke a procedure that allowed a judge to receive, by closed circuit television, the testimony of a child who is alleged to be a victim of child abuse. However, the judge must first find that the testimony would result in the child suffering such distress that the child could not reasonably communicate in person. Craig objected on Confrontation Clause grounds, which the trial court overruled, finding that while the

statute took away face-to-face confrontation, the defense could still observe the girl and cross examine her and the jury could ascertain her demeanor. The judge then found that the testimony would cause a degree of emotional distress that allowed for the invocation of the statute, and he granted the closed circuit testimony. Eventually, Craig was convicted on all counts.

ISSUE: Is the Confrontation Clause of the Sixth Amendment violated when a judge allows a child to testify against a defendant, outside their presence, by closed circuit television?

HOLDING: No.

RATIONALE: "Although face-to-face confrontation forms 'the core of the values furthered by the Confrontation Clause . . .' we have nevertheless recognized that it is not the *sine qua non* of the confrontation right."

"For this reason, we have never insisted on an actual face-to-face encounter at trial in every instance in which testimony is admitted against a defendant. Instead, we have repeatedly held that the Clause permits, where necessary, the admission of certain hearsay statements against a defendant despite the defendant's inability to confront the declarant at trial."

"We have accordingly stated that a literal reading of the Confrontation Clause would 'abrogate virtually every hearsay exception, a result long rejected as unintended and too extreme. . . .' Thus, in certain narrow circumstances, 'competing interests, if "closely examined," may warrant dispensing with confrontation at trial. . . .' Given our hearsay cases, the word 'confronted,' as used in the Confrontation Clause, cannot simply mean face-to-face confrontation, for the Clause would then, contrary to our cases, prohibit the admission of any accusatory hearsay statement made by an absent declarant. . . ."

"In sum, our precedents establish that 'the Confrontation Clause reflects a *preference* for face-to-face confrontation at trial . . .' a preference that 'must occasionally give way to considerations of public policy and the necessities of the case. . . .' [W]e cannot say that such confrontation is an indispensable element of the Sixth Amendment's guarantee of the right to confront one's accusers. Indeed, one commentator has noted that '[i]t is all but universally assumed that there are circumstances that excuse compliance with the right of confrontation.'"

"This interpretation of the Confrontation Clause is consistent with our cases holding that other Sixth Amendment rights must also be interpreted in the context of the necessities of trial and the adversary process. . . . We see no reason to treat the face-to-face component of the confrontation right any differently. . . ."

"Maryland's statutory procedure . . . prevents a child witness from seeing the defendant as he or she testifies against the defendant at trial. We find it significant . . . that Maryland's procedure preserves all of the other elements of the confrontation right. . . . We are therefore confident that use of the one-way closed circuit television procedure . . . does not impinge upon the truth-seeking or symbolic purposes of the Confrontation Clause."

"We likewise conclude today that a State's interest in the physical and psychological well-being of child abuse victims may be sufficiently important to outweigh, at least in some cases, a defendant's right to face his or her accusers in court. That a significant majority of States have enacted statutes to protect child witnesses from the trauma of giving testimony in child abuse cases attests to the widespread belief in the importance of such a public policy."

"[W]e conclude that where necessary to protect a child witness from trauma that would be caused by testifying in the physical presence of the defendant, at least where such trauma would impair the child's ability to communicate, the Confrontation Clause does not prohibit use of a procedure that, despite the absence of face-to-face confrontation, ensures the reliability of the evidence by subjecting it to rigorous adversarial testing. . . ."

C. Waiver of Right to Be Present

1. Voluntary Absence

Taylor v. United States, 414 U.S. 17 (1973)

Vote: 9-0

FACTS: Taylor failed to return for the afternoon session of his trial on four charges of selling cocaine. He was present when the morning session ended, when the court announced the afternoon schedule, and when he was told by his attorney to return at the appointed time. The judge then recessed the trial until the following morning when Taylor's wife testified that she had left court the previous day with Taylor; that they had separated after sharing a taxi; that he had not seemed ill; and, finally, that she had not heard from him since. The judge then denied a motion for mistrial by his attorney, who asserted that the jurors' minds would be tainted by Taylor's absence and that continuation of the trial deprived him of his Sixth Amendment right to confront the witnesses against him. Relying upon rules that provided that a defendant's voluntary absence should not prevent the continuation of the trial, the court found that Taylor had absented himself voluntarily. During the rest of the trial, the court admonished the jury not to infer guilt from Taylor's absence and ultimately, Taylor was found guilty of all charges.

ISSUE: Is the Sixth Amendment right to be present and to confront witnesses at trial violated if the accused is voluntarily absent from the proceedings?

HOLDING: No.

RATIONALE: "There is no challenge to the trial court's conclusion that petitioner's absence from the trial was voluntary, and no claim that the continuation of the trial was not authorized by Rule 43. Nor are we persuaded that Rule 43 is unconstitutional or that petitioner was deprived of any constitutional rights in the circumstances before us. Rule 43 . . . reflects the long-standing rule recognized by this Court in *Diaz v. United States*, 223 U.S. 442 (1912) 'where the offense is not capital and the accused is not in custody, the prevailing rule has been, that if, after the trial has begun in his presence, he voluntarily absents himself, this does not nullify what has been done or prevent the completion of the trial, but, on the contrary, operates as a waiver of his right to be present and leaves the court free to proceed with the trial. . . .'"

"Petitioner, however, insists that his mere voluntary absence from his trial cannot be construed as an effective waiver, that is, 'an intentional relinquishment or abandonment of a known right or privilege.'"

"[W]e cannot accept this position. . . . The right at issue is the right to be present, and the question becomes whether that right was effectively waived by his voluntary absence. Consistent with Rule 43 and Diaz, we conclude that it was."

"It seems equally incredible to us, as it did to the Court of Appeals, 'that a defendant who flees from a courtroom in the midst of a trial—where judge, jury, witnesses, and lawyers are present and ready to continue—would not know that as a consequence the trial could continue in his absence. . . .' Moreover, no issue of the voluntariness of his disappearance was ever raised. As was recently noted, 'there can be no doubt whatever that the governmental prerogative to proceed with a trial may not be defeated by conduct of the accused that prevents the trial from going forward.'"

2. Unruly Behavior and Trial Proceedings

Illinois v. Allen, 397 U.S. 337 (1970)
Vote: 9-0
FACTS: William Allen entered a bar and after ordering a drink, took $200 from the bartender at gunpoint. At the trial, Allen was allowed to defend himself after refusing a lawyer, but one was appointed for him as an advisor. During voir dire, Allen verbally abused the judge after he was told to confine his questions to the qualifications of the prospective jurors. The judge ordered the appointed lawyer to take over. Allen stated that the attorney would not represent him and then threatened the judge's life. Allen then tore his file and the judge warned him that he would be removed from the court if he continued. Allen continued his abuse stating that no trial would take place and that the court could do whatever it liked to discipline him. After further abuse, Allen was removed and voir dire continued.

Before the jury was brought in for the afternoon trial, Allen complained about his attorney and the fairness of the trial. He also said he wanted to be present during the trial, and the judge stated that as long as he "behaved himself" he would be allowed to stay. Allen's lawyer then moved to have him removed, whereupon Allen began to protest, threatening to stop the trial by continuously talking and asking for his relatives to be allowed to testify for him. The trial judge then ordered Allen removed, and he was only brought in for purposes of identification during the prosecution's case. During one appearance, he again verbally abused the judge, but after the prosecution rested, the judge told Allen that if he conducted himself properly he would be allowed to stay. After Allen gave his assurance, he was permitted to return to the courtroom, with the rest of the trial conducted by his appointed lawyer. Eventually he was convicted of armed robbery.
ISSUE: Is the Sixth Amendment right to be present at trial violated when the accused is removed for unruly conduct?

HOLDING: No.

RATIONALE: "We cannot agree that the Sixth Amendment, the cases upon which the Court of Appeals relied, or any other cases of this Court so handicap a trial judge in conducting a criminal trial. . . . [W]e explicitly hold today that a defendant can lose his right to be present at trial if, after he has been warned by the judge that he will be removed if he continues his disruptive behavior, he nevertheless insists on conducting himself in a manner so disorderly, disruptive, and disrespectful of the court that his trial cannot be carried on with him in the courtroom."

"It is essential to the proper administration of criminal justice that dignity, order, and decorum be the hallmarks of all court proceedings in our country. The flagrant disregard in the courtroom of elementary standards of proper conduct should not and cannot be tolerated. We believe trial judges confronted with disruptive, contumacious, stubbornly defiant defendants must be given sufficient discretion to meet the circumstances of each case."

"But our courts, palladiums of liberty as they are, cannot be treated disrespectfully with impunity. Nor can the accused be permitted by his disruptive conduct indefinitely to avoid being tried on the charges brought against him. It would degrade our country and our judicial system to permit our courts to be bullied, insulted, and humiliated and their orderly progress thwarted and obstructed by defendants brought before them charged with crimes. As guardians of the public welfare, our state and federal judicial systems strive to administer equal justice to the rich and the poor, the good and the bad, the native and foreign born of every race, nationality, and religion. Being manned by humans, the courts are not perfect and are bound to make some errors. But, if our courts are to remain what the Founders intended, the citadels of justice, their proceedings cannot and must not be infected with the sort of scurrilous, abusive language and conduct paraded before the Illinois trial judge in this case."

D. Defendant Opportunity for Cross-Examination

Kentucky v. Stincer, 482 U.S. 730 (1987)

Vote: 6-3

FACTS: Sergio Stincer was indicted for committing first-degree sodomy with three young children. After the jury was sworn, but before evidence was presented, the court conducted an in-chambers hearing to determine if the two young girls were competent to testify. Stincer's lawyer objected when Stincer was excluded from the hearing. The two girls were examined separately and the judge, prosecutor, and Stincer's lawyer asked questions to determine if they were capable of recalling facts and whether they understood the difference between telling the truth and telling a lie. The two children were not asked about the testimony they would give at trial. The judge found that the girls were competent, and Stincer's lawyer did not object.

Before each of the girls began their testimony, the prosecutor repeated some of the questions about their background that they had been asked at the hearing. Both girls testified that Stincer had used a sock and inserted his genitals into their mouths. On cross-examination, Stincer's lawyer repeated some of the questions from the hearing that were designed to ascertain their ability to tell the truth. After the testimony of the girls was concluded, Stincer's lawyer did not request that the judge reconsider his competency rulings. Stincer was eventually convicted.

ISSUE: Is the Sixth Amendment right of an accused to confront witnesses violated when he is excluded from a hearing held to determine the competency of child witnesses?

HOLDING: No.

RATIONALE: "Although claims arising under the Confrontation Clause may not always fall neatly into one of these two categories, these cases reflect the Confrontation Clause's functional purpose in ensuring a defendant an opportunity for cross-examination. . . . Of course, the Confrontation Clause guarantees only 'an *opportunity* for effective cross-examination, not cross-examination that is effective in whatever way, and to whatever extent, the defense might wish. . . .' This limitation is consistent with the concept that the right to confrontation is a functional one for the purpose of promoting reliability in a criminal trial."

"[I]t is more useful to consider whether excluding the defendant from the hearing interferes with his opportunity for effective cross-examination. No such interference occurred when respondent was excluded from the competency hearing of the two young girls in this case. After the trial court determined that the two children were competent to testify, they appeared and testified in open court. At that point, the two witnesses were subject to full and complete cross-examination, and were so examined. . . . There was no Kentucky rule of law, nor any ruling by the trial court, that restricted respondent's ability to cross-examine the witnesses at trial."

"[Q]uestions at a competency hearing usually are limited to matters that are unrelated to the basic issues of the trial. Children often are asked their names, where they go to school, how old they are, whether they know who the judge is, whether they know what a lie is, and whether they know what happens when one tells a lie."

"At the close of the children's testimony, respondent's counsel, had he thought it appropriate, was in a position to move that the court reconsider its competency rulings on the ground that the direct and cross-examination had elicited evidence that the young girls lacked the basic requisites for serving as competent witnesses. Thus, the critical tool of cross-examination was available to counsel as a means of establishing that the witnesses were not competent to testify, as well as a means of undermining the credibility of their testimony."

"Because respondent had the opportunity for full and effective cross-examination of the two witnesses during trial, and because of the nature of the competency hearing at issue in this case, we conclude that respondent's rights under the Confrontation Clause were not violated by his exclusion from the competency hearing of the two girls."

E. Hearsay and Confrontation

1. Spousal Recorded Testimony

Crawford v. Washington, 541 U.S. 36 (2004)

Vote: 9-0

FACTS: Kenneth Lee was stabbed at his apartment, and police arrested Michael D. Crawford later that night. After giving Crawford and his wife, Sylvia, *Miranda* warnings, detectives interrogated each of them twice. Crawford eventually confessed that he and Sylvia had looked for Lee because Crawford was upset over an incident in which Lee had tried to rape Sylvia. The two had found him at his apartment, and a fight ensued in which Lee was stabbed and Crawford's hand was cut. Sylvia corroborated Crawford's story, but her account of the fight itself was different—particularly with respect to whether Lee had drawn a weapon before Crawford assaulted him. Crawford was charged with assault and attempted murder. He claimed self-defense. Sylvia did not testify because of the marital privilege, which bars a spouse from testifying without the other spouse's consent. In Washington, the privilege does not extend to out-of-court statements admissible under a hearsay exception. The State played Sylvia's tape-recorded statements as evidence that the stabbing was not in self-defense, even though Crawford did not have the ability to cross-examine. The jury convicted Crawford of assault, and on appeal Crawford argued that the admission of the tape-recorded statement violated his right to cross-examine witnesses against him.

ISSUE: Does the playing of defendant's spouse's tape-recorded statement violate the Sixth Amendment right to confront witnesses at trial?

HOLDING: Yes.

RATIONALE: "As the English authorities . . . reveal, the common law in 1791 conditioned admissibility of an absent witness's examination on unavailability and a prior opportunity to cross-examine. The Sixth Amendment therefore incorporates those limitations. The numerous early state decisions applying the same test confirm that these principles were received as part of the common law in this country."

"[T]here is scant evidence that exceptions were invoked to admit *testimonial* statements against the accused in a *criminal* case."

"Our later cases conform to *Mattox* [*v. United States,* 156 U.S. 237 (1895)]'s holding that prior trial or preliminary hearing testimony is admissible only if the defendant had an adequate opportunity to cross-examine. . . . Even where the defendant had such an opportunity, we excluded the testimony where the government had not established unavailability of the witness."

"Our cases have thus remained faithful to the Framers' understanding: Testimonial statements of witnesses absent from trial have been admitted only where the declarant is unavailable, and only where the defendant has had a prior opportunity to cross-examine."

"Where testimonial statements are involved, we do not think the Framers meant to leave the Sixth Amendment's protection to the vagaries of the rules of evidence, much less to amorphous notions of 'reliability. . . .' It commands, not that evidence be reliable, but that reliability be assessed in a particular manner: by testing in the crucible of cross-examination."

"Dispensing with confrontation because testimony is obviously reliable is akin to dispensing with jury trial because a defendant is obviously guilty. This is not what the Sixth Amendment prescribes."

"That inculpating statements are given in a testimonial setting is not an antidote to the confrontation problem, but rather the trigger that makes the Clause's demands most urgent. It is not enough to point out that most of the usual safeguards of the adversary process attend the statement, when the single safeguard missing is the one the Confrontation Clause demands."

"The Framers . . . were loath to leave too much discretion in judicial hands."

"Where testimonial evidence is at issue, however, the Sixth Amendment demands what the common law required: unavailability and a prior opportunity for cross-examination."

2. Emergency and Evidentiary Statements

Davis v. Washington 126 S.Ct. 2266 (2006)
Vote: 8-1
FACTS: A 911 call operator reversed a call and Michelle McCottry answered and proceeded to detail a fight that she had with Davis in which he assaulted her and left injuries. The operator asker her questions about who Davis was, what he was doing, and the nature of their fight. Police arrived and took note of her injuries and her desire to get her things and her children out of the apartment. Davis was charged with felony violation of a domestic no-contact order. The prosecution's only witnesses were the two officers that arrived on the scene. Both officers testified that McCottry had recent injuries, but neither could testify as to the cause of the injuries. McCottry did not appear, but the trial court admitted the recorded 911 call as testimony. Davis objected, arguing that his right to confront the witnesses against him was violated, but to no avail. The Washington Court of Appeals and the Supreme Court of Washington both affirmed.
ISSUE: Are statements nontestimonial for purposes of the Sixth Amendment Confrontation Clause when they are made during an emergency situation and testimonial when the purpose of interrogation is to prove events for use in a criminal case?
HOLDING: Yes.
RATIONALE: "A critical portion of this holding, and the portion central to resolution of the two cases now before us, is the phrase 'testimonial statements.' Only statements of this sort cause the declarant to be a 'witness' within the meaning of the Confrontation Clause. . . . It is the testimonial character of the statement that separates it from other hearsay that, while subject to traditional limitations upon hearsay evidence, is not subject to the Confrontation Clause."

"Without attempting to produce an exhaustive classification of all conceivable statements . . . as either testimonial or nontestimonial, it suffices to decide the present cases to hold as follows: Statements are nontestimonial when made in the course of police interrogation under circumstances objectively indicating that the primary purpose of the interrogation is to enable police assistance to meet an ongoing emergency. They are testimonial when the circumstances objectively indicate that there is no such ongoing emergency, and that the primary purpose of the interrogation is to establish or prove past events potentially relevant to later criminal prosecution."

"We are not aware of any early American case invoking the Confrontation Clause or the common-law right to confrontation that did not clearly involve testimony as thus defined. Well into the 20th century, our own Confrontation Clause jurisprudence was carefully applied only in the testimonial context."

F. Defendant Right to Compulsory Process

United States v. Valenzuela-Bernal, 458 U.S. 858 (1982)
Vote: 7-2
FACTS: Valenzuela-Bernal entered the United States illegally from Mexico and was taken by smugglers to a house in Escondido, California. In exchange for his not having to pay the smugglers, he agreed to drive five others to Los Angeles. Agents tried to stop his car at a checkpoint after they noticed five people lying down inside the car, but Valenzuela-Bernal accelerated and drove through. Agents gave chase, and Valenzuela-Bernal stopped and fled on foot with the five passengers. Subsequently, three of the passengers and Valenzuela-Bernal were apprehended by Border Patrol agents. Valenzuela-Bernal admitted his illegal entry into the country and explained his reason for not stopping: "I was bringing the people [and] I already knew I had had it—too late—it was done." The three passengers also admitted that they were illegally in the country and each identified Valenzuela-Bernal as the driver. An Assistant U.S. Attorney concluded that two passengers had no evidence material to the prosecution or defense of Valenzuela-Bernal so they were deported. The third, Morales, was detained to provide a basis for establishing that Valenzuela-Bernal had transported the aliens.

Valenzuela-Bernal was indicted for illegally transporting Enrique Romero-Morales. He moved to dismiss the indictment, claiming that deporting the two passengers violated his Sixth Amendment right to compulsory process for obtaining favorable witnesses. He was then found guilty after a bench trial, but his conviction was overturned on appeal.
ISSUE: Does the deportation of alien witnesses violate the Sixth Amendment right to compulsory process for obtaining favorable witnesses if there is no showing that the evidence lost would be both material and favorable to the defense?
HOLDING: No.
RATIONALE: "Congress has adopted a policy of apprehending illegal aliens at or near the border and deporting them promptly. Border Patrol agents are authorized by statute to make warrantless arrests of aliens suspected of 'attempting to enter the

United States in violation of . . . law . . .' and are directed to examine them without 'unnecessary delay' to determine whether 'there is prima facie evidence establishing' their attempted illegal entry. . . . Aliens against whom such evidence exists may be granted immediate voluntary departure from the country. . . . Thus, Congress has determined that prompt deportation, such as occurred in this case, constitutes the most effective method for curbing the enormous flow of illegal aliens across our southern border."

"In addition to satisfying immigration policy, the prompt deportation of alien witnesses who are determined by the Government to possess no material evidence relevant to a criminal trial is justified by several practical considerations. . . . Thus, the detention of alien eyewitnesses imposes substantial financial and physical burdens upon the Government, not to mention the human cost to potential witnesses who are incarcerated though charged with no crime."

"Congress' immigration policy and the practical considerations discussed above demonstrate that the Government had good reason to deport respondent's passengers once it concluded that they possessed no evidence relevant to the prosecution or the defense."

"The only recent decision of this Court dealing with the right to compulsory process guaranteed by the Sixth Amendment suggests that more than the mere absence of testimony is necessary to establish a violation of the right. . . . Indeed, the Sixth Amendment does not by its terms grant to a criminal defendant the right to secure the attendance and testimony of any and all witnesses: it guarantees him 'compulsory process for obtaining *witnesses in his favor*. . . .' [R]espondent cannot establish a violation of his constitutional right to compulsory process merely by showing that deportation of the passengers deprived him of their testimony. He must at least make some plausible showing of how their testimony would have been both material and favorable to his defense."

"To summarize, the responsibility of the Executive Branch faithfully to execute the immigration policy . . . justifies the prompt deportation of illegal-alien witnesses upon the . . . good-faith determination that they possess no evidence favorable to the defendant. . . . The mere fact that the Government deports such witnesses is not sufficient to establish a violation of the Compulsory Process Clause of the Sixth Amendment. . . . A violation of these provisions requires some showing that the evidence lost would be both material and favorable to the defense."

G. Right to Counsel

1. Limitations Due to Conflict of Interest

Wheat v. United States, 486 U.S. 153 (1988)
Vote: 5-4
FACTS: Over a period of years, a drug distribution ring transported marijuana from Mexico and other locations to Southern California. Mark Wheat was an intermediary

who stored the marijuana in his home and then distributed it to customers in the re-
gion. Juvenal Gomez-Barajas was also involved and was acquitted on drug charges
overlapping with those against Wheat. To avoid a second trial on other charges, he offered to plead guilty, but by the beginning of Wheat's trial, the court had not accepted
the plea.

Javier Bravo, a third member of the conspiracy, decided to plead guilty to one count
of transporting 2,400 pounds of marijuana from Los Angeles to a home controlled by
Victor Vidal. At the conclusion of Bravo's proceedings, Gomez-Barajas and Bravo's attorney, Eugene Iredale, notified the court that he had been contacted by Wheat and had
been asked to take his case, after which the prosecution became concerned about a conflict of interest. At a hearing, the prosecution objected to Wheat's proposed use of
Iredale on the ground that his representation of Gomez-Barajas and Bravo created a
conflict of interest because if Gomez-Barajas's plea agreement did not work out, he
would be tried and be represented by Iredale, who would also be representing Wheat.
As a result, he would not be allowed to cross-examine Wheat and therefore be prevented from effectively representing Gomez-Barajas. Additionally, Iredale's representation of Bravo would affect his ability to represent Wheat because some of the marijuana
transported by Bravo was given to Wheat, preventing him from examining Bravo.
Wheat then argued his right to have counsel of his own choosing and the willingness
of the three defendants to waive the right to conflict-free counsel, stating that the prosecution's assertions were only speculative. After hearing from each side, the court
found that the conflict existed and denied Wheat's request to hire Iredale. Wheat was
then convicted of conspiracy to possess more than 1,000 pounds of marijuana with intent to distribute and five counts of possessing marijuana with intent to distribute.

ISSUE: Can a court deny an accused's waiver of his right to conflict-free counsel by refusing to permit the accused's proposed substitution of attorneys?

HOLDING: Yes.

RATIONALE: "[W]hile the right to select and be represented by one's preferred attorney is comprehended by the Sixth Amendment, the essential aim of the Amendment is
to guarantee an effective advocate for each criminal defendant rather than to ensure
that a defendant will inexorably be represented by the lawyer whom he prefers."

"The Sixth Amendment right to choose one's own counsel is circumscribed in several important respects. Regardless of his persuasive powers, an advocate who is not a
member of the bar may not represent clients (other than himself) in court. Similarly, a
defendant may not insist on representation by an attorney he cannot afford or who for
other reasons declines to represent the defendant. Nor may a defendant insist on the
counsel of an attorney who has a previous or ongoing relationship with an opposing
party, even when the opposing party is the Government. The question raised in this
case is the extent to which a criminal defendant's right under the Sixth Amendment to
his chosen attorney is qualified by the fact that the attorney has represented other defendants charged in the same criminal conspiracy."

"For these reasons we think the district court must be allowed substantial latitude in
refusing waivers of conflicts of interest not only in those rare cases where an actual conflict may be demonstrated before trial, but in the more common cases where a poten-

tial for conflict exists which may or may not burgeon into an actual conflict as the trial progresses. In the circumstances of this case, with the motion for substitution of counsel made so close to the time of trial, the District Court relied on instinct and judgment based on experience in making its decision. We do not think it can be said that the court exceeded the broad latitude which must be accorded it in making this decision."

2. Right to Confer with Counsel

a. During Overnight Recess

Geders v. United States, 425 U.S. 80 (1976)
Vote: 8-0

FACTS: A grand jury in Florida indicted Geders and others with conspiracy to import and illegal importation of a controlled substance into the United States and with possession of marihuana. Geders testified in his own defense, and before he finished the court recessed for the night. After the jury left, the prosecutor asked the judge to instruct Geders not to discuss the case overnight with anyone. The judge had given the same instruction to all witnesses whose testimony was interrupted by a recess. Geders's attorney objected, explaining that he believed he had a right to confer with his client about matters other than the cross-examination, and that he wished to discuss the trial. The judge doubted that Geders would be able to confine the conversation, saying: "I think he would understand it if I told him just not to talk to you; and I just think it is better that he not talk to you about anything." The judge suggested that he could still have an opportunity to speak with Geders, and he indicated that he would grant a recess the next day so that he could do so after his testimony ended. Geders's lawyer continued to object but agreed that he would follow the judge's order. When court convened, Geders's attorney reopened his direct examination of Geders and the recross-examination finished soon after. The judge then called the lunch break, and Geders was permitted to confer with his attorney during the recess. The trial concluded the following day, and Geders was convicted of all charges.

ISSUE: Does a judge's order directing a defendant not to consult his attorney during an overnight recess deprive him of the Sixth Amendment right to assistance of counsel?

HOLDING: Yes.

RATIONALE: "There are other ways to deal with the problem of possible improper influence on testimony or 'coaching' of a witness short of putting a barrier between client and counsel for so long a period as 17 hours. The opposing counsel in the adversary system is not without weapons to cope with 'coached' witnesses. A prosecutor may cross-examine a defendant as to the extent of any 'coaching' during a recess, subject, of course, to the control of the court. Skillful cross-examination could develop a record which the prosecutor in closing argument might well exploit by raising questions as to the defendant's credibility. . . . In addition the trial judge, if he doubts that defense counsel will observe the ethical limits on guiding witnesses, may direct that the examination of the witness continue without interruption until completed. If the judge considers the risk high he may arrange the sequence of testimony so that direct and cross-examination of a witness will be completed without interruption. That this would not be feasible in some cases due to the length of direct and cross-examination does not alter the availability, in most cases, of a solution that does not cut off communication for so long a period as presented by this record."

"To the extent that conflict remains between the defendant's right to consult with his attorney during a long overnight recess in the trial, and the prosecutor's desire to cross-examine the defendant without the intervention of counsel, with the risk of improper 'coaching,' the conflict must, under the Sixth Amendment, be resolved in favor of the right to the assistance and guidance of counsel."

"We hold that an order preventing petitioner from consulting his counsel 'about anything' during a 17-hour overnight recess between his direct and cross-examination impinged upon his right to the assistance of counsel guaranteed by the Sixth Amendment."

b. During Brief Recess while Accused Is in the Middle of Testimony

Perry v. Leeke, 488 U.S. 272 (1989)
Vote: 6-3
FACTS: Perry was tried and convicted by a jury of participating in a murder, kidnapping, and sexual assault. His defense was that he had not taken an active part in the abduction or the homicide and that he was forced to commit the sexual assault. Evidence indicated that he was mildly retarded and that he was nonviolent but could be easily influenced. He took the stand and began to testify after a lunch break. After his direct testimony, the trial judge called a fifteen-minute recess, and, without advance notice, told him that he was not allowed to talk to anyone, including his lawyer, during the break. When the trial resumed, Perry's lawyer moved for a mistrial, but the judge denied the motion, explaining that Perry "was in a sense then a ward of the Court. He was not entitled to be cured or assisted or helped approaching his cross examination."
ISSUE: Does a judge's order directing a defendant not to consult his attorney during a fifteen-minute recess deprive him of the Sixth Amendment right to assistance of counsel?
HOLDING: No.
RATIONALE: "The distinction rests instead on the fact that when a defendant becomes a witness, he has no constitutional right to consult with his lawyer while he is testifying. He has an absolute right to such consultation before he begins to testify, but neither he nor his lawyer has a right to have the testimony interrupted in order to give him the benefit of counsel's advice."

"The reason for the rule is one that applies to all witnesses—not just defendants. It is a common practice for a judge to instruct a witness not to discuss his or her testimony with third parties until the trial is completed. Such nondiscussion orders are a corollary of the broader rule that witnesses may be sequestered to lessen the danger that their testimony will be influenced by hearing what other witnesses have to say, and to increase the likelihood that they will confine themselves to truthful statements based on their own recollections. . . . [W]hen he assumes the role of a witness, the rules that generally apply to other witnesses—rules that serve the truth-seeking function of the trial—are generally applicable to him as well. Accordingly, it is entirely appropriate for a trial judge to decide, after listening to the direct examination of any witness, whether the defendant or a nondefendant, that cross-examination is more likely to elicit truthful responses if it goes forward without allowing the witness an opportunity to consult with third parties, including his or her lawyer."

"In other words, the truth-seeking function of the trial can be impeded in ways other than unethical 'coaching.' Cross-examination often depends for its effectiveness on the ability of counsel to punch holes in a witness' testimony at just the right time, in just the right way. Permitting a witness, including a criminal defendant, to consult with counsel after direct examination but before cross-examination grants the witness an opportunity to regroup and regain a poise and sense of strategy that the unaided witness would not possess. This is true even if we assume no deceit on the part of the witness; it is simply an empirical predicate of our system of adversary rather than inquisitorial justice that cross-examination of a witness who is uncounseled between direct examination and cross-examination is more likely to lead to the discovery of truth than is cross-examination of a witness who is given time to pause and consult with his attorney."

"[W]e think the judge must also have the power to maintain the status quo during a brief recess in which there is a virtual certainty that any conversation between the witness and the lawyer would relate to the ongoing testimony."

"We merely hold that the Federal Constitution does not compel every trial judge to allow the defendant to consult with his lawyer while his testimony is in progress if the judge decides that there is a good reason to interrupt the trial for a few minutes."

3. Juveniles

In re Gault, 387 U.S. 1 (1967)
Vote: 7-2
FACTS: Gerald Francis Gault and Ronald Lewis, were arrested by the Sheriff of Gila County in Arizona. Gault was still on probation as a result of his having been with another boy who had stolen a wallet from a woman's purse. The police were led to the boys after a complaint by a neighbor about a lewd phone call. When Gault was arrested, both of his parents were at work and no notice was given that he was being taken to the Children's Detention Home. After his brother discovered that he was in custody, he and his mother went there, and upon their arrival, Probation Officer Flagg told Mrs. Gault why her son was there and that a hearing would be held the following day. Flagg filed a petition with the court that was not given to the Gaults. The petition only stated that Gault needed protection and that he was a delinquent and asked for a hearing. Flagg provided an affidavit in support of it.

Officers Flagg and Henderson, Gault, his mother, and brother appeared before the judge for the hearing. The woman who complained of the rude call was not present.

No one was sworn in, no transcript was taken, and no written record provided. From the oral testimony of those present, it was determined that Gault was questioned about the call, but disagreement existed as to his level of involvement. Officer Flagg stated that Gault had admitted making the lewd comments, while the judge testified that Gault had made one of them. At the conclusion of the hearing, the judge said he would "think about it" and Gault was taken back to detention. A few days later he was sent home.

At a separate hearing, Gault, his friend, Gault's parents, his friend's father, Flagg, and Henderson appeared before the judge. Testimony again differed as to Gault's involvement in the call. The complainant was again not present and the judge told Mrs. Gault that she did not have to be.

At the conclusion of the hearing, a report was filed by the officers with the court but not given to the Gaults. The charge listed was lewd phone calls, and Gault was then committed to the school for delinquents. A habeas corpus petition was then filed for Gault.

The judge testified that his determination that Gault was a habitual problem was based upon the fact that Gault had stolen a baseball glove and lied to police about it. He also stated that no charges were ever filed and no hearing was ever held in that incident. He also testified that Gault had admitted to making other nuisance calls. The petition for relief was then rejected. An appeal was made to the Supreme Court arguing that such unlimited discretion of a court to commit a juvenile without notice of the charges, right to counsel, right to confront witnesses, right to exercise the privilege to be free from self-incrimination, a right to a transcript of the proceedings, and a right to appeal all violate Due Process.

ISSUE: Does a delinquency hearing, which may result in commitment, violate due process if the accused is not advised of his right to counsel?

HOLDING: Yes.

RATIONALE: In *Kent v. United States* [383 U.S. 541 (1966)] . . . we said that 'there is no place in our system of law for reaching a result of such tremendous consequences without ceremony—without hearing, without effective assistance of counsel, without a statement of reasons.'"

"The probation officer cannot act as counsel for the child. His role in the adjudicatory hearing, by statute and in fact, is as arresting officer and witness against the child. Nor can the judge represent the child. There is no material difference in this respect between adult and juvenile proceedings of the sort here involved. In adult proceedings, this contention has been foreclosed by decisions of this Court. A proceeding where the issue is whether the child will be found to be 'delinquent' and subjected to the loss of his liberty for years is comparable in seriousness to a felony prosecution. The juvenile needs the assistance of counsel to cope with problems of law, to make skilled inquiry into the facts, to insist upon regularity of the proceedings, and to ascertain whether he has a defense and to prepare and submit it. The child 'requires the guiding hand of counsel at every step in the proceedings against him.'"

"During the last decade, court decisions, experts, and legislatures have demonstrated increasing recognition of this view. In at least one-third of the States, statutes now provide for the right of representation by retained counsel in juvenile delinquency proceedings, notice of the right, or assignment of counsel, or a combination of these. In other States, court rules have similar provisions."

"The President's Crime Commission has recently recommended that in order to assure 'procedural justice for the child,' it is necessary that 'Counsel . . . be appointed as a matter of course wherever coercive action is a possibility, without requiring any affirmative choice by child or parent.'"

"We conclude that the Due Process Clause of the Fourteenth Amendment requires that in respect of proceedings to determine delinquency which may result in commitment to an institution in which the juvenile's freedom is curtailed, the child and his parents must be notified of the child's right to be represented by counsel retained by them, or if they are unable to afford counsel, that counsel will be appointed to represent the child."

"They had a right expressly to be advised that they might retain counsel and to be confronted with the need for specific consideration of whether they did or did not choose to waive the right. If they were unable to afford to employ counsel, they were entitled in view of the seriousness of the charge and the potential commitment, to appointed counsel, unless they chose waiver."

4. Right to Counsel and Probation Revocation/Sentencing Hearings

Mempa v. Rhay, 389 U.S. 128 (1967)
Vote: 9-0
FACTS: Jerry Douglas Mempa was convicted in the Spokane County Superior Court of "joyriding" based on his guilty plea. He was then given probation for two years on the condition that he spend thirty days in jail, but the imposition of the sentence was deferred. About four months later, the prosecutor moved to revoke Mempa's probation due to his involvement in a burglary. A hearing was held, and Mempa, who was seventeen at the time, was accompanied by his stepfather. He was not represented by counsel and was not asked whether he wished to have counsel appointed. At the hearing, Mempa was asked if he had been involved in the burglary and he answered that he had. A probation officer testified without cross-examination that Mempa had been involved in the burglary and had previously denied it. Without asking Mempa if he had anything to say or any evidence to provide, the court immediately revoked his probation and sentenced him to ten years, but stated that it would recommend to the parole board that he serve only a year. Mempa filed a petition for a writ of habeas corpus, claiming that he had been deprived of his right to counsel at the proceeding at which his probation was revoked and sentence imposed.
ISSUE: Does an accused have the right to counsel at a probation revocation or sentencing hearing?
HOLDING: Yes.
RATIONALE: "There was no occasion in Gideon to enumerate the various stages in a criminal proceeding at which counsel was required, but *Townsend* [*v. Burke*, 334 U.S.

736 (1948)], *Moore* [*v. Michigan*, 355 U.S. 155 (1957)], and *Hamilton* [*v. Alabama*, 368 U.S. 52 (1961)], when the *Betts* [*v. Brady*, 316 U.S. 455 (1942)] requirement of special circumstances is stripped away by *Gideon* [*v. Wainwright*, 372 U.S. 335 (1963)], clearly stand for the proposition that appointment of counsel for an indigent is required at every stage of a criminal proceeding where substantial rights of a criminal accused may be affected. In particular, *Townsend*, illustrates the critical nature of sentencing in a criminal case and might well be considered to support by itself a holding that the right to counsel applies at sentencing."

"[T]he necessity for the aid of counsel in marshaling the facts, introducing evidence of mitigating circumstances and in general aiding and assisting the defendant to present his case as to sentence is apparent."

"Even more important in a case such as this is the fact that certain legal rights may be lost if not exercised at this stage."

"The two foregoing factors assume increased significance when it is considered that, as happened in these two cases, the eventual imposition of sentence on the prior plea of guilty is based on the alleged commission of offenses for which the accused is never tried."

"All we decide here is that a lawyer must be afforded at this proceeding whether it be labeled a revocation of probation or a deferred sentencing. We assume that counsel appointed for the purpose of the trial or guilty plea would not be unduly burdened by being requested to follow through at the deferred sentencing stage of the proceeding."

5. Right to Counsel in Capital Crimes

Powell v. Alabama, 287 U.S. 45 (1932)
Vote: 7-2
FACTS: The defendants, Charlie Weems, Ozie Powell, Clarence Norris, Olen Montgomery, Willie Roberson, Haywood Patterson, Andrew Wright, Leroy Wright, and Eugene Williams, all African Americans, were on a train traveling through Alabama with white boys and girls. A fight took place between the defendants and several white boys, in the course of which the white boys, with the exception of one, were thrown off the train. The two girls, Ruby Bates and Victoria Price, testified that each of them was assaulted by six different men in turn, and they identified the seven defendants as having been among them. Orville Gilley was the only one of the white boys to testify. Before the train reached Scottsboro, a sheriff's posse seized the defendants and two others. Both girls and the defendants then were taken to Scottsboro. Word of the allegations preceded them, and they were met by a large crowd. As the attitude of the community was one of great hostility, the sheriff called the militia to assist in safeguarding the prisoners. It was noted that every step taken from the arrest to the sentence was accompanied by the military. The record does not disclose the defendants' ages, except that one of them was nineteen. They were all illiterate.

Powell and several others were charged with the rape of the two white girls. The men were indicted and arraigned, and they pleaded not guilty on the same day. No attorneys were appointed despite the fact that the record indicated that they had been. The judge stated in court prior to trial that he was appointing all members of the bar to help the defendants, and one attorney volunteered to help.

The state moved to try the cases separately. As the trials proceeded, each defendant was read the charges and he pleaded not guilty, with each trial lasting only one day. Under the law at the time, the jury could fix the punishment for rape from ten years to death. Each of the juries found the defendant guilty and sentenced him to death. The trial court overruled the requests for new trials and imposed the recommended sentences.

ISSUE: Does an indigent accused have the right to appointed counsel in a capital case?

HOLDING: Yes.

RATIONALE: "As early as 1758, Blackstone, although recognizing that the rule was settled at common law, denounced it as not in keeping with the rest of the humane treatment of prisoners by the English law. 'For upon what face of reason,' he says 'can that assistance be denied to save the life of a man, which yet is allowed him in prosecutions for every petty trespass?'"

"Similarly, in South Carolina the original Constitution of 1776 did not contain the provision as to counsel, but it was provided as early as 1731 . . . that every person charged with treason, murder, felony, or other capital offense, should be admitted to make full defense by counsel learned in the law. In Virginia there was no constitutional provision on the subject, but as early as August, 1734 . . . there was an act declaring that in all trials for capital offenses the prisoner, upon his petition to the court, should be allowed counsel."

"[W]e are of opinion that, under the circumstances just stated, the necessity of counsel was so vital and imperative that the failure of the trial court to make an effective appointment of counsel was likewise a denial of due process within the meaning of the Fourteenth Amendment. . . . All that it is necessary now to decide, as we do decide, is that in a capital case, where the defendant is unable to employ counsel, and is incapable adequately of making his own defense because of ignorance, feeble-mindedness, illiteracy, or the like, it is the duty of the court, whether requested or not, to assign counsel for him as a necessary requisite of due process of law; and that duty is not discharged by an assignment at such a time or under such circumstances as to preclude the giving of effective aid in the preparation and trial of the case. To hold otherwise would be to ignore the fundamental postulate, already adverted to, 'that there are certain immutable principles of justice which inhere in the very idea of free government which no member of the Union may disregard.'"

6. Federal Defendants

Johnson v. Zerbst, 304 U.S. 458 (1938)
Vote: 6-2
FACTS: Johnson and Bridwell were arrested in Charleston, South Carolina, and charged with possessing and passing counterfeit twenty-dollar bills while on leave.

They were kept in jail, given notice of the indictment, arraigned, tried, convicted, and sentenced two days later in the United States District Court and transported to Atlanta. While counsel represented them in the preliminary hearings, they were not present for their trial. Neither defendant had relatives, friends, or acquaintances in Charleston, and both had little education and were without funds. They stated that they had never been guilty of or charged with any offense before. In the habeas hearing, evidence showed that no request was directed to the judge to appoint counsel, but that such request was made to the district attorney, who stated that in South Carolina the court did not appoint counsel unless the defendant was charged with a capital crime. Bridwell testified that he didn't feel that he was a criminal, despite what the prosecution said about him. While they were in jail they asked the guard to call an attorney for them, and they were not allowed to contact one on their own. Both petitions for habeas corpus relief had been turned down. They argued that their right to assistance of counsel was violated.

ISSUE: Does an indigent federal defendant have the right to appointed counsel?

HOLDING: Yes.

RATIONALE: "The 'right to be heard would be, in many cases, of little avail if it did not comprehend the right to be heard by counsel. Even the intelligent and educated layman has small and sometimes no skill in the science of law. If charged with a crime, he is incapable, generally, of determining for himself whether the indictment is good or bad. He is unfamiliar with the rules of evidence. Left without the aid of counsel he may be put on trial without a proper charge, and convicted upon incompetent evidence, or evidence irrelevant to the issue or otherwise inadmissible. He lacks both the skill and knowledge adequately to prepare his defense, even though he may have a perfect one. He requires the guiding hand of counsel at every step in the proceedings against him.' The Sixth Amendment withholds from federal courts, in all criminal proceedings, the power and authority to deprive an accused of his life or liberty unless he has or waives the assistance of counsel."

"The constitutional right of an accused to be represented by counsel invokes, of itself, the protection of a trial court, in which the accused—whose life or liberty is at stake—is without counsel. This protecting duty imposes the serious and weighty responsibility upon the trial judge of determining whether there is an intelligent and competent waiver by the accused. While an accused may waive the right to counsel, whether there is a proper waiver should be clearly determined by the trial court, and it would be fitting and appropriate for that determination to appear upon the record."

7. Right to Counsel in State Court

a. Appointed Counsel and Due Process

Gideon v. Wainwright, 372 U.S. 335 (1963)

Vote: 9-0

FACTS: Clarence Earl Gideon was charged in a Florida court with breaking and entering into a poolroom with intent to commit a misdemeanor, which was a felony. Without any money or a lawyer, Gideon asked the judge to appoint a lawyer for him. The judge refused, citing state law that only allowed for appointed counsel in capital cases. Gideon defended himself and conducted many of the activities that a lawyer would have, such as making an opening statement, cross-examining the State's witnesses, presenting witnesses on his own behalf, and reasserting his innocence. The jury convicted him, and he was sentenced to five years in the state prison. He then filed an appeal arguing that the failure of the state to provide counsel for him at his trial violated his rights.

ISSUE: Does the Sixth Amendment provision that an accused has the right to assistance of counsel apply to the states via the Fourteenth Amendment?

HOLDING: Yes.

RATIONALE: "We accept *Betts v. Brady* [316 U.S. 455 (1942)]'s assumption, based as it was on our prior cases, that a provision of the Bill of Rights which is 'fundamental and essential to a fair trial' is made obligatory upon the States by the Fourteenth Amendment. We think the Court in Betts was wrong, however, in concluding that the Sixth Amendment's guarantee of counsel is not one of these fundamental rights. Ten years before *Betts*, this Court, after full consideration of all the historical data examined in Betts, had unequivocally declared that 'the right to the aid of counsel is of this fundamental character. . . .' While the Court at the close of its Powell opinion did by its language, as this Court frequently does, limit its holding to the particular facts and circumstances of that case, its conclusions about the fundamental nature of the right to counsel are unmistakable."

"[T]he Court in *Betts* made an abrupt break with its own well-considered precedents. In returning to these old precedents, sounder we believe than the new, we but restore constitutional principles established to achieve a fair system of justice. Not only these precedents but also reason and reflection require us to recognize that in our adversary system of criminal justice, any person haled into court, who is too poor to hire a lawyer, cannot be assured a fair trial unless counsel is provided for him. This seems to us to be an obvious truth. . . . That government hires lawyers to prosecute and defendants who have the money hire lawyers to defend are the strongest indications of the widespread belief that lawyers in criminal courts are necessities, not luxuries. The right of one charged with crime to counsel may not be deemed fundamental and essential to fair trials in some countries, but it is in ours. This noble ideal cannot be realized if the poor man charged with crime has to face his accusers without a lawyer to assist him."

b. Representation and Incarceration

Argersinger v. Hamlin, 407 U.S. 25 (1972)
Vote: 9-0

FACTS: Argersinger was charged in Florida with carrying a concealed weapon, punishable by imprisonment up to six months, a $1,000 fine, or both. He had a bench trial and did not have a lawyer. He was convicted and sentenced to serve ninety days in jail, Argersinger brought a habeas corpus petition alleging he was unable as an indigent layman to raise a sufficient defense without an appointed lawyer and that one should have been provided for him.

ISSUE: Can a person be incarcerated if they were not provided a lawyer at trial?

HOLDING: No.

RATIONALE: "We reject, therefore, the premise that since prosecutions for crimes punishable by imprisonment for less than six months may be tried without a jury, they may also be tried without a lawyer."

"The requirement of counsel may well be necessary for a fair trial even in a petty-offense prosecution. We are by no means convinced that legal and constitutional questions involved in a case that actually leads to imprisonment even for a brief period are any less complex than when a person can be sent off for six months or more."

"The trial of vagrancy cases is illustrative. While only brief sentences of imprisonment may be imposed, the cases often bristle with thorny constitutional questions."

"Beyond the problem of trials and appeals is that of the guilty plea, a problem which looms large in misdemeanor as well as in felony cases. Counsel is needed so that the accused may know precisely what he is doing, so that he is fully aware of the prospect of going to jail or prison, and so that he is treated fairly by the prosecution."

"We must conclude, therefore, that the problems associated with misdemeanor and petty offenses often require the presence of counsel to insure the accused a fair trial. Mr. Justice Powell suggests that these problems are raised even in situations where there is no prospect of imprisonment. . . . And, as we said in *Baldwin* [*v. New York*, 399 U.S. 66 (1970)] . . . , 'the prospect of imprisonment for however short a time will seldom be viewed by the accused as a trivial or "petty" matter and may well result in quite serious repercussions affecting his career and his reputation.'"

"We hold, therefore, that absent a knowing and intelligent waiver, no person may be imprisoned for any offense, whether classified as petty, misdemeanor, or felony, unless he was represented by counsel at his trial."

c. Appointed Counsel and Authorized Imprisonment

Scott v. Illinois, 440 U.S. 367 (1979)

Vote: 5-4

FACTS: Aubrey Scott was convicted of shoplifting merchandise valued at less than $150 and fined $50 after a bench trial. The statute set the maximum penalty at a $500 fine or one year in jail, or both. Scott argued that a line of cases that culminated with *Argersinger* required that states must provide counsel whenever imprisonment is an authorized penalty.

ISSUE: Are the states required to provide appointed counsel for indigent defendants if a statute merely authorizes incarceration, even if only a fine is imposed?

HOLDING: No.

RATIONALE: "We agree with the Supreme Court of Illinois that the Federal Constitution does not require a state trial court to appoint counsel for a criminal defendant such as petitioner."

"There is considerable doubt that the Sixth Amendment itself, as originally drafted by the Framers of the Bill of Rights, contemplated any guarantee other than the right of an accused in a criminal prosecution in a federal court to employ a lawyer to assist in his defense."

"[W]e conclude today that *Argersinger* [v. *Hamlin*, 407 U.S. 25 (1972)] did indeed delimit the constitutional right to appointed counsel in state criminal proceedings. . . . [W]e believe that the central premise of *Argersinger*—that actual imprisonment is a penalty different in kind from fines or the mere threat of imprisonment—is eminently sound and warrants adoption of actual imprisonment as the line defining the constitutional right to appointment of counsel. *Argersinger* has proved reasonably workable, whereas any extension would create confusion and impose unpredictable, but necessarily substantial, costs on 50 quite diverse States. We therefore hold that the Sixth and Fourteenth Amendments to the United States Constitution require only that no indigent criminal defendant be sentenced to a term of imprisonment unless the State has afforded him the right to assistance of appointed counsel in his defense."

8. Effective Assistance of Counsel

a. The Test for Ineffective Assistance of Counsel

Strickland v. Washington, 466 U.S. 668 (1984)
Vote: 7-2
FACTS: During a ten-day period, Washington committed three murders, torture, kidnapping, assaults, attempted murders, attempted extortion, and theft. After his accomplices were arrested, he surrendered and confessed to some of the crimes. He was indicted for kidnapping and murder and provided a lawyer. Counsel actively pursued pretrial motions and discovery but limited his efforts after Washington confessed to the other two murders. The indictment was then modified to reflect additional charges. Washington waived his right to a jury trial and pleaded guilty to all charges. He told the judge that he had no prior record, that his crimes were motivated by his inability to support his family, and that he accepted responsibility for them. The judge made no statement about his sentence.

Washington waived his right to a jury for sentencing and opted to be sentenced by the judge. In preparing for the sentencing, counsel spoke with Washington about his background. He also spoke with his wife and mother but did not follow up on an attempt to meet them. He did not seek out character witnesses, nor did he request a psychiatric examination since he felt that Washington was not mentally ill. He relied on the plea discussion with the judge for information about Washington, thereby preventing cross-examination by the prosecution. He also did not request a presentence report because he knew that it would undermine Washington's claim of having no significant criminal history. At the sentencing, Washington's lawyer based his argument on the information provided at the plea discussion and on the contention that Washington's remorse, surrender, and duress, should mitigate to save his life. He did not cross-examine any of the State's witnesses at this stage. The judge found several aggravating circumstances with respect to each of the murders and nothing in mitigation. He then sentenced Washington to death on each of the murders and to prison for the other offenses.

On appeal, Washington argued ineffective assistance of counsel at the sentencing on several grounds, arguing that his lawyer failed to: ask for a continuance to prepare for sentencing, request a psychiatric report, present character witnesses, seek a presentence report, present meaningful arguments to the judge, and investigate the medical reports or cross-examine the medical experts. In support of the claim, Washington submitted affidavits from people who said that they would have testified if asked to do so. He also submitted one psychiatric report and one psychological report stating that he was 'chronically frustrated and depressed because of his economic dilemma' at the time of his crimes. The court denied his request for relief.

ISSUE: Is the test for ineffective assistance of counsel that the defendant must show that the lawyer was not functioning so as to provide reasonably effective assistance and that the lawyer's errors were so serious that but for those errors the result of the trial would have been different?

HOLDING: Yes.

RATIONALE: "Counsel, however, can also deprive a defendant of the right to effective assistance."

"A convicted defendant's claim that counsel's assistance was so defective as to require reversal of a conviction or death sentence has two components. First, the defendant must show that counsel's performance was deficient. This requires showing that counsel made errors so serious that counsel was not functioning as the 'counsel' guaranteed the defendant by the Sixth Amendment. Second, the defendant must show that the deficient performance prejudiced the defense. This requires showing that counsel's errors were so serious as to deprive the defendant of a fair trial, a trial whose result is reliable. Unless a defendant makes both showings, it cannot be said that the conviction or death sentence resulted from a breakdown in the adversary process that renders the result unreliable."

"As all the Federal Courts of Appeals have now held, the proper standard for attorney performance is that of reasonably effective assistance. . . . When a convicted defendant complains of the ineffectiveness of counsel's assistance, the defendant must show that counsel's representation fell below an objective standard of reasonableness."

"Thus, a court deciding an actual ineffectiveness claim must judge the reasonableness of counsel's challenged conduct on the facts of the particular case, viewed as of the time of counsel's conduct. A convicted defendant making a claim of ineffective assistance must identify the acts or omissions of counsel that are alleged not to have been the result of reasonable professional judgment. The court must then determine whether, in light of all the circumstances, the identified acts or omissions were outside the wide range of professionally competent assistance."

"Accordingly, any deficiencies in counsel's performance must be prejudicial to the defense in order to constitute ineffective assistance under the Constitution."

"The defendant must show that there is a reasonable probability that, but for counsel's unprofessional errors, the result of the proceeding would have been different. A reasonable probability is a probability sufficient to undermine confidence in the outcome."

"When a defendant challenges a conviction, the question is whether there is a reasonable probability that, absent the errors, the factfinder would have had a reasonable doubt respecting guilt. When a defendant challenges a death sentence such as the one at issue in this case, the question is whether there is a reasonable probability that, absent the errors, the sentencer—including an appellate court, to the extent it independently reweighs the evidence—would have concluded that the balance of aggravating and mitigating circumstances did not warrant death."

"The principles governing ineffectiveness claims should apply in federal collateral proceedings as they do on direct appeal or in motions for a new trial."

b. Counsel Falling Below Standards and Prejudicing the Jury

Wiggins v. Smith, 539 U.S. 510 (2003)
Vote: 7-2

FACTS: Police discovered Florence Lacs drowned in the bathtub of her ransacked apartment in Woodlawn, Maryland. The State indicted Kevin Wiggins and filed a notice of intention to seek the death penalty. Two public defenders, Carl Schlaich and Michelle Nethercott, assumed responsibility for his case. Wiggins elected to be tried before a judge. He was found guilty of first-degree murder, robbery, and two counts of theft. Wiggins elected to be sentenced by a jury, and his lawyers filed a motion to bifurcate the sentencing so that they could show that he did not do the killing and to present a mitigation case. The court denied the motion and sentencing began. Nethercott told the jury they would hear evidence suggesting that someone else killed Lacs and then explained that the judge would instruct them to weigh Wiggins's clean record as a factor against a death sentence. She also stated that she was going to discuss Wiggins's difficult life, but she never did.

Before closing arguments, Schlaich made a proffer to the court, detailing the mitigation case counsel would have presented had the court granted their motion. At no point did Schlaich proffer any evidence of Wiggins's psychological problems, his capacity for empathy, and his desire to function properly. As a result, the jury sentenced him to death. With new counsel, Wiggins challenged the adequacy of his representation at sentencing.

ISSUE: Does the failure of an attorney to present mitigating life history information at the sentencing phase of a death case meet the test of ineffective assistance of counsel when the attorneys promised that they would be providing such evidence?

HOLDING: Yes.

RATIONALE: "We established the legal principles that govern claims of ineffective assistance of counsel in *Strickland v. Washington*, 466 U.S. 668 (1984). An ineffective assistance claim has two components: A petitioner must show that counsel's performance was deficient, and that the deficiency prejudiced the defense. . . . To establish deficient performance, a petitioner must demonstrate that counsel's representation 'fell below an objective standard of reasonableness.'"

"[W]e focus on whether the investigation supporting counsel's decision not to introduce mitigating evidence of Wiggins' background *was itself reasonable*. . . . In assessing counsel's investigation, we must conduct an objective review of their performance, measured for 'reasonableness under prevailing professional norms.'"

"The record demonstrates that counsel's investigation drew from three sources. Counsel arranged for William Stejskal, a psychologist, to conduct a number of tests on petitioner."

"Counsel had available to them the written PSI, which included a one-page account of Wiggins' 'personal history' noting his 'misery as a youth . . .' and observing that he spent most of his life in foster care."

"Counsel's decision not to expand their investigation beyond the PSI and the DSS records fell short of the professional standards that prevailed. . . . [S]tandard practice in Maryland in capital cases at the time . . . included the preparation of a social history report. Counsel chose not to commission such a report. Counsel's conduct similarly fell short of the standards for capital defense work. . . . Despite these well-defined norms . . . counsel abandoned their investigation of petitioner's background after having acquired only rudimentary knowledge of his history from a narrow set of sources."

"The scope of their investigation was also unreasonable in light of what counsel actually discovered. . . . The records revealed . . . : Petitioner's mother was a chronic alcoholic; Wiggins was shuttled from foster home to foster home . . . while there; he had frequent, lengthy absences from school; and, on at least one occasion, his mother left him and his siblings alone for days without food. . . . As the Federal District Court emphasized, any reasonably competent attorney would have realized that pursuing these leads was necessary to making an informed choice among possible defenses, particularly given the apparent absence of any aggravating factors in petitioner's background."

"[D]uring the sentencing proceeding itself . . . Nethercott entreated the jury to consider . . . that Kevin Wiggins has had a difficult life, counsel never followed up on that suggestion. . . ."

"Counsel's pursuit of bifurcation until the eve of sentencing and their partial presentation of a mitigation case suggest that their incomplete investigation was the result of inattention, not reasoned strategic judgment."

"The mitigating evidence counsel failed to discover and present in this case is powerful. . . . Wiggins experienced severe privation and abuse in the first six years of his life while in the custody of his alcoholic, absentee mother. He suffered physical torment, sexual molestation, and repeated rape during his subsequent years in foster care. The time Wiggins spent homeless, along with his diminished mental capacities, further augment his mitigation case. Petitioner thus has the kind of troubled history we have declared relevant to assessing a defendant's moral culpability."

"Given both the nature and the extent of the abuse petitioner suffered, we find there to be a reasonable probability that a competent attorney, aware of this history, would have introduced it at sentencing in an admissible form."

"We further find that had the jury been confronted with this considerable mitigating evidence, there is a reasonable probability that it would have returned with a different sentence."

"Moreover . . . Wiggins does not have a record of violent conduct that could have been introduced by the State to offset this powerful mitigating narrative . . . the mitigating evidence in this case is stronger, and the State's evidence in support of the death penalty far weaker, than in *Williams* [*v. Taylor*, 529 U.S. 362 (2000)], where we found prejudice as the result of counsel's failure to investigate and present mitigating evidence. . . . We thus conclude that the available mitigating evidence, taken as a whole, 'might well have influenced the jury's appraisal' of Wiggins' moral culpability."

9. Right to Act as Own Counsel

a. Right to Defend Oneself at Trial

Faretta v. California, 422 U.S. 806 (1975)
Vote: 6-3
FACTS: Anthony Faretta was charged with grand theft in Los Angeles and at his arraignment, the judge appointed the public defender to represent him. However, Faretta requested that he be permitted to represent himself. The judge found that Faretta had represented himself once before, that he had a high school education, and that he did not want to be represented by the public defender because he felt that it had a heavy case load. The judge stated that he believed Faretta was "making a mistake." Nevertheless, the judge accepted Faretta's waiver but indicated that he might reverse this ruling if it appeared that Faretta was unable to represent himself. Prior to trial, the judge asked Faretta how his defense was proceeding, and after consideration of his answers, the judge ruled that Faretta had not made an intelligent and knowing waiver and ruled that Faretta had no right to conduct his own defense. The judge then appointed the public defender to represent Faretta and Faretta's subsequent request to act as co-counsel was rejected, as were his efforts to make motions on his own behalf. Throughout the trial, the judge required that Faretta's defense be conducted only through the appointed lawyer. Faretta was subsequently convicted.
ISSUE: Does a defendant have a constitutional right to act as his own lawyer?
HOLDING: Yes.
RATIONALE: "In the federal courts, the right of self-representation has been protected by statute since the beginnings of our Nation. Section 35 of the Judiciary Act of 1789 enacted by the First Congress and signed by President Washington one day before the Sixth Amendment was proposed, provided that 'in all the courts of the United States, the parties may plead and manage their own causes personally or by the assistance of such counsel. . . .' The right is currently codified in 28 U.S.C. § 1654."

"With few exceptions, each of the several States also accords a defendant the right to represent himself in any criminal case. The constitutions of 36 States explicitly confer that right. Moreover, many state courts have expressed the view that the right is also supported by the Constitution of the United States."

"For example . . . the Court held that the Confrontation Clause of the Sixth Amendment gives the accused a right to be present at all stages of the proceedings where fundamental fairness might be thwarted by his absence. This right to 'presence' was based upon the premise that the 'defense may be made easier if the accused is permitted to be present at the examination of jurors or the summing up of counsel, for it will be in his power, if present, to give advice or suggestion or even to supersede his lawyers altogether and conduct the trial himself.'"

"The United States Court of Appeals have repeatedly held that the right of self-representation is protected by the Bill of Rights. . . . The right to the assistance of counsel . . . was intended to supplement . . . and not to impair 'the absolute and primary right to conduct one's own defense in propria persona.'"

"This Court's past recognition of the right of self-representation, the federal-court authority holding the right to be of constitutional dimension, and the state constitutions pointing to the right's fundamental nature form a consensus not easily ignored. . . . We confront here a nearly universal conviction, on the part of our people as well as our courts, that forcing a lawyer upon an unwilling defendant is contrary to his basic right to defend himself if he truly wants to do so."

"This consensus is soundly premised. The right of self-representation finds support in the structure of the Sixth Amendment, as well as in the English and colonial jurisprudence from which the Amendment emerged."

"The Sixth Amendment does not provide merely that a defense shall be made for the accused; it grants to the accused personally the right to make his defense. It is the accused, not counsel, who must be 'informed of the nature and cause of the accusation,' who must be 'confronted with the witnesses against him,' and who must be accorded 'compulsory process for obtaining witnesses in his favor.' Although not stated in the Amendment in so many words, the right to self-representation—to make one's own defense personally—is thus necessarily implied by the structure of the Amendment. The right to defend is given directly to the accused; for it is he who suffers the consequences if the defense fails."

"[W]here the defendant will not voluntarily accept representation by counsel, the potential advantage of a lawyer's training and experience can be realized, if at all, only imperfectly. To force a lawyer on a defendant can only lead him to believe that the law contrives against him. Moreover, it is not inconceivable that in some rare instances, the defendant might in fact present his case more effectively by conducting his own defense. . . . And although he may conduct his own defense ultimately to his own detriment, his choice must be honored out of 'that respect for the individual which is the lifeblood of the law.'"

b. Right to Defend Oneself on Appeal

Martinez v. Court of Appeal, 528 U.S. 152 (2000)
Vote: 9-0
FACTS: Salvador Martinez described himself as a self-taught paralegal with twenty-five years' experience at different firms. While an office assistant in Santa Ana, California,

he was accused of converting $6,000 of a client's money to his own use. He was charged with grand theft and the fraudulent appropriation of property. He chose to represent himself at trial before a jury and the jury acquitted him of grand theft, but convicted him of embezzlement. The jury also found that he had three prior convictions, and under California's "three strikes" law, the court imposed a mandatory sentence of twenty-five years to life. Martinez filed an appeal and a motion to represent himself, but the appellate courts denied it, stating that no right existed to defend oneself on appeal.

ISSUE: Does an appellant have the right to defend himself on appeal?

HOLDING: No.

RATIONALE: "Our conclusion in *Faretta* [*v. California*, 422 U.S. 806 (1975)] . . . was confined to the right to defend oneself at trial. We now address . . . whether the reasoning in support of that holding also applies when the defendant becomes an appellant. . . . We have concluded that it does not."

"Therefore, while *Faretta* is correct in concluding that there is abundant support for the proposition that a right to self-representation has been recognized for centuries, the original reasons for protecting that right do not have the same force when the availability of competent counsel for every indigent defendant has displaced the need—although not always the desire—for self-representation."

"We are not aware of any historical consensus establishing a right of self-representation on appeal. We might, nonetheless, paraphrase *Faretta* and assert: No State or Colony ever forced counsel upon a convicted appellant, and no spokesman ever suggested that such a practice would be tolerable or advisable. . . . Historical silence . . . has no probative force in the appellate context because there simply was no long-respected right of self-representation on appeal. In fact, the right of appeal itself is of relatively recent origin."

"Thus, unlike the inquiry in *Faretta*, the historical evidence does not provide any support for an affirmative constitutional right to appellate self-representation."

"The Sixth Amendment identifies the basic rights that the accused shall enjoy in 'all criminal prosecutions.' They are presented strictly as rights that are available in preparation for trial and at the trial itself. The Sixth Amendment does not include any right to appeal."

"In light of our conclusion that the Sixth Amendment does not apply to appellate proceedings . . . we are entirely unpersuaded that the risk of either disloyalty or suspicion of disloyalty is a sufficient concern to conclude that a constitutional right of self-representation is a necessary component of a fair appellate proceeding."

"No one, including Martinez and the *Faretta* majority, attempts to argue that as a rule *pro se* representation is wise, desirable or efficient."

"The requirement of representation by trained counsel implies no disrespect for the individual inasmuch as it tends to benefit the appellant as well as the court. . . . Considering the change in position from defendant to appellant, the autonomy interests that survive a felony conviction are less compelling than those motivating the decision in *Faretta*. Yet the overriding state interest in the fair and efficient administration of justice remains as strong as at the trial level."

"For the foregoing reasons, we conclude that neither the holding nor the reasoning in *Faretta* requires California to recognize a constitutional right to self-representation on direct appeal from a criminal conviction. . . . Its impact on the law will be minimal, because a lay appellant's rights to participate in appellate proceedings have long been limited by the well-established conclusions that he has no right to be present during appellate proceedings . . . or to present oral argument."

14

Juries and Trial Issues

A S THE TITLE SUGGESTS, this chapter is concerned with matters dealing with the jury and the trial. At this stage of the process, decisions are made as to who will sit on a jury and whether or not that process was fairly implemented. The determination of guilt or innocence is also something that is considered at this stage. So a defendant will know whether or not his or her defense strategy was successful. As at all of the other stages of the criminal process, the accused has certain rights that must be protected. The Supreme Court, as it has done at all of the other points in the process, has also made some important decisions in this area.

For example, the Court has maintained that the right to a jury trial is fundamental to the American sense of criminal processing. However, the Court has allowed for some exceptions to this rule such as delinquency proceedings and minor offenses. In addition, an accused can also waive his or her right to a jury trial.

Jury size and selection has also been an important area of concern for the Supreme Court. In this regard it has ruled on how big juries can be before they can render a constitutionally acceptable verdict. Jury selection turns on the matter of how people can be lawfully excluded, and the Court has stated that while people cannot be excluded because of their race, they can be excluded if they are averse to certain types of sentences, such as the death penalty.

The Court has also stated that juries of certain size in particular kinds of cases must be unanimous. For example, in serious cases twelve-member juries must be unanimous, but in others, they do not need to be. However, if a court is utilizing a six-person jury, that jury must always be unanimous. Finally, the Court has also made pronouncements with regard to jury instructions and how they are to be administered prior to the jury being sequestered for deliberations.

A. Jury Trials

Duncan v. Louisiana, 391 U.S. 145 (1968)
Vote: 7-2
FACTS: Gary Duncan asked for a jury against a charge of simple battery but was denied. Testimony at trial showed that Duncan, while driving, saw his cousins by the side of the road with four white boys. Duncan knew that his cousins had reported racial incidents at school, so he stopped the car, got out, and approached the boys. Witnesses said that Duncan and the white boys spoke to each other, that Duncan encouraged his cousins to leave with him, and that Duncan was going to leave with his cousins. The white boys testified that Duncan slapped Herman Landry on the elbow, while Duncan's cousins testified that he had merely touched him. The judge concluded that the State had proved that Duncan had committed simple battery, and found him guilty. The conviction was punishable by a maximum of two years in prison and a $300 fine. Duncan was sentenced to serve sixty days and to pay a fine of $150.
ISSUE: Does the Fourteenth Amendment guarantee the application of the Sixth Amendment right to a jury trial to the states in all serious criminal cases?
HOLDING: Yes.
RATIONALE: "The test for determining whether a right extended by the Fifth and Sixth Amendments with respect to federal criminal proceedings is also protected against state action by the Fourteenth Amendment has been phrased in a variety of ways in the opinions of this Court. . . . The claim before us is that the right to trial by jury guaranteed by the Sixth Amendment meets these tests. . . . Because we believe that trial by jury in criminal cases is fundamental to the American scheme of justice, we hold that the Fourteenth Amendment guarantees a right of jury trial in all criminal cases which—were they to be tried in a federal court—would come within the Sixth Amendment's guarantee."

"[J]ury trial in criminal cases had been in existence in England for several centuries and carried impressive credentials traced by many to Magna Carta. Its preservation and proper operation as a protection against arbitrary rule were among the major objectives of the revolutionary settlement which was expressed in the Declaration and Bill of Rights of 1689."

"Jury trial came to America with English colonists, and received strong support from them. Royal interference with the jury trial was deeply resented."

"The constitutions adopted by the original States guaranteed jury trial. Also, the constitution of every State entering the Union thereafter in one form or another protected the right to jury trial in criminal cases."

"Even such skeletal history is impressive support for considering the right to jury trial in criminal cases to be fundamental to our system of justice."

"We are aware of prior cases in this Court in which the prevailing opinion contains statements contrary to our holding today that the right to jury trial in serious criminal cases is a fundamental right and hence must be recognized by the States as part of their obligation to extend due process of law to all persons within their jurisdiction. . . .

None of these cases, however, dealt with a State which had purported to dispense entirely with a jury trial in serious criminal cases. . . . Respectfully, we reject the prior dicta regarding jury trial in criminal cases."

"A right to jury trial is granted to criminal defendants in order to prevent oppression by the Government. . . . Providing an accused with the right to be tried by a jury of his peers gave him an inestimable safeguard against the corrupt or overzealous prosecutor and against the compliant, biased, or eccentric judge. If the defendant preferred the common-sense judgment of a jury to the more tutored but perhaps less sympathetic reaction of the single judge, he was to have it. Beyond this, the jury trial provisions in the Federal and State Constitutions reflect a fundamental decision about the exercise of official power—a reluctance to entrust plenary powers over the life and liberty of the citizen to one judge or to a group of judges. Fear of unchecked power, so typical of our State and Federal Governments in other respects, found expression in the criminal law in this insistence upon community participation in the determination of guilt or innocence. The deep commitment of the Nation to the right of jury trial in serious criminal cases as a defense against arbitrary law enforcement qualifies for protection under the Due Process Clause of the Fourteenth Amendment, and must therefore be respected by the States."

"[T]he most recent and exhaustive study of the jury in criminal cases concluded that juries do understand the evidence and come to sound conclusions in most of the cases presented to them and that when juries differ with the result at which the judge would have arrived, it is usually because they are serving some of the very purposes for which they were created and for which they are now employed."

"It is doubtless true that there is a category of petty crimes or offenses which is not subject to the Sixth Amendment jury trial provision and should not be subject to the Fourteenth Amendment jury trial requirement here applied to the States. Crimes carrying possible penalties up to six months do not require a jury trial if they otherwise qualify as petty offenses. . . . But the penalty authorized for a particular crime is of major relevance in determining whether it is serious or not and may in itself, if severe enough, subject the trial to the mandates of the Sixth Amendment."

B. Aggregate Petty Charges and the Right to Trial

Lewis v. United States, 518 U.S. 322 (1996)
Vote: 7-2
FACTS: Ray A. Lewis was a mail handler for the postal service. One day he was observed by inspectors opening mail and pocketing their contents. The next day, the inspectors routed mail containing marked bills through Lewis's station. After observing him open the mail and remove the money, the inspectors arrested him. He was charged with two counts of obstructing the mail, with each count carrying a maximum sentence of six months. Lewis requested a jury, but the judge granted a prosecutorial motion for a

bench trial. She explained that because she would not sentence Lewis to more than six months, he was not entitled to a jury trial.

ISSUE: Does a defendant who is prosecuted in a single proceeding for multiple petty offenses have a constitutional right to a jury trial where the aggregate prison term authorized for the offenses exceeds six months?

HOLDING: No.

RATIONALE: "We conclude that no jury trial right exists where a defendant is prosecuted for multiple petty offenses. The Sixth Amendment's guarantee of the right to a jury trial does not extend to petty offenses, and its scope does not change where a defendant faces a potential aggregate prison term in excess of six months for petty offenses charged."

"Petitioner argues that, where a defendant is charged with multiple petty offenses in a single prosecution, the Sixth Amendment requires that the aggregate potential penalty be the basis for determining whether a jury trial is required. Although each offense charged here was petty, petitioner faced a potential penalty of more than six months' imprisonment; and, of course, if any offense charged had authorized more than six months' imprisonment, he would have been entitled to a jury trial. The Court must look to the aggregate potential prison term to determine the existence of the jury trial right, petitioner contends, not to the 'petty' character of the offenses charged."

"We disagree. The Sixth Amendment reserves the jury trial right to defendants accused of serious crimes. As set forth above, we determine whether an offense is serious by looking to the judgment of the legislature, primarily as expressed in the maximum authorized term of imprisonment. Here, by setting the maximum authorized prison term at six months, the Legislature categorized the offense of obstructing the mail as petty. The fact that petitioner was charged with two counts of a petty offense does not revise the legislative judgment as to the gravity of that particular offense, nor does it transform the petty offense into a serious one, to which the jury trial right would apply. We note that there is precedent at common law that a jury trial was not provided to a defendant charged with multiple petty offenses."

"To be sure, in the cases in which we sought to determine the line between 'petty' and 'serious' for Sixth Amendment purposes, we considered the severity of the authorized deprivation of liberty as an indicator of the legislature's appraisal of the offense. . . . But it is now settled that a legislature's determination that an offense carries a maximum prison term of six months or less indicates its view that an offense is 'petty. . . .' Where we have a judgment by the legislature that an *offense* is 'petty,' we do not look to the potential prison term faced by a *particular defendant* who is charged with more than one such petty offense."

"Where the offenses charged are petty, and the deprivation of liberty exceeds six months only as a result of the aggregation of charges, the jury trial right does not apply. As petitioner acknowledges, even if he were to prevail, the Government could properly circumvent the jury trial right by charging the counts in separate informations and trying them separately."

C. Legislative Intent and Offense Seriousness

Blanton v. City of North Las Vegas, 489 U.S. 538 (1989)
Vote: 9-0
FACTS: Melvin R. Blanton and Mark D. Fraley were charged with driving under the influence of alcohol (DUI) in separate incidents. Neither had prior DUI convictions. The court denied their requests for a jury trial, but on appeal, the court denied Blanton's request but granted Fraley's. Blanton then appealed to the Supreme Court of Nevada, as the City of North Las Vegas did with regard to Fraley. The Supreme Court concluded that the Constitution does not guarantee a right to a jury trial for a DUI offense because the maximum term of incarceration is six months and the maximum possible fine is $1,000. However, the court may order the defendant to perform forty-eight hours of work dressed in clothes that identify him as a DUI offender. The defendant also loses his license for ninety days, and must attend an alcohol abuse course. Repeat offenders are subject to increased penalties.
ISSUE: Are offenders charged under a DUI statute that allows for punishment up to six months, fines, automatic revocation of their driver's licenses and community service entitled to a jury trial as required by the Sixth Amendment?
HOLDING: No.
RATIONALE: "The issue in this case is whether there is a constitutional right to a trial by jury for persons charged under Nevada law with driving under the influence of alcohol (DUI). . . . We hold that there is not."

"Although we did not hold in *Baldwin* [*v. New York,* 399 U.S. 66 (1970)] that an offense carrying a maximum prison term of six months or less automatically qualifies as a 'petty' offense . . . we do find it appropriate to presume for purposes of the Sixth Amendment that society views such an offense as 'petty.' A defendant is entitled to a jury trial in such circumstances only if he can demonstrate that any additional statutory penalties, viewed in conjunction with the maximum authorized period of incarceration, are so severe that they clearly reflect a legislative determination that the offense in question is a 'serious' one. This standard, albeit somewhat imprecise, should ensure the availability of a jury trial in the rare situation where a legislature packs an offense it deems 'serious' with onerous penalties that nonetheless 'do not puncture the 6-month incarceration line.'

"The maximum authorized prison sentence for first-time DUI offenders does not exceed six months. A presumption therefore exists that the Nevada Legislature views DUI as a 'petty' offense for purposes of the Sixth Amendment. Considering the additional statutory penalties as well, we do not believe that the Nevada Legislature has clearly indicated that DUI is a 'serious' offense."

"Viewed together, the statutory penalties are not so severe that DUI must be deemed a 'serious' offense for purposes of the Sixth Amendment. It was not error, therefore, to deny petitioners jury trials."

D. Right to Trial in Juvenile Proceedings

McKeiver v. Pennsylvania, 403 U.S. 528 (1971)
Vote: Split
FACTS: Joseph McKeiver participated with twenty or thirty youths who pursued three teenagers and took twenty-five cents from them. He had never been arrested before, and the testimony of two of the victims was suspect. Edward Terry hit an officer with his fists and with a stick when the officer broke up a fight that he was watching.

In addition, Barbara Burrus and about forty-five other black children, ranging in age from eleven to fifteen years, were the subjects of juvenile court summonses with the charges arising out of demonstrations by black adults and children protesting school assignments and a school consolidation plan. The same lawyer appeared for all the juveniles, and a request for a jury trial in each case was denied. The juveniles and adults were observed walking along the highway singing, shouting, clapping, and playing basketball, which interfered with traffic. They were taken into custody when they refused to leave the highway, and delinquency petitions were filed for those under sixteen. In each case, the court found that the juvenile had committed an act for which an adult could have been punished and declared each child a delinquent and entered custody orders against them. However, the orders were suspended, and the children were placed on probation and required to follow a set of rules, including obeying a curfew and going to school. All of the cases were consolidated under McKeiver.
ISSUE: Does a juvenile have the right to a jury trial in a delinquency proceeding?
HOLDING: No.
RATIONALE: "[W]e conclude that trial by jury in the juvenile court's adjudicative stage is not a constitutional requirement. We so conclude for a number of reasons."

"The Court has refrained . . . from taking the easy way with a flat holding that all rights constitutionally assured for the adult accused are to be imposed upon the state juvenile proceeding."

"There is a possibility, at least, that the jury trial, if required as a matter of constitutional precept, will remake the juvenile proceeding into a fully adversary process and will put an effective end to what has been the idealistic prospect of an intimate, informal protective proceeding."

"The Task Force Report, although concededly pre-[*In re Gault*, 387 U.S. 1 (1967)], is notable for its not making any recommendation that the jury trial be imposed upon the juvenile court system. This is so despite its vivid description of the system's deficiencies and disappointments. Had the Commission deemed this vital to the integrity of the juvenile process, or to the handling of juveniles, surely a recommendation or suggestion to this effect would have appeared. The Court specifically has recognized by dictum that a jury is not a necessary part even of every criminal process that is fair and equitable. . . ."

"The imposition of the jury trial on the juvenile court system would not strengthen greatly, if at all, the factfinding function, and would, contrarily, provide an attrition of the juvenile court's assumed ability to function in a unique manner. It would not remedy the defects of the system."

"[W]e are particularly reluctant to say . . . that the system cannot accomplish its rehabilitative goals. . . . We are reluctant to disallow the States to experiment further and to seek in new and different ways the elusive answers to the problems of the young, and we feel that we would be impeding that experimentation by imposing the jury trial."

"Of course there have been abuses. . . . We refrain from saying at this point that those abuses are of constitutional dimension. They relate to the lack of resources and of dedication rather than to inherent unfairness."

"If the jury trial were to be injected into the juvenile court system as a matter of right, it would bring with it into that system the traditional delay, the formality, and the clamor of the adversary system and, possibly, the public trial. It is of interest that these very factors were stressed by the. . . . Senate when . . . it recommended, and Congress then approved . . . the abolition of the jury trial in the juvenile court."

E. Limitation of the Jury Waiver

Singer v. United States, 380 U.S. 24 (1965)
Vote: 9-0
FACTS: Singer was charged with thirty violations of the mail fraud statute, as it was alleged that he used the mail to trick amateur songwriters into sending him money for the marketing of their songs. At trial, he offered a request to waive a trial by jury 'for the purpose of shortening the trial.' The trial court was willing to approve it, but the Government refused to consent, and Singer was subsequently convicted by a jury on all but one of the counts. Singer challenged a Federal Rule of Procedure that stated that a jury trial could only be waived if both the prosecution and the court agreed. He argued that the Constitution gave a defendant in a federal case the right to waive a jury trial whenever he believes it to be in his interest, regardless of whether the prosecution and the court agree.
ISSUE: Does the Constitution grant a defendant in a federal case the right to waive a jury trial, even if the court and prosecution do not consent?
HOLDING: No.
RATIONALE: "We have examined petitioner's arguments and find them to be without merit. We can find no evidence that the common law recognized that defendants had the right to choose between court and jury trial. Although instances of waiver of jury trial can be found in certain of the colonies prior to the adoption of the Constitution, they were isolated instances occurring pursuant to colonial 'constitutions' or statutes and were clear departures from the common law. There is no indication that the colonists considered the ability to waive a jury trial to be of equal importance to the right to demand one. Having found that the Constitution neither confers nor recognizes a right of criminal defendants to have their cases tried before a judge alone, we also conclude that Rule 23 (a) sets forth a reasonable procedure governing attempted waivers of jury trials."

"Thus, as late as 1827 the English common law gave criminal defendants no option as to the mode of trial. The closest the common law came to such a procedure was that of the 'implied confession' . . . by which defendants accused of minor offenses did not explicitly admit their guilt but threw themselves on the King's mercy and expressed their willingness to submit to a small fine. Despite the 'implied confession,' the court heard evidence and could discharge the defendant if it found the evidence wanting. . . . It cannot seriously be argued that this obscure and insignificant procedure, having no applicability to serious offenses, establishes the proposition that at common law defendants had the right to choose the method of trial in all criminal cases."

"However, from 1692 on, in light of increasing hostility to the Crown, the colonists of Massachusetts stressed their right to trial by jury, not their right to choose between alternate methods of trial."

"The most that can be said for these examples is that they . . . in no way show that there was any general recognition of a defendant's right to be tried by the court instead of by a jury. Indeed, if there had been recognition of such a right, it would be difficult to understand why Article III and the Sixth Amendment were not drafted in terms which recognized an option."

"In no known federal criminal case in the period immediately following the adoption of the Constitution did a defendant claim that he had the right to insist upon a trial without a jury."

"'Before any waiver can become effective, the consent of government counsel and the sanction of the court must be had, in addition to the express and intelligent consent of the defendant.'"

"In *Adams v. United States ex rel. McCann*, 317 U.S. 269 [(1942)], this Court reaffirmed the position taken in *Patton* [*v. United States*, 281 U.S. 276 (1930)] that 'one charged with a serious federal crime may dispense with his Constitutional right to jury trial, where this action is taken with his express, intelligent consent, where the Government also consents, and where such action is approved by the responsible judgment of the trial court.'"

"[I]t has long been accepted that the waiver of constitutional rights can be subjected to reasonable procedural regulations."

<hr>

F. Jury Size

1. How Small Can a Jury Be?

Williams v. Florida, 399 U.S. 78 (1970)
Vote: 7-2
FACTS: Prior to his trial for robbery in Florida, Williams filed a motion to impanel a twelve-person jury instead of the six-person provided by law in all but capital cases, which was denied. He was eventually convicted, but on appeal he argued that his Sixth Amendment right to a jury trial was violated because he was not given a twelve-member jury.

ISSUE: Does a decision by a state to provide a six-member jury instead of twelve violate the Sixth Amendment right to a jury trial?

HOLDING: No

RATIONALE: "We hold that the 12-man panel is not a necessary ingredient of 'trial by jury,' and that respondent's refusal to impanel more than the six members provided for by Florida law did not violate petitioner's Sixth Amendment rights as applied to the States through the Fourteenth."

"As introduced by James Madison in the House, the Amendment . . . that finally emerged from the Committee was the version that ultimately became the Sixth Amendment, ensuring an accused 'the right to a speedy and public trial, by an impartial jury of the State and district wherein the crime shall have been committed, which district shall have been previously ascertained by law. . . .'"

"Three significant features may be observed in this sketch of the background of the Constitution's jury trial provisions. First, even though the vicinage requirement was as much a feature of the common-law jury as was the 12-man requirement, the mere reference to 'trial by jury' in Article III was not interpreted to include that feature. . . . Second, provisions that would have explicitly tied the 'jury' concept to the 'accustomed requisites' of the time were eliminated. . . . Finally, contemporary legislative and constitutional provisions indicate that where Congress wanted to leave no doubt that it was incorporating existing common-law features of the jury system, it knew how to use express language to that effect. Thus, the Judiciary bill, signed by the President on the same day that the House and Senate finally agreed on the form of the Amendments to be submitted to the States, provided in certain cases for the narrower 'vicinage' requirements that the House had wanted to include in the Amendments."

"But there is absolutely no indication in 'the intent of the Framers' of an explicit decision to equate the constitutional and common-law characteristics of the jury. . . . The relevant inquiry, as we see it, must be the function that the particular feature performs and its relation to the purposes of the jury trial. Measured by this standard, the 12-man requirement cannot be regarded as an indispensable component of the Sixth Amendment."

"[T]he essential feature of a jury obviously lies in the interposition between the accused and his accuser of the commonsense judgment of a group of laymen. . . . The performance of this role is not a function of the particular number of the body that makes up the jury. . . . But we find little reason to think that these goals are in any meaningful sense less likely to be achieved when the jury numbers six, than when it numbers 12—particularly if the requirement of unanimity is retained."

"In short, neither currently available evidence nor theory suggests that the 12-man jury is necessarily more advantageous to the defendant than a jury composed of fewer members."

"We conclude, in short, as we began: the fact that the jury at common law was composed of precisely 12 is a historical accident, unnecessary to effect the purposes of the jury system and wholly without significance. . . . To read the Sixth Amendment as forever codifying a feature so incidental to the real purpose of the Amendment is to ascribe a blind formalism to the Framers. . . . [W]e conclude that petitioner's Sixth

Amendment rights, as applied to the States through the Fourteenth Amendment, were not violated by Florida's decision to provide a six-man rather than a 12-man jury."

2. Is a Jury of Less Than Six Members Constitutional?

Ballew v. Georgia, 435 U.S. 223 (1978)
Vote: 9-0
FACTS: Claude Davis Ballew was the manager of the Paris Adult Theatre when two investigators from the Fulton County Solicitor General's office viewed a film entitled *Behind the Green Door*. After viewing it on different occasions and securing warrants for its seizure, they arrested Ballew and a cashier. Ballew was then charged with two misdemeanor charges of "distributing obscene materials." After his motion for a twelve-person jury was denied, he was informed that five-member juries were used for misdemeanor offenses. He was subsequently convicted of the charges. On appeal he argued that the use of the five-member jury deprived him of his Sixth and Fourteenth Amendment right to a trial by jury.
ISSUE: Does a jury that consists of only five people violate the right to trial by jury?
HOLDING: Yes.
RATIONALE: "[W]e now hold that the five member jury does not satisfy the jury trial guarantee of the Sixth Amendment, as applied to the States through the Fourteenth."

"Williams held that . . . this purpose could be fulfilled by a jury of six members."

"We face . . . the . . . question whether a further reduction in the size of the . . . . jury . . . inhibits the functioning of the jury."

"First, recent empirical data suggest that progressively smaller juries are less likely to foster effective group deliberation. At some point, this decline leads to inaccurate factfinding and incorrect application of the common sense of the community to the facts. . . . The smaller the group, the less likely are members to make critical contributions necessary for the solution of a given problem. Because most juries are not permitted to take notes . . . memory is important for accurate jury deliberations. . . . Furthermore, the smaller the group, the less likely it is to overcome the biases of its members to obtain an accurate result."

"Second, the data now raise doubts about the accuracy of the results achieved by smaller and smaller panels. Statistical studies suggest that the risk of convicting an innocent person (Type I error) rises as the size of the jury diminishes. Because the risk of not convicting a guilty person (Type II error) increases with the size of the panel, an optimal jury size can be selected . . . [and] . . . that the optimal jury size was between six and eight."

"Another doubt about progressively smaller juries arises from the increasing inconsistency that results from the decreases."

"Third, the data suggest that the verdicts of jury deliberation in criminal cases will vary as juries become smaller, and that the variance amounts to an imbalance to . . . the defense."

"Fourth, what has just been said about . . . juries' decrease in size foretells problems . . . for the representation of minority groups in the community. The Court repeatedly has held that meaningful community participation cannot be attained with the exclusion of minorities or other identifiable groups from jury service."

"Fifth, several authors have identified in jury research methodological problems tending to mask differences in the operation of smaller and larger juries."

"While we adhere to, and reaffirm our holding in *Williams v. Florida* [399 U.S. 78 (1970)], these studies, most of which have been made since *Williams* was decided in 1970, lead us to conclude that the purpose and functioning of the jury in a criminal trial is seriously impaired, and to a constitutional degree, by a reduction in size to below six members. . . . Because of the fundamental importance of the jury trial to the American system of criminal justice, any further reduction that promotes inaccurate and possibly biased decision making, that causes untoward differences in verdicts, and that prevents juries from truly representing their communities, attains constitutional significance."

"The point that is to be made, of course, is that a reduction in size from six to five or four or even three would save the States little. They could reduce slightly the daily allowances, but with a reduction from six to five the saving would be minimal. If little time is gained by the reduction from 12 to 6, less will be gained with a reduction from 6 to 5."

"Petitioner, therefore, has established that his trial on criminal charges before a five-member jury deprived him of the right to trial by jury guaranteed by the Sixth and Fourteenth Amendments."

G. Jury Selection

1. Representativeness

Taylor v. Louisiana, 419 U.S. 522 (1975)

Vote: 8-1

FACTS: Billy J. Taylor was indicted for aggravated kidnapping. He moved to quash the jury venire beginning his trial, alleging that women were systematically excluded from the venire because they had to declare in writing that they wanted to serve prior to their being selected, and as a result, he would be deprived of his right to "a fair trial by jury of a representative segment of the community." Taylor's motion was denied, and he was eventually tried, convicted, and sentenced to death. On appeal, the Supreme Court of Louisiana held that the provisions requiring a woman to declare in writing that she wished to serve on a jury prior to her selection were valid.

ISSUE: Does a provision that requires women to declare in writing that they wish to serve on a jury before they can be selected to do so violate an accused's Sixth Amendment right to a jury that is representative of the community?

HOLDING: Yes.

RATIONALE: "The unmistakable import of this Court's opinions . . . is that the selection of a petit jury from a representative cross section of the community is an

essential component of the Sixth Amendment right to a jury trial. Recent federal legislation governing jury selection within the federal court system has a similar thrust."

"The right to a proper jury cannot be overcome on merely rational grounds. There
must be weightier reasons if a distinctive class representing 53% of the eligible jurors
is for all practical purposes to be excluded from jury service. No such basis has been
tendered here."

"Accepting . . . the view that the Sixth Amendment affords the defendant in a
criminal trial the opportunity to have the jury drawn from venires representative of the
community, we think it is no longer tenable to hold that women as a class may be excluded or given automatic exemptions based solely on sex if the consequence is that
criminal jury venires are almost totally male. . . . If at one time it could be held that
Sixth Amendment juries must be drawn from a fair cross section of the community but
that this requirement permitted the almost total exclusion of women, this is not the
case today. Communities differ at different times and places. What is a fair cross section at one time or place is not necessarily a fair cross section at another time or a different place."

"[A]s we have said, Louisiana's special exemption for women operates to exclude
them from petit juries, which in our view is contrary to the command of the Sixth and
Fourteenth Amendments."

"It should also be emphasized . . . we impose no requirement that petit juries actually chosen must mirror the community and reflect the various distinctive groups in
the population. Defendants are not entitled to a jury of any particular composition . . .
but the jury wheels, pools of names, panels, or venires from which juries are drawn
must not systematically exclude distinctive groups in the community and thereby fail
to be reasonably representative thereof."

2. Exclusion of Jurors and the Death Penalty

Lockhart v. McCree, 476 U.S. 162 (1986)
Vote: 6-3
FACTS: A gas station in Camden, Arkansas, was robbed, and Evelyn Boughton, the
owner, was shot and killed. That same afternoon, Ardia McCree was arrested in Hot
Springs, Arkansas, after a police officer saw him driving a car matching a witness's description of that used by Boughton's killer. McCree admitted that he had been at
Boughton's shop at the time of the murder but claimed that a tall, black stranger, wearing an overcoat, asked him for a ride and then took McCree's rifle out of the car and
used it to kill Boughton. McCree also claimed that the stranger rode with McCree to a
dirt road, got out of the car, and walked away with the rifle. Two eyewitnesses contradicted McCree's story, stating that they saw only one person in the car. The police also
found McCree's rifle and a bank bag from the shop alongside the road. Based on ballistics tests, an FBI agent testified that the bullet that killed Boughton had been fired
from McCree's rifle. McCree was charged with capital felony murder. The trial judge, at
voir dire removed for cause, over McCree's objections, eight prospective jurors who

stated that they could not under any circumstances vote for the death penalty. McCree was convicted, but the judge rejected the State's request for the death penalty, opting to set McCree's punishment at life imprisonment without parole. McCree filed a habeas corpus petition claiming that the removal of the prospective jurors that were against the death penalty violated the Sixth and Fourteenth Amendments rights to a fair trial. ISSUE: Is the Sixth Amendment right to a fair trial violated when a judge allows the removal for cause of prospective jurors whose opposition to the death penalty is so strong that it would prevent or substantially impair their duties at the sentencing phase of the trial?

HOLDING: No.

RATIONALE: "McCree concedes, as he must, that 'nullifiers' may properly be excluded from the guilt-phase jury, and studies that fail to take into account the presence of such 'nullifiers' thus are fatally flawed."

"In our view, groups defined solely in terms of shared attitudes that would prevent or substantially impair members of the group from performing one of their duties as jurors, such as the '*Witherspoon* [*v. Illinois*, 391 U.S. 510 (1968)]-excludables' at issue here, are not 'distinctive groups' for fair-cross-section purposes."

"The group of 'Witherspoon-excludables' involved in the case at bar differs significantly from the groups we have previously recognized as 'distinctive.' 'Death qualification,' unlike the wholesale exclusion of blacks, women, or Mexican-Americans from jury service, is carefully designed to serve the State's concededly legitimate interest in obtaining a single jury that can properly and impartially apply the law to the facts of the case at both the guilt and sentencing phases of a capital trial. There is very little danger . . . that 'death qualification' was instituted as a means for the State to arbitrarily skew the composition of capital-case juries."

"In sum, '*Witherspoon*-excludables,' or for that matter any other group defined solely in terms of shared attitudes that render members of the group unable to serve as jurors in a particular case, may be excluded from jury service without contravening any of the basic objectives of the fair-cross-section requirement."

"McCree argues that his jury lacked impartiality because the absence of '*Witherspoon*-excludables' 'slanted' the jury in favor of conviction."

"We do not agree. McCree's 'impartiality' argument apparently is based on the theory that, because all individual jurors are to some extent predisposed toward one result or another, a constitutionally impartial *jury* can be constructed only by 'balancing' the various predispositions of the individual *jurors*. Thus, according to McCree, when the State 'tips the scales' by excluding prospective jurors with a particular viewpoint, an impermissibly partial jury results. We have consistently rejected this view of jury impartiality"

"On a more practical level, if it were true that the Constitution required a certain mix of individual viewpoints on the jury, then trial judges would be required to undertake the Sisyphean task of 'balancing' juries, making sure that each contains the proper number of Democrats and Republicans, young persons and old persons, white-collar executives and blue-collar laborers, and so on. Adopting McCree's concept of jury impartiality would also likely require the elimination of peremptory challenges, which are commonly used by both the State and the defendant to attempt to produce a jury favorable to the challenger."

"In our view, it is simply not possible to define jury impartiality, for constitutional purposes, by reference to some hypothetical mix of individual viewpoints. . . . [T]he Constitution presupposes that a jury selected from a fair cross section of the community is impartial, regardless of the mix of individual viewpoints actually represented on the jury, so long as the jurors can . . . properly carry out their sworn duty to apply the law to the facts of the particular case."

3. Exclusion of Jurors and Race

Batson v. Kentucky, 476 U.S. 79 (1986)
Vote: 7-2
FACTS: James Kirkland Batson, a black man, was indicted on charges of second-degree burglary and receipt of stolen goods. On the first day of the trial, the judge conducted voir dire of the venire, excused some jurors for cause, and permitted the attorneys to exercise peremptory challenges. The prosecutor used his to strike all four blacks on the venire, and a white jury was thus selected. Batson's lawyer moved to discharge the jury on the ground that the removal of the black veniremen violated Batson's rights under the Sixth and Fourteenth Amendments to a jury drawn from a cross section of the community, and under the Fourteenth Amendment to equal protection of the laws. The judge stated that the lawyers were allowed to use their peremptory challenges to "strike anybody they want to" and then denied the motion, reasoning that the cross-section requirement applies to selection of the venire, not to selection of the jury. The jury convicted Batson of both charges, but on appeal, he continued to argue that the prosecution's use of its peremptory challenges to exclude the black veniremen was unconstitutional.
ISSUE: Does the use of peremptory challenges to exclude potential jurors because of their race violate equal protection of the law?
HOLDING: Yes.
RATIONALE: "In *Swain v. Alabama* [380 U.S. 202 (1965)], this Court recognized that a 'State's purposeful or deliberate denial to Negroes on account of race of participation as jurors in the administration of justice violates the Equal Protection Clause. . . .' This principle has been 'consistently and repeatedly' reaffirmed, in numerous decisions of this Court both preceding and following *Swain*. We reaffirm the principle today."

"But the defendant does have the right to be tried by a jury whose members are selected pursuant to nondiscriminatory criteria. . . . The Equal Protection Clause guarantees the defendant that the State will not exclude members of his race from the jury venire on account of race . . . or on the false assumption that members of his race as a group are not qualified to serve as jurors."

"Racial discrimination in selection of jurors harms not only the accused whose life or liberty they are summoned to try. Competence to serve as a juror ultimately depends on an assessment of individual qualifications and ability impartially to consider evidence presented at a trial. . . . A person's race simply 'is unrelated to his fitness as a juror. . . .' As long ago as *Strauder* [*v. West Virginia*, 100 U.S. 303 (1880)], therefore, the Court recognized that by denying a person participation in jury service on account of his race, the State unconstitutionally discriminated against the excluded juror."

"The harm from discriminatory jury selection extends beyond that inflicted on the defendant and the excluded juror to touch the entire community. Selection procedures that purposefully exclude black persons from juries undermine public confidence in the fairness of our system of justice."

"It was impermissible for a prosecutor to use his challenges to exclude blacks from the jury 'for reasons wholly unrelated to the outcome of the particular case on trial' or to deny to blacks 'the same right and opportunity to participate in the administration of justice enjoyed by the white population.'"

"Just as the Equal Protection Clause forbids the States to exclude black persons from the venire on the assumption that blacks as a group are unqualified to serve as jurors . . . so it forbids the States to strike black veniremen on the assumption that they will be biased in a particular case simply because the defendant is black. The core guarantee of equal protection, ensuring citizens that their State will not discriminate on account of race, would be meaningless were we to approve the exclusion of jurors on the basis of such assumptions, which arise solely from the jurors' race."

H. Adult Trial and Juvenile Adjudication Issues

1. Standard of Evidence for Juveniles

In re Winship, 397 U.S. 358 (1970)
Vote: 6-3
FACTS: During an adjudicatory hearing conducted pursuant to a New York delinquency statute, the judge determined that Samuel Winship had entered a locker and stolen $112 from a woman's purse. The delinquency petition alleged that if the offense had been committed by an adult, it would have constituted the crime of larceny. The judge admitted that the State did not prove its case beyond a reasonable doubt but rejected the argument that such a standard of proof was necessary in delinquency hearings, stating that another law made only a preponderance of evidence the standard of proof. At the dispositional hearing, Winship was ordered placed in a training school, subject to extensions, until his eighteenth birthday. The decision was affirmed on appeal.
ISSUE: Is proof beyond a reasonable doubt the required standard during a proceeding for a juvenile if he is charged with an act that would constitute a crime if committed by an adult?
HOLDING: Yes.
RATIONALE: "The requirement that guilt of a criminal charge be established by proof beyond a reasonable doubt dates at least from our early years as a Nation. The 'demand for a higher degree of persuasion in criminal cases was recurrently expressed from

ancient times, [though] its crystallization into the formula "beyond a reasonable doubt" seems to have occurred as late as 1798. It is now accepted in common law jurisdictions as the measure of persuasion by which the prosecution must convince the trier of all the essential elements of guilt.'"

"The reasonable-doubt standard is indispensable, for it 'impresses on the trier of fact the necessity of reaching a subjective state of certitude of the facts in issue.'"

"It is also important in our free society that every individual going about his ordinary affairs have confidence that his government cannot adjudge him guilty of a criminal offense without convincing a proper factfinder of his guilt with utmost certainty."

"Lest there remain any doubt about the constitutional stature of the reasonable-doubt standard, we explicitly hold that the Due Process Clause protects the accused against conviction except upon proof beyond a reasonable doubt of every fact necessary to constitute the crime with which he is charged."

"We turn to the question whether juveniles, like adults, are constitutionally entitled to proof beyond a reasonable doubt when they are charged with violation of a criminal law. The same considerations that demand extreme caution in factfinding to protect the innocent adult apply as well to the innocent child."

"Nor do we perceive any merit in the argument that to afford juveniles the protection of proof beyond a reasonable doubt would risk destruction of beneficial aspects of the juvenile process. Use of the reasonable-doubt standard during the adjudicatory hearing will not disturb New York's policies that a finding that a child has violated a criminal law does not constitute a criminal conviction, that such a finding does not deprive the child of his civil rights, and that juvenile proceedings are confidential. Nor will there be any effect on the informality, flexibility, or speed of the hearing at which the factfinding takes place. And the opportunity during the post-adjudicatory or dispositional hearing for a wide-ranging review of the child's social history and for his individualized treatment will remain unimpaired. Similarly, there will be no effect on the procedures distinctive to juvenile proceedings that are employed prior to the adjudicatory hearing."

"We conclude . . . that the observance of the standard of proof beyond a reasonable doubt 'will not compel the States to abandon or displace any of the substantive benefits of the juvenile process.'"

"In sum, the constitutional safeguard of proof beyond a reasonable doubt is as much required during the adjudicatory stage of a delinquency proceeding as are those constitutional safeguards applied in [*In re Gault*, 387 U.S. 1 (1967)]—notice of charges, right to counsel, the rights of confrontation and examination, and the privilege against self-incrimination."

2. Commenting on the Refusal to Testify

Griffin v. California, 380 U.S. 609 (1965)
Vote: 6-2
FACTS: Griffin was convicted of first-degree murder after a jury trial. He did not testify at the guilt phase of the trial, but did at the penalty phase. The trial judge instructed

the jury at the guilt phase that a defendant has a constitutional right not to testify. However, the judge also stated: "As to any evidence or facts against him which the defendant can reasonably be expected to deny or explain because of facts within his knowledge, if he does not testify or if, though he does testify, he fails to deny or explain such evidence, the jury may take that failure into consideration as tending to indicate the truth of such evidence and as indicating that among the inferences that may be reasonably drawn therefrom those unfavorable to the defendant are the more probable."

Griffin had been seen with the dead woman the evening of her death, with the evidence placing him with her in the alley where her body was found, and the prosecutor made much of Griffin's failure to testify. The prosecutor stated that Griffin would know about how the woman was injured but would not talk about it. Griffin was convicted and sentenced to death, and the conviction was affirmed on appeal.

ISSUE: Does a comment by the prosecution that the defendant failed to testify for specific reasons violate a defendant's Fifth Amendment right to be free from Self-Incrimination?

HOLDING: Yes.

RATIONALE: "If this were a federal trial, reversible error would have been committed. . . . But that is the beginning, not the end, of our inquiry. The question remains whether, statute or not, the comment rule, approved by California, violates the Fifth Amendment."

"We think it does. It is in substance a rule of evidence that allows the State the privilege of tendering to the jury for its consideration the failure of the accused to testify. No formal offer of proof is made as in other situations; but the prosecutor's comment and the court's acquiescence are the equivalent of an offer of evidence and its acceptance. The Court in the *Wilson* [*v. United States*, 149 U.S. 60 (1893)] case stated: 'the act was framed with a due regard also to those who might prefer to rely upon the presumption of innocence . . . and not wish to be witnesses. It is not every one who can safely venture on the witness stand though entirely innocent of the charge against him. Excessive timidity, nervousness when facing others and attempting to explain transactions of a suspicious character, and offences charged against him, will often confuse and embarrass him to such a degree as to increase rather than remove prejudices against him. It is not every one, however honest, who would, therefore, willingly be placed on the witness stand. The statute, in tenderness to the weakness of those who from the causes mentioned might refuse to ask to be a witness, particularly when they may have been in some degree compromised by their association with others, declares that the failure of the defendant in a criminal action to request to be a witness shall not create any presumption against him.'"

"For comment on the refusal to testify is a remnant of the 'inquisitorial system of criminal justice . . .' which the Fifth Amendment outlaws. It is a penalty imposed by courts for exercising a constitutional privilege."

"We said in *Malloy v. Hogan* [378 U.S. 1 (1964)] the same standards must determine whether an accused's silence in either a federal or state proceeding is justified. We take that in its literal sense and hold that the Fifth Amendment, in its direct application to the Federal Government, and in its bearing on the States by reason of the Fourteenth

Amendment, forbids either comment by the prosecution on the accused's silence or instructions by the court that such silence is evidence of guilt."

3. Use of an Alias by a Witness against the Defendant

Smith v. Illinois, 390 U.S. 129 (1968)
Vote: 8-1
FACTS: At trial, the main witness against Smith was "James Jordan," who testified that, with marked money provided by two Chicago officers, he had bought a bag of heroin from Smith in a restaurant. The officers corroborated the transaction, but only "Jordan" and Smith testified to the activity inside the restaurant, and Smith's version was completely different. Smith's lawyer asked "Jordan" if that was his real name, and he admitted, over the prosecutor's objection, that it was not. He was then asked what his real name was, and the judge sustained the prosecutor's objection. He was then asked where he lived, and again the judge sustained the objection. Smith was convicted of selling drugs, and on appeal he argued that his right to confront the witnesses against him was violated when a prosecution witness was allowed to avoid telling the court his real name.
ISSUE: Is a defendant's Sixth Amendment right to confront the witnesses against him violated when a witness is allowed to keep his identity secret at trial?
HOLDING: Yes.
RATIONALE: "Yet when the credibility of a witness is in issue, the very starting point in 'exposing falsehood and bringing out the truth' through cross-examination must necessarily be to ask the witness who he is and where he lives. The witness' name and address open countless avenues of in-court examination and out-of-court investigation. To forbid this most rudimentary inquiry at the threshold is effectively to emasculate the right of cross-examination itself."

"In *Alford v. United States*, 282 U.S. 687 [(1931)], this Court almost 40 years ago unanimously reversed a federal conviction because the trial judge had sustained objections to questions by the defense seeking to elicit the 'place of residence' of a prosecution witness over the insistence of defense counsel that 'the jury was entitled to know 'who the witness is, where he lives and what his business is. . . .'"

"The question 'Where do you live . . . ?' was an essential step in identifying the witness with his environment, to which cross-examination may always be directed."

"In *Pointer v. Texas* [380 U.S. 400 (1965)], the Court made clear that 'the right of an accused to be confronted with the witnesses against him must be determined by the same standards whether the right is denied in a federal or state proceeding. . . .' [W]e . . . hold that the petitioner was deprived of a right guaranteed to him under the Sixth and Fourteenth Amendments of the Constitution."

4. Jury Inquiries of the Judge and Defense Notification

Rogers v. United States, 422 U.S. 35 (1975)
Vote: 9-0

FACTS: A jury convicted George Rogers on five charges of knowingly and willfully making oral threats "to take the life of or to inflict bodily harm upon the President of the United States." The jury retired for deliberation at 3:00 p.m. on the second day of his trial, and about two hours later, at 4:55 p.m., the jury sent a note, signed by the foreman, to the judge, asking if the court would "accept the Verdict—'Guilty as charged with extreme mercy of the Court.'" The judge instructed the marshal who delivered the note to tell the jury that he would accept such a verdict. However, he did so without notifying Rogers or his lawyer.

ISSUE: Is a judge's acceptance of a note from a jury requesting if the judge will accept a particular verdict reversible error if the judge does not inform the defense of the request?

HOLDING: Yes.

RATIONALE: "[T]he communication from the jury in this case was tantamount to a request for further instructions. However, we need not look solely to our prior decisions for guidance as to the appropriate procedure in such a situation. Federal Rule Crim. Proc. 43 guarantees to a defendant in a criminal trial the right to be present 'at every stage of the trial including the impaneling of the jury and the return of the verdict.' Cases interpreting the Rule make it clear . . . that the jury's message should have been answered in open court and that petitioner's counsel should have been given an opportunity to be heard before the trial judge responded."

"Although a violation of Rule 43 may in some circumstances be harmless error . . . the nature of the information . . . in addition to the manner in which it was conveyed, does not permit that conclusion in this case. The trial judge should not have confined his response to the jury's inquiry to an indication of willingness to accept a verdict with a recommendation of 'extreme mercy. . . .' [T]he court should have reminded the jury that the recommendation would not be binding. . . . In addition, the response should have included the admonition that the jury had no sentencing function and should reach its verdict without regard to what sentence might be imposed."

"The fact that the jury . . . returned a verdict of 'guilty with extreme mercy' within five minutes 'after being told unconditionally and unequivocally that it could recommend leniency . . .' strongly suggests that the trial judge's response may have induced unanimity by giving . . . the impression that the recommendation might be an acceptable compromise. We acknowledge that the comments of the trial judge upon receiving the verdict may be said to have put petitioner's counsel on notice that the jury had communicated with the court, but the only indication that the court had unilaterally communicated with the jury comes from the note itself, which the court correctly ordered to be filed in the record, with a notation as to the time of receipt and the court's response. It appears, however, that petitioner's counsel was not aware of the . . . communication until after we granted . . . certiorari. In such circumstances . . . we conclude that the combined effect of the District Court's errors was so fraught with potential prejudice as to require us to notice them notwithstanding petitioner's failure to raise the issue in the Court of Appeals or in this Court."

5. Jury Instructions and Possible Consequences of a Guilty Verdict

Shannon v. United States, 512 U.S. 573 (1994)
Vote: 7-2
FACTS: A police officer stopped Terry Lee Shannon, a convicted felon, on a street in Tupelo, Mississippi. For reasons not explained, the officer asked him to accompany him to the station to speak with a detective. After telling the officer that he did not want to live, Shannon walked across the street, pulled a pistol, and shot himself in the chest. He survived and was indicted for unlawful possession of a firearm by a felon. At trial, he raised the insanity defense and asked the judge to instruct the jury that he would be involuntarily committed if the jury returned a "not guilty by reason of insanity" (NGI) verdict. The judge refused, and the jury returned a guilty verdict. Shannon's conviction was affirmed on appeal, and he contended that an instruction informing the jury of the consequences of an NGI verdict is required under the Insanity Defense Reform Act (IDRA) whenever requested by the defendant. He also argued that such an instruction is required as a matter of general federal criminal practice.
ISSUE: Are federal courts required to instruct the jury regarding the consequences to the defendant of a verdict of "not guilty by reason of insanity"?
HOLDING: No.
RATIONALE: "Before the IDRA was enacted, the Federal Courts of Appeals generally disapproved of instructing the jury concerning the post-trial consequences of an insanity acquittal. . . . The courts in general gave two reasons for disapproving such instructions. First, they pointed out that . . . the consequences of an insanity acquittal were far from certain. Second, they concluded that such instructions would run afoul of the . . . principle that a jury is to base its verdict on the evidence before it, without regard to the possible consequences of the verdict."

"It is well established that when a jury has no sentencing function, it should be admonished to 'reach its verdict without regard to what sentence might be imposed. . . .' The principle that juries are not to consider the consequences of their verdicts is a reflection of the basic division of labor in our legal system between judge and jury. The jury's function is to find the facts and to decide whether, on those facts, the defendant is guilty of the crime charged. . . . Moreover, providing jurors sentencing information . . . distracts them from their factfinding responsibilities, and creates a strong possibility of confusion."

"To determine whether Congress intended courts to depart from the principle that jurors are not to be informed of the consequences of their verdicts, we turn first, as always, to the text of the statute. . . . The text of the Act gives no indication that jurors are to be instructed regarding the consequences of an NGI verdict."

"We are not aware of any case . . . in which we have given authoritative weight to a single passage of legislative history that is in no way anchored in the text of the statute. On its face, the passage Shannon identifies does not purport to explain or interpret any provision of the IDRA."

"Even assuming Shannon is correct that some jurors will harbor the mistaken belief that defendants found NGI will be released into society immediately . . . the jury in his case was instructed 'to apply the law as [instructed] regardless of the consequence,' and that 'punishment . . . should not enter your consideration or discussion. . . .' Although it may take effort on a juror's part to ignore the potential consequences of the verdict, the effort required in a case in which an NGI defense is raised is no different from that required in many other situations."

"We also are not persuaded that the instruction Shannon proposes would allay the fears of the misinformed juror about whom Shannon is concerned. 'If the members of a jury are so fearful of a particular defendant's release that they would violate their oaths by convicting [the defendant] solely in order to ensure that he is not set free, it is questionable whether they would be reassured by anything short of an instruction strongly suggesting that the defendant, if found NGI, would very likely be civilly committed for a lengthy period.'"

"Jurors may be as unfamiliar with other aspects of the criminal sentencing process as they are with NGI verdicts. But, as a general matter, jurors are not informed of mandatory minimum or maximum sentences, nor are they instructed regarding probation, parole, or the sentencing range accompanying a lesser included offense. . . . In short, if we pursue the logic of Shannon's position, the rule against informing jurors of the consequences of their verdicts would soon be swallowed by the exceptions."

"Finally . . . the IDRA was the product of a thorough and exhaustive review of the insanity defense as used in the federal courts. . . . Congress certainly could have included a provision requiring the instruction Shannon seeks. For whatever reason, Congress chose not to do so. Under these circumstances, we are reluctant to depart from well-established principles of criminal practice without more explicit guidance from Congress."

6. Verdict

a. Unanimity and Twelve-Member Juries

Apodaca v. Oregon, 406 U.S. 404 (1972)
Vote: 5-4
FACTS: Robert Apodaca, Henry Morgan Cooper Jr., and James Arnold Madden were convicted respectively of assault with a deadly weapon, burglary in a dwelling, and grand larceny before separate juries, all of which returned less-than-unanimous verdicts. The vote in the cases of Apodaca and Madden was eleven to one, while for Cooper it was ten to two, the minimum under Oregon law for sustaining a conviction. Their convictions were affirmed on appeal, so they claimed at the Oregon Supreme Court that conviction by a less-than-unanimous jury violates the right to trial by jury in criminal cases specified by the Sixth Amendment.

ISSUE: Does the conviction by a jury of less than a unanimous vote violate the Sixth Amendment right to trial?

HOLDING: No.

RATIONALE: "In *Williams v. Florida*, 399 U.S. 78 (1970), we had occasion to consider . . . whether the Sixth Amendment's right to trial by jury requires that all juries consist of 12 men. . . . [W]e concluded that it was not of constitutional stature. We reach the same conclusion today with regard to the requirement of unanimity."

"As we observed in *Williams*, one can draw conflicting inferences from this legislative history. . . . One possible inference is that Congress eliminated references to unanimity . . . because those requisites were thought already to be implicit in the very concept of jury. A contrary explanation, which we found in *Williams* to be the more plausible, is that the deletion was intended to have some substantive effect. . . . [T]he Framers explicitly rejected the proposal and instead left such specification to the future."

"A requirement of unanimity, however, does not materially contribute to the exercise of this commonsense judgment. . . . In terms of this function we perceive no difference between juries required to act unanimously and those permitted to convict or acquit by votes of 10 to 2 or 11 to 1. Requiring unanimity would obviously produce hung juries in some situations where nonunanimous juries will convict or acquit. But in either case, the interest of the defendant in having the judgment of his peers interposed between himself and the officers of the State who prosecute and judge him is equally well served."

"Petitioners also cite quite accurately a long line of decisions of this Court upholding the principle that the Fourteenth Amendment requires jury panels to reflect a cross section of the community. . . . They then contend that unanimity is a necessary precondition for effective application of the cross-section requirement, because a rule permitting less than unanimous verdicts will make it possible for convictions to occur without the acquiescence of minority elements within the community."

"All that the Constitution forbids, however, is systematic exclusion of identifiable segments of the community from jury panels and from the juries ultimately drawn from those panels."

b. Constitutionality of Jury Votes of 9-3 to Convict

Johnson v. Louisiana, 406 U.S. 356 (1972)

Vote: 5-4

FACTS: The victim of an armed robbery identified Johnson from photographs as having committed the crime. Johnson was arrested at his home and was then identified at a lineup, at which he had counsel, by the victim of a different robbery. It is the second robbery that is at issue. Johnson pleaded not guilty, was tried by a twelve-man jury, and was convicted by a nine-to-three verdict. The Louisiana courts rejected his claims that such a verdict violated his constitutional rights to due process and equal protection.

ISSUE: Do state provisions that allow for guilty verdicts of nine to three for conviction violate the Due Process and Equal Protection Clauses of the Fourteenth Amendment?

HOLDING: No.

RATIONALE: "We conclude, therefore, that, as to the nine jurors who voted to convict, the State satisfied its burden of proving guilt beyond any reasonable doubt."

"Of course, the State's proof could perhaps be regarded as more certain if it had convinced all 12 jurors. . . . But the fact remains that nine jurors—a substantial majority of the jury—were convinced by the evidence. In our view disagreement of three jurors does not alone establish reasonable doubt, particularly when such a heavy majority of the jury, after having considered the dissenters' views, remains convinced of guilt. That rational men disagree is not in itself equivalent to a failure of proof by the State, nor does it indicate infidelity to the reasonable-doubt standard."

"We conclude, therefore, that verdicts rendered by 9 out of 12 jurors are not automatically invalidated by the disagreement of the dissenting three. Appellant was not deprived of due process of law."

"Appellant also attacks as violative of the Equal Protection Clause the provisions of Louisiana law requiring unanimous verdicts in capital . . . cases, but permitting less-than-unanimous verdicts in cases such as his. We conclude, however, that the Louisiana statutory scheme serves a rational purpose and is not subject to constitutional challenge."

"In order to 'facilitate, expedite, and reduce expense in the administration of criminal justice . . .' 9 jurors rather than 5 or 12 were required for a verdict. We discern nothing invidious in this classification. We have held that the States are free under the Federal Constitution to try defendants with juries of less than 12 men. . . . Three jurors here voted to acquit, but from what we have earlier said, this does not demonstrate that appellant was convicted on a lower standard of proof. To obtain a conviction in any of the categories under Louisiana law, the State must prove guilt beyond reasonable doubt, but the number of jurors who must be so convinced increases with the seriousness of the crime and the severity of the punishment that may be imposed. We perceive nothing unconstitutional or invidiously discriminatory, however, in a State's insisting that its burden of proof be carried with more jurors where more serious crimes or more severe punishments are at issue."

15

Posttrial Procedures

IN THIS FINAL CHAPTER, we examine several remaining issues. Unlike chapter 14, where the focus was on matters that were related to the jury and trial, this chapter examines activities that take place after the trial has been completed and the verdict has been reached. These matters are designed to ensure that the accused, perhaps now the convict, was treated fairly and that all the information pertaining to his or her case was heard and properly considered. As we have said before, it is the accused that enjoys protections against overzealous governmental prosecution. To make sure that those protections have not been violated, additional actions can be taken.

For example, the Supreme Court has heard a number of cases that deal directly with the sentencing hearing. The Court has stated that certain kinds of information, such as past acquittals, can be heard at such a proceeding. Conversely, the Court has also pointed out that assumptions and statements based on untruths cannot be factored into the sentencing process. Additionally, the Court has also ruled on whether the intention of the offender to select a particular victim because of their race can be considered. Further, the Court has stated that the defendant has a right to counsel at the sentencing. In a very recent case, the Court has also had the occasion to determine whether or not judges or juries can impose a sentence upon a convict that exceeds state guidelines.

As a further layer of protection for the accused, the Supreme Court has also ruled that those who have been convicted have the opportunity to attack the conviction based upon various legal issues. One of these actions is called an appeal, and the Court has stated that a convicted offender has a constitutional right to only one. If the person desires to file more than one, he or she must do so with his or her own resources. Another way to attack a conviction is to argue that the state is illegally detaining you, even after you have been sentenced and incarcerated. This is a habeas corpus proceeding and when translated the phrase roughly means "bring the body here."

A. Sentencing

1. Can Information Concerning Acquittals Be Considered?

United States v. Watts, 519 U.S. 148 (1997)

Vote: 7-2

FACTS: Police discovered cocaine base in the kitchen and two loaded guns and ammunition in a bedroom closet of Vernon Watts's house. A jury convicted Watts of possessing cocaine base with intent to distribute, but acquitted him of using a firearm in relation to a drug crime. Despite his acquittal, the federal court found by a preponderance of the evidence that Watts had possessed the guns in connection with the drug offense. As a result, the judge factored in two extra points to his offense level under the U.S. Sentencing Guidelines. The sentence was vacated by the court of appeals, which held that a judge may not rely on any facts on which a defendant was acquitted. The Government argued that the judge was permitted to enhance the sentence because it did not require the connection between the drug offense and possession of the gun. The appellate court rejected this argument and stated that the judge had considered evidence that the jury rejected.

ISSUE: Can a judge consider the underlying conduct of a defendant who has been acquitted on one charge and convicted on another in enhancing the sentence if the government proves the underlying events of the acquitted charge by a preponderance of the evidence?

HOLDING: Yes.

RATIONALE: "We begin our analysis with 18 U.S.C. §3661, which codifies the longstanding principle that sentencing courts have broad discretion to consider various kinds of information. The statute states: 'No limitation shall be placed on the information concerning the background, character, and conduct of a person convicted of an offense which a court of the United States may receive and consider for the purpose of imposing an appropriate sentence.'"

"Indeed, under the pre-Guidelines sentencing regime, it was 'well established that a sentencing judge may take into account facts introduced at trial relating to other charges, even ones of which the defendant has been acquitted.'"

"The Guidelines did not alter this aspect of the sentencing court's discretion."

"Section 1B1.3, in turn, describes in sweeping language the conduct that a sentencing court may consider in determining the applicable guideline range. The commentary to that section states: 'Conduct that is not formally charged or is not an element of the offense of conviction may enter into the determination of the applicable guideline sentencing range . . .' With respect to certain offenses . . . USSG §1B1.3(a)(2) requires the sentencing court to consider 'all acts and omissions . . . that were part of the same course of conduct or common scheme or plan as the offense of conviction.'"

"Although Justice Stevens' dissent . . . argues that the court must close its eyes to acquitted conduct at earlier stages of the sentencing process because the 'broadly inclusive language of §3661' is incorporated only into §1B1.4 of the Guidelines. This argument ignores §1B1.3 which, as we have noted, directs sentencing courts to consider all other related conduct, whether or not it resulted in a conviction."

"[W]e have held that application of the preponderance standard at sentencing generally satisfies due process. . . . We therefore hold that a jury's verdict of acquittal does not prevent the sentencing court from considering conduct underlying the acquitted charge, so long as that conduct has been proved by a preponderance of the evidence."

2. Information That Cannot Be Considered

a. Untrue Assumptions

Townsend v. Burke, 334 U.S. 736 (1948)
Vote: 6-3
FACTS: Townsend was arrested on June 3, 1945, and indicted for burglary and armed robbery. He confessed the next day and was sentenced on June 5, after pleading guilty to two charges of robbery and two charges of burglary and not guilty to others. During the discussions surrounding the plea, the judge recited several past charges against Townsend, one of which had been dismissed and others of which he was acquitted. He did not have a lawyer at the sentencing. He argued that this violated his right to counsel since the accusations made by the judge concerning his record could not be corrected by counsel.
ISSUE: Can a judge take into consideration information that is not true in a sentencing proceeding?
HOLDING: No.
RATIONALE: "In that, and in earlier cases, we have indicated, however, that the disadvantage from absence of counsel, when aggravated by circumstances showing that it resulted in the prisoner actually being taken advantage of, or prejudiced, does make out a case of violation of due process."

"The trial court's facetiousness casts a somewhat somber reflection on the fairness of the proceeding when we learn from the record that actually the charge of receiving the stolen saxophone had been dismissed and the prisoner discharged by the magistrate. But it savors of foul play or of carelessness when we find from the record that, on two other of the charges which the court recited against the defendant, he had also been found not guilty. . . . We are not at liberty to assume that items given such emphasis by the sentencing court, did not influence the sentence which the prisoner is now serving."

"We believe that on the record before us, it is evident that this uncounseled defendant was either overreached by the prosecution's submission of misinformation to the court or was prejudiced by the court's own misreading of the record. Counsel, had any been present, would have been under a duty to prevent the court from proceeding on such false assumptions and perhaps under a duty to seek remedy elsewhere if they persisted. Consequently, on this record we conclude that, while disadvantaged by lack of counsel, this prisoner was sentenced on the basis of assumptions concerning his criminal record which were materially untrue. Such a result, whether caused by carelessness or design, is inconsistent with due process of law, and such a conviction cannot stand."

"It is not the duration or severity of this sentence that renders it constitutionally invalid; it is the careless or designed pronouncement of sentence on a foundation so extensively and materially false, which the prisoner had no opportunity to correct by the services which counsel would provide, that renders the proceedings lacking in due process."

b. Intention of Offender to Select Victim Due to Race

Wisconsin v. Mitchell, 508 U.S. 476 (1993)
Vote: 9-0
FACTS: A group of young black men, including Todd Mitchell, gathered at an apartment in Kenosha, Wisconsin. Several discussed a scene from the motion picture *Mississippi Burning,* in which a white man beat a black boy who was praying. Mitchell asked: "Do you all feel hyped up to move on some white people?" Shortly thereafter the men left the apartment. A white boy approached the group on the opposite side of the street, and as the boy walked by, Mitchell said: "You all want to fuck somebody up? There goes a white boy; go get him." Mitchell pointed in the boy's direction, and the group ran at the boy, beat him, and stole his shoes. The boy was rendered comatose for four days. Mitchell was convicted of aggravated battery, but because the jury found that Mitchell selected his victim because of his race, the maximum sentence for the offense was increased to seven years under a statute that enhances the maximum penalty whenever the defendant "[i]ntentionally selects the person against whom the crime . . . is committed . . . because of the race, religion, color, disability, sexual orientation, national origin, or ancestry of that person." Mitchell was then sentenced to four years' imprisonment for the aggravated battery. He appealed his conviction and sentence, challenging the constitutionality of the penalty-enhancement law.
ISSUE: Can a sentence be enhanced for an offense under a state "hate crime" law?
HOLDING: Yes.
RATIONALE: "The question presented in this case is whether this penalty enhancement is prohibited by the First and Fourteenth Amendments. We hold that it is not."

"Mitchell argues that the Wisconsin penalty-enhancement statute is invalid because it punishes the defendant's discriminatory motive, or reason, for acting. But motive plays the same role under the Wisconsin statute as it does under federal and state antidiscrimination laws, which we have previously upheld against constitutional challenge."

"Nothing in our decision last Term in *R.A.V.* [*v. St. Paul,* 505 U.S. 377 (1992)] compels a different result here."

"[W]hereas the ordinance struck down in *R.A.V.* was explicitly directed at expression (i.e., 'speech' or 'messages') . . ., the statute in this case is aimed at conduct unprotected by the First Amendment."

"Moreover, the Wisconsin statute singles out for enhancement bias-inspired conduct because this conduct is thought to inflict greater individual and societal harm. For example, according to the State and its amici, bias-motivated crimes are more likely to provoke retaliatory crimes, inflict distinct emotional harms on their victims, and incite community unrest . . . The State's desire to redress these perceived harms provides an adequate explanation for its penalty-enhancement provision over and above mere disagreement with offenders' beliefs or biases."

"Finally, there remains to be considered Mitchell's argument that the Wisconsin statute is unconstitutionally overbroad because of its 'chilling effect' on free speech"

"The sort of chill envisioned here is far more attenuated and unlikely than that contemplated in traditional 'overbreadth' cases. . . . We are left, then, with the prospect of a citizen suppressing his bigoted beliefs for fear that evidence of such beliefs will be introduced against him at trial if he commits a more serious offense against person or property. This is simply too speculative. . . ."

"Evidence of a defendant's previous declarations or statements is commonly admitted in criminal trials subject to evidentiary rules dealing with relevancy, reliability, and the like. Nearly half a century ago, in *Haupt v. United States*, 330 U.S. 631 (1947), we rejected a contention similar to that advanced by Mitchell here."

3. Do Judges or Juries Have the Authority to Increase Sentences beyond State Guidelines?

Blakely v. Washington, 542 U.S. 296 (2004)
Vote: 5-4
FACTS: Ralph Howard Blakely Jr. married Yolanda in 1973 despite his having been diagnosed with psychological and personality disorders. Yolanda filed for divorce, and in 1998, Blakely abducted her from their home at knifepoint, bound her with duct tape, and forced her into a wooden box in his truck. During the abduction, he implored her to dismiss the divorce proceedings. When their son, Ralphy, returned home from school, Blakely ordered him to follow in another car, threatening to harm Yolanda with a shotgun if he refused. Ralphy escaped and sought help when they stopped at a gas station, but Blakely continued with Yolanda to a friend's house in Montana, where he was finally arrested after the friend called police. He was then charged with first-degree kidnapping, but the State reduced the charge to second-degree kidnapping involving domestic violence and use of a firearm (a Class B felony) after a plea agreement. The case then proceeded to sentencing. State law provided that "[n]o person convicted of a [class B] felony shall be punished by confinement . . . exceeding . . . a term of ten years." Washington's Sentencing Reform Act specified that for Blakely's offense a judge may impose a sentence above the standard range if he finds "substantial and compelling reasons" for doing so. The Act lists aggravating factors that justify such a departure, and when a judge imposes an exceptional sentence, he must set forth findings and conclusions that support it. On the basis of other state statutes allowing in some cases an 'exceptional sentence' exceeding the general statutory limit, the judge imposed a ninety-month prison sentence on the ground that the accused had acted with 'deliberate cruelty,' which was a statutorily enumerated ground for an enhanced sentence in a domestic-violence case.

ISSUE: Can a judge impose an "enhanced" sentence after making a judicial determination of an aggravating factor that the jury did not find?

HOLDING: No.

RATIONALE: "This case requires us to apply the rule we expressed in *Apprendi v. New Jersey*, 530 U.S. 466 (2000): 'Other than the fact of a prior conviction, any fact that increases the penalty for a crime beyond the prescribed statutory maximum must be submitted to a jury, and proved beyond a reasonable doubt.' This rule reflects two long-standing tenets of common-law criminal jurisprudence: that the 'truth of every accusation' against a defendant 'should afterwards be confirmed by the unanimous suffrage of twelve of his equals and neighbors.'"

"In this case, petitioner was sentenced to more than three years above the 53-month statutory maximum of the standard range because he had acted with 'deliberate cruelty.' The facts supporting that finding were neither admitted by petitioner nor found by a jury. . . . Our precedents make clear, however, that the 'statutory maximum' for *Apprendi* purposes is the maximum sentence a judge may impose *solely on the basis of the facts reflected in the jury verdict or admitted by the defendant*. . . . In other words, the relevant 'statutory maximum' is not the maximum sentence a judge may impose after finding additional facts, but the maximum he may impose *without* any additional findings. When a judge inflicts punishment that the jury's verdict alone does not allow, the jury has not found all the facts 'which the law makes essential to the punishment . . .' and the judge exceeds his proper authority."

"Because the State's sentencing procedure did not comply with the Sixth Amendment, petitioner's sentence is invalid."

"Just as suffrage ensures the people's ultimate control in the legislative and executive branches, jury trial is meant to ensure their control in the judiciary. . . . *Apprendi* carries out this design by ensuring that the judge's authority to sentence derives wholly from the jury's verdict. Without that restriction, the jury would not exercise the control that the Framers intended."

"As *Apprendi* held, every defendant has the *right* to insist that the prosecutor prove to a jury all facts legally essential to the punishment. Under the dissenters' alternative, he has no such right. That should be the end of the matter."

"The Framers would not have thought it too much to demand that, before depriving a man of three more years of his liberty, the State should suffer the modest inconvenience of submitting its accusation to 'the unanimous suffrage of twelve of his equals and neighbors.'"

4. Guilty Plea and Waiver of Privilege against Self-Incrimination

Mitchell v. United States, 526 U.S. 314 (1999)

Vote: 5-4

FACTS: Amanda Mitchell and twenty-two others were indicted for offenses arising from a conspiracy to distribute cocaine. The leader, Harry Riddick, obtained cocaine and resold it through couriers, including Mitchell, and she was charged with conspiring to distribute five or more kilograms of cocaine and with three counts of distributing cocaine within 1,000 feet of a school or playground. In 1995, without an agreement, she plead guilty to all four charges and reserved the right to contest the drug quantity. The district court advised her the drug quantity would be determined at her sentencing. Before accepting the plea, the judge informed her of the possible penalties and told her that by pleading guilty, she would waive the right to remain silent.

After the Government explained the charges, the judge asked her if she committed the offenses, to which Mitchell replied, "Some of it." She indicated that she was present for a transaction but never delivered the cocaine. She then on two separate occasions restated her desire to plead guilty. When several of Mitchell's codefendants went on trial, some of them testified that Mitchell was a regular seller. One gave specifics as to the amounts she sold and the frequency of her selling but conceded that he had never seen her sell. Both parties referred to Alvitta Mack's testimony that, as an informant, she had made drug buys of two ounces each from Mitchell. The defense did nothing to question the testimony but argued that it was the only clear evidence pertaining to amount for sentencing purposes. The judge then stated that as a consequence of her plea Mitchell had no right to remain silent and that he found credible the testimony indicating she had been a regular drug courier and that she had sold more than the five-kilogram threshold, thus mandating a minimum ten-year sentence. The judge admitted that Mitchell's silence was a factor in his decision.

ISSUE: Does a guilty plea serve as a waiver of the privilege against self-incrimination at sentencing?

HOLDING: No.

RATIONALE: "The Government maintains that petitioner's guilty plea was a waiver of the privilege against compelled self-incrimination with respect to all the crimes comprehended in the plea. We hold otherwise and rule that petitioner retained the privilege at her sentencing hearing."

"Nor does Federal Rule of Criminal Procedure 11, which governs pleas, contemplate the broad waiver the Government envisions."

"Neither the Rule itself nor the District Court's explication of it indicates that the defendant consents to take the stand in the sentencing phase or to suffer adverse consequences from declining to do so. Both the Rule and the District Court's admonition were to the effect that by entry of the plea petitioner would surrender the right 'at trial' to invoke the privilege. As there was to be no trial, the warning would not have brought home to petitioner that she was also waiving the right to self-incrimination at sentencing. The purpose of Rule 11 is to inform the defendant of what she loses by forgoing the trial, not to elicit a waiver of the privilege for proceedings still to follow."

"Rule 11 does not prevent the defendant from relying upon the privilege at sentencing."

"Treating a guilty plea as a waiver of the privilege at sentencing would be a grave encroachment on the rights of defendants. . . . Were we to accept the Government's position, prosecutors could indict without specifying the quantity of drugs involved, obtain a guilty plea, and then put the defendant on the stand at sentencing to fill in the drug quantity. The result would be to enlist the defendant as an instrument in his or her own condemnation, undermining the long tradition and vital principle that criminal proceedings rely on accusations proved by the Government. . . ."

"The centerpiece of the Third Circuit's opinion is the idea that the entry of the guilty plea completes the incrimination of the defendant, thus extinguishing the privilege. Where a sentence has yet to be imposed, however, this Court has already rejected the proposition that 'incrimination is complete once guilt has been adjudicated . . .' and we reject it again today."

"It is true, as a general rule, that where there can be no further incrimination, there is no basis for the assertion of the privilege. We conclude that principle applies to cases in which the sentence has been fixed and the judgment of conviction has become final."

"Where the sentence has not yet been imposed a defendant may have a legitimate fear of adverse consequences from further testimony. As the Court stated in *Estelle* [*v. Smith*, 451 U.S. 454 (1981)]: 'Any effort by the State to compel [the defendant] to testify against his will at the sentencing hearing clearly would contravene the Fifth Amendment. . . .' *Estelle* was a capital case, but we find no reason not to apply the principle to noncapital sentencing hearings as well."

"To maintain that sentencing proceedings are not part of 'any criminal case' is contrary to the law and to common sense."

"Our holding today is a product of existing precedent, not only *Griffin* [*v. California*, 380 U.S. 609 (1965)] but also by *Estelle*, in which the Court could 'discern no basis to distinguish between the guilt and penalty phases of respondent's capital murder trial so far as the protection of the Fifth Amendment privilege is concerned. . . .'"

"The Government retains the burden of proving facts relevant to the crime at the sentencing phase and cannot enlist the defendant in this process at the expense of the self-incrimination privilege."

5. Introduction of New Testimonial Evidence at the Sentencing Phase of Capital Trials

Oregon v. Guzek 546 U.S. 517 (2006)
Vote: 8-0
FACTS: Guzek and two others burglarized the Houser home. One associate killed Rod Houser, and Guzek killed Lois Houser. Police traced Guzek and his friends after they found out that Guzek held a grudge against the family. At trial, the associates painted Guzek as the ringleader.

Guzek's defense was partially based on an alibi that his grandfather and mother supported. The court convicted Guzek, and sentenced him to death. On appeal, the Oregon Supreme Court ordered a new sentencing proceeding, and Guzek was again sentenced to death. He again appealed, and the Oregon Supreme Court again ordered resentencing. Guzek was sentenced to death a third time. He again appealed, and the Oregon Supreme Court addressed the admissibility of live testimony from Guzek's mother about his alibi. It held that the Eighth and Fourteenth Amendments provided

Guzek a constitutional right to introduce this evidence at his sentencing proceeding.
ISSUE: Does a defendant have Eighth and Fourteenth Amendment rights to live testimony from a witness at his capital sentencing proceeding?
HOLDING: No.
RATIONALE: "We can find nothing in the Eighth or Fourteenth Amendments that provides a capital defendant a right to introduce new evidence of this kind at sentencing."

"We cannot agree with the Oregon Supreme Court that our previous cases have found in the Eighth Amendment a constitutional right broad enough to encompass the evidence here at issue."

"[T]his Court decided *Franklin v. Lynaugh* . . . , and that case makes clear, contrary to the Oregon Supreme Court's understanding, that this Court's previous cases had *not* interpreted the Eighth Amendment as providing a capital defendant the right to introduce at sentencing evidence designed to cast 'residual doubt' on his guilt of the basic crime of conviction. The *Franklin* plurality said it was 'quite doubtful' that any such right existed. . . . And two other Members of the Court added that 'our cases' do not support any such 'right to reconsideration by the sentencing body of lingering doubts about . . . guilt.'"

"[T]he Court's statements on the matter make clear that the Oregon Supreme Court erred in interpreting *Green* as providing a capital defendant with a constitutional right to introduce residual doubt evidence at sentencing."

"But the Eighth Amendment does not deprive the State of its authority to set reasonable limits upon the evidence a defendant can submit, and to control the manner in which it is submitted. Rather, 'States are free to structure and shape consideration of mitigating evidence "in an effort to achieve a more rational and equitable administration of the death penalty."'"

"Third, the negative impact of a rule restricting defendant's ability to introduce *new* alibi evidence is minimized by the fact that Oregon law gives the defendant the right to present to the sentencing jury *all* the evidence of innocence from the original trial regardless."

"The legitimacy of these trial management and evidentiary considerations, along with the typically minimal adverse impact that a restriction would have on a defendant's ability to present his alibi claim at resentencing convinces us that the Eighth Amendment does not protect defendant's right to present the evidence at issue here."

6. Imposition of the Death Sentence on Juveniles

Roper v. Simmons 543 U.S. 551 (2005)
Vote: 5-4
FACTS: At the age of 17, Simmons committed murder after discussing the plan with his friends. Simmons assured his friends they could "get away with it" because they were minors. The three met at about 2 a.m. on the night of the murder, but one left. Simmons and another entered Crook's home and Mrs. Crook called out, "Who's

there?" Simmons later admitted that he wanted to kill Mrs. Crook due to a previous car accident. The two bound Mrs. Crook with duct tape, put her in her minivan and drove to a park. They then covered her head with a towel, tied her hands and feet with wire, wrapped her face in duct tape and threw her from a bridge, drowning her. Mr. Crook reported his wife missing after returning from an overnight trip. After his arrest, Simmons confessed and agreed to do a videotape reenactment of the crime.

The State charged Simmons with burglary, kidnapping, stealing, and murder in the first degree and sought the death penalty. Both sides in the case addressed Simmons's age, and the defense argued that his youth should be a mitigating factor. The jury convicted him after it agreed to three aggravating circumstances, and the judge imposed death. Simmons argued that the reasoning that the Court used to disallow death sentences for the mentally retarded also applied to criminals who committed their crimes when they were under eighteen.

ISSUE: Does the Eighth Amendment protection against cruel and unusual punishment prohibit the imposition of the death penalty on offenders who committed their crimes when they were under eighteen?

HOLDING: Yes.

RATIONALE: "The evidence of national consensus against the death penalty for juveniles is similar, and in some respects parallel, to the evidence *Atkins* held sufficient to demonstrate a national consensus against the death penalty for the mentally retarded."

"Thirty States prohibit the juvenile death penalty, including 12 that have rejected it altogether and 18 that maintain it but, by express provision or judicial interpretation, exclude juveniles from its reach."

"Congress considered the issue when enacting the Federal Death Penalty Act in 1994, and determined that the death penalty should not extend to juveniles."

"Three general differences between juveniles under 18 and adults demonstrate that juvenile offenders cannot with reliability be classified among the worst offenders. Juveniles' susceptibility to immature and irresponsible behavior means 'their irresponsible conduct is not as morally reprehensible as that of an adult. . . .' Their own vulnerability and comparative lack of control over their immediate surroundings mean juveniles have a greater claim than adults to be forgiven for failing to escape negative influences in their whole environment. . . . The reality that juveniles still struggle to define their identity means it is less supportable to conclude that even a heinous crime committed by a juvenile is evidence of irretrievably depraved character. The *Thompson* plurality recognized the import of these characteristics with respect to juveniles under 16 . . . [and the] same reasoning applies to all juvenile offenders under 18."

"When a juvenile offender commits a heinous crime, the State can exact forfeiture of some of the most basic liberties, but the State cannot extinguish his life and his potential to attain a mature understanding of his own humanity."

"The age of 18 is the point where society draws the line for many purposes between childhood and adulthood. It is, we conclude, the age at which the line for death eligibility ought to rest."

7. Harmless Error and Judicial Fact-Finding

Washington v. Recuenco 126 S.Ct. 2546 (2006)
Vote: 7-2

FACTS: Recuenco fought with his wife, and after smashing their stove, he threatened her with a gun. He was arrested and charged with assault with a deadly weapon. The trial court accepted a motion by the defense to submit a form to the jury that directed it to make a determination as to whether Recuenco was "armed with a deadly weapon at the time of the commission of the crime." A firearm qualifies as such a weapon under Washington law. However, nothing in the form required the jury to find that Recuenco had engaged in assault with a "firearm" specifically. The jury convicted Recuenco and found, by way of the form, that he had been armed with a deadly weapon. The State sought the lower end of the sentence for the charge but asked for a three-year enhancement for the firearm instead of the one-year that would have normally come with the jury finding of Recuenco being "armed with a deadly weapon." Thus the trial court, rather than the jury, found that Recuenco was armed with a "firearm," and it imposed a sentence of thirty-nine months.

During the course of the appellate process the Supreme Court held that any fact that increased the sentence must be submitted to a jury, and that the maximum sentence that could be imposed was that which was based upon the facts studied by the verdict of the jury or admitted to by the defendant.

ISSUE: Is the harmless-error rule applicable to a trial court's error in applying a sentencing enhancement that was not submitted to the jury?

HOLDING: Yes.

RATIONALE: "Failure to submit a sentencing factor to the jury, like failure to submit an element to the jury, is not structural error."

"'[I]f the defendant had counsel and was tried by an impartial adjudicator, there is a strong presumption that any other [constitutional] errors that may have occurred are subject to harmless-error analysis. . . .' Only in rare cases has this Court held that an error is structural, and thus requires automatic reversal."

"We recently considered whether an error similar to that which occurred here was structural in *Neder*. . . . At Neder's trial, the District Court instructed the jury that it 'need not consider' the materiality of any false statements to convict Neder of the tax offenses or bank fraud, because materiality 'is not a question for the jury to decide.' The court also failed to include materiality as an element of the offenses of mail fraud and wire fraud. We determined that the District Court erred because . . . materiality is an element of the tax offense that must be found by the jury. . . . We nonetheless held that harmless-error analysis applied to these errors, because 'an instruction that omits an element of the offense does not *necessarily* render a criminal trial fundamentally unfair or an unreliable vehicle for determining guilt or innocence.'"

"'[A]ny possible distinction between an "element" of a felony offense and a "sentencing factor" was unknown to the practice of criminal indictment, trial by jury, and judgment by court as it existed during the years surrounding our Nation's founding. . . .' Assigning this distinction constitutional significance cannot be reconciled with our recognition in *Apprendi* that elements and sentencing factors must be treated the same for Sixth Amendment purposes."

⟵

B. Probation Revocation

1. Can Probation Be Revoked for Failure to Pay a Fine?

Bearden v. Georgia, 461 U.S. 660 (1983)
Vote: 9-0
FACTS: Bearden was indicted for burglary and theft by receiving stolen property. He pleaded guilty, and was sentenced. Pursuant to the First Offender's Act, the trial court did not enter a judgment of guilt but deferred and sentenced Bearden to three years' probation for the burglary and a concurrent one-year probation for the theft charge. As a condition of probation, the court ordered Bearden to pay a $500 fine and $250 in restitution. He was to pay $100 that day, $100 the next day, and the $550 balance within four months. He borrowed money from his parents and paid the first $200. However, he was laid off, and with only a ninth-grade education and an inability to read, he was unable to find work. He also had no other income or assets to speak of. Shortly before the balance came due, he notified the probation office he was going to be late with his payment because he could not find a job. After a hearing, the court revoked probation for failure to pay and entered a conviction. Bearden was sentenced to serve the remaining portion of probation in prison. The Georgia Court of Appeals rejected Bearden's claim that imprisoning him for inability to pay the fine violated the Equal Protection Clause of the Fourteenth Amendment.
ISSUE: Can a court revoke probation automatically if a person cannot pay a fine?
HOLDING: No.
RATIONALE: "We conclude that the trial court erred in automatically revoking probation because petitioner could not pay his fine, without determining that petitioner had not made sufficient bona fide efforts to pay or that adequate alternative forms of punishment did not exist."

"Most relevant to the issue here is the holding in *Williams v. Illinois*, 399 U.S. 235 (1970), that a State cannot subject a certain class of convicted defendants to a period of imprisonment beyond the statutory maximum solely because they are too poor to pay the fine."

"The rule of *Williams* and *Tate* [*v. Short*, 401 U.S. 395 (1971)], then, is that the State cannot 'impos[e] a fine as a sentence and then automatically conver[t] it into a jail term solely because the defendant is indigent and cannot forthwith pay the fine in full. . . .' Both *Williams* and *Tate* carefully distinguished this substantive limitation on the imprisonment of indigents from the situation where a defendant was at fault in failing to pay the fine."

"But if the probationer has made all reasonable efforts to pay the fine or restitution, and yet cannot do so through no fault of his own, it is fundamentally unfair to revoke probation automatically without considering whether adequate alternative methods of punishing the defendant are available. This lack of fault provides a 'substantial reaso[n] which justifie[s] or mitigate[s] the violation and make[s] revocation inappropriate.'"

"[A] probationer who has made sufficient bona fide efforts to pay his fine and restitution, and who has complied with the other conditions of probation, has demonstrated a willingness to pay his debt to society and an ability to conform his conduct to social norms. The State nevertheless asserts three reasons why imprisonment is required to further its penal goals."

"First, the State argues that revoking probation furthers its interest in ensuring that restitution be paid to the victims of crime. . . . Such a goal is fully served, however, by revoking probation only for persons who have not made sufficient bona fide efforts to pay."

"Second, the State asserts that its interest in rehabilitating the probationer and protecting society requires it to remove him from the temptation of committing other crimes. This is no more than a naked assertion that a probationer's poverty by itself indicates he may commit crimes in the future and thus that society needs for him to be incapacitated. . . . But it must be remembered that the State is seeking here to use as the *sole* justification for imprisonment the poverty of a probationer who, by assumption, has demonstrated sufficient bona fide efforts to find a job and pay the fine and whom the State initially thought it unnecessary to imprison. Given the significant interest of the individual in remaining on probation . . . the State cannot justify incarcerating a probationer who has demonstrated sufficient bona fide efforts to repay his debt to society, solely by lumping him together with other poor persons and thereby classifying him as dangerous. This would be little more than punishing a person for his poverty."

"Third, and most plausibly, the State argues that its interests in punishing the lawbreaker and deterring others from criminal behavior require it to revoke probation for failure to pay a fine or restitution. . . . This interest can often be served fully by alternative means."

2. How Much Due Process Is Required for Probation Revocation?

Gagnon v. Scarpelli, 411 U.S. 778 (1973)
Vote: 8-1
FACTS: Gerald Scarpelli pleaded guilty to armed robbery in Wisconsin, but the judge imposed a suspended fifteen-year sentence and gave him seven years probation instead. Scarpelli signed an agreement and a permit allowing him to reside in Illinois. Police caught Scarpelli and Fred Kleckner in the course of a burglary, and Scarpelli admitted that he and Kleckner had broken into the house to steal merchandise or money. Wisconsin then revoked his probation without a hearing.
ISSUE: Is a probationer entitled to a preliminary and final hearing and a lawyer if he is indigent before probation is formally revoked?
HOLDING: Yes.
RATIONALE: "Probation revocation, like parole revocation, is not a stage of a criminal prosecution, but does result in a loss of liberty. Accordingly, we hold that a probationer, like a parolee, is entitled to a preliminary and a final revocation hearing."

"At the preliminary hearing, a probationer or parolee is entitled to notice of the alleged violations of probation or parole, an opportunity to appear and to present evidence in his own behalf, a conditional right to confront adverse witnesses, an independent decisionmaker, and a written report of the hearing. . . . The final hearing is a less summary one because the decision under consideration is the ultimate decision to revoke rather than a mere determination of probable cause, but the 'minimum requirements of due process' include very similar elements: '(a) written notice of the claimed violations of (probation or) parole; (b) disclosure to the (probationer or) parolee of evidence against him; (c) opportunity to be heard in person and to present witnesses and documentary evidence; (d) the right to confront and cross-examine adverse witnesses (unless the hearing officer specifically finds good cause for not allowing confrontation); (e) a "neutral and detached" hearing body such as a traditional parole board, members of which need not be judicial officers or lawyers; and (f) a written statement by the factfinders as to the evidence relied on and reasons for revoking (probation or) parole.'"

"[P]etitioner argues that counsel need never be supplied. What this argument overlooks is that the effectiveness of the rights guaranteed by *Morrissey* [*v. Brewer*, 408 U.S. 471 (1972)] may in some circumstances depend on the use of skills which the probationer or parolee is unlikely to possess. Despite the informal nature of the proceedings and the absence of technical rules of procedure or evidence, the unskilled or uneducated probationer or parolee may well have difficulty in presenting his version of a disputed set of facts where the presentation requires the examining or cross-examining of witnesses or the offering or dissecting of complex documentary evidence."

"In some cases . . . the probationer's or parolee's version of a disputed issue can fairly be represented only by a trained advocate."

C. Appeals

1. Is Court-Appointed Counsel a Constitutional Right?

Ross v. Moffitt, 417 U.S. 600 (1974)
Vote: 6-3
FACTS: Ross pleaded not guilty to forgery and uttering a forged instrument. He was represented by appointed counsel. Upon his conviction he appealed to the North Carolina Court of Appeals, where he was again given a court-appointed lawyer. Following affirmance of his conviction, respondent sought to continue the process to the North Carolina Supreme Court, but his lawyer was told that the State was not required to provide counsel.
ISSUE: Is a state required to provide court-appointed counsel for indigents for discretionary appeals after the appeal of right or for appeals to the Supreme Court?
HOLDING: No.

RATIONALE: "We do not believe that the Due Process Clause requires North Carolina to provide respondent with counsel on his discretionary appeal to the State Supreme Court."

"[I]t is ordinarily the defendant, rather than the State, who initiates the appellate process, seeking not to fend off the efforts of the State's prosecutor but rather to overturn a finding of guilt made by a judge or a jury below. The defendant needs an attorney on appeal not as a shield to protect him against being 'haled into court' by the State and stripped of his presumption of innocence, but rather as a sword to upset the prior determination of guilt. . . . The fact that an appeal has been provided does not automatically mean that a State then acts unfairly by refusing to provide counsel to indigent defendants at every stage of the way. . . . Unfairness results only if indigents are singled out by the State and denied meaningful access to the appellate system because of their poverty."

"The Fourteenth Amendment 'does not require absolute equality or precisely equal advantages. . . .' It does require that the state appellate system be 'free of unreasoned distinctions . . .' and that indigents have an adequate opportunity to present their claims fairly within the adversary system. . . . In this case we do not believe that the Equal Protection Clause, when interpreted in the context of these cases, requires North Carolina to provide free counsel for indigent defendants seeking to take discretionary appeals to the North Carolina Supreme Court, or to file petitions for certiorari in this Court."

"North Carolina has followed the mandate of *Douglas* [*v. California*, 372 U.S. 353 (1963)] and authorized appointment of counsel for a convicted defendant appealing to the intermediate Court of Appeals, but has not gone beyond *Douglas* to provide for appointment of counsel for a defendant who seeks either discretionary review in the Supreme Court of North Carolina or a writ of certiorari here."

"We do not believe that it can be said, therefore, that a defendant in respondent's circumstances is denied meaningful access to the North Carolina Supreme Court simply because the State does not appoint counsel to aid him in seeking review in that court. At that stage he will have, at the very least, a transcript or other record of trial proceedings, a brief on his behalf in the Court of Appeals setting forth his claims of error, and in many cases an opinion by the Court of Appeals disposing of his case. These materials, supplemented by whatever submission respondent may make pro se, would appear to provide the Supreme Court of North Carolina with an adequate basis for its decision to grant or deny review."

"[T]he fact that a particular service might be of benefit to an indigent defendant does not mean that the service is constitutionally required. The duty of the State under our cases is not to duplicate the legal arsenal that may be privately retained by a criminal defendant in a continuing effort to reverse his conviction, but only to assure the indigent defendant an adequate opportunity to present his claims fairly in the context of the State's appellate process."

"The suggestion that a State is responsible for providing counsel to one petitioning this Court simply because it initiated the prosecution which led to the judgment sought to be reviewed is unsupported by either reason or authority. . . . [T]his Court has followed a consistent policy of denying applications for appointment of counsel by persons seeking to file jurisdictional statements or petitions for certiorari in this Court. . . . In the light of these authorities, it would be odd, indeed, to read the Fourteenth Amendment to impose such a requirement on the States."

2. Conflict of Interest in Representation

Holloway v. Arkansas, 435 U.S. 475 (1978)
Vote: 6-3
FACTS: Welch, Campbell, and Holloway entered a Little Rock, Arkansas, restaurant and terrorized the employees. During the robbery, one of two female employees was raped once; the other, twice. Each of the three were charged with one count of robbery and two counts of rape, and the court appointed a public defender to represent all three. The three were arraigned and pleaded not guilty. The lawyer asked the judge to appoint separate lawyers because the defendants mentioned a possible conflict of interest. After conducting a hearing, the judge declined to appoint separate counsel. Before the jury was selected, the lawyer again asked to have separate counsel appointed due to a concern that the information that he had would preclude his cross-examination of his clients.

At trial, various employees identified Holloway, Welch, and Campell as committing various offenses for which they were being tried. On the second day of trial, the lawyer advised the judge that all three men wanted to testify, against his advice, and that a conflict would arise as a result. The judge told the lawyer that it was fine for them to testify. Holloway stated that he was at his brother's house at the time of the robbery. When Welch tried to testify, he denied being at the restaurant, at which time Holloway interrupted and asked if he could object. The judge said that the lawyer would object and that he could not. The lawyer again explained the conflict and the judge told him to proceed. Welch proceeded to testify and denied any involvement in any of the crimes, as did Campbell. The jury rejected the testimony and convicted the men of all charges. On appeal to the Arkansas Supreme Court, the men argued that their representation by one lawyer, over their objection, violated the guarantee of effective assistance of counsel.
ISSUE: Is the failure of a judge to appoint separate counsel or to conduct a hearing to determine if separate counsel are needed to avoid a conflict of interest for more than one defendant in the same trial, a deprivation of the effective assistance of counsel?
HOLDING: Yes.
RATIONALE: "More than 35 years ago, in *Glasser v. United States*, 315 U.S. 60 (1942), this Court held that by requiring an attorney to represent two codefendants whose interests were in conflict the District Court had denied one of the defendants his Sixth Amendment right to the effective assistance of counsel."

"This Court held that 'the "Assistance of Counsel" guaranteed by the Sixth Amendment contemplates that such assistance be untrammeled and unimpaired by a court order requiring that one lawyer should simultaneously represent conflicting interests.'"

"We hold that the failure, in the face of the representations made by counsel weeks before trial and again before the jury was empaneled, deprived petitioners of the guarantee of 'assistance of counsel.'"

"'Of equal importance with the duty of the court to see that an accused has the assistance of counsel is its duty to refrain from . . . *insisting, or indeed, even suggesting, that counsel undertake to concurrently represent interests which might diverge from those of his first client, when the possibility of that divergence is brought home to the court.*'"

"Additionally, since the decision in *Glasser,* most courts have held that an attorney's request for the appointment of separate counsel, based on his representations as an officer of the court regarding a conflict of interests, should be granted. . . . In so holding, the courts have acknowledged and given effect to several interrelated considerations. An 'attorney representing two defendants in a criminal matter is in the best position professionally and ethically to determine when a conflict of interest exists or will probably develop in the course of a trial. . . .' Second, defense attorneys have the obligation, upon discovering a conflict of interests, to advise the court at once of the problem. Finally, attorneys are officers of the court, and 'when they address the judge solemnly upon a matter before the court, their declarations are virtually made under oath. . . .' We find these considerations persuasive."

"Nor does our holding preclude a trial court from exploring the adequacy of the basis of defense counsel's representations regarding a conflict of interests without improperly requiring disclosure of the confidential communications of the client."

D. Habeas Corpus

1. Fair Opportunity for Litigation and Habeas Corpus

Stone v. Powell, 428 U.S. 465 (1976)
Vote: 6-3
FACTS: Lloyd Powell and three companions entered a liquor store, where Powell became involved in an altercation with Gerald Parsons, the manager, over the theft of a bottle of wine. In the scuffling, Powell shot and killed Parsons's wife. An officer of the Henderson, Nevada, police subsequently arrested Powell for violation of the vagrancy ordinance, and in the search discovered a revolver with six expended cartridges in the cylinder. Powell was extradited and convicted of second-degree murder. Powell's accomplices testified against him, and a criminologist testified that the revolver found on Powell was the gun used to kill Parsons's wife. The court rejected Powell's contention that testimony by the officer as to the revolver should have been excluded because the vagrancy ordinance was unconstitutional. Powell filed a petition for a writ of habeas corpus arguing that the testimony concerning the revolver should have been excluded as the fruit of an illegal search. He argued that his arrest had been unlawful because the Henderson ordinance was vague and that the arresting officer lacked probable cause to believe that he was violating it. The district court concluded that the arresting officer

had probable cause. The Court of Appeals for the Ninth Circuit reversed, agreeing that the ordinance was vague and that Powell's arrest was illegal.

ISSUE: If a state court has provided fair opportunity to litigate a Fourth Amendment claim, is a state prisoner entitled to federal habeas relief on the ground that evidence admitted at trial was obtained via an illegal search or seizure?

HOLDING: No.

RATIONALE: "The discussion in *Kaufman* [*v. United States*, 394 U.S. 217 (1969)] of the scope of federal habeas corpus rests on the view that the effectuation of the Fourth Amendment, as applied to the States through the Fourteenth Amendment, requires the granting of habeas corpus relief when a prisoner has been convicted in state court on the basis of evidence obtained in an illegal search or seizure since those Amendments were held in *Mapp v. Ohio*, 367 U.S. 643 (1961), to require exclusion of such evidence at trial and reversal of conviction upon direct review. Until these cases we have not had occasion fully to consider the validity of this view. . . . Upon examination, we conclude, in light of the nature and purpose of the Fourth Amendment exclusionary rule, that this view is unjustified. We hold, therefore, that where the State has provided an opportunity for full and fair litigation of a Fourth Amendment claim, the Constitution does not require that a state prisoner be granted federal habeas corpus relief on the ground that evidence obtained in an unconstitutional search or seizure was introduced at his trial."

"In this context the contribution of the exclusionary rule, if any, to the effectuation of the Fourth Amendment is minimal, and the substantial societal costs of application of the rule persist with special force."

2. Habeas Corpus Restrictions and the Miranda Warnings

Withrow v. Williams, 507 U.S. 680 (1993)
Vote: 5-4

FACTS: Police officers in Romulus, Michigan, learned that Robert Allen Williams Jr. might have information about a double murder. Two officers went to his house and asked him to the station for questioning, and he agreed to go. The officers searched Williams, but did not handcuff him, and went to the station in an unmarked car. Sergeant David Early, testified that Williams was not under arrest, although a report indicated that he was. At the station, Williams first denied involvement but soon implicated himself, and the officers continued questioning him, assuring him that their concern was the "shooter." The officers decided not to advise Williams of his *Miranda* rights and Early stated: "You know everything that went down. You just don't want to talk about it. What it's gonna amount to is you can talk about it now and give us the truth and we're gonna check it out and see if it fits or else we're simply gonna charge you and lock you up and you can just tell it to a defense attorney and let him try and prove differently." Williams then admitted he had given the weapon to the killer, who had called him and told him where he had discarded the evidence. He also maintained that he had not been present at the scene.

At this point, forty minutes after they had begun questioning, the officers Mirandized Williams, but he waived the rights and made more inculpatory statements. Williams then admitted that he had driven the murderer to and from the scene, had witnessed the crimes, and had helped the murderer dispose of evidence. He was formally charged with murder shortly thereafter. Before trial, Williams moved to suppress his responses to the officers and the court suppressed some of the statements as the products of improper delay in arraignment under Michigan law but not others. A bench trial led to Williams's conviction on two counts each of first-degree murder and possession of a firearm during the commission of a felony. Williams then petitioned for a writ of habeas corpus, alleging a violation of his *Miranda* rights as a ground for relief.

ISSUE: Does the restriction on granting habeas relief to a defendant that had a fair opportunity to litigate a Fourth Amendment claim apply to *Miranda* violations?

HOLDING: No.

RATIONALE: "Today we hold that *Stone* [*v. Powell*, 428 U.S. 465 (1976)]'s restriction on the exercise of federal habeas jurisdiction does not extend to a state prisoner's claim that his conviction rests on statements obtained in violation of the safeguards mandated by *Miranda v. Arizona*, 384 U.S. 436 (1966)."

"'Prophylactic' though it may be, in protecting a defendant's Fifth Amendment privilege against self-incrimination, *Miranda* safeguards 'a fundamental *trial* right.'"

"Nor does the Fifth Amendment 'trial right' protected by *Miranda* serve some value necessarily divorced from the correct ascertainment of guilt. "'[A] system of criminal law enforcement which comes to depend on the 'confession' will, in the long run, be less reliable and more subject to abuses" than a system relying on independent investigation.' By bracing against 'the possibility of unreliable statements in every instance of in-custody interrogation,' *Miranda* serves to guard against 'the use of unreliable statements at trial.'"

"Finally, and most importantly, eliminating review of *Miranda* claims would not significantly benefit the federal courts in their exercise of habeas jurisdiction, or advance the cause of federalism in any substantial way."

"One might argue that tension results between the two judicial systems whenever a federal habeas court overturns a state conviction on finding that the state court let in a voluntary confession obtained by the police without the *Miranda* safeguards. And one would have to concede that this has occurred in the past, and doubtless will occur again. It is not reasonable, however, to expect such occurrences to be frequent enough to amount to a substantial cost of reviewing *Miranda* claims on habeas. . . . And if, finally, one should question the need for federal collateral review of requirements that merit such respect, the answer simply is that the respect is sustained in no small part by the existence of such review. 'It is the occasional abuse that the federal writ of habeas corpus stands ready to correct.'"

3. Restrictions on the Writ of Habeas Corpus

Felker v. Turpin, 518 U.S. 651 (1996)
Vote: 9-0

FACTS: Ellis Wayne Felker approached Jane W. as she got out of her car and claimed to be lost. He induced her to go to his trailer, where he raped and sodomized her. She escaped and notified police when he fell asleep. He was convicted of aggravated sodomy. When Felker was paroled four years later, he met Joy Ludlam, a waitress, and offered her a job at "The Leather Shoppe," a business he owned, in order to induce her to visit him. Her body was discovered in a creek, and analysis showed that she had been beaten, raped, sodomized, and strangled. Police discovered hair like Felker's on her body and clothes, hair resembling Ludlam's in his bedroom, and fibers like those in her coat in his car. Felker's neighbor reported seeing Ludlam's car at Felker's house the day she disappeared. Felker was convicted of murder, rape, aggravated sodomy, and false imprisonment and sentenced to death on the murder charge. The Georgia Supreme Court affirmed and the Supreme Court denied two petitions.

Felker then filed a petition for a writ of habeas corpus in the U.S. District Court for the Middle District of Georgia, which was denied. He filed another after that. These appeals come under Title I of the Antiterrorism and Effective Death Penalty Act of 1996, which changes the law dealing with the authorization of federal courts to grant habeas relief. The Act went into effect shortly before Felker was scheduled to be executed, and it concerns conditions under which second habeas applications by state prisoners must be dismissed. Felker argued that the three-judge panel's ability to determine whether an application meets the requirements of law, plus the fact that its decisions are not appealable, amounts to a suspension of the writ of habeas corpus.

ISSUE: Do the limitations of successive appeals under the Antiterrorism and Effective Death Penalty Act amount to a suspension of the writ of habeas corpus?

HOLDING: No.

RATIONALE: "The Act requires a habeas petitioner to obtain leave from the court of appeals before filing a second habeas petition in the district court. But this requirement simply transfers from the district court to the court of appeals a screening function which would previously have been performed by the district court as required by 28 U.S.C. §2254 Rule 9(b). The Act also codifies some of the preexisting limits on successive petitions, and further restricts the availability of relief to habeas petitioners. But we have long recognized that 'the power to award the writ by any of the courts of the United States, must be given by written law . . .' and we have likewise recognized that judgments about the proper scope of the writ are 'normally for Congress to make.'"

"The new restrictions on successive petitions constitute a modified res judicata rule, a restraint on what is called in habeas corpus practice 'abuse of the writ.' In *McCleskey v. Zant*, 499 U.S. 467 (1991), we said that 'the doctrine of abuse of the writ refers to a complex and evolving body of equitable principles informed and controlled by historical usage, statutory developments, and judicial decisions. . . .' The added restrictions which the Act places on second habeas petitions are well within . . . this evolutionary process, and we hold that they do not amount to a 'suspension' of the writ contrary to Article I, §9."

4. Timeliness of Habeas Corpus Petitions

Evans v. Chavis 546 U.S. 189 (2006)
Vote: 9-0
FACTS: Chavis filed a state habeas corpus petition on May 14, 1993, that the trial court denied. The California Court of Appeal also denied him on September 29, 1994. Chavis then waited more than three years before filing a petition in the California Supreme Court, which was denied in April of 1998. After a second batch of state petitions, Chavis filed a federal petition in 2000. The State asked the court to dismiss it on the ground that it was untimely under the Antiterrorism and Effective Death Penalty Act (AEDPA), which gives one year to file federal petitions, and Chavis had filed his more than four years after AEDPA became effective. However, the federal courts had to calculate how many days the state applications had been "pending" in the state courts and add those days to the one-year limitation. The Ninth Circuit held that the state court petition was "pending" for purposes of AEDPA from the time the California Court of Appeal issued its opinion in 1994 to the time Chavis petitioned the California Supreme Court in 1997. Under that determination, the federal petition was timely.

ISSUE: Does a state prisoner that files a habeas petition in a state supreme court three years after being denied in a lower court file an untimely federal petition?

HOLDING: Yes.

RATIONALE: "In *Saffold*, we held that (1) only a *timely* appeal tolls AEDPA's 1-year limitations period for the time between the lower court's adverse decision and the filing of a notice of appeal in the higher court; (2) in California, 'unreasonable' delays are not timely. . . . In addition, we referred to a Ninth Circuit case holding that a 4-year delay was reasonable as an example of what the law forbids the Ninth Circuit to do."

"[W]e see no alternative way of applying state law to a case like this one but for the Ninth Circuit simply to ask and to decide whether the state prisoner made the relevant filing within a reasonable time. In doing so, the Circuit must keep in mind that, in *Saffold*, we held that timely filings in California (as elsewhere) fell within the federal tolling provision *on the assumption* that California law in this respect did not differ significantly from the laws of other States."

"[W]e find the Ninth Circuit's reasoning in conflict with our *Saffold* holding. . . . We are convinced that the law does not permit a holding that Chavis's federal habeas petition was timely."

"Thus, viewing every disputed issue most favorably to Chavis, there remains a totally unexplained, hence unjustified, delay of at least six months."

"Six months is far longer than the . . . 'short period[s] of time' 30 to 60 days, that most States provide for filing an appeal to the state supreme court. . . . Nor do we see how an unexplained delay of this magnitude could fall within the scope of the federal statutory word 'pending' as interpreted in *Saffold*."

5. Invalidation of Aggravating Factors and Habeas Relief

Brown v. Sanders 546 U.S. 212 (2006)
Vote: 5-4
FACTS: Sanders and another broke into Boender's home, where they bound and blindfolded him and his girlfriend, Janice. Both victims were then struck on the head and Boender died. Sanders was convicted of first-degree murder, attempted murder, robbery, burglary, and attempted robbery.

The jury found four "special circumstances," each of which rendered Sanders eligible for death. At the penalty phase, the jury found two additional aggravating factors from a different list that it was required to consider and sentenced Sanders to death. The California Supreme Court invalidated two of the four special circumstances but affirmed the death sentence. Sanders then filed a habeas petition arguing that the jury's consideration of invalid special circumstances made his death sentence unconstitutional.
ISSUE: Is the invalidation of two aggravating factors sufficient for habeas relief if other aggravating factors are valid?
HOLDING: No.
RATIONALE: "We think it will clarify the analysis, and simplify the sentence-invalidating factors we have hitherto applied to nonweighing States . . . if we are henceforth guided by the following rule: An invalidated sentencing factor . . . will render the sentence unconstitutional by reason of its adding an improper element to the aggravation scale in the weighing process *unless* one of the other sentencing factors enables the sentencer to give aggravating weight to the same facts and circumstances."

"As we have explained, such skewing will occur, and give rise to constitutional error, only where the jury could not have given aggravating weight to the same facts and circumstances under the rubric of some other, valid sentencing factor."

"As the California Supreme Court noted, however, 'the jury properly considered two special circumstances [eligibility factors] (robbery-murder and witness-killing). . . .' These are sufficient to satisfy *Furman*'s narrowing requirement, and alone rendered Sanders eligible for the death penalty."

E. May Enemy Combatants Challenge Their Designation in U.S. Courts?

Hamdi v. Rumsfeld, 542 U.S. 507 (2004)
Vote: 6-3
FACTS: Yaser Esam Hamdi, an American citizen, was classified as an "enemy combatant" for taking up arms with the Taliban. He was captured in Afghanistan in 2001 and detained in Charleston, South Carolina. Hamdi's father filed a habeas petition alleging that the Government held his son in violation of the Fifth and Fourteenth Amendments. The Government contended, in the Michael Mobbs Declaration, that Hamdi was affiliated with the Taliban military and that he surrendered an assault rifle. The U.S. District Court for the Eastern District of Virginia found that the Mobbs Declara-

tion did not support Hamdi's detention, and ordered the Government to turn over evidence that led it to believe that Hamdi was an "enemy combatant." It also ordered that Hamdi be given counsel and that Hamdi have access to him.

ISSUE: Does a U.S. citizen detained as an "enemy combatant" have the right to a hearing to challenge that designation?

HOLDING: Yes.

RATIONALE: "Most notably, § 2243 provides that 'the person detained may, under oath, deny any of the facts set forth in the return or allege any other material facts,' and § 2246 allows the taking of evidence in habeas proceedings by deposition, affidavit, or interrogatories."

"The simple outline of § 2241 makes clear both that Congress envisioned that habeas petitioners would have some opportunity to present and rebut facts and that courts in cases like this retain some ability to vary the ways in which they do so as mandated by due process."

"[T]he circumstances surrounding Hamdi's seizure cannot in any way be characterized as 'undisputed,' as 'those circumstances are neither conceded in fact, nor susceptible to concession in law, because Hamdi has not been permitted to speak for himself or even through counsel as to those circumstances. . . .' An assertion that one *resided* in a country in which combat operations are taking place is not a concession that one was '*captured* in a zone of active combat operations in a foreign theater of war,' and certainly is not a concession that one was 'part of or supporting forces hostile to the United States or coalition partners' and 'engaged in an armed conflict against the United States.' Accordingly, we reject any argument that Hamdi has made concessions that eliminate any right to further process."

"[W]e believe that neither the process proposed by the Government nor the process apparently envisioned by the District Court below strikes the proper constitutional balance when a United States citizen is detained in the United States as an enemy combatant."

"We therefore hold that a citizen-detainee seeking to challenge his classification as an enemy combatant must receive notice of the factual basis for his classification, and a fair opportunity to rebut the Government's factual assertions before a neutral decisionmaker. . . . 'For more than a century the central meaning of procedural due process has been clear: "Parties whose rights are to be affected are entitled to be heard; and in order that they may enjoy that right they must first be notified. . . ."' These essential constitutional promises may not be eroded."

F. Do Foreign Nationals at Guantanamo Bay Have the Right to Use U.S. Courts to Challenge Their Detention?

Rasul v. Bush, 542 U.S. 466 (2004)

Vote: 6-3

FACTS: Habeas corpus petitioners are two Australian citizens, Mamdouh Habib and David Hicks, and Shafiq Rasul, Fawzi Khalid Abdullah Fahad Al Odah, and ten other

Kuwaiti citizens who were captured abroad during hostilities between the United States and the Taliban. Since 2002, the U.S. military has held them—and 640 other non-Americans—at the Naval Base at Guantanamo Bay. Petitioners filed suits under federal law challenging the legality of their detention, alleging that they had never been combatants against the United States or engaged in terrorist acts, and that they have never been charged, permitted to consult counsel, or provided access to courts or other tribunals.

ISSUE: Do U.S. courts have jurisdiction to consider the legal challenges of foreign nationals captured abroad and detained at U.S. military bases in other countries?

HOLDING: Yes.

RATIONALE: "The United States exercises 'complete jurisdiction and control' over the Guantanamo Base, and may continue to do so permanently if it so chooses. . . . Respondents themselves concede that the habeas statute would create federal-court jurisdiction over the claims of an American citizen held at the base. . . . Considering that § 2241 draws no distinction between Americans and aliens held in federal custody, there is little reason to think that Congress intended the statute's geographical coverage to vary depending on the detainee's citizenship. Aliens held at the base, like American citizens, are entitled to invoke the federal courts' authority under § 2241."

"Application of the habeas statute to persons detained at the base is consistent with the historical reach of the writ of habeas corpus. At common law, courts exercised habeas jurisdiction over the claims of aliens detained within sovereign territory of the realm, as well as the claims of persons detained in the so-called 'exempt jurisdictions,' where ordinary writs did not run, and all other dominions under the sovereign's control. . . . Later cases confirmed that the reach of the writ depended not on formal notions of territorial sovereignty, but rather on the practical question of 'the exact extent and nature of the jurisdiction or dominion exercised in fact by the Crown.'"

"We therefore hold that § 2241 confers on the District Court jurisdiction to hear petitioners' habeas corpus challenges to the legality of their detention at the Guantanamo Bay Naval Base."

Index

About the Author

Michael A. Cretacci, Ph.D., is assistant professor of criminal justice at the State University of New York College at Buffalo. He received his M.S. in criminal justice from the State University of New York College at Buffalo and his Ph.D. in criminal justice from the State University of New York at Albany. He has published in the areas of police history, social control theory, and criminal procedure. His teaching interests include criminological theory, policing, profiling, criminal procedure, and multicide.